MANET by himself

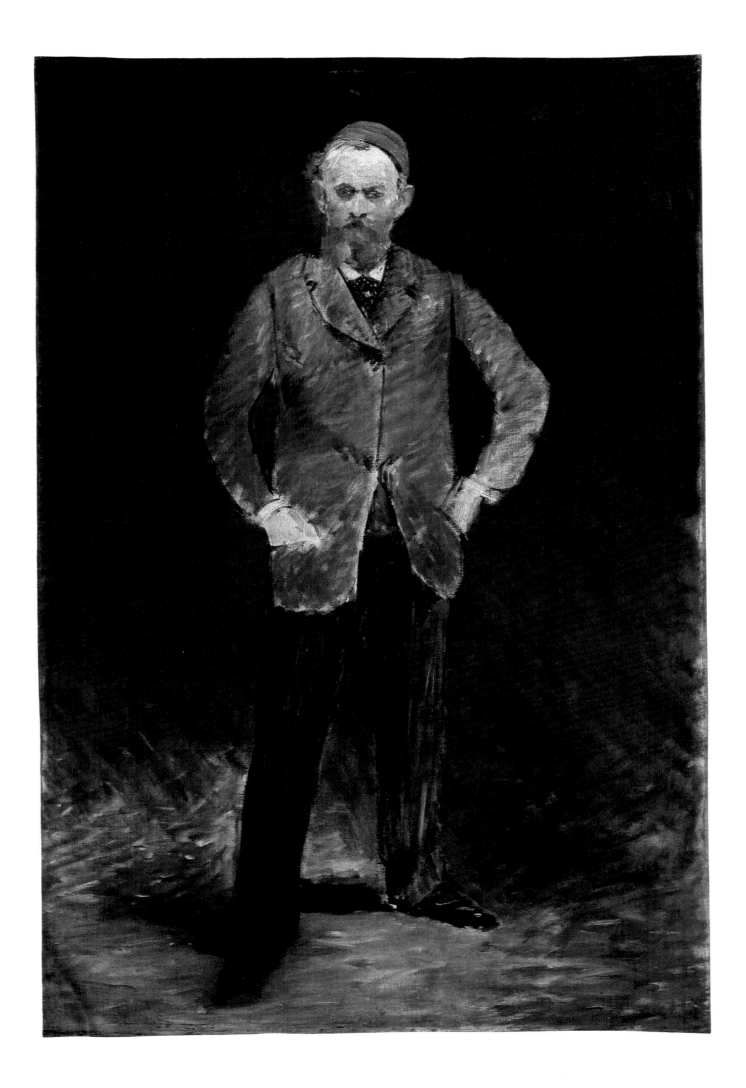

Edited by Juliet Wilson-Bareau

Correspondence & conversation

MANET by himself

Paintings, pastels, prints & drawings

LITTLE, BROWN AND COMPANY

BOSTON   NEW YORK   LONDON

For my father Paul Bareau at 90 and in memory of my mother

A LITTLE, BROWN Book

First published in Great Britain in 1991
by Macdonald & Co (Publishers)
Reprinted 1995 by Little, Brown and Company

This edition published in 2000 by Little, Brown and Company (UK)

Copyright © 1991, 1995 Little, Brown and Company (UK)

A CIP catalogue record for this book is available
from the British Library

ISBN 0-316-85505-7

Editorial Direction: Lewis Esson Publishing
Editor: Sarah Chapman
Design: Studio Gossett
Picture Research: Philippa Thomson
Translation: Juliet Wilson-Bareau
Production by Omnipress
Printed in Spain

Little, Brown and Company (UK)
Brettenham House
Lancaster Place
London WC2E 7EN

FRONTISPIECE: SELF-PORTRAIT WEARING A
SKULL-CAP, c.1878

Acknowledgements

I am indebted to Françoise Cachin, Charles Stuckey and John
House for a broadening understanding of Manet's art as a
'whole' and to Richard Kendall for the opportunity to present
it here. The final result owes much to the support of everyone
at Macdonald; Lewis Esson balanced sympathetic understanding and creative editorial control, with the help of Sarah Chapman; Andrew Gossett proved his commitment to finding the
most stimulating and intelligent solution to every aspect of the
book's design; and Philippa Thomson's outstanding organization and tact as picture coordinator played an essential part
in establishing the visual quality of the book. The documents
and reproductions, many of them unpublished, have been
made available thanks to the generosity and support of curators, particularly those in museums and libraries in Paris, and
of private collectors. I am very grateful to them all.

The publications of many scholars have contributed to this
presentation, but in a series committed to the general reader
the text is only indirectly annotated. If colleagues find this
book useful, it will be a measure of my debt to their work. All
detailed study of Manet's art is inevitably based on the monumental *catalogue raisonné* by Denis Rouart and Daniel Wildenstein, published in 1975, and Daniel Wildenstein's generous
cooperation in preparing the present publication is warmly
acknowledged.

My friend Ralph Manheim knows how much the translation
of Manet's correspondence and conversation owes to his rare
ear, and Michael Pakenham at the University of Exeter was
immensely helpful.

I would particularly like to express my debts, direct or
indirect, to Kathy Adler, Lloyd Austin and Richard Ormond in
Great Britain; to Colette Becker, Huguette Berès, Thierry
Bodin, Jean-Paul Bouillon, Eric Buffetaud, François Chapon,
Dominique Cordellier, Eric Darragon, Jeanne Haour, Waring
Hopkins, Jean-Claude Leblond-Zola, Pierre Lévy, Henri
Loyrette, Hélène Portiglia, Hubert Prouté, Anne Roquebert,
Yves Rouart, Robert and Manuel Schmit, Lucien Scheler and
the late Clément Tempelaere in France; to Matthias Frehner
and Samuel Josefowitz in Switzerland; and to Inge Dupont, Jay
Fisher, Richard Parks, Theodore Reff, John Rewald, Joe Rishel
and Barbara Shapiro in the United States. I would also like to
thank all those who agreed anonymously to the reproduction of
works or documents in their collections.

Contents

Preface

Although the idea of an edition of Manet's letters was discussed by Berthe Morisot and Stéphane Mallarmé just four years after the artist's death in 1883, no collected correspondence has yet appeared and this is the first time that the letters have been used on their own to tell the story of the artist's life. Etienne Moreau-Nélaton and Adolphe Tabarant drew on parts of the correspondence for their biographies published in 1926 and 1947 respectively. Moreau-Nélaton had access to the family correspondence and documents inherited by Julie Rouart, the daughter of Eugène Manet and Berthe Morisot (part of which is now deposited at the Musée Marmottan, Paris). He also reproduced some of Manet's letters to Fantin-Latour and to Eva Gonzalès and her husband Henri Guérard, as well as letters from other private collections, and made use of the extensive public collections in Paris archives and libraries. Tabarant, drawing on material from the other side of the Manet family, was able to acquire and make use of the important group of documents that came from Suzanne Manet and her son Léon Leenhoff (now preserved in the Pierpont Morgan Library in New York).

Many of these letters have been reproduced in later biographies and collections of documents (including Eric Darragon's admirably balanced selection in his recent *Manet*, Paris 1989). The letters written during Manet's early voyage to Rio, most of those sent from Paris during the Siege of 1870–71, and many of the enchanting illustrated letters sent from Bellevue in the summer of 1880 have been the subject of separate publications. Furthermore, the letters to Baudelaire have long been available in Claude Pichois' edition, those to Zola were edited by Colette Becker and published in their entirety in the catalogue of the 1983 centenary exhibition, while the letters to Mallarmé, many of them reproduced in L. J. Austin's monumental Mallarmé correspondence, have recently become available for study (acquired by the Musée Stéphane Mallarmé for the poet's home on the banks of the Seine).

Collected together, transcribed from or checked against the original manuscripts wherever possible in preparation for this publication, Manet's letters still present many problems and require much further research. They are unevenly spread over the artist's life, with concentrations in the periods when he and his correspondents were apart. The voyage to Rio and the Siege of Paris provide the most substantial groups, from which representative extracts have been selected here. The relatively few letters from the period of intense activity in the early 1860s are usefully supplemented here, as elsewhere, by Manet's conversations recorded by his friends. Degas disliked Antonin Proust's *Souvenirs*, first published in 1897, because he thought they imposed an 'attitude' on Manet – 'Manet was much nicer, much more natural', he told Daniel Halévy. However, Manet's speech as recorded by Proust (from notes made at the time, according to Proust himself) often corresponds to a remarkable

extent with the tone and phrasing of his letters or relates unmistakably to contemporary documents. The degree of authenticity of the various writers' records and 'souvenirs' can thus be tested against the letters themselves.

The choice of what to include in this book was often difficult to make. Some interesting and very revealing letters are undated and as yet undatable and have therefore been excluded. Others remain obscure without explanation or the inclusion of the other side of the correspondence, while a number of Manet's allusions have so far resisted efforts to elucidate them. Although some tentative dates and readings proposed here may well prove erroneous, wherever possible dates have been checked for accuracy through postmarks, types of paper, computation of day/date relationships or the date of documents referred to in the text, the writer and recipients of all letters being in Paris unless otherwise stated (though Manet's autograph indications of 'Paris' are included). The selection of letters and documents includes items such as the list of pictures sold to Durand-Ruel in 1872, reproduced for the first time in the exact form of Manet's lost original document. It aims to cover as many aspects of his life and art as possible within the space available, and concentrates on the more personal aspects of Manet's views and feelings and his involvement with his art.

The choice of works to parallel the texts has been made with an eye to Manet's crucial relationship with the Paris Salon. All his works submitted to the Salon, whether accepted or rejected, are included here (though one is seen in a different version, one in a different medium), as well as intended submissions such as *The Execution of Maximilian* and an unrealized scene of the execution of Communards in *The Barricade*. Some works proved unobtainable, others did not fit in for one reason or another, and the generous number of reproductions seems all too soon too few to express a rounded view of the 'whole' Manet.

Juliet Wilson-Bareau

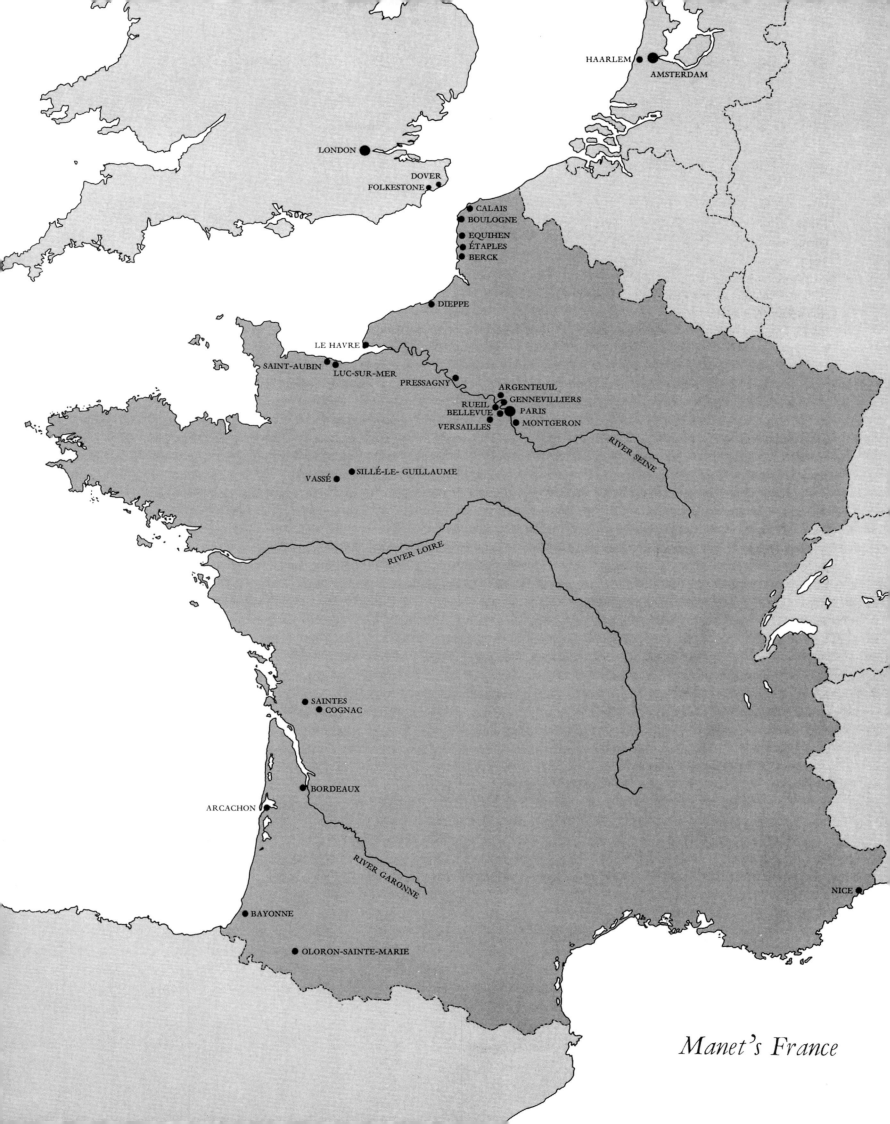

HAARLEM
AMSTERDAM

LONDON

DOVER
FOLKESTONE

CALAIS
BOULOGNE
EQUIHEN
ÉTAPLES
BERCK

DIEPPE

LE HAVRE
SAINT-AUBIN
LUC-SUR-MER
PRESSAGNY
ARGENTEUIL
GENNEVILLIERS
RUEIL
BELLEVUE   PARIS
VERSAILLES   MONTGERON

RIVER SEINE

VASSÉ SILLÉ-LE- GUILLAUME

RIVER LOIRE

SAINTES
COGNAC

BORDEAUX

ARCACHON

RIVER GARONNE

NICE

BAYONNE

OLORON-SAINTE-MARIE

Manet's France

Introduction

At the Paris Salon of 1865, Edouard Manet's *Olympia* (*85*) and his *Jesus Mocked by the Soldiers* (*84*) caused a storm of outraged protest. In the same gallery of the huge exhibition building were two seascapes signed 'Claude Monet'. It was the younger artist's first appearance at the Salon and a number of people mistook his boldly painted canvases with their otherwise unknown signature for works by the notorious Manet. To be complimented on works he had not painted, while being attacked and ridiculed for those he had, not unnaturally upset the older artist who wondered whether the newcomer was deliberately taking advantage of the stir he had caused. At the following Salon the initial confusion between the two artists was again vividly expressed when Monet exhibited a striking full-length study of *Camille* (Kunsthalle, Bremen). It recalled works like Manet's *Street Singer* (*61*), and the caricaturist André Gill featured it with the caption: 'Monet or Manet? – Monet. But it is to *Manet* that we owe this *Monet*; bravo! *Monet*; thank you! *Manet*.'

This confusion has tended to persist until our own day. As a towering figure in the Impressionist movement, Monet has achieved much wider public recognition than Manet, largely through the popularity of his landscape paintings. Since Monet was active over a period of some sixty-five years, they represent through sheer numbers a much more easily identifiable body of work, reinforced in the public mind by the memorable repetition of motifs in his celebrated 'series' paintings – the grainstacks and poplars, the façade of Rouen cathedral and the lily pond at Giverny. Manet, on the other hand, rarely repeated himself, and always maintained that he had no intention of doing so. In the course of his brief career between 1860 and 1883, a span of little more than twenty years, his work presented an astonishing variety of motifs and apparently bewildering changes in style. This is particularly true of his early work in which many influences made themselves felt. In *The Old Musician* (*51*) of 1862, which clearly reflects compositions by seventeenth-century French and Spanish Masters, the Le Nain brothers and Velasquez, the figures were modelled by vagrants, rag-pickers and gypsies whom Manet encountered in Paris. The blending of influences is also true of the period in the mid-1870s when Manet was contributing to the emerging Impressionist style and painted alongside Monet and Renoir at Argenteuil (*160*, *161*); at the same time he was redefining his own interests as a painter of urban life and Parisian types, as theme which came to be influenced more by Mallarmé's idealistic vision of a new democratic society than by Zola's harsher, bleaker naturalism.

Manet's approach to picture-making was determined largely by two overriding ambitions: to work in a truly modern style and present himself as an artist who could hold his own in all the categories of painting to be found in the official Paris Salon. His earliest 'trial runs' for the Salon (*40*, *41*) and the works he submitted to the Salon jury in the 1860s drew on his knowledge of Italian and particularly Venetian art of the Renaissance and on his lifelong admiration for seventeenth-century Dutch and Spanish painting. Through their example, and in opposition to current academic teaching and accepted artistic modes, he aimed at revitalizing and modernizing the grand traditions of religious, mythological and historical painting in a specifically French context. He also wanted to make his mark on portraiture, land- (or rather sea-) scape and genre. He had a clear and particular vision of what he took to be the enduring qualities of French art, from Clouet to Chardin, and admired the landscapes of Corot, Daubigny and above all Jongkind. He respected the tremendous innovations of Courbet and his search for truth, but saw Courbet's painting as too dark and heavy-handed to be able to bring about the revolution of which he dreamed. Courbet was Manet's great precursor, and Manet's several recorded references to him suggest that he was the contemporary who most impressed the young artist in his early years. Courbet's work caused a scandal whenever it was shown during the 1850s, in the Salons and in his famous *Pavillon du Réalisme*, erected alongside the official buildings of the great *Exposition universelle* of 1855. As an art student during these years (between 1850 and 1856) Manet was inevitably impressed by the energy and independence with which Courbet confronted the pictorial conventions of his day in a painting like the huge *Burial at Ornans* (Musée d'Orsay). However, if he admired Courbet's uncompromising scenes of everyday life, often presented on a monumental scale, Manet certainly found the provincial artist's deliberately earthy realism at odds with his own taste.

The seemingly confusing sequence of styles and motifs in Manet's art reflects not only his far-reaching ambitions and the fact that his methods were constantly under review, but also that 'scholarship' has not entirely caught up with him: the chronology of his life is not sufficiently well documented, nor is the sequence of his work completely clear. To some extent this is because the artist was the opposite of a programmatic painter: he believed in spontaneity and impulse, and his search for solutions, in his deliberately unauthoritarian and open-minded vision of the world, led him to cut, alter and repaint canvases throughout his career. For example, an early study of the woman who was to become his wife (*45*) is a repainted fragment of what was probably a large 'Venetian' composition in the style of Tintoretto; where a sketch and a large surviving fragment give us a fair impression of another of Manet's ambitious early compositions (*40*, *41*), we have only x-ray evidence and caricatures to suggest what the *Incident in a Bullfight*, shown at the Salon of 1864, looked like before the cutting out and repainting of the two surviving fragments (*71*, *72*); and we have to rely on a watercolour replica to judge the effect of the great panoramic racecourse scene painted that same year (*92*,

94). Only in recent years have the early *Déjeuner sur l'herbe* (*58*) and the late *Bar at the Folies-Bergère* (*228*) revealed the astonishing stages of their development, and even with the existence of a composition sketch, three full-scale canvases and a lithograph, our understanding of the complex development of his *Execution of Maximilian* (*22, 95, 96*) is still incomplete. Many cut or altered canvases remain to be reconstructed or understood through patient examination in the laboratory, while changes to many others probably lie unsuspected beneath the deceptively fresh surfaces that Manet was able to impart even to his most radically repainted works.

With an artist such as Manet a date on a work normally indicates the year of its completion, not necessarily that of its actual execution. The *Déjeuner sur l'herbe* and *Olympia*, both dated 1863, were almost certainly executed over quite a long time, and *Olympia* (*85*) was probably retouched – possibly even with the addition of the infamous black cat – just before the picture was sent to the Salon of 1865. Many paintings would have been in progress at the same time in Manet's studio and it was natural that he should review and revise his work before its exhibition or sale. He certainly retouched canvases before his major one-man exhibition in 1867, and a specific instance has proved that he did so when selling a group of twenty-five works of all periods to Durand-Ruel in 1872, updating an early canvas whose original design, now known from an x-ray image, is reflected in the 1862 etching of *The Urchin* (*18*).

During the first half of the 1860s a number of Manet's major works were shown in Louis Martinet's spacious exhibition galleries on the boulevard des Italiens, and he occasionally exhibited in French provincial towns and foreign Salons. Throughout his life, however, the Paris Salon remained his principal goal. In the spring of 1859, three or four years after leaving the studio of the highly regarded artist Thomas Couture, Manet submitted his *Absinthe Drinker* (*50*) to the Salon jury. It was rejected, to his chagrin, but at the following Salon two years later he showed the double portrait of his parents (*48*) and his celebrated *Spanish Singer* (*56*), both dated 1860. They caused a considerable stir, and the *Spanish Singer* earned him an honourable mention, the only time Manet's work was officially recognized until he received a second-class medal at the Salon of 1881.

The Salon became Manet's battleground, and most of his major compositions were intended for its walls. It was the most important artistic event of the Parisian year and from 1863, without a break except in 1871 after the 'terrible year' of the Franco-Prussian War and the Commune, the Salon was held annually, during May and June. Manet's letters reflect his preparations during the preceding autumn and winter, and his feverish activity and anxiety as the sending-in date drew near. The most recent *catalogue raisonné* of Manet's work (Rouart and Wildenstein, 1975) lists 430 paintings of which some two-

thirds are copies, sketches or minor works, or paintings left unfinished at his death. Of the remaining, more substantial pictures, Manet sent thirty-eight to the Salon between 1859 and 1882, of which twenty-seven were accepted and a further three hung in the Salon des Refusés of 1863. He was advised not even to submit the *Execution of Maximilian* (*96*) in 1869, and in 1867 and 1878, the years when Paris hosted an *Exposition universelle*, he decided not to risk rejection by the jury. On the first occasion he mounted his own one-man exhibition in a temporary pavilion (the 'chapel' next to Courbet's vast 'cathedral' on the same occasion), while in 1878 he planned a more ambitious show but finally thought better of it. Only after the award of a medal in 1881 were his works automatically accepted, and it was by then too late – the Salon of 1882 was to be his last.

The Salon was the equivalent of the 'blockbuster' exhibition of today. It was visited by hundreds of thousands of people (some half-million by the mid-1870s), most of whom probably rarely, if ever, set foot in museums and galleries at other times and whose contact with contemporary art was likely to be limited to illustrated magazines and reproductive prints and photographs of the most widely acclaimed works. Daumier and other caricaturists regularly mocked this ignorant, bourgeois public, sometimes tiresomely pretentious, sometimes touchingly naïve, which demanded charming or improving subjects, responding to sentimental themes and nudes as daring as might be so long as they were presented in a suitably tasteful, usually mythological, guise. 'Pictures that tell a story' were popular too, scenes from history or the Bible or depictions of contemporary life. Portraits were also a constant feature, and were admired for the sitters' position and personality, their beauty or fine clothes.

The huge crowds of visitors to the Salon made their way past thousands of paintings, as well as works in other media including sculpture. Paintings were arranged principally in alphabetical order in the vast galleries of a building near the Champs Elysées (close to the Grand Palais where important exhibitions are held today). Manet's paintings appeared alongside those of other artists whose names began with M, larger canvases hanging above smaller ones, and all arranged in serried ranks up to the ceiling, with no space between the frames. Today's major exhibitions rarely exceed three hundred items, whereas the numbers of Manet's paintings in the Salon catalogues, mid-way through the alphabet, give an idea of the huge numbers exhibited on the Salon walls. For example, his two works in the 1861 Salon (*48, 56*) were numbered 2098 and 2099 (all his Salon catalogue numbers are given in the picture list at the end of this volume), and those in other Salons usually came between 1200 and 1500. Only in the famous Salon des Refusés of 1863 did the numbers drop dramatically, with Manet's three entries, including the celebrated *Déjeuner sur l'herbe*, numbered

363 to 365 (57, 58 and 60) in a catalogue listing only some six hundred paintings from the three thousand which had been rejected by the official Salon (though more, uncatalogued, works were in fact shown).

If a newcomer or relatively unknown artist wanted to make an impact in these conditions, even if he was favoured with a reasonably good position by the hanging committee, it was essential to create pictures that would stand out from the mass of works around them and catch the public's eye. Size was one factor, alluring or sensational subject matter another. Neither of these characteristics, though much exploited by regular Salon exhibitors, offers any intrinsic artistic merit. Manet, a painter to his fingertips, who set great store by 'sincerity' in art, counted above all on the style and aesthetic qualities of his work when seen in what might often be a poor position and at a considerable distance.

Through his use of simple compositional structures, clear bold colours and, in his earlier years, a distinctively broad, flat handling of paint, Manet's work creates a powerful visual impact. Its effect on the crowded Salon walls, among paintings by artists of what he termed the 'brown-sauce school' or the providers of 'frothy' nudes, must have been astonishing. It is difficult to sense this impact today when works are seen in carefully controlled environments, displayed in the airy, well-lit spaces of the world's great galleries. Even so, a wall of some of Manet's finest paintings, in the Metropolitan Museum in New York, can still produce a sense of shock: *The Spanish Singer* (56), for all its early date, has a striking immediacy, provoking the spectator's response not so much to the figure represented – there is no sentimental appeal, no anecdotal story line – but to an all-pervading sense of vitality through the picture's bold clear-cut design, fresh colour, strong contrasts and confident brushwork. *Mlle V . . . in the Costume of an Espada* (57), which flanked the *Déjeuner sur l'herbe* (58) together with the *Young Man in the Costume of a Majo* (60) in the Salon des Refusés in 1863, shows a model posturing in the fancy-dress trappings of a 'matador' against a background drawn from several of Goya's bullfighting prints. The subject is given credibility through a bold handling of paint and vivid touches of colour harmonizing with black and brown to create an image of compelling charm and liveliness, in spite of its inherent absurdity. In the *Young Woman with a Parrot* (89), shown at the Salon of 1868, we are confronted by the same model, Victorine, as an up-to-date Parisienne, her simple peignoir of pink satin, the bird on its perch and half-peeled orange conjured up with the breadth and assurance of handling that Manet had just experienced in Velasquez's paintings during his visit to Spain.

Paintings like these – so forceful even in a modern museum display – inevitably jumped off the Salon walls, too bold, too startling in their deceptively simple technique to be ignored. And these were paintings of unobjectionable subjects, unlike the *Déjeuner sur l'herbe* (58) or *Olympia* (85) whose subject matter was bound – if not actually calculated – to outrage the moral sentiments of the day, since prudery flourished in France under the Second Empire just as in Victorian England. Manet's religious paintings were also considered shocking. The *Dead Christ and the Angels* (81), a subject for which he was ridiculed by the arch-realist Courbet, and his *Jesus Mocked by the Soldiers* (84), offended public opinion and the critics at the Salons of 1864 and 1865. Even today these compositions are less easy to accommodate than Manet's secular subjects. Although they were certainly of great significance for him (he maintained years later that he still longed to paint a crucifixion), he never repeated his experiments with images whose powerful, naïve handling and bold colour were wildly at variance with the expectations of the Salon public.

The outrage created by Manet's works and the violent tones in which critics and caricaturists responded to them in the Press led to a general assumption that Manet must be the type of artist, hirsute and shirt-sleeved, beer-drinking and pipe-smoking, bohemian and revolutionary, that the public had long identified with Courbet. In fact, nothing could have been farther from the truth. Those who knew Manet were always impressed by his elegance and charm. He could be sharp-tongued and impatient, and occasionally gave way to attacks of depression and nervous outbursts which irritated both Baudelaire and Berthe Morisot's highly critical mother at different times. But all his friends testified to his goodness and generosity of spirit. The actress and model Ellen Andrée recalled him as an altogether 'superior' person compared with other artists she had known, including the sophisticated but bear-like Degas. Manet's graceful good breeding went hand in hand with his naturalness and spontaneity, and was also combined with the affectations of a slightly rollicking gait and a 'low' Parisian manner of speech and cutting wit. Although Jacques-Émile Blanche remembered him always immaculately dressed and proud of his 'pretty feet in English ankle boots', Léon Leenhoff recalled being told as a boy how Manet disliked wearing shoes after the months he spent at sea on his youthful voyage to Rio. He combined simplicity and elegance, and the rare critics who wrote favourably about his art were always at pains to stress the agreeable character and correct appearance of the man.

If Manet and his art have been regarded as something of an enigma, this partly reflects his emergence from a traditional, though liberal, bourgeois context as a highly unconventional, adventurous and sensitive artistic personality. Even as a schoolboy, reading Diderot's *Salons* in the history class, Manet responded bluntly to his strictures about contemporary artists painting hats that were bound to become outmoded: 'That's extremely stupid – one should be of one's own time and do what one sees, without worrying about questions of fashion.'

Mallarmé, years later, suggested that if Manet could bring the public to see 'the true beauties of the people . . . as they are, the graces which exist in the bourgeoisie will then be recognized and taken as worthy models in art'.

Manet's earliest letters, to his parents, show him strongly attached to his family, addressing his father and mother with the familiar *tu* in direct and affectionate though very respectful terms. His father, a decorated and highly regarded official in the Ministry of Justice, wanted his eldest son to follow him in the legal profession. He compromised to the extent of agreeing that he might take up a naval career, and when the young Manet continued to fail his examinations – through lack of application rather than any intellectual dullness – his father accompanied him to Le Havre where Manet embarked on a training ship for Rio de Janeiro, six weeks before his seventeenth birthday. This voyage lasted seven months and was followed by another failure to secure entry to the *École navale*. Manet was then allowed to follow his inclinations, encouraged by his uncle Edmond Fournier, and became an art student.

With his schoolfriend Antonin Proust, who was to leave the extensive 'souvenirs' from which so much of our knowledge of the artist is derived, Manet enrolled in the studio of Thomas Couture, a curiously dissident 'academic' artist who had acquired a great reputation with his vast *Romans of the Decadence* (Musée d'Orsay) at the Salon of 1847, but was then thwarted in his plans to complete the even larger *Enrolment of the Volunteers* (Musée départemental, Beauvais), an ambitious celebration of Republican virtues begun under the Second Republic in 1848, but which could no longer be encouraged by Napoleon III after the *coup d'état* of 1851 and the installation of the Second Empire. Manet's references to the time he spent in Couture's studio are almost totally negative, and he might be said to have learnt how not to paint from his example. In particular, Couture's moralizing, allegorizing conception of art must have been completely antipathetic, in spite of their shared Republican views, to Manet who believed in the virtues of spontaneity and truth to life. Perhaps partly as a result of his affectionate but oppositional relationship with his father whose political views were hardly less liberal than his own (and who on occasion even backed his art student son against the stubborn teacher), Manet cultivated an informed scepticism, an elegant, ironic detachment that counterbalanced an essential naïvety, to which Proust referred, and his passionately held beliefs about life and art. He painted a penetrating study of his parents (criticized in a Salon review as unfilial in its harsh realism) in a double portrait (*48*) that shows his strong-willed mother deferring to the husband who cannot or will not meet his son's gaze.

Manet described this and many of his other paintings as straightforward responses to the subjects in front of him. His own writings reveal little of what he later referred to as his 'innermost thoughts' and intentions, and he seems to have been hardly less reticent, in spite of his reputation for strong views and verbal fireworks, in his conversations with friends and colleagues. But although Manet failed to expatiate on the meaning of his art, his written and recorded opinions and his manner of expressing them combine with our knowledge of the paintings and the way he worked on them to provide useful clues. Jacques-Émile Blanche, who knew Manet when he had abandoned his overt references to the art of the past and was immersed in the realities of life in Paris under the Third Republic, considered Manet's views on art to be nothing but a collection of charmingly naïve statements, the equivalent of an amateur Communard's views on revolution. Mallarmé, however, who went to Manet's studio every day for many years, wrote articles which certainly express the artist's views since they include phrases that are almost identical to those attributed to Manet by Proust.

Manet's early years, when he was trying to make his way as a young artist in Paris, remain haphazardly and incompletely documented through his own or his correspondents' letters. We learn relatively little about his student days, virtually nothing about his earliest exhibition at Martinet's or in the Salon, or the sending of a picture (*41*) to the St Petersburg (Leningrad) Academy in 1861; nothing at all, from him, about the *Déjeuner sur l'herbe* or his other paintings in the Salon des Refusés. It is thanks to Baudelaire's absence in Belgium that he, Manet and their friends wrote letters about the Salons of 1864 and 1865, and about Manet's noisy reception there in 1865 and subsequent journey to Spain. Similarly, Manet's absence in Boulogne during the summer months of 1868 was responsible for a burst of correspondence from the bored artist exiled from Paris and anxious for news.

Although there are inevitable gaps in terms of factual reporting at some periods of Manet's career, the writings and recorded conversations still provide remarkable insights into his personality and activities. As with the long letters written to his family on the voyage to Rio, it was during the seemingly endless months of the siege of Paris by the Prussian army that Manet took up his pen, often daily, to describe life in the beleaguered city, to express his anxieties or convey reassurances to his wife and mother whom he had sent with Léon (his wife's son) to the western Pyrenees. Like the letters from the young naval cadet to his parents, these missives, many of them sent by balloon from the besieged city, provide coded information about relationships with his family and friends as well as his own personal views. They show him sometimes at loggerheads with his brothers and occasionally irritated by his mother when she would not follow his advice, but also coming to realize how much he depended on his wife for whom he expresses increasing tenderness and affection.

It may seem strange that Manet, a handsome and eligible

bachelor, should have committed himself to a Dutchwoman who was two years his senior and had an illegitimate son, almost certainly not his. Suzanne Leenhoff was an excellent pianist who came to the Manet household to give lessons to Edouard and his brother Eugène while the former was still an art student. Unknown even to Manet's close friends and relations, Suzanne became his companion and they moved into an apartment in the Batignolles district. They lived together from 1860 and it is probably from this date that Suzanne appears as a nude model in his work (*38–44*). In October 1863, a full year after the death of Manet's father (and probably corresponding to his mother's period of official mourning), Manet astonished possibly more people than Baudelaire, who referred to Manet's departure for Holland 'to bring back *his wife*'.

Later, in 1866, the couple took up residence with Mme Manet at 49 rue St Pétersbourg, together with Léon (born in 1852) who was always presented to the rest of the world as Suzanne's younger brother. Some time between 1863 and 1866 (when Zola described it as one of four 'barely dry' canvases in the studio), Manet painted a strong, sober portrait of his widowed mother (*49*), a spirited woman of considerable character and charm. Referred to even by herself as Mme Manet-maman, she treated Suzanne like a daughter and was particularly fond of the young Léon. She loved entertaining and held soirées twice a week, inviting her three sons' friends on Thursdays and her own and later her daughter-in-law's lady friends on Tuesdays. The Thursday gatherings included politicians, artists, writers, musicians and composers. Baudelaire was a regular guest in the early years and also corresponded with Mme Manet, inviting himself to dinner and expressing his admiration and affection for her son. As well as close family friends and relations such as Commandant Hippolyte Lejosne and Paul Meurice, Antonin Proust and Émile Ollivier, and the lawyer cousins Jules de Jouy and Ambroise Adam, artists like Astruc and Fantin, Bracquemond and Degas, writers and critics such as Champfleury, Duranty, Zola and Duret, were all invited to these soirées in the 1860s. In the 1870s Mme Manet's receptions were attended by the politicians Clemenceau and Gambetta, the poets Mallarmé and de Banville, fashionable artists such as Chaplin and de Nittis, and even false friends like the critic Albert Wolff.

There were also musical evenings at their own or friends' homes. The celebrated guitarist Jaime Bosch, who dedicated one of his solo pieces to Manet (*122*), played for the Manet and Meurice families, and later for the Charpentiers. Suzanne Manet and Mme Meurice performed on the piano, while others sang. In a letter to Baudelaire, by then in Belgium, Mme Meurice described a splendid reception given by Mme Manet senior, at which 'Mme Manet [the artist's wife] played like an angel, M. Bosch scratched his guitar like a treasure, Cherubini-Astruc sang and the Commandante Thérèse [Lejosne] did the

same'. In another letter she comments on the musical tastes of the group for whom she played every fortnight: 'for Manet it has to be *Haydn*; *Beethoven* for Bracquemond; *Haendel* for Champfleury; even Fantin has his God: *Schumann*. Come' – she exhorts Baudelaire – 'and I'll play Wagner.'

Manet's mother not only ruled the family's social life at home but also attempted to keep a firm grip on her son's affairs. In a detailed 'Statement for my son Edouard from 25 September 1862, the date of his father's death, to 1866', she noted the monies he had received from his father's estate, her gift of 10,000 francs on his marriage, his sale to her of his share in the family estate at Gennevilliers (just north of Paris) and the rent received from it over four years – a total of nearly 80,000 francs. She concluded that this amounted to '19,871 francs per year', adding 'It seems to me high time to call a halt on this ruinous downhill path.' This was a year before the expenses of his private exhibition in a pavilion alongside the *Exposition universelle* of 1867 forced Manet to borrow more than 18,000 francs from his mother. Underpinned by the family fortune and living, as he did for the rest of his life, under the same roof as his mother, Manet was never threatened by the poverty which Monet experienced to an extreme degree and which Manet and his brother Gustave were able to alleviate by lending the younger artist money on many occasions. At the same time his own account books and notes show that he was constantly borrowing money or raising loans from various sources, both private and commercial, while also lending not only to Monet but to other friends, including Baudelaire and even Zola on one occasion.

The 'ruinous downhill path' which so alarmed his mother was no doubt seen by her as part of a lifestyle over which she had little or no control. Her charming, elegant son left the family home each day to pursue his activities as an artist in town, in his own and his colleagues' studios, in the Café de Bade and Tortoni's on the chic boulevard des Italiens and, in the more bohemian Batignolles and Clichy district, at the Friday gatherings in the Café Guerbois or later at the Nouvelle-Athènes. Mme Manet's alarm was expressed at the end of the period, between 1863 and 1865, when Manet's appearance in the annual Salons inevitably provoked a storm of abuse and ridicule. If his critical reception improved slightly after 1867, it did not prevent him from challenging his friend Duranty to a duel after a press review he judged to be insultingly cool. The incident took place at the Café Guerbois in February 1870 and after the duel, at which Zola acted as one of Manet's seconds, the artist's mother wrote to Fantin, inviting him to dinner, 'since Edouard, thank goodness, has given up going to that dreadful café' and would otherwise be unable to see him, begging Fantin to 'Help us keep him away from that place which is so dangerous for someone of his lively, spontaneous temperament.'

Mme Manet's constant presence, her affection for her son and daughter-in-law and their knowledge that they could always turn to her for financial support, must have contributed to Manet's self-confidence and his refusal to toe the official line. At the same time his material debts and sense of moral obligation to his widowed mother, as well as his deep affection and respect for her, may help to explain the fact that he persisted in seeking success in the official, socially acceptable arena of the Salon, as well as his constant longing for recognition and rewards, his gratitude to those who voted him a medal, albeit second class, in 1881, and his delight at being awarded the Legion of Honour – all of which appeared entirely contemptible to the gruff, uncompromising Degas.

For a man of his extreme sensitivity, who struggled all his life and began to achieve recognition only when he was too ill to be able to make the most of it, Manet seems to have chosen an ideal companion in Suzanne Leenhoff. He told Baudelaire, just before leaving for his wedding in Holland, that his wife-to-be was 'good-looking, very good-natured and a very fine musician'. On their return to Paris, Suzanne was introduced to the Manet family's friends and relations. A cousin, Ambroise Adam (*62*), commented ironically that 'the young bride... is 27, looks 30 and is pretty *forte* even on the *piano*. She has a fine musical talent, but as a Dutchwoman she is the shape and size appropriate to her country; besides that she seems fair and gentle.' Suzanne's ample form expanded over the years (*27*) and Manet urged her, during the family's evacuation from Paris in 1870, to take exercise as well as practise her piano. The sharp-tongued Mme Morisot referred to the shock Manet must have experienced at seeing Suzanne again after her 'bucolic blooming' in the Pyrenees, adding that she was by then, some six months later, somewhat recovered. That Manet was very fond of his placid, good-natured wife is certain, and his portraits of her bear this out (*26, 27, 111, 112*). He was also proud of her pianistic talent and evidently took particular pleasure in depicting her confident, muscular hands which figure prominently in the portraits.

Manet spent much of his time with his male friends and models and, later, with the actresses and demi-mondaines who posed for many of his major paintings as well as for more intimate portraits and pastels. The painter Giuseppe de Nittis, who was frequently in his company in the late 1870s, felt certain that in spite of appearances Manet remained faithful to his wife. He told a story about Manet following a slender, pretty, coquettish young woman in the street. 'Suddenly his wife came up to him and said, laughing, "There, I've caught you this time." "Well, that's funny!" said Manet, "I though it was you!" But the truth is that Mme Manet was a rather hefty, placid Dutchwoman who looked nothing like a skinny little Parisienne. She told the story herself, in her smiling, good-humoured way.'

His mother's strength of character and his wife's even temper no doubt helped Manet to overcome the nervous excitement and the tendency to depression that sometimes alarmed those who were closest to him. If he was destroyed by syphilis like his father, as Philippe Burty and Edmond de Goncourt implied, there is little sign that it affected his artistic output until the very end. In his last years, after the onset of serious disorders, he struggled not to appear handicapped and refused to admit to the world at large that he was ill. From the difficult beginnings of his career to its premature end, his devoted wife must have provided a consoling pillow from which he could arise each day to throw himself, as Mallarmé so vividly recalled, at the canvas before him in the studio, or give vent to brilliant verbal displays in conversation with his friends.

It is customary nowadays to consider both the aesthetic form and the thematic content of a work of art in terms of its social and political context and to consider both the viewing public and the 'consumer', whether state or private patron, for whom it was intended. Attention to the social and political frameworks within which Manet operated have confirmed his well-known Republican sympathies and thrown a new light on many of his images. A print of an apparently innocent café scene turns out to have been published in a radical journal that upheld the deported Communard Henri Rochefort, whose return to Paris Manet celebrated in 1880–81 (*224, 225*); *Masked Ball at the Opera* has recently been interpreted in terms of political allegory long recognized in the lithograph of *Polichinelle* (*156, 157*); Manet's views of the rue Mosnier are now seen as subtle but specific references to the political nature of the *Fête de la Paix* of 1878 and the radical Parisian poor (*178–81*).

Nineteenth-century art is also now discussed in terms of 'gender', that is, as the product of almost exclusively male artists for predominantly male viewers, critics and clients. From this viewpoint much of the art of the Salons is seen to be profoundly sexist in character. The Salon exhibitions always included an orgy of nudities, aimed at a viewer cast in the role of voyeur, and offering a variety of submissive, yielding female forms with vaguely classical associations, labelled 'Diana' and 'Venus' (there were dozens of these in the Salon of 1863), 'Sappho' and 'Psyche', or simply 'Nymph' and 'Bacchante', while the Bible provided 'Daughters of Eve' or the ever popular, voluptuously repentant 'Magdalene'. Courbet, as a realist, threw off much of the pretence. Nevertheless, in his own robustly sensual manner and in a rather different mode, he produced nudes for public consumption in the Salon and elsewhere that were as erotically available as any by Baudry and Cabanel, and almost as unrealistically 'chaste' and idealized in what they lacked, through concealment or the depilatory conventions of the day. And this was the man who mocked Manet for painting angels with wings.

Conventions of any kind were anathema to Manet and his own strategy was to concentrate on their destruction. His most notorious pictures in the 1860s were the *Déjeuner sur l'herbe* (*58*) and *Olympia* (*85*); in the 1870s, the *Masked Ball at the Opera* (*157*) and *Nana* (*171*). The nudes in the *Déjeuner sur l'herbe* and *Olympia* were both considered shocking. In the first, a classical nymph borrowed from Raphael (by way of Marcantonio's engraving and with reference to the Giorgione in the Louvre) is metamorphosed into a naked woman picnicking with two fully dressed young men; in the second, *Olympia*, in the guise of a reclining 'Venus' or Renaissance courtesan borrowed from Titian (the celebrated *Venus of Urbino* copied by Manet (*36*) in the Uffizi), is presented as a contemporary prostitute or courtesan with a suitably evocative name. In the later works, the *Opera Ball* shows a licentious carnival scene, with men in evening dress ogling and fumbling the women in masks and outrageous fancy dress, while *Nana* depicts a celebrated *grande cocotte* in her boudoir.

Manet was not simply content to interrogate his parents (*48*), his wife and other portrait sitters, he responded to the personalities of all his models, even when they were 'only' artists' models. It is surely no accident that Victorine is always so recognizable in Manet's paintings, so particularized in her femininity, serenity and slightly quizzical charm. He is alert to the specific characteristics, both physical and psychological, of other models, too. If *Nana* (*171*) is a 'fictionalized' representation of Henriette Hauser, the mistress of the Prince of Orange, posed in the artist's studio (with props which appear in other pictures) as if in an episode from Zola's *L'Assommoir*, she is also seen as very much herself, a pert and knowing demi-mondaine comfortable with her own curvaceous form and with her recreated but authentic-looking milieu. (Banned from the Salon in 1877, the picture caused a sensation in the window of a fashionable gift shop.)

Preferring the more opulent and cultivated charms of the demi-mondaines of the Third Republic, like Henriette Hauser and his close friend Méry Laurent (*230*), even Mallarmé could see *Olympia* only as a 'wan, wasted courtesan', and most recent critics have interpreted the early nudes as harsh images of contemporary sexuality, analysing them in terms of power and class and money. In front of the paintings themselves, however, a different impression may well emerge. The early nudes and earlier and later figure studies, whether of men or women, the prostitutes and tramps, artists and 'actresses', can also be seen as exercises in open-minded dialogue, in civilized communication at the heart of what is often read as cold or provocative confrontation. In the *Déjeuner* the relationships of the figures carry connotations of quiet conversation and friendship in keeping with their classical source rather than of the dangerous immorality evoked by similar situations shown in popular prints, which led to expectations that Manet's painting does not in fact fulfil. Victorine's gaze, so often perceived, both then and now, as shockingly, immodestly direct and cool, is surely that of the real Victorine posing for Manet in his studio, her nudity as 'borrowed' for the occasion as the clothes she has discarded. As *Olympia*, Victorine is a calm, cool but also radiant figure, her alertness and firm contours conveying a sense of youthful self-assurance rather than any hard or threatening persona. She plays for Manet the role of modern courtesan or prostitute, and he observes her precisely as he has posed her, in the cold north light of his studio, paying homage to Titian (more clearly still in the early stages of the painting as seen in the x-ray image) and allowing the interplay between the model and his own ideas to generate changes like the transformation of Titian's sleeping lapdog into the hissing, challenging cat. The striking position of Olympia's hand, which has been the subject of so much debate, also serves to emphasize the presence of the real Victorine. A new interpretation of the nude that rejected the false trappings of classical allegory and took account of modern social mores could only, in the France of the 1860s, show a naked prostitute on a bed; the hand acknowledges what could not be shown when an artist refused to compromise with draperies or indulge in the smooth euphemisms of academic convention.

By combining an insistence on the personality and physical presence of his female models with an insistence on the painting as surface, as a patterning of paint on canvas, Manet emphasizes the model herself as true subject rather than mere object, guarding her integrity through ambiguities in relation to her secondary, representational role. Indeed, he distances her in many instances from her anecdotal setting and from the intrusive viewer's eye, not only by blurring the physical details and preventing her from being fully 'grasped' in a visual sense, but also by fending off the voyeur – either directly, through the protective hand and the aggression of the cat in *Olympia*, or indirectly through a neutralizing male presence: the two relaxed young men in the *Déjeuner sur l'herbe*, the unconcerned man about town in the background of *The Balcony* (*102*), the seated beau – all the more significant for being a last-minute introduction – in *Nana*, where the cocotte's lively glance would otherwise have implicated only the viewer. Finally – but only because it was his last great Salon painting – the real barmaid from the Folies-Bergère, who may or may not be a prostitute, confronts the viewer with 'Olympian' calm, a girl whose divorce from the representation of her real-life situation behind the fictitious bar in Manet's studio is signified by her own displaced reflection, just as the viewer actually looking at the picture is replaced by the client whose reflection appears at the extreme limit of the canvas and our consciousness.

Apart from his *Nana*, another overtly erotic female is the curious *Young Woman Reclining in Spanish Costume* (*67*), an image from the early 1860s that evokes Baudelaire and Goya as well as

Guys and Devéria and has an inscrutable, faintly perverse aura. However, the relationship between Manet and his models usually suggests a friendly complicity. There is no sense of either aggressive intrusion or intrusive idealization. Though the faces and figures, whether male or female, do not actively seek our sympathy or impose their own mood, save perhaps in the *Spanish Singer* (*56*) and *Le bon bock* (*151*) which are somewhat untypical in this respect, we are left in no doubt about the spontaneous nature and self-assured charm of Victorine, about the placid gentleness of the artist's wife, the tense and moody intelligence of Berthe Morisot as she appears in *The Balcony* (*102*) and *Repose* (*106*), or the self-willed, upper-class independence of Mlle Lemonnier, pursed lips and firm little double chin belying the romantic effect of her pastel portrait (*210*), vignetted like a retouched society photograph. Indeed, the sharp characterization in many of the later pastel portraits, some of actresses and demi-mondaines, others from the ranks of the fashionable bourgeoisie, suggests that they are part of a gallery of types and characters which Manet would have introduced into the paintings he did not live to create, just as pastels of Méry Laurent and Jeanne Demarsy served as models for the background of *A Bar at the Folies-Bergère* (*288*).

Mallarmé wrote about Manet in relation to his own ambitious projects for a new art – in his case a dramatic art – for a new, democratic society (one recalls the reference, in 1868, to discussions with Degas about an 'art within reach of the lower classes'). Manet's essentially humane and democratic attitudes, his often-stated refusal to depart from his own spontaneous responses to contemporary life which he regarded as the only possible subject of art, underlie his deliberately but often misleadingly naïve and direct interpretations of the world in which he lived. In all his paintings he surrounds the models before him with subtle signs and symbols from both past and present. His art is informed by intelligence and tact and wit – 'You must always lead the dance and provide entertainment. Don't make it a chore, no, never a chore!' – as much as by his clear commitment to a new, democratic and Republican order. The ambiguities in his art were a way of ensuring that he himself retained his liberty while offering his work up to the expectations and desires of each spectator. This is the meaning of the clash of contradictory views still heard today, which ensures that Manet's art will remain open to interpretations extending far beyond the confines of his studio or the specific context of his times.

Apart from school reports about his lack of application and poor handwriting, little is known about Manet's early years until his voyage to Rio on a naval training ship in 1848–9. The long letters he wrote to his family reveal a lively, outspoken sixteen-year-old of acute visual sensitivity, responding with interest and amusement to life on board ship and in Rio and its surroundings.

As a student with Thomas Couture until he was just twenty-four, he rejected the idea of copying from the antique and offended his teacher by getting the studio models to take up natural poses or even keep their clothes on. He studied the art of the past, copying in museums and churches, and in the print and drawing cabinets of Paris and Florence, and kept abreast of the contemporary scene through the Salons and other exhibitions and through studying the works of Delacroix and other artists in the Musée du Luxembourg. By 1859, at the age of twenty-seven, he was ready to make his Salon début. Although the Absinthe Drinker (50) *was rejected by the jury, it marked the start of Manet's studies of contemporary Parisian types, a lifelong interest that he shared with Baudelaire as an observant* flâneur.

In the early 1860s Manet was observing bathers by the Seine and dreaming of a nude composition which he was to realize in the Déjeuner sur l'herbe (58). *In 1861 he sketched a quick portrait of his cousin* Ambroise Adam (62) *in a country garden, and his success at the Salon with the* Spanish Singer (56) *that year no doubt gave him the confidence to attempt more ambitious paintings directly inspired by life in the city. The* Old Musician (51), *in which the figure of the absinthe drinker reappears, was among a group of paintings exhibited in March 1863 at Martinet's galleries on the boulevard des Italiens. A study of Léon Leenhoff (54), also included, may have been shown there on an earlier occasion, since a letter from Manet suggests that it was exhibited on its own. Other canvases depicted urban images (61, 65), the Spanish dancers who had performed in Paris the previous winter (see 68–70) and the provocative* Young Woman Reclining in Spanish Costume (67), *which was etched by Félix Bracquemond, the colleague who helped Manet with his prints and made a pastel portrait of him in 1864.*

The shows at Martinet's galleries were part of Manet's strategy to gain support for his Salon pictures. In 1863, however, his three works were rejected and shown in the Salon des Refusés (57, 58, 60); his cousin Adam noted that 'The poor boy has one of the best positions but would rather have had a less good one in the real Salon.' At the Salon of 1864 he was strongly criticized for his Incident in a Bullfight, *subsequently cut and reworked (see 71, 72), and for* The Dead Christ and the Angels (81). *That summer, however, Manet scored a topical success with his depiction of the sinking of a Confederate ship by a United States corvette off Cherbourg. The* Combat of the Kearsarge and the Alabama (75) *was exhibited by Cadart and favourably reviewed by Philippe Burty. While on holiday at Boulogne he also produced a series of seascapes (see 73–6) in the vigorous style which led to the confusion of his work with that of Monet.*

Early in 1865 Manet evidently thought of using Martinet's galleries again as a trailer for the Salon, and may even have considered showing Olympia (85) *there, since it seems unlikely that the 'reclining woman' in the list sent to Martinet would have been the picture (67) already seen there in 1863. Disagreements with Martinet apparently led Manet to withdraw the pictures he planned to show. His Salon entries,* Jesus Mocked by the Soldiers (84) *and* Olympia (85), *caused uproar when they were shown, and prompted*

Manet to make an excursion to Spain. *After an initially unpromising encounter with Théodore Duret (24) in Madrid, the two men apparently went straight to the Prado museum, where they wrote their names in the visitors' book on 1 September 1865. Study of Velasquez and Goya led Manet to abandon the more traditional Salon subjects:* The Fifer *(14) and* The Tragic Actor *(88), inspired by Velasquez, were rejected by the jury in 1866, and he decided not to run that risk the following year, on the occasion of the* Exposition universelle. *Zola who had come to Manet's defence in* L'Événement *in 1866, published a long critical study of the artist on 1 January 1867. Manet determined to hold his own show, with a catalogue in which he spelt out his own aims and with a reprint of Zola's article. The slim booklet in blue paper wrappers appears as Manet's signature in the portrait for which Zola posed in January 1868 (91). The setting created by Manet in his studio includes the writer's paraphernalia, a Japanese screen and an actor print with reproductions after a Velasquez in the Prado and* Olympia. *Manet's letter to Zola (here redated thanks to the watermark) also refers to a portrait of 'Madame', Zola's companion who later became his wife (192).*

During the Exposition universelle *of 1867, news reached Paris of the execution of the Habsburg Archduke Maximilian who had been installed as Emperor of Mexico. This followed the withdrawal of the French troops that had guaranteed the régime, and the episode became a focus for Napoleon III's Republican critics. Manet decided to make it the subject of a history painting for the Salon, and painted three full-scale versions with the help of a much altered sketch (95). He was unofficially advised that his final version (96) would not be accepted for the Salon of 1869 and was also prevented from publishing a lithograph of the execution (22). The year 1867 also saw the death of Baudelaire in Paris. Manet attended his funeral and offered to donate his etched portraits of the poet for a memorial publication (17). In the summer of 1868 Manet spent two months at Boulogne and made a brief excursion to London.*

From 1868 to 1873 all Manet's Salon submissions were accepted. They included his portrait of Zola (91), the first appearance of Berthe Morisot, in The Balcony *(102), and a formal portrait of* Eva Gonzalès *(107), Berthe Morisot's rival as Manet's pupil. This was shown in 1870, together with* The Music Lesson *(110), for which Zacharie Astruc (90) posed. Manet himself sat for Fantin-Latour's group portrait* A Studio in the Batignolles *(Musée d'Orsay), which shows him painting a portrait of Astruc, watched by Renoir, Zola, Bazille and Monet. Manet was now widely recognized as the leader of these younger artists. Although Bazille was killed that year in the Franco-Prussian War, Monet and Renoir went on to develop the style known as Impressionism, and painted with Manet at Argenteuil in the 1870s.*

In February 1870 Manet fought a duel with the critic Duranty. In March he joined in the agitation led by Jules de La Rochenoire (211) to reform the election of the Salon jury. During a politically disturbed and anxious summer, France declared war on Prussia, Napoleon III's army was defeated and on 4 September the Empire was officially replaced by the new Republic, proclaimed in Paris by Gambetta. Resistance to the occupying Prussian forces led to further conflict. Paris organized its defences and Manet sent his family to the country, remaining in Paris as a volunteer gunner in the National Guard and later as a cavalry officer attached to the general staff. Increasing hardships were experienced in the besieged city and Manet described these in letters to his wife and mother whom he rejoined after the surrender of Paris.

[Le Havre,] Saturday [9 December 1848]

To Mme Auguste Manet   Dear Mother, if I hadn't been afraid of another separation
and the goodbyes which are always so upsetting, I would regret your not having come with
me to Le Havre; you would have seen our splendid ship where we're going to be really
comfortable; we won't have just the bare necessities, there will even be a certain amount of
luxury . . .

I don't know if we'll be leaving tomorrow, but we're embarking at 4 o'clock, prepared to sail
on a favourable wind. . . . There are 26 men on board including a cook and a Negro *maître
d'hôtel*. We've even got a very pretty saloon aft with a piano in it.

Goodbye, Mother dear, with much love

your respectful son, Edouard M.

*

[Le Havre,] Friday [15 December 1848]

I'm now going to say a final goodbye; we're quite definitely
leaving at nine o'clock tomorrow . . . Papa will come and say goodbye to me on board
tomorrow; I'm very glad he has been here until my departure, he's been so good to me
throughout our stay.

The weather is superb for our departure tomorrow, the sea looks as if it's going to be calm.
We're all delighted to be leaving even though we're extremely well off here from every point of
view, because we're looked after by four poor little ship's boys and two apprentices whose
training consists of kicks and beatings, and I assure you it makes them remarkably obedient.
Our *maître d'hôtel*, who is a Negro, as I told you, and is responsible for their training, gives
them a terrific licking if they don't behave; for our part, we don't take advantage of our right
to hit them, we're keeping that in reserve for special occasions . . .

*

On board the *Havre et Guadeloupe*, Friday 22 December [1848]

I can finally put pen to paper to write to you and tell you
what I've been doing since my departure; I wanted to write down what we have done day by
day, but was prevented by seasickness and bad weather . . .

We left Le Havre, with our colours flying, to the sound of two gunshots, and said a noisy
goodbye to the townspeople who had crowded on to the jetty to watch us leave; the weather
was superb, the sea very calm, I wasn't sick that whole day, and felt very proud of it because
most of my shipmates were hanging over the rails. At eight in the evening we sighted the
Harfleur lighthouse; from then on we were out of sight of land. I'll skip the next three or four
days; I was horribly seasick. The weather was dreadful; it's impossible to form an idea of the
sea if you haven't seen it as wild as we did, you can't imagine the mountains of water that
surround you and suddenly almost engulf the whole ship, and the wind that whistles in the
rigging and is sometimes so strong that they have to reef in all the sails. At those times,
believe me, I really missed the comforts of home; we got out of the Channel all right, but the
headwinds forced us up as far as the coast of Ireland which was way off course. Then, I can tell

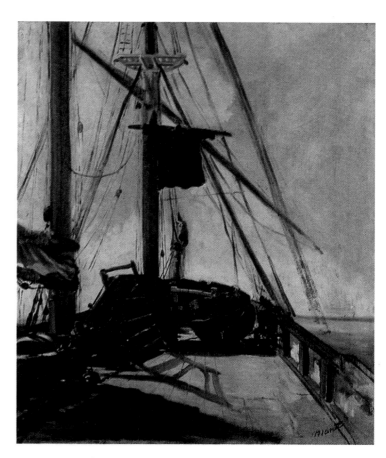

1   THE SHIP'S DECK, c.1868

you, we saw the Ocean in all its fury . . . It seems to me I've been on board for months; a sailor's life is so boring! Nothing but sea and sky, always the same thing, it's stupid; we can't do a thing, our teachers are sick and the rolling is so bad that you can't stay below deck. Sometimes at dinner we all fall on top of each other and the platters full of food with us . . .

Sunday 17

The wind changed again during the night which was dreadful; one poor sailor had a pulley fall on his head, but it didn't prevent him working as usual the next day. All these fellows are really amazing, they're always good-humoured, always jolly, in spite of the toughness of their job, because it's no fun taking in a reef perched on a yard that is sometimes under water, working day and night in all kinds of weather; the fact is that they all hate their job.

At dinner this evening we had champagne, 6 to a bottle, the captain joined us for a drink, we drank his health . . . We're all delighted with M. Besson: he is always polite and very nice to us though he's quite capable of making himself respected. One can't say the same of the second-in-command, he's a real brute, an old sea-dog who keeps you on your toes and pushes you around like anything.

In the evenings after dinner we all get together on the poop deck and sing . . . we've got some musicians on board . . .

Friday 22

There's a ship in sight; we're going to signal it and hand over our letters.

Goodbye dear Mother, with much love to you and papa, granny, my brothers, Jules. . . .

your respectful son, EDOUARD MANET

In sight of the island of Madeira, on board the *Havre et Guadeloupe*, 30 December [1848]

Friday 22 December

To Mme Auguste Manet   Dear Mother, They hurried us so much this morning to finish our letters that I couldn't tell you about our meeting with the ship we sighted. As soon as we saw it we put on all sail; the wretch, thinking we were chasing him, clapped canvas to his backside, sorry, it's the customary expression. To set his mind at rest, we hoisted our flag; reassured, he hoisted his – it was a Portuguese brig – and hailed us. . . . we gave the captain presents, a Dutch cheese, two fresh loaves and two bottles of Cognac that made the whole crew very happy . . .

Sunday 24

We've had a lovely Christmas celebration; at midnight we had a tremendous *réveillon*; the captain made us a present of six bottles of champagne, 4 Savoy cakes and two packets of Havana cigars; and we had hot chocolate . . . After going through all the songs we know, we went to bed at 4 in the morning. . . .

Monday 25

We hope to sight Madeira soon; how glad we'll be to see land! . . . We've finally caught a tuna, a beautiful fish; I can't tell you it's a delicious fish, because it's being cooked for the officers.

Tuesday 26

. . . This evening the sea was more phosphorescent than usual, the boat seemed to be plunging through a sea of fire, it was quite beautiful.

Wednesday 27

What a wonderful day! We're past the coast of Portugal; so the sun is getting hotter, and they took advantage of it this morning to wash the ship's boys: they put a big basin of water on deck and threw the 3 brats in, a sailor scrubbed them with a pumice stone and black as they had been before, they came out as white as snow. . . .

Thursday 28

We've had a fine day, the sea was calm enough for us to do some fencing. . . . I seem to be good at it and hope to master the art by the end of our trip.

At 4 o'clock, they harpooned some *porpoises*. They are huge creatures, schools of 10 or 12 swim around the ship, especially the bows; they swim like lightning and are a very difficult target. . . .

Saturday 30, 4 o'clock in the morning

What an exciting night! at midnight or 1 o'clock, the look-out began to cry land-ho; everyone rushed on deck, it was Porto-Santo; some way off we could make out a thin black line: Madeira. We'll be there today.

Goodbye, Mother dear . . .

P.S. I would like Papa to register me to take the examination in Paris. I very much hope there will be a letter from you in Rio de Janeiro.

*

In sight of Santa-Cruz, Tenerife, on board the *Havre et Guadeloupe*, 6 January 1849

Saturday evening 30 December [1848]

Dear Mother, At two in the morning, as I told you in my last letter, the look-out cried land-ho. We came a little closer, then we waited for daybreak and saw the island of *Porto-Santo*; . . . it's a mountainous island, surrounded by rocks and inhabited only by fishermen . . .

I've drawn a view of the island. My drawing will give you a clear idea of it. It's a very exact representation. There has been a magnificent catch today, the sailmaker harpooned a huge *porpoise*, we had a hard time getting it on board, it's an extraordinary fish, it has a sort of duck's bill and a jaw set with a row of little sharp, white teeth; we ate some, the flesh tastes like beef, it's not bad at all . . .

Sunday 31 December

All hope is lost, we won't be putting into port at Madeira, we've been tacking all day long, the winds are still against us . . . we've lost sight of Porto-Santo and are nearing the coasts of Africa; we're all very sad, because we had counted on posting our letters and taking on plenty of oranges.

Monday 1 January 1849

I'm wishing you a Happy New Year, dear Father and Mother, from far far away . . .

This is how we spent our New Year's Day on board: at 6 o'clock in the morning, the sailors came down to our quarters and woke us up with a million good wishes, they brought a superb porpoise pâté that they themselves had made, it was delicious . . . we went up to the poop deck to wish the Captain a Happy New Year; he served madeira and did the honours very well. . . . at 3 o'clock a storm got up . . . and everyone went below; that didn't prevent us enjoying ourselves in the evening. We had invited the whole crew to dinner, we'd been given champagne, and one of the sailors, who knows almost all the operas and comic operas, sang us his whole repertory until half-past eight. We all went to bed delighted with our evening. . . .

Friday 5 January [1849]

. . . tomorrow around ten or 11 o'clock we should drop anchor off Santa Cruz de Tenerife; that's where we'll post our letters, and probably take on fresh rations; they hope to get us oranges which are very cheap there; I'll get a sailor to buy me some native pipes which I'm told are very good; tell Papa and Edmond and the smokers among our friends that I'll bring some back for them. . . .

Goodbye, dear Mother, with my fondest love and to Papa, my brothers, Granny.

EDOUARD M.

*

The voyage to Rio, 1848–1849

TO AUGUSTE MANET Dear Papa, another disappointment; after tacking all day long off Santa Cruz, we had to leave without dropping anchor. The winds were against us. Still, we had a perfect view of the island of Tenerife, there's nothing finer than its famous mountain, 11,130 feet high, with its summit covered in snow . . . It's been a month since we left, though this voyage normally takes 12 days . . .

Monday 8 January

At 5 o'clock this afternoon we crossed the tropic of Cancer; we're now only some 520 leagues from the Line, and we've been promised a magnificent baptism. . . .

Wednesday 10 January

We met two English ships today . . . We've not had the luck to meet a French mailboat which could end our anxiety about what's happening and what has happened in Paris, we can only guess what consequences the election of one president or another might have. . . .

Sunday 21 and Monday 22 January

We'll be crossing the Line tomorrow, and we've been having preliminary ceremonies today. At midday an astrologer, the son-in-law of old Father Line, came down from the main mast followed by his assistant; he got the Captain to go up on the poop deck, calculated the height of the sun, and indicated the course to steer. Then, after joking with the Captain, he climbed back up where he had come from to find out whether Father Line would allow us to cross his domains . . .

This morning, the 22nd, we were forbidden to go forward; . . . at last the procession appears . . . a priest, a choirboy; Father Line and his wife, all got up you can't imagine how; the god Neptune, a barber, two policemen and finally the devil and his son. The procession climbed up to the poop deck; Father Line paid his respects to the Captain and introduced his better half, then the priest delivered the funniest sermon and the first baptism got under way . . . this is what they do to baptise you: first you're taken to an altar for confession; the priest makes you take all sorts of vows followed by communion; then you're put into the hands of the barber who applies paint all over your face and neck, etc., then scrapes your skin as hard as he can with a wooden razor two feet long, but that's not all; one of the men asks you to wash in a big basin of water near the altar; suspecting nothing, I approached the basin, but he grabbed me by the legs and threw me into a nosedive that I'm not likely to forget. After this trial, most people think that's all, but you haven't taken two steps outside the tent when you fall into the arms of the devil who is actually our Negro and who daubs you from top to bottom with his tail soaked in pitch. Once we had all been baptised, we all took buckets and soaked each other . . .

Tuesday 30

For two or three days we've been repainting the ship; we want to arrive in Rio looking as smart as possible . . .

Let me remind you, dear Papa, how much I would like to take my exams in Paris, it's much the best thing; I don't want to sit them in the provinces . . .

In the Rio de Janeiro roads, 5 February 1849

To Mme Auguste Manet   We've finally cast anchor in the Rio roads after 2 months at sea and a lot of bad weather. . . . The Captain went ashore this evening and brought back a dozen letters, I hoped one of them might be from you, but my luck wasn't in . . .

. . . On Sunday after Mass . . . I went ashore with M. Jules Lacarrière, a young man of my age. He took me to his mother who has a dress shop on Ouvidor Road and owns a small Brazilian-style country house 5 minutes from Rio; I . . . was received with open arms, in the nicest possible way. After lunch I went off with my new friend to explore the town. It's quite big, but with very small streets; for an artistically minded European it has a very special character; in the street you encounter only Negroes and Negresses; Brazilian men don't go out much and ladies even less . . . In this country all the Negroes are slaves; they all look downtrodden; it's extraordinary what power the whites have over them; I saw a slave market, a rather revolting spectacle for people like us; the Negroes wear trousers, sometimes a cotton jacket, but as slaves they're not allowed to wear shoes. The Negresses are generally naked to the waist, some with a scarf tied at the neck and falling over their breasts, they are usually ugly, though I have seen some quite pretty ones . . . Some wear turbans, others do their frizzy hair in elaborate styles and almost all wear petticoats adorned with monstrous flounces.

Most Brazilian women are very pretty; they have superb dark eyes and hair to match . . . they never go out alone but are always followed by their black maid or accompanied by their children . . .

. . . There's something very comical about the Brazilian militia, the Brazilians also have a national guard, there is a press law in this country and it's in force at the present moment, because there have been disorders in Bahia and they keep sending troops there.

I wish you would write a really nice letter to my hostess and thank her for the way she has looked after me . . . don't be put off by the fact that she owns a dress shop, she is quite exceptional and her son is a pupil at the Jouffroy boarding school, a delightful boy and better brought up, I can assure you, than many of us. . . .

We haven't been able to find a drawing teacher in Rio, and the Captain has asked me to give my shipmates lessons, so now they've set me up as a drawing teacher: I may say that I acquired quite a reputation during the voyage, all the officers and tutors asked me to do caricatures of them and even the Captain wanted one as a New Year's gift; I was lucky enough to carry it all off to everyone's satisfaction. . . .

The Carnival of Rio is something quite special. On the Sunday before Lent I spent the whole day walking around town. At 3 o'clock, all the Brazilian ladies are at their front doors or on their balconies, bombarding every gentleman who passes with multicoloured wax balls filled with water; these are called *limons*.

In several streets I was subjected to the customary bombardment. My pockets were filled with *limons* and I gave as good as I got, which is the proper thing to do. This game went on until 6 o'clock in the evening, when everything quietened down and then there was a masked ball something like our Opera balls . . . We spent Shrove Tuesday in the country. It was a delightful outing . . . unfortunately there are enormous quantities of snakes and you have to take great care when walking in the undergrowth . . .

Your respectful son, Edouard Manet

*

The voyage to Rio, 1848–1849

In the Rio de Janeiro roads, Monday 26 February [1849]

TO JULES DE JOUY   I was delighted to get your letter ... I wonder if you'll be able to decipher my scrawl and my impressions; I must confess I found the early days pretty grim ... more than once I wondered: *what on earth have I let myself in for*, but the bad days are over, we're all hardened sailors now. ...

In telling you about Rio I'll be more or less repeating what I said in my letter to my mother ... All the Negroes in Rio are slaves. The slave trade flourishes here. As for the Brazilians, they are spineless and seem to have little energy, their women are generally very good-looking but don't deserve the reputation for looseness they've acquired in France; there's nothing so prudish or stupid as a Brazilian lady ...

Now that I know Rio inside out, I long to be back with you all in France.

Why are you moving house? That surprises me. Are you really worried about your job? With your knowledge of politics, how do you feel about the election of L[ouis] Napoleon; for goodness' sake don't go and make him emperor, that would be too much of a good thing.

So poor Eugène is despondent as usual, what a funny boy he is, it doesn't make sense, because everything seems to be going well for him this year. ...

Yours ever, EDOUARD MANET

*

In the Rio de Janeiro roads, on board the *Havre et Guadeloupe*, 11 March 1849

TO EUGÈNE MANET   My dear brother, I'm taking advantage of a ship leaving for Le Havre to write you a few lines, thinking that you'll be as pleased to get a letter from me as I would have been to get one from you. We've almost come to the end of our cruise, since we'll be leaving Rio on 10 April ... I'll be very glad to see the harbour at Le Havre, I can assure you, although I'm now quite used to life at sea ...

Well, believe it or not, I'm more bored since I've been at Rio than I was on the high seas, looking at land and not being able to get there except on Thursdays and Sundays; at the time of writing, I haven't been ashore for two weeks. On an excursion to the country with people from the town, I was bitten on the foot by some snake, my foot got terribly swollen, it was agony, but now I'm over it. ... in the end I haven't really enjoyed my stay in the roadstead; I've been harassed, a bit roughed up; and have more than once been tempted to jump ship ...

I have no hope of passing this year, on board ship it's even harder to concentrate than on land ...

To judge by Mother's letter, you're finding maths difficult, but don't let it get you down; everyone feels the same way at first. Be sure to remember me to my friends at the Collège Rollin ...

Jules has written to me, as you know; he tells me he's leaving the rue Guénégaud, but he seemed so well settled there. I was hoping that in spite of Louis Napoleon he would still have his job in the legal administration when I return. ...

I hope to bring you back a monkey, I've been promised one. Every time I go walking in the woods or in some virgin forest, I think of Papa and start looking for canes; I've found some good ones. ...

*

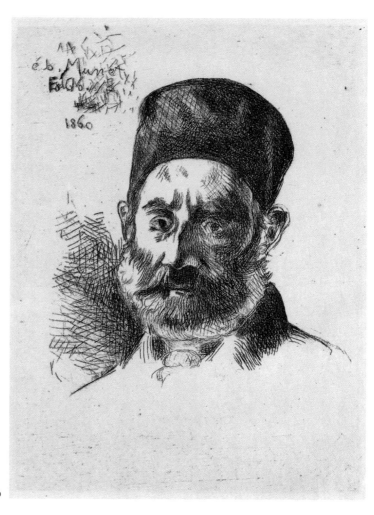

2 AUGUSTE MANET, d.1860

In the Rio de Janeiro roads, on board the *Havre et Guadeloupe*, 22 March 1849

Dear Papa, I thought the letter Eugène received would be
the last I would write you, but now there's another opportunity...

So you've had more excitement in Paris; try and keep a decent republic against our return,
for I fear L[ouis] Napoleon is not a good republican....

Your respectful son, E. MANET

*

[1849]

RECORDED BY ANTONIN PROUST   ...my father sent me off as a naval apprentice bound for
Rio de Janeiro. Captain Besson, who had seen me painting during the voyage, said to me when
we reached Rio: 'Since you can paint, young man, you can repaint these Dutch cheeses which
have been discoloured by seawater. Here's a pot of red lead and some brushes'. I went to work.
On our arrival at anchorage, the cheeses glistened like tomatoes. The natives, especially the
Negroes, rushed to buy them and devoured them down to the rind, regretting only that there
weren't any more.

Several days later, the authorities issued an announcement to reassure the population which
had been alarmed by some mild cases of cholera. The announcement attributed them to
overindulgence in unripened fruit. Naturally I had my own ideas about this. But in business
discretion is essential. I didn't say a word and... from then on the captain treated me with
exceptional consideration and he for one was convinced of my talent.

Couture's studio, 1850–1856, and early years as an artist

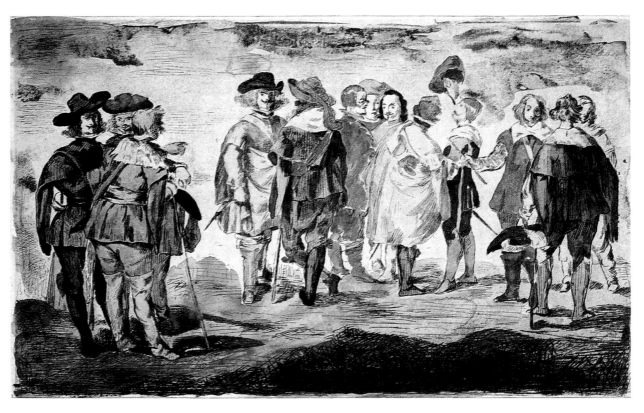

3   THE LITTLE CAVALIERS, AFTER VELASQUEZ C.1861–2

[1850s]

RECORDED BY CHARLES TOCHÉ   The day I enrolled in Couture's studio, they gave me an antique cast to copy. I turned it around in every direction. It looked more interesting upside down. In the end, after two or three attempts, I gave up the idea of getting anything out of Antiquity. But I learnt a great deal on my trip to Brazil. I spent endless nights looking at the play of light and shade in the ship's wake. And in the daytime, from the upper deck, I would keep my eyes on the horizon. That's how I learnt how to capture a sky.

*

[1850s]

RECORDED BY ANTONIN PROUST   [In Couture's studio]   I don't know what I'm doing here. Everything we're looking at is absurd. The light is all wrong, the shadows are wrong. When I get to the studio, I feel I'm entering a tomb. Of course I know we can't have models undressing in the street. But there's the countryside and in the summer at least we could do nude studies out in the open, since the nude, we're told, is the Alpha and Omega in art. . . .

[To life models in 'antique' poses]   Can't you behave naturally? Do you stand like that when you go to buy a bunch of radishes at your greengrocer's? . . .

We're not in Rome. We don't want to go to Rome. We're in Paris and we intend to stay here. . . .

[To a fellow student]   Do you take me for a history painter? . . . Reconstructing historical figures – what a joke! Do you base a man's portrait on his hunting licence? There's only one good way. Capture what you see in one go. When it's right, it's right. When it's wrong, you start again. Anything else is nonsense.

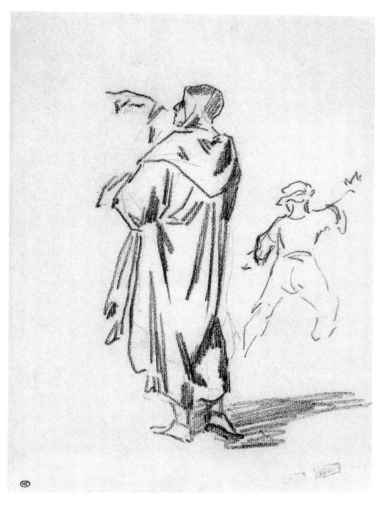

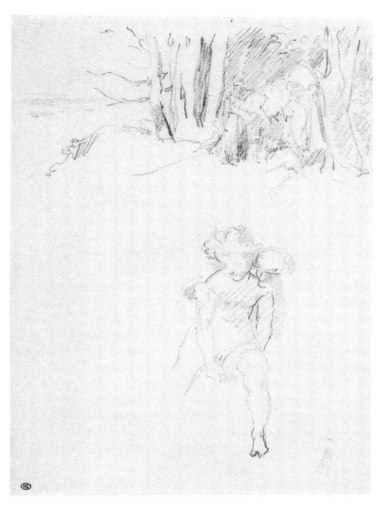

4 AFTER ANDREA DEL SARTO'S GAMBLERS STRUCK
   BY LIGHTNING (DETAIL), 1857

5 AFTER ANDREA DEL SARTO'S ST JOHN BAPTISING
   THE PEOPLE (DETAIL), 1857

[On Delacroix] . . . there's a real masterpiece in the Luxembourg, and that's the *Barque of Dante*. Suppose we call on Delacroix on the pretext of asking his permission to copy the *Barque*.

. . . It's not Delacroix who is cold, it's his theories that are chilling. Still, let's copy the *Barque* (*31*). It's a real piece of painting.

[On Velasquez's *Cavaliers* (*52*)] Now . . . that's good clean work. It puts you off the brown-sauce school . . . Velasquez, El Greco, Valdés Leal, Herrera the Elder, they're really impressive, I'm not making a case for Murillo, I don't like him, nor Zurbarán. But what about Ribera and Goya, you know what Reynolds said of Goya: 'He's a Spanish painter, but of the Gibraltar school.' That soapy Englishman could do with a few painters of Goya's calibre!

[On Courbet's *Burial at Ornans*, Salon of 1852] Yes, the *Burial* is very good. It can't be said often enough that it is very good, because it's better than anything else. But between ourselves, it still doesn't go far enough. It is too dark.

*

Florence, 19 November 1857

TO THE PRESIDENT OF THE ACADEMY   Messrs Eugène Brunet and Edouard Manet from Paris respectfully beg permission from the President of the Academy to work for 30 days in the cloister of the Annunziata (*4, 33, 34*).

E. MANET   EUG. BRUNET

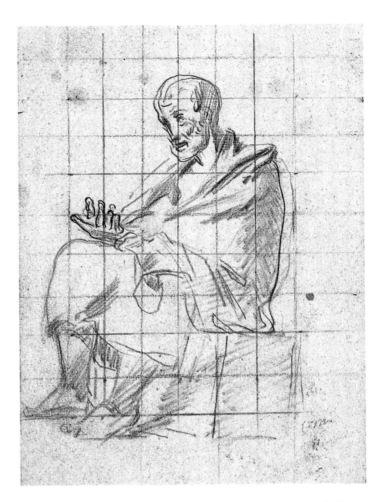

6   AFTER AN ENGRAVED COPY OF GIULIO ROMANO'S
BATHSHEBA (DETAIL), c.1858–60

7   AFTER A HELLENISTIC CARVING OF CHRYSIPPOS, c.1858–60

25 November 1858

TO THE BIBLIOTHÈQUE IMPÉRIALE CURATOR   M. Edouard Manet, artist, domiciled in Paris at 52 rue de la Victoire, respectfully begs the curator to grant him a student card that will enable him to work in the Print Room [see (6)].

*

[1858–60]

RECORDED BY ANTONIN PROUST   [After a row with Couture]   All right then, I'll do a picture that will really amaze him.

[On Couture's response to the *Absinthe Drinker* (50)] Well, that's that, I was silly enough to make him a few concessions and foolishly laid in my picture according to his formula. That's all over now. It's a good thing he spoke to me as he did. It's put me back on my feet again. . . .

[After the Salon jury's verdict]   I heard it three days ago. I didn't want to tell you. So he got them to throw it out. I can imagine what he must have said about it to his old cronies. But what comforts me is that Delacroix thought it was good. Yes, because I've definitely been told that Delacroix liked it. He's a horse of a different colour from Couture. I don't care for his technique. But he knows what he wants and gets it. That's something.

[On Baudelaire's contention that you must be yourself]   That's what I've always told you, my dear Baudelaire, but surely I was being myself in the *Absinthe Drinker*? . . .

[On the *Absinthe Drinker*]   I've painted a Parisian type, observed in Paris and executed with the same naïve technique that I found in Velasquez's [*Cavaliers* (52)]. They don't understand it.

Perhaps they'll understand better if I paint a Spanish type.

[On the *Spanish Singer* (*56*)]   I think that's just about right, isn't it! When I was painting this figure, I was thinking about the Madrid masters and about Hals as well. You know, I can't believe that Hals wasn't in fact a Spaniard. Which wouldn't be so surprising, since he came from Malines [Mechelen, in the Spanish Netherlands].

Renaud de Vilbac called in yesterday. All he could see was that my *Guitarrero* was playing a guitar strung for the right hand with his left hand. What do you think of that? Just imagine, I painted the head in a single sitting. After two hours at it, I looked in my little black mirror, and it worked. I didn't add a single brushstroke.

[On the portrait of his parents (*48*)]   As for my mother and father, I posed them in the most straightforward way, just as you see them there.

[On the river bank at Argenteuil]   It seems I've got to do a nude. All right, I'll let them have one.

When we were in [Couture's] studio, I copied Giorgione's women, the women with the musicians [*Le Concert champêtre*]. It's a really dark picture in which the ground has come through. I want to make a new version [see (*58*)], with a transparent atmosphere, with figures like those you can see over there. They'll tear me apart. They'll say I'm being influenced by the Italians after being influenced by the Spanish masters. . . .

[On Titian and the Italian primitives]   I detest everything unnecessary, but it's so difficult to distinguish just what is necessary. We've been perverted by all the artistic tricks of the trade. How to get rid of them? Who's going to give us back a clear, direct kind of painting and do away with the frills? The one true way is to go straight ahead, without worrying about what people are going to say.

[On French painters]   You can certainly get effects by laying on the colours with a palette knife, with plenty of bitumen in the underlying layers, but what does it add up to? Courbet (*8*) quite likes these tricks, but he treats them in the right way, as something of a joke. The other day he called at Deforge's shop. Diaz was there. 'How much do you want for your Turk?' he asked Diaz, pointing to one of his pictures on display. Diaz replied, 'It's not a Turk, it's a Virgin.' 'Well that's no good to me, I wanted a Turk,' said Courbet and went back to the café with his friends, shouting with laughter. . . . But however much he jeers, he is still very much a Frenchman and a great painter. When all is said and done there is a basic honesty in this country that always brings us back to the truth, however dazzling the displays put on by the acrobats. Look at artists like the Le Nain brothers, Watteau, Chardin, even David: they all have a feeling for truth.

*

[c.1860–61/1863?]

To Louis Martinet   Monsieur Martinet, You have asked the price of the picture exhibited in your gallery (*Boy holding a sword*) (*54*). I would like *one thousand* francs for it but I authorize you, *if you see fit*, to let it go for eight hundred.

Edouard Manet

*

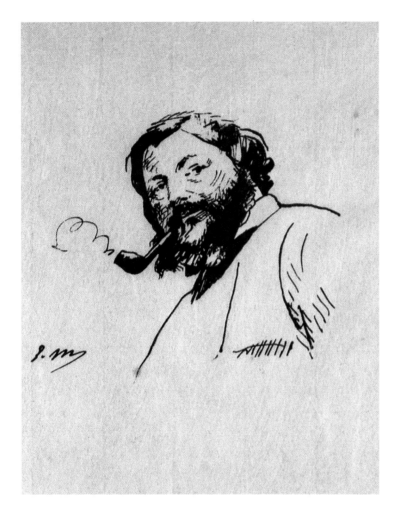

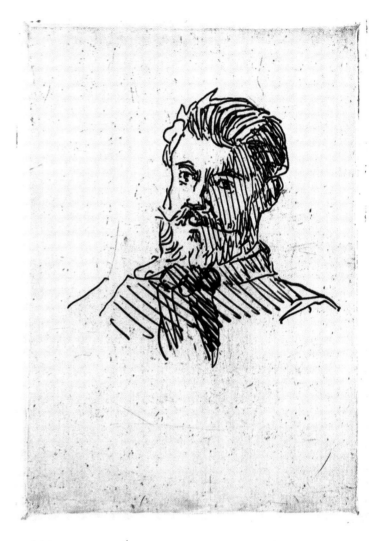

8 PORTRAIT OF GUSTAVE COURBET, 1878

9 PORTRAIT OF FÉLIX BRACQUEMOND, c.1868

[before May 1864]

TO FÉLIX BRACQUEMOND . . . I'm in my studio every day until four o'clock and on Tuesdays you'll find me at home from five o'clock on. But I'd like to see you to settle on a day each week for the sittings. It's not much, but it will give you time to finish my portrait for the [Salon] exhibition and, considering how late I am, I won't lose too much time.

Yours, ED. MANET

*

Saturday evening [1864]

I was expecting you today, I was going to compliment you on your portrait. I'm only sorry that you didn't work up the hands as much as you have the head, which is really very good and will do you great credit. . . .

*

[1864]

I thought I would see you at the Café de Bade to discuss the etching proof you sent me [after (67)]. I think a background is needed, the sofa should be treated rather more vigorously, the curtain removed, and perhaps the whole should be reworked a little more freely.

If you're dining in Montmartre tomorrow, drop in at my studio. I'll be there all day.

[Boulogne-sur-mer, after 17 July 1864]

Although I'm enjoying my seaside holiday, I miss our discussions on Art with a capital A, and besides there's no Café de Bade here.

I've done some studies of small boats on the open sea. On Sunday I went to see the *Kearsarge*, which was lying at anchor off Boulogne. I'll bring back a study. If you hear any news, let me know. I'm always avid for news; is our friend Baudelaire back in Paris?

Give my warm regards to Lejosne, Fioupou, Stevens, all the Café de Bade crowd.

*

Boulogne-sur-mer [after 18 July 1864]

TO PHILIPPE BURTY

I've just read your complimentary lines about my picture (75) in *La Presse* [of 18 July]. I'm grateful to you and hope the proverb 'one swallow doesn't make a summer' will not apply to us!

The *Kearsarge* was anchored off Boulogne last Sunday and I went to see her; I had formed a pretty accurate view of her, and in fact have now painted her as she looks out at sea (76) — you'll be able to judge.

*

Tuesday 14 [February 1865]

TO CHARLES BAUDELAIRE [in Brussels]

I went to see Lemère and Marcellin [sic] yesterday evening. Lemère seems favourably inclined and thinks that *Faure* might be the publisher to take it on. . . .

Mme Meurice has asked me to tell you they've heard that Lacroix has asked Judith to translate an English author, Mathurin [sic] I think. I'm not sure of the spelling. Meurice says you are the only person capable of translating the book. Lévy, who has heard about this and is always keen to go against Lacroix, is quite capable of asking *you* to do the translation. What do you think?

The good Commandant Lejosne, who seems a bit of a fool to me, continues to be concerned, or to pretend to be concerned, over the health of his formidable wife, but I hope for our friend's sake that he's a victim of and not an accessory to her ridiculous behaviour.

We are all painting like mad. Fantin is preparing a *Toast to Truth*, to be drunk by his friends of course. I think he will let us in for some hard knocks. I haven't painted out the sketch of Adèle and I'll be sending Martinet nine *new* canvases for the exhibition that will be opening on Sunday; these are in addition to what I'll be sending to the Palais de l'Industrie [for the Salon]. I'm very late, but you can see I've not been wasting my time.

Bracquemond will probably be going to Brussels to engrave some pictures by Leys. Fioupou sends his regards and asks you to buy him any Directoire or First Republic fashion plates you may come across.

You never told me whether you received the music I ordered from the publisher on the place de la Madeleine, did he send it? He told me he would have to order it from Germany, he was sold out.

You mention the *Revue de Paris*, it seems pretty poor to me and unlikely to survive for long.

EDOUARD MANET

[15–17 February 1865]

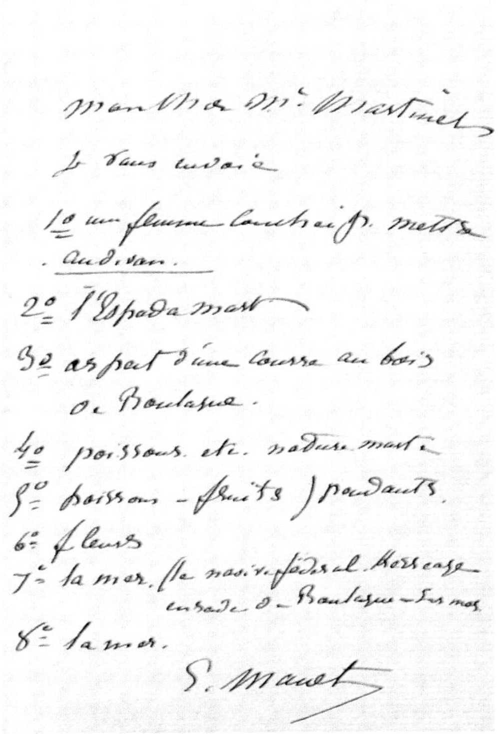

TO LOUIS MARTINET

My dear M. Martinet, I'm sending you

1   a reclining woman (67?/85?) to put *in the Oriental room*
2   the dead Matador (72)
3   view of a race in the Bois de Boulogne [see (92)]
4   fish etc. still life
5   fish – fruit: pendants (77, 78)
6   flowers (80)
7   the sea (the Union ship *Kearsarge* at anchor off Boulogne-sur-mer) (76)
8   the sea

E. MANET

10   LETTER TO LOUIS MARTINET, February 1865

[March–April 1865?]

TO FÉLIX BRACQUEMOND

Thank you for thinking of my exhibition. I'm all ready. But whom should I contact? Should I go and see Petit? Would it be better to call on Chesneau who has shown some sympathy for me and might be able to ward off the hostility of that rotten old de N[ieuwerkerke]. Why don't you come to the Café de Bade before dinner on Tuesday, or write and tell me what you think. I've had a letter from Baudelaire who sends his regards.

*

[c.25 March 1865]

TO CHARLES BAUDELAIRE [in Brussels]

You are very wise and I was wrong to get upset, my picture was accepted just as I was writing to you. In fact, from what I hear, it won't be too bad a year; it's a *Jesus mocked by the soldiers* (84) and I think it's the last time I'll be going in for that sort of subject [see (81)]. So you didn't in fact know that Th. Gautier was on the jury. I didn't send him your letter, it was no longer necessary and it's better not to use letters of recommendation when there's no need to.

I've recently had quite a surprise. M. *Ernest Chesneau* bought a picture from me, two flowers in a vase, a little thing I showed at Cardart's, perhaps it will bring me luck.

I've just finished the *Mystery of Maria Roget* because I began at the end, I'm always so curious, and I'm amazed that idiot Vilmessant [sic] didn't want it. It's original and amusing.

E. MANET

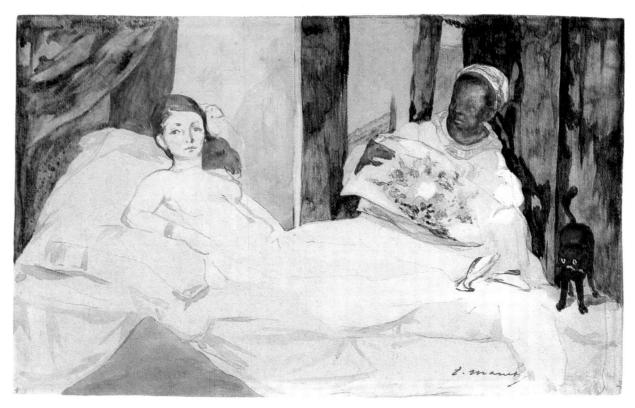

II   OLYMPIA, c.1863–5

[early May 1865]

I wish I had you here, my dear Baudelaire, insults are
beating down on me like hail, I've never been through anything like it. Verwée will tell you all
about it, he has sent in two remarkable pictures which are much appreciated.

I wish I could have your sound judgment on my pictures (*84, 85*) because all this uproar is
upsetting, and obviously someone must be wrong; Fantin has been an angel, he has been
standing up for me, which is all the nicer of him considering that his own picture this year [*The
Toast*], though good in many ways, is less effective than last year's (and he knows it).

You must be finding your prolonged stay over there very fatiguing, I can't wait to see you
back, like all your friends.

How are your negotiations with Lemer getting on? I wish our newspapers and journals
would give us more of your work, for example some of the poetry you must have written over
this last year.

The Academy in London has rejected my pictures.

ED. MANET

*

[1865]

RECORDED BY ANTONIN PROUST   [On public reaction to *Olympia* (85)]   That kind . . . I know
them. They need something frothy. I can't provide that particular article. There are specialists
who can.

*

[1865]

RECORDED BY THÉODORE DURET   [At the Salon of 1865]   Who is this Monet whose name
sounds just like mine and who is taking advantage of my notoriety?

*

The visit to Spain, September 1865

To Zacharie Astruc [at Fontainebleau]   What a good letter, really detailed, really clear, I'm delighted with it and am encouraged to set off all by myself; you are the only companion I would have wished for. If I had sold *Olympia* (*85*) which I was on the point of doing recently, I would have treated myself to the pleasure of your company. But I had the cheek to ask ten thousand francs for it. So that's for another day. I should be going with Champfleury and Stevens, but they keep putting it off... Anyway they're a bloody bore. Excuse the unseemly language, but since my letter is not for publication, I can say what I please; I'm tempted to leave immediately, the day after tomorrow perhaps, I simply can't wait to see all those wonderful things and go to *Maître* Velasquez for advice.

Your itinerary seems excellent; I'll follow it precisely though I'm told there's cholera at Marseilles, which may prevent me from taking that route home....

Give Mme Astruc all our good wishes for the arrival of your heir. We would love the same thing to happen to us....

ED. MANET

*

[1 September 1865]

Recorded by Théodore duret   [On their meeting in Madrid]   Well Sir, is it just to annoy me, to make an ass of me that you pretend to enjoy this revolting food and keep calling the waiter back every time I send him away?... You must have recognized me, you must know who I am?...

[On Duret's denial]   Ah! you've come from Portugal, well! I've just come from Paris.

*

Grand Hôtel de Paris, Puerta del Sol, Madrid, Sunday morning [3 September 1865]

To Henri Fantin-Latour   How I miss you here and how happy it would have made you to see Velasquez who all by himself makes the journey worthwhile; the artists of all the other schools around him in the museum at Madrid, who are extremely well represented, all look like shams. He is the supreme artist; he didn't surprise me, he enchanted me. The full-length portrait we have in the Louvre is not from his hand [see (*12*)]. Only the *Infanta* is indisputable. There is a huge painting here, full of little figures like those in the Louvre picture called the *Cavaliers* (*52*), but with figures of women as well as men, perhaps of higher quality and above all completely unrestored. The landscape in the background is by a pupil of Velasquez.

The most extraordinary piece in this splendid *œuvre* and possibly the most extraordinary piece of painting that has ever been done is the picture described in the catalogue as a portrait of a famous actor at the time of Philip IV; the background disappears, there's nothing but air surrounding the fellow, who is all in black and appears alive; and the *Spinners*, the fine portrait of Alonso Cano; *las Meninas* (the dwarfs) [sic], another extraordinary picture; the philosophers, both amazing pieces; all the dwarfs, one in particular seen sitting full face with his hands on his hips, a choice picture for a true connoisseur; his magnificent portraits – one would have to go

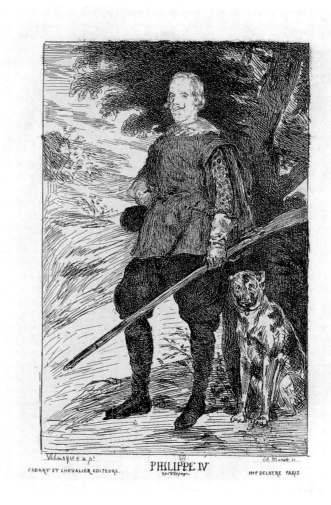

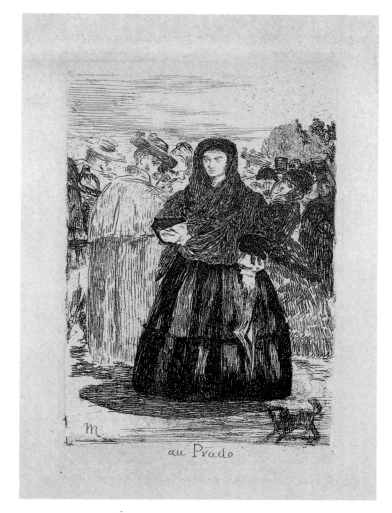

12 AFTER VELASQUEZ'S PHILIP IV IN HUNTING DRESS, 1862   13 AU PRADO (ON THE PRADO), c.1863

through them all, they are all masterpieces; a portrait of Charles V by Titian, which is highly regarded and which I'm sure I would have admired anywhere else, seems wooden to me here.

Then there's Goya, the most original next to the master whom he imitated too closely in the most servile sense of imitation. But still he's tremendously spirited. The museum has two fine equestrian portraits by him, done in the manner of Velasquez, though much inferior. What I've seen by Goya so far hasn't greatly appealed to me; in a day or so I'm to see a splendid collection of his work at the Duke of Osuna's.

I'm disappointed; the weather is terrible this morning and I'm afraid the bullfight which should take place this evening and which I'm so much looking forward to may be postponed, till heaven knows when. Tomorrow I am going on an excursion to Toledo where I'm told I shall see both *Greco* and Goya very well represented.

Madrid is a pleasant town, full of entertaining things to do. The Prado, a charming promenade full of pretty women all in mantillas (*13, 19*). . . . in the street one still sees a lot of local costumes, and the bullfighters are also strikingly dressed.

Goodbye for now, my dear Fantin, greetings and yours ever,

E. MANET

. . . The day I arrived in Madrid I met a Frenchman [Théodore Duret (*24*)] who is interested in art and who knew me. So I am not alone.

The return from Spain

To CHARLES BAUDELAIRE [in Brussels]   I got back from Madrid only yesterday, and my wife has just given me your letter. What a bore that your affairs are not settled, you seem to be detained endlessly over there and I'm very much afraid that the Garnier-Lemer negotiations may not come to anything, they seem to be dragging on for ever. I don't expect to be back in Paris before the end of September, I need to take a rest here after my trip which was very hurried and tiring.

I'm afraid I can't become the proud owner of your portrait by Courbet and I'm very sorry, but it occurs to me that Lejosne might be willing and able to do so; I would certainly discuss it with him if I were in Paris and I suggest you write to him about it.

At last, my dear Baudelaire, I've really come to know Velasquez and I tell you he's the greatest artist there has ever been; I saw 30 or 40 of his canvases in Madrid, portraits and other things, all masterpieces; he's greater than his reputation and compensates all by himself for the fatigue and problems that are inevitable on a journey in Spain. I saw some interesting things by Goya, some of them very fine, including an incredibly charming portrait of the Duchess of Alba dressed as a *majo* [sic].

One of the finest, most curious and most terrifying sights to be seen is a bullfight. When I get back I hope to put on canvas the brilliant, glittering effect and also the drama of the *corrida* I saw. And the *Prado*, too, where every evening one can see the most attractive women in Madrid, all wearing mantillas over their hair. But although this country provides a feast for the eyes, one's stomach suffers tortures. When you sit down to table you want to vomit rather than eat. I had to leave alone after waiting for Stevens and Champfleury, another pair I won't rely on in future, not even to cross the Boulevard.

Goodbye for now, my dear Baudelaire, warmest regards, and believe me, no one but you can look after your affairs properly, don't count on others; no good can come of your staying in that wretched country.

E. MANET

Here's my address: at the château de Vassé, c/o M. Fournier, near Sillé-le-Guillaume (Sarthe).

*

To ZACHARIE ASTRUC   I'm back from my Spanish tour and am staying on here for a few days. I'm planning to take a bit of a rest, because I had a great deal to see in a short time and came back to the family worn out. Your advice and excellent instructions guided me during my stay, so it's to you, first and foremost, that I owe an account of what I found there. What thrilled me most in Spain and made the whole trip worthwhile were the works of Velasquez. He's the greatest artist of all; he came as no surprise, however, for I discovered in his work the fulfilment of my own ideals in painting, and the sight of those masterpieces gave me enormous hope and courage . . . I was not at all impressed by Ribera and Murillo. They are definitely second-rate artists. Compared to Velasquez's portrait of the *Duke of Olivares*, Titian's *Charles V* looks like a dummy on a rocking horse. There were only two painters, apart from the Master, who attracted me: Greco whose work is bizarre, but includes some very fine portraits (I didn't like his *Christ* at Burgos at all) and Goya whose masterpiece seems to me to be in the Academy (*The Duchess of Alba* [in fact the *Clothed Maja*], what a stunning creation). I must have asked a dozen times or more at the Café Suisse for the artist García Martínez; he was not in Madrid, so I didn't manage to see the Osuna Gallery [at La Alameda].

Like you, I admired Toledo, Valladolid and San Pablo, Burgos and its cathedral. But what horrible food in that country . . . ! It's a great pity. I stayed a week in Madrid and had plenty of time to see everything, the Prado with all those mantillas was absolutely delightful, but the outstanding sight is the bullfight. I saw a magnificent one, and when I get back to Paris I plan to put a quick impression on canvas: the colourful crowd, and the dramatic aspect as well, the picador and horse overturned, with the bull's horns ploughing into them and the horde of *chulos* trying to draw the furious beast away (*86*, *87*).

Write to me, my dear fellow, if you have time . . . I went off on my own, as I think I told you; what would Stevens and Champfleury have done in Spain anyway? . . .

EDOUARD MANET

*

Paris, 13 October [1865]

TO THÉODORE DURET [in Saintes]   I would have written to you earlier to say how interesting I found your articles on Spain, but I was not yet back in Paris when your packet reached me. On my return from the Sarthe, I went down with the illness [mild cholera] that most Parisians are suffering from at the moment and we were spending a few days with friends in the country; I'm better now and will soon be back at work. I have, however, already painted *The bullring in Madrid* (*86*) since my return; I would love to have your dauntingly frank opinion of it on your next trip to Paris. I must say that I very much hope there will be a follow-up to your articles and that you will go on to talk about Spain from the artistic and political points of view, with special emphasis on Velasquez, Goya and Greco! so make sure you send me the texts.

It will be nice to see you again and have a chat about our adventures in Spain, but I warn you in advance, you will never get me to agree that we ate a decent lunch in Toledo.

ED. MANET

*

[c.25 October 1865]

TO CHARLES BAUDELAIRE [in Brussels]   I've been back in Paris for quite some time now, after falling victim to the current epidemic; fortunately my family is all right. It's a long time since I had any news from you. I've tried to see Lemer on several occasions but can't get hold of him. Are there any new developments on that front? I was delighted to hear that Victor Hugo can't do without you now; I'm not surprised; he's bound to find the company of someone like you more attractive than that of his usual crowd of lionizers. Couldn't he put you in touch with his publishers?

I'm sure you want to come back to Paris as soon as possible and will pray that the year 1866 does not find you still in Brussels. . . .

ED. MANET

Paris, 27 March [1866]

To CHARLES BAUDELAIRE [in Brussels]   It's a very long time since I had any news from you; let me know before too long how you are and what you're up to. I'm still waiting for the book you said was on the way [*Les Épaves*], and my mouth has been watering at the thought of having something new of yours to read.

I've sent two pictures to the Salon; I'll have them photographed and send you prints; there's a portrait of *Rouvière* in the rôle of *Hamlet* (*88*), which I call the Tragic Actor to escape criticism from people who may not find it a good likeness – and a Fifer from the light-infantry guards (*14*), but you have to see the paintings to get a proper idea of them.

Madame Meurice sends her good wishes and would like a letter from you; her portrait by Bracquemond will be in the Salon. . . .

Yours ever, ED. MANET

*

Monday 7 May [1866]

To ÉMILE ZOLA   Dear Monsieur Zola, I don't know where to find you to shake your hand and tell you how proud and happy I am to be championed by a man of your talent, what a splendid article [in *L'Événement*, 7 May], a thousand thanks.

Your previous article (*Le moment artistique*) [4 May] was quite remarkable and made a great impression. I would like to consult you about something. Where could we meet? I'm at the Café de Bade, 26 boulevard des Italiens, every day from 5.30 to 7 o'clock, if that should suit you.

Until then, I am, dear sir, . . . your much obliged and appreciative

EDOUARD MANET

*

34 boulevard des Batignolles, Paris, 16 June [1866]

To AUGUSTE POULET-MALASSIS [in Brussels]   My dear Sir, Asselineau tells me you are willing to part with the portrait of Baudelaire by Courbet. Since I would very much like to have it but am unable to find . . . the sum you are asking, may I suggest exchanging it for a painting I once gave to Baudelaire but which has remained in my possession (a woman dressed as a *majo*, lying on a red couch) (*67*). I believe it has some merit, and it has even had the honour of being engraved by our friend Bracquemond. I shall be delighted if such an exchange proves feasible and sufficiently to your liking.

I must thank you . . . for the beautiful copy of *Les Épaves* with the kind inscription from its talented publisher; I found it most flattering.

ED. MANET

I am sending a photograph to remind you of the painting in question.

*

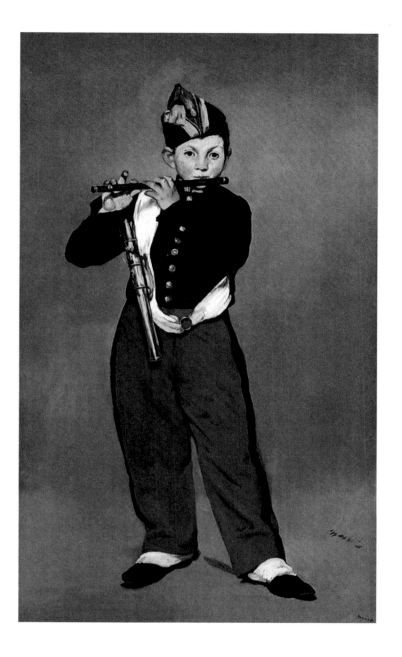

14   THE FIFER, 1866

Monday 15 October [1866]

To Émile Zola   My dear Zola, Well here indeed is a friend I would never
have suspected; new ones seem to be appearing every day and I attribute much of this to your
bold stand.

I would have written to you sooner but was caught up in our move on my return from the
country, goodness what a bore it is, but it's just about finished now. Would you like to come to
the studio on Thursday at 1 or 2 o'clock, as you please? Friday, if Thursday is inconvenient for
you. We must have a talk about the 'Stories for Ninon'.

Yours ever, ED. MANET

*

81 rue Guyot, Monday 15 October 1866

TO ERNEST CHESNEAU   I would very much like to show you some pictures that I
have put on display in my studio, and if it is not too presumptuous I would suggest you pick
an afternoon, when I will be delighted to see you here.

ED. MANET

*

Tuesday 16 October [1866]

TO NADAR   I accept your invitation to dinner on Friday but fear I am
taking advantage of your kind hospitality. If you could come that day and collect me at the
studio (81 rue Guyot), where I would like to show you some pictures that I have put on
display, we could then go on together to pick up our friend Baudelaire?

E. MANET

Don't come any later than 4.30 because I can only do the honours here in daylight – drop me a
line to let me know.

*

Friday [late 1866]

TO PHILIPPE BURTY   I'm sorry you didn't come yesterday. I wasn't able to ask
Zola for news of your book – he also has friends in on Thursdays, but I'll write to him about it.
    The little girl deserves more than a study and I think a full-length portrait might do quite a
bit for my reputation. I'm at your disposal but before we start you should think about the
actual length of time I will need; I only hope the child won't be too bored by it – for me, you
understand, it would be pure pleasure.

E. MANET

Do what you like with my woodblock, you can even efface it.

*

Saturday [late 1866]

TO ÉMILE ZOLA   I'm greatly put out by the coincidence that prevents your
coming to us on Thursdays. The people who do come are very surprised not to see you and I'm
often asked: Why can't we see M. Zola? So do try and come next Thursday, it would give us
great pleasure.
    Burty wants me to ask whether you have received his book. Not having your address, he
sent it to you at *Le Figaro*, and would very much like to know if you will be reviewing it
somewhere. In short, he hopes you will – so much for that. You certainly have a reputation as a
man of influence; my friend Zacharie Astruc has asked me to find out whether you could
persuade Hachette to publish a book of his verse?

E. MANET

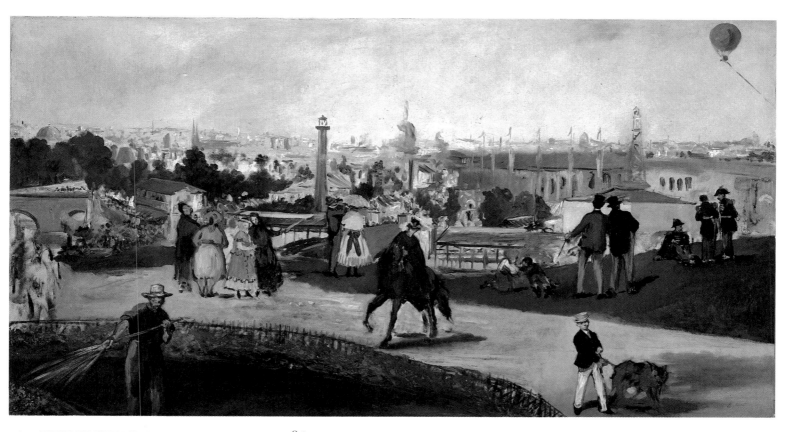

15   VIEW OF THE EXPOSITION UNIVERSELLE, 1867

Wednesday 2 January [1867]

What a splendid New Year's gift you've made me; I'm delighted by your remarkable article. It comes just at the right moment since I've not been deemed worthy of the benefits enjoyed by so many others, namely, the advantage of submitting works by list. Furthermore, I have so little confidence in our judges that I wouldn't dream of sending them my pictures. They could easily play me the trick of accepting just one or two, and then, as far as the public is concerned, I might as well throw the rest away.

I've decided to hold a one-man exhibition. I have at least forty-odd pictures I can show, and have already been offered sites in very good locations near the Champ de Mars. I'm going to go all out, and with the support of people like you, it should be a success. . . .

E. MANET

Everyone here is delighted with the article [in *La Revue du XIXe siècle*, 1 January] and sends their thanks.

*

Manet's retrospective exhibition, 1867

[February–March 1867]

To Émile Zola   I must say that I would be very pleased to see your
pamphlet about me on sale at my exhibition and I hope and trust that a great many copies
would be sold, it's quite likely, and after all nothing ventured nothing gained.

If my etched portrait appeals to you, I would even suggest having it as a frontispiece. Tell
me what you think and let me know the size of the booklet so that I can arrange for the
printing of the etching.

Ed. Manet

Shall we do this as a joint venture?

I'm reopening my letter, recalling that I recently made a woodblock after *Olympia* (*11, 85*),
intended for Lacroix's *Paris-Guide*. If it didn't cost too much we could insert it. Furthermore,
since the woodblock is ours, we can always put it to good use at some other time. I'll write to
an engraver skilled enough to make a good job of it. R.S.V.P.

*

Sunday evening [February–March 1867]

On second thoughts, I think it might be in poor taste, and
strain our resources to no great advantage, to reprint such an outspoken eulogy of me and sell
it at my own exhibition. I shall need your friendship and your valiant pen so much in the
future that I ought to exercise the greatest discretion in making public use of them. I may be
violently attacked, so it might be better to keep your or our forces in reserve until then.

We can always bring out the first pamphlet at the end of the exhibition if it is successful. In
that case it will be taken more as a collector's item.

I'm planning to come and see you anyway and bring you up to date on my various projects.

Ed. Manet

*

Tuesday evening [19? February 1867]

To Henri Fantin-Latour   Bracquemond told me yesterday that you're counting on
doing my portrait [for the Salon] this week, so let's set a date for Thursday (the day after
tomorrow) because otherwise I won't be able to make it until 7 or 8 March. I'm terribly
behindhand.

Manet

Tell my maid if that's all right. And let me know what time you want me to come.

*

Paris, May 1867

To the Public at Manet's Exhibition   [Preface to the exhibition catalogue]   Since 1861 M. Manet has exhibited or attempted to exhibit his work.

This year he has decided to present a retrospective exhibition of his work directly to the public.

On his first appearance in the Salon, M. Manet received an official distinction [for (56)], but since then his work has been so often rejected by the jury that he feels that if any attempt to do something new in art involves a struggle, it should at least be conducted fairly, that is, the artist should be enabled to show his work.

Otherwise, the artist could too easily find himself alone, with no outlet for his art. He would be obliged to stack up his canvases or roll them up and put them away in the attic.

The fact is that official acceptance, encouragement and rewards are seen by a certain section of the public as a guarantee of talent, and this public is accordingly predisposed for or against the accepted or rejected works. But on the other hand, the artist is told that it is the spontaneous reactions of this same public that lie behind the jury's negative response to his canvases.

That being the case, the artist has been advised to wait. To wait for what? Until juries cease to exist?

He has thought it preferable to appeal directly to the public.

The artist is not saying: Come and see perfect works; rather: Come and see honest works.

One effect of the honesty of these works is that they may appear to suggest a protest, whereas the artist has been concerned only to convey his impressions.

M. Manet has never wished to make a protest. The protests have in fact been made against M. Manet, who did not expect them. They have had their source in the traditional teachings concerning composition, technique and the formal aspect of a picture. Those who have been brought up on these principles countenance no others, since such principles foster impatience and intolerance. These people acknowledge the value of nothing that falls foul of their theories and instead of offering criticism, condemn it out of hand.

It is a vital matter, a *sine qua non* for an artist to be able to exhibit his work, since after repeated viewing, surprise and even shock will give way to familiarity. Little by little, understanding and acceptance will follow.

Time, too, works on pictures with an invisible polishing tool, smoothing away their inital asperities.

To exhibit is to find friends and allies for the fight.

M. Manet has always recognized talent wherever found; he has never wanted to do away with the painting of the past or aimed at creating a new kind of art. He has simply tried to be himself and no one else.

Furthermore, M. Manet has found powerful supporters, and he is aware that the opinion of undeniably talented people is growing daily more favourable.

It remains only for the artist to win over the public that has been supposedly turned into an enemy.

*

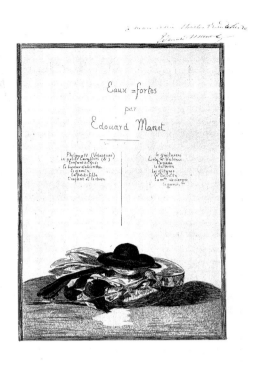

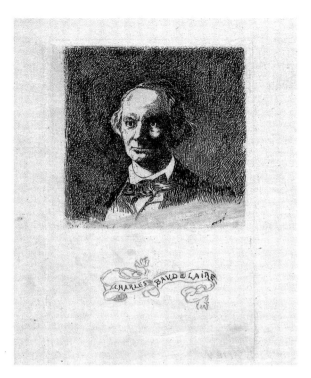

16   COVER FOR A SET OF PRINTS, c.1863

17   PORTRAIT OF CHARLES BAUDELAIRE, c.1868

[1866–early 1867?]

TO CHARLES ASSELINEAU   If you see our friend Baudelaire, tell him not to be cross with me, I've been ill myself and am so busy at the moment that from day to day I keep putting off visiting him; actually, I've had what sounds like good news of him from various quarters.

ED. MANET

*

Tuesday 10 September [1867]

TO NADAR   You spoke most eloquently in defence of our poor friend Baudelaire [at his funeral] yesterday; you are a man of true feeling. I had already been touched by the loving care shown him in your home by you and your family.

With my warmest regards, my dear Nadar,   EDOUARD MANET

*

49 rue St Pétersbourg [after September 1867]

TO CHARLES ASSELINEAU   I believe you are currently planning an edition of the works of Baudelaire? If there is to be a frontispiece portrait to the *Spleen de Paris*, I have a Baudelaire wearing a hat, as if going for a stroll (*64*), which might not be bad at the beginning of this volume, and I have yet another, more substantial image of him, bare-headed (*17*), that would look well in a volume of verse – I would very much like to take this on and naturally, in putting myself forward, I would *give* you my plates.

ED. MANET

[late 1867]

TO ÉMILE ZOLA

I've just finished *Thérèse Raquin* and want to congratulate you warmly. It's a very well-constructed and very interesting novel.

Yours ever, ED. MANET

*

Tuesday 8 [January 1868]

I'm delighted to be able to do something that will give you pleasure and am entirely at your disposal. Would you like to have the first sitting *next Monday*, at half past twelve at the latest? We can decide then on the days for Madame and on yours (*91*).

E. MANET

*

[*L'Événement illustré*, 10 May 1868]

RECORDED BY ÉMILE ZOLA

[During the portrait sessions (*91*)]   ...I can't do anything without the model. I don't know how to invent. So long as I tried to paint according to the lessons I had learnt, I produced nothing worthwhile. If I amount to anything today, I put it down to precise interpretation and faithful analysis.

*

[April–May 1868?]

TO ÉMILE ZOLA

I forgot to send you Champfleury's address. It's 20 rue de Boulogne [for Bruxelles]. Do come to the Café Guerbois on Friday evening, but not too late.

E. MANET

*

[late April–May 1868]

Bravo, my dear Zola, it's a splendid preface [to the second edition of *Thérèse Raquin*] and you are standing up not only for a group of writers but for a whole group of artists as well. I must say that someone who can fight back as you do must really enjoy being attacked.

EDOUARD MANET

*

[December 1868]

...I'm in the middle of *Madeleine Férat* and don't want to wait till I've finished to congratulate you. The redheaded woman is portrayed so well it makes one jealous, and the descriptions of the love scenes are enough to deflower any virgin who reads them.

E. MANET

49 rue St Pétersbourg, Monday 10 [June 1867]

TO A PATRON

Dear Sir, I cannot let you have the print *Little cavaliers* (*3*); the copperplate has met with an accident and will take rather a long time to repair, but I would urge you to choose one or other of two etchings after pictures that are included in my exhibition, the *Spanish singer* (*56, 121*) and *The urchin* (*18*). Personally, I prefer *The urchin* as an example of printmaking, but do, please, follow your own inclination and let me know your decision so that I can send the plate to Delâtre at 303 rue St Jacques.

Yours faithfully, EDOUARD MANET

*

Cercle de l'Union Artistique [June 1868]

TO THÉODORE DURET

I think one could do a small full-length portrait to the size you want (*24*); a head on its own is always rather dull – as to the rest it will be whatever you are able or willing to make it, there should be no obligations between friends.

If you would like to make a start on Sunday, I'll be at my studio from midday onwards.

ED. MANET

*

[late June–July 1868]

TO PHILIPPE BURTY

All right, I'll do an etching for M. Renaud's sonnet (*19*). Be kind enough to send me the largest plate that is allowed and tell me when it has to be ready.

ED. MANET

18   LE GAMIN (THE URCHIN), 1862

19   FLEUR EXOTIQUE (EXOTIC FLOWER), 1868

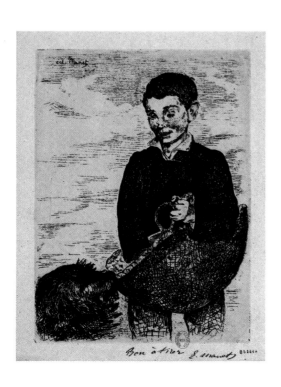

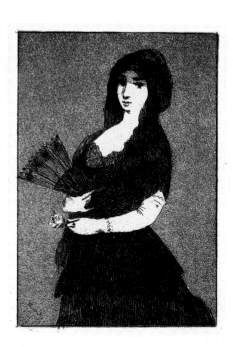

c/o M. Leblond, 162 rue de Boston, Boulogne-sur-mer, 29 July [1868]

To Edgar Degas   I'm planning to make a little trip to London, tempted by
the low cost of the journey; do you want to come along? You can go from Paris to London 1st
class return for 31 francs 50; buy your ticket from M. Spiers, 13 rue de la Paix. I think we
should explore the terrain over there since it could provide an outlet for our products.

I can't afford to spend more than three or four days in England.

Let me know immediately because I will write and tell Legros what day we'll be arriving
so that he can act as our interpreter and guide. If you can persuade Fantin to come with you,
that would be delightful.

Regards to Duranty, Fantin, Zola, if you see them tell them I'll be writing to them one of
these days.

I'm enclosing a list of departure times.

By leaving on Saturday 1 August at 4 in the afternoon, we can embark the same evening on
the midnight boat.

I wouldn't really be able to get away after that until the end of August because of a move
we're obliged to make here – whereas now we would be able to see the picture exhibition
[at the Royal Academy] which is still open.

Let me know by return and keep the luggage to a minimum.

Edouard Manet

*

2 rue Napoléon, Boulogne-sur-mer, Sunday [10? August 1868]

To Henri Fantin-Latour   I wanted to write to you from London but was so busy
during my two days there that I didn't have a moment, I won't say not to think of my friends,
but to write to them; I would have loved to have had you with me on this little trip and de
Gas was really silly not to have come with me. I was enchanted by London, by the welcome
I got from everyone I visited, Legros was very kind and helpful. The excellent Edwards was
charming and asked me to tell you that there are opportunities for you there right now and
that you should come over – Wisthler [sic] wasn't in London so I couldn't see him, I was very
disappointed about it, he was on an excursion on a yacht.

But I believe there is something to be done over there; the feel of the place, the atmosphere,
I liked it all and I'm going to try and show my work there next year – among other things, you
should exhibit my portrait, it would be good for both of us.

Goodbye for now, my dear Fantin, send me your news, tell me what's happening in Paris,
tell me about yourself and about our friends – warm regards to Duranty.

. . . ever yours, Edouard Manet

Until the 17th of this month no. 2 rue Napoléon, after the 17th 156 rue de Boston

*

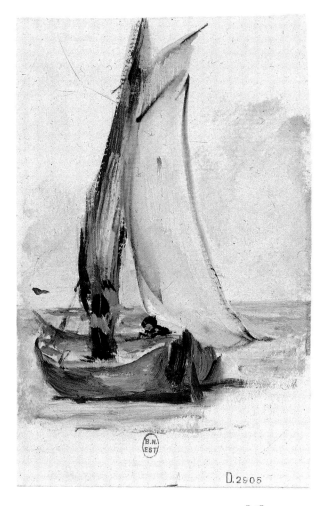

20   FISHING BOAT ON THE BEACH, c.1868–73

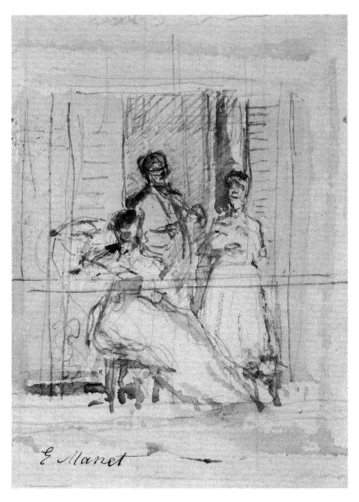

21   SKETCH FOR THE BALCONY, 1868

2 bis rue Napoléon, Boulogne-sur-mer [5–16 August 1868]

TO ÉMILE ZOLA   I should be very glad to hear from you and learn what
you're up to. Tell me, too, about our young friend Guillemet. I would be pleased if he could ask
Monet how my exhibition [of *The Dead Man* (72)] is going at Le Havre.

I went to London a few days ago and was delighted with the trip. I was very well received.
I feel there is an opening for me over there, and I'm going to try it out next season.

I saw some artists who were very kind and strongly recommended me to exhibit! they're not
given to the sort of petty jealousy we have over here, most of them are real gentlemen.

I wanted to write to you from London but stayed for only two days that were so busy
I didn't have a moment to get down to it.

Goodbye for now, my dear Zola, write to me as soon as you can.

Until the 17th, 2 bis rue Napoléon; from then on, 156 rue de Boston.

ED. MANET

I believe we might find a suitable occasion to distribute the pamphlet over there.

*

[156 rue de Boston,] Boulogne-sur-mer, 26 August [1868]

To Henri Fantin-Latour   It's clear, my dear Fantin, that you Parisians have all the entertainment you could wish for but I have no one here to talk to; so I envy your being able to discuss with that famous aesthetician Degas the question of whether or not it is advisable to put art within reach of the lower classes, by turning out pictures for sixpence apiece. I haven't been able to discuss painting with anyone from outside since I've been here – good old Duranty, who will turn into a billiards champion at the rate he's going, is wrong about my grand projects, he imagines me painting pictures on a grand scale – absolutely not, I've been complaining long enough at being in that situation; I am now concerned to earn some money and since I think, like you, that there's not much to be done in our stupid country overrun by government bureaucrats, I want to try exhibiting in London next year. Millet was well advised not to go fishing for that tarnished bauble [the cross of the Legion of Honour] that's only fit for children or the Cassagnacs of this world, and I shan't think well of him if he wears it. It seems that Daubigny's son met with a pretty cool reception, he deserves it, he has no talent and his father is a boor. I think that if we resolved to stick together and above all not to get discouraged, we would be able to react against all this mediocrity which is only held together by consensus. I agree with you, the young Morisot girls are charming, it's a pity they're not men; but being women, they could still do something in the cause of painting by each marrying an academician and bringing discord into the camp of those old dodderers, though that would be asking for considerable self-sacrifice – meanwhile, give them my respects.

I'm impatient to get back to Paris because I'm not producing anything here, two months is definitely too long. I've had a letter from Bracquemond who is going to Balleroy to do a painting, I wonder if it's the portrait of the countess? The lucky fellow is quite capable of that.

Tell Degas it's about time he wrote to me, I gather from Duranty he's becoming a painter of 'high life'; why not? It's too bad he didn't come to London, those well-trained horses would have inspired a few pictures. Have you heard anything about the Stevens and whether they still entertain?

Now then, my dear Fantin, don't spend too much time running off to sit at Antiope's feet [Correggio's picture in the Louvre], and let's make a rendezvous for next year in London.

MANET

*

[early 1869]

To Émile Zola   Would you be so kind as to write to *Bournat*, Deputy to the legislature and President of the Société artistique des Bouches-du-Rhône.

I shall write to Ollivier asking him to recommend me.

I have sent the *Spanish singer* (56) and the *Boy with a sword* (54) [exhibited in Marseilles from December 1868].

ED. MANET

*

49

The 'Maximilian affair', 1869

[January 1869]

To Émile Zola   Have a look at the enclosed letter and let me have it back in
a sealed envelope with your views.

    It sounds as if the authorities want to push me into a difficult situation over my lithograph
(*22*) which was already giving me cause for concern. I thought they could stop it from being
published but not from being printed. Anyway, it's a good mark for the work since it bears
no title of any kind. I was waiting for a publisher before getting the stone lettered – death of
Max. etc.

    I feel it might be a good idea to write a few lines about this ludicrously small-minded
procedure. What do you think?

Ed. Manet

*

[early February? 1869]

To Théodore Duret   I am sending you the short note you asked for.   E.M.

    We understand that M. Manet has been refused permission for the printing of a lithograph
he has just made representing the [mas(sacre) *deleted*] execution of Maximilian (*95, 96*). We are
surprised at the action of the authorities in banning a purely artistic work.

*

Thursday 18 February [1869]

To Philippe Burty   My Maximilian affair is getting more complicated – the
printer [Lemercier] refuses to give me back the stone and is asking for permission to efface it.
Obviously I refuse; nor, it goes without saying, will I take steps as he advises towards getting
the ban lifted, and I had him served with papers yesterday. That's where the matter stands –
but it seems to me of some interest to know how it may develop. I should imagine one can't
destroy a printing block, stone, etc. without a court order, and without publication there can
be no punishable offence.

    I'm sending you these fresh details in case you think it advisable to mention them.

    It's the kind of question that is important to settle in the interest of any artist who might
find himself in the same situation.

Ed. Manet

*

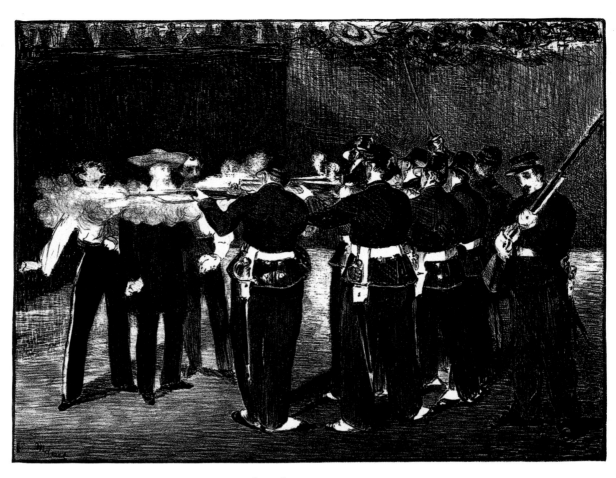

22   THE EXECUTION OF MAXIMILIAN, 1867–8

Saturday [20 or 27 February 1869]

TO LEMERCIER & CO.   Dear Sir, Would you kindly have my stone ready by *Monday*. I shall send someone to fetch it.

You complain about my behaviour towards you; you have no doubt forgotten that you refused to hand over the stone. I do not imagine that, as you seem to imply in your last letter, it was fear of not being paid that made you act in this way – in any event, for whatever reason, you are charging me 35 fr. 50 for a stone worth 29 fr. Would you please look into this.

I have had three trial proofs. I had asked for 4 but learnt that one had been given to a Mr R. I trust you will not charge me for it.

Yours faithfully, E. MANET

A duel with Duranty, 1870

[23 February 1870]

RECORDED BY ANTONIN PROUST   There was only one thing I was afraid of, that my thrusts would pass over his head. I was so springy! I can't tell you what trouble I went to, the day before the duel, to find a pair of really broad, roomy shoes in which I would feel quite comfortable. In the end, I found a pair in the Passage Jouffroy. After the duel, I was going to give them to Duranty but he refused them because his feet were larger than mine. We have wondered ever since how we could have been silly enough to want to run each other through.

Eva Gonzalès as pupil and model, 1869–1870

[c.1868–70]

RECORDED BY PHILIPPE BURTY   [A lesson in still-life painting for Eva Gonzalès]   Get it down quickly. Don't worry about the background. Just go for the tonal values. You see? When you look at it, and above all when you think how to render it as you see it, that is, in such a way that it makes the same impression on the viewer as it does on you, you don't look for, you don't see the lines on the paper over there do you? And then, when you look at the whole thing, you don't try to count the scales on the salmon. Of course not. You see them as little silver pearls against grey and pink – isn't that right? – look at the pink of this salmon, with the bone appearing white in the centre and then greys like shades of mother of pearl [see (*104*)]! And the grapes, now do you count each grape? Of course not. What strikes you is their clear amber colour, and the bloom which models the form by softening it. What you have to decide with the cloth is where the highlights come and then the planes which are not in direct light. Half-tones are for the *Magasin pittoresque* engravers. The folds will come by themselves if you put them in their proper place [see (*105*)]. Ah! M. Ingres, there's the man! We're all just children. There's the one who knew how to paint materials! Ask Bracquemond . . . Above all keep your colours fresh! . . .

*

Thursday [June–July? 1869]

TO MME EMMANUEL GONZALÈS   If Mlle Gonzalès and you are still of the same mind, I would be very happy to start the portrait (*107*) on Sunday at whatever time suits you – it seems more convenient to do it at home at 49 rue de St Pétersbourg, where there is a small room that I can use as a studio. If you agree, I shall send someone on Sunday morning to pick up Mademoiselle Gonzalès' dress.

ED. MANET

*

Wednesday evening [January–February? 1870]

TO EVA GONZALÈS   Dear Mademoiselle, I am really embarrassed at having to ask you to put off tomorrow's sitting until Saturday, but a letter has come this afternoon from Astruc (the devil take him) who has found some excuse or other to come on Thursday instead of Saturday. I'm too busy to make an issue of it and there are some people you have to take when you can . . .

ED. MANET

*

[1 March 1870]

To Jules de La Rochenoire   My dear La Rochenoire, Would you send me 5 or 6 projects and as many jury lists – I'll get in touch with papers where I have contacts.

E. Manet

*

Saturday [12 March 1870]

To Émile Zola   The artist's committee which has voted for the enclosed list has asked me to do what I can to publicize it. Could you have a short note published in *Le Rappel* and *La Cloche* in more or less these terms:

The project put forward by the committee presenting the following list for the jury is quite unbiased. All artists should vote for the following names – the list follows.

I've received notice to attend this evening a meeting of 150 artists, which has been brought forward. Candidates are invited to appear and give their views on the organization or disorganization of the arts.

I haven't a minute to myself and am running very late.

E. Manet

At *La Cloche* it's Montrosier who looks after the arts; he's very nice.

*

Saturday [postmarked (Sunday) 20 March 1870]

To Jules de La Rochenoire   Our list has no hope of getting through unless we take really drastic measures before it is too late. I am inclined to burn our boats by putting the following notice in all the papers and sending it to the homes of all artists *who have to go before the jury:*

All those who are afraid of being *rejected should vote for the following persons who believe in the right of every artist to show his work in the most favourable conditions* followed by the list of candidates.

Too bad if those idiots don't vote for us – we're on the right side and in any event we'll be fighting for truth. If one of the names on the list looks like dropping out, I have an excellent, indeed a *major* recruit – more news later.

Manet

*

Théodore Duret, critic and patron

[May–June 1870?]

To Théodore Duret   Thank you for your excellent article about me. – You love painting, you have a real feeling for it, so you write about it very well.

Unfortunately art critics as enlightened as you are as rare as true artists.

Edouard Manet

*

[September? 1870]

My dear Duret, since it is very pleasant and most unusual to sell one's painting to someone who really appreciates it and I'm quite certain that you understand the qualities of the piece you've requested [*The Torero Saluting*], I shall let you have it for twelve hundred francs, since it's you, but I want the price to remain between ourselves. I'll be at the studio tomorrow at dinner time.

Ed. Manet

I wouldn't let anyone have such a major figure for less than 2500 so if the price suits you I wouldn't want it known that you had acquired it for less than 2000.

23   WOMAN PLAYING A GUITAR, c.1867–8

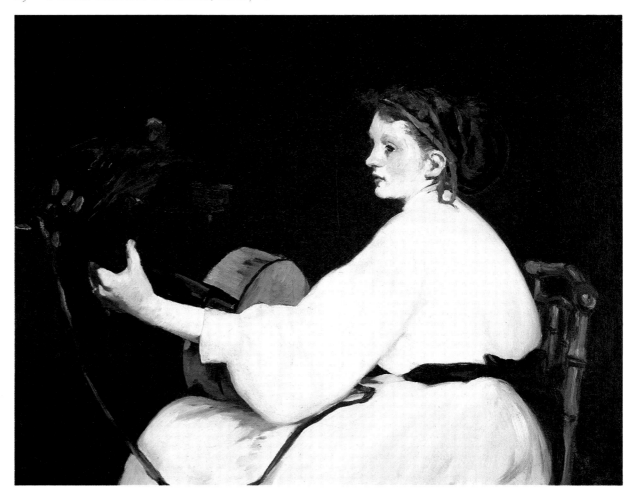

9 a.m. Saturday 10 [September 1870]

TO SUZANNE MANET [at Oloron-Sainte-Marie]   How is it that I haven't yet received a telegram announcing your arrival? If circumstances were not what they are, I would be really worried. . . .

I'm glad I persuaded you to go – Paris is in a state of abysmal gloom. I'm surprised we haven't had to lodge any militiamen, everyone in the neighbourhood has them. . . .

I have no idea what is going to happen. I've just seen Gustave who is sure [the Prussians] won't get here and that there'll be peace negotiations . . .

The women are up in arms; in Montmartre they've taken on the rôle of the police and are trying to prevent the men from staying home. The theatres are closed.

My regards to you all, give mother a kiss for me. Tell Léon to behave like a man . . . Thank M. Lailhacar. I'll put as much as I can into safekeeping. . . . I hope this won't last long.

Your husband, EDOUARD MANET

*

Paris, 10 September [1870]

TO EVA GONZALÈS [in Dieppe]   My mother and my wife left on Thursday, I sent them off with Léon to the Basses-Pyrénées where I hope they will be quite safe. I think we poor Parisians are going to be caught up in a terrible drama – death and destruction, looting and carnage will be inevitable if Europe doesn't intervene in time – militiamen are arriving from every corner of France, some are assigned to billets, others camp out on the squares and boulevards, Paris is a sorry sight – A lot of people are leaving . . . Madame Stevens is in Brussels, Mme and Mlle Morisot are staying, I believe . . . Champfleury has left, it's a debacle and people are storming the railway stations . . .

EDOUARD MANET

*

Paris, Sunday [11 September 1870]

TO SUZANNE MANET   Why haven't we heard from you? . . . We're expecting the Prussians any day now – the preparations for defence are most impressive . . . Jules [De Jouy] is leaving this morning to join you. . . . If there were any risk of fire in this quarter, I would have the pianos moved to his home, I don't think the shells will reach as far as that. . . .

A letter has come for you from Mlle Gonzalès. I opened it and have sent her your address. Yesterday evening Eugène and I paid the Morisots a short visit. . . .

I see that Léon forgot one of his woollen shirts . . .

EDOUARD MANET

*

Paris, Tuesday [13 September 1870]

Your letter has arrived and I'm surprised you haven't yet had my two letters and the papers I've been sending every day. This morning I took Eugène to the Ministry of the Interior to see Gambetta and try to get him a job. . . . I shall probably have your pianos taken to Jules's place, and some of my pictures sent to him and some to Duret; I'm very glad you're all right. . . .

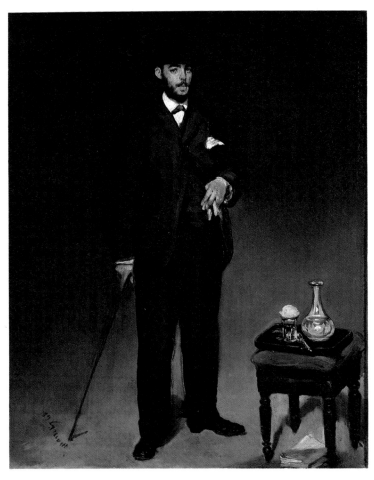

24   PORTRAIT OF THÉODORE DURET, d.1868

25   LETTER TO THÉODORE DURET, 16 September 1870?

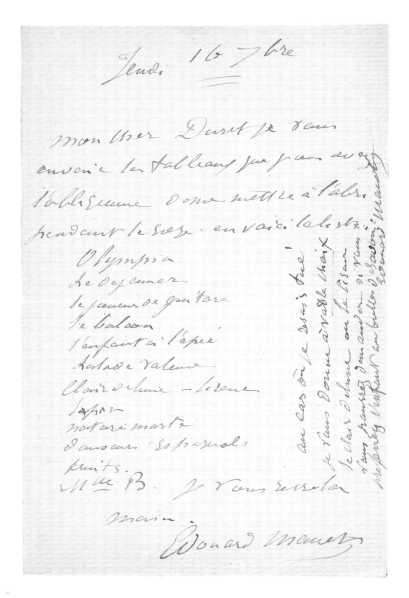

Thursday [15 or Friday] 16 September [1870]

My dear Duret I am
sending you the pictures you have
kindly offered to shelter
during the siege – here is the list:
Olympia (*85*)
The luncheon (*103*)
the guitar player (*56*)
the balcony (*102*)
the boy with a sword (*54*)
Lola de Valence [see (*69*)]
Moonlight (*98*) – Reader
rabbit
still life (*104*)
Spanish dancers [see (*70*)]
fruit (*105*)
Mlle B. (*106*)

In the event of my death, you can take *your choice* of
Moonlight (*98*) or the Reader, or if you prefer you can
ask for the Boy with the soap bubbles.

Greetings, EDOUARD MANET

EDOUARD MANET

Paris, Thursday 15 September [1870]

To Suzanne Manet

I've just got home and though it's half past eleven, I'm writing to you because I want my letter to go off first thing in the morning . . . It's sad to come home alone every evening and find no one in . . . You shouldn't feel guilty for not having stayed on. For one thing, women would only get in the men's way . . . and in any case, very few women have stayed behind – many of the men have left too, but I think they'll pay for it on their return. I went to the meeting at Belleville with Eugène this evening and they read out the names of those who were absent, they wanted to post them up in the Paris streets and confiscate their property on behalf of the nation.

That's how we usually spend the evenings. Yesterday we were with Degas and Eugène at a public meeting at the Folies-Bergère where we heard General Cluseret speak. It's all very interesting. The present provisional government is very unpopular and it looks as if the true republicans are planning its overthrow after the war. . . .

I went to Gennevilliers with Gustave this morning and we came back via Asnières; it's a sad sight. Everyone has left, all the trees have been chopped down, everything has been burnt and the grainstacks are on fire in the fields. . . .

*

Paris, midday Tuesday 20 [September 1870]

We've reached the decisive moment . . . There's fighting everywhere, all round Paris. The enemy caused fairly heavy losses yesterday; the militia faced their fire with courage enough, but unfortunately the troops of the line gave way. I haven't written these last few days because I was on guard at the fortifications – it's very tiring and very hard. One sleeps on straw, and there's not even enough of that to go round . . .

Edouard Manet

*

Paris, 24 [September 1870]

I hope this letter will reach you. . . . Everyone is furious at Bismarck's response and his outrageous pretensions – Paris is determined to defend itself to the last and I think their audacity will cost them dearly. . . .

I was on guard at the ramparts yesterday and the day before. We heard the guns going all night long. We're all getting quite used to the noise. . . .

Edouard Manet

*

Letters sent by balloon from Paris under siege

To Suzanne Manet   I'm tormented by the thought that you're without news of us. – A balloon carrying letters is due to leave tomorrow, and I've been promised that mine will be on it so I hope it will reach you. – It is still impossible to make firm predictions, but Paris is tremendously well defended. There are now four hundred thousand armed National Guardsmen, without counting the *Garde mobile* and the regiment. If the provinces came to our aid, I think we could get the better of the Prussians. – We're all three in very good health.

     M. Aubry had a stroke last Thursday, and is paralysed down one side....

Your husband, Edouard Manet

*

Paris, Friday 30 September [1870]

It's a long time since I heard from you....

     Some of my letters should have reached you via the balloons that have left Paris. I think there's one leaving tomorrow or the day after.... The Prussians seem to be regretting their decision to besiege Paris. They must have thought it would be easier than it is. It's true that we can't have milk with our coffee now; the butchers are only open three days a week, people queue up outside (*115*) from four in the morning and there's nothing left for the latecomers.

     We eat meat only once a day and I believe all sensible Parisians must be doing the same....

     I've seen the Morisot ladies who are probably going to make up their minds to leave Passy which is likely to be bombarded.... Paris nowadays is a huge camp. From five in the morning until evening, the militia and the national guards who are not on duty do drill and are turning into real soldiers. Otherwise life is very boring in the evening – all the café-restaurants are closed after ten o'clock, one just has to go to bed....

Your loving husband, Edouard

*

Paris, 5 October [1870]

My dear Suzanne, ... Don't worry, we're not in any danger. ... We can't really say what's happening here since letters that leave by balloon could fall into enemy hands. ...

My dear mother, I've been trying recently to get Eugène a post in the Ministry of the Interior. They've nothing that would suit him at the moment but there's a chance of something at the National Defence ministry where I went this morning. I asked if he could be appointed second-in-command of a sector ... It would give him connections and he might be able to get some kind of mission. It's true that the only way to leave Paris is by balloon and getting back again means risking one's neck, but in present conditions one just has to take risks. I'm trying to get Gustave going but that's pretty difficult.

Your son, Edouard

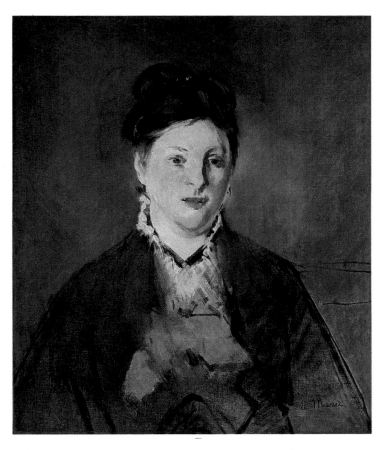

26   PORTRAIT OF MME SUZANNE MANET, c.1870

Paris, 23 October [1870]

The weather is terrible today, my dear Suzanne. It's impossible to set foot outside, particularly since my foot is only just getting better and I can only wear very light shoes. That didn't prevent me going to M. Aubry's funeral yesterday. You must have seen from the papers that the Paris army made a concerted attack on the enemy positions on Friday. The fighting went on all day long and I believe the Prussians sustained great losses – ours were not so high but poor Cuvelier, Degas' friend, was killed; Leroux was wounded and I think taken prisoner. We're beginning to have enough of being boxed in here without any outside contacts... A smallpox outbreak is spreading and at the moment we're down to 75 grams of meat per person, while milk is only available to children and the sick. ...

I spent a long time, my dear Suzanne, looking for your photograph – I eventually found the album in the table in the drawing room, so I can look at your comforting face from time to time. I woke up last night thinking I heard you calling me... People who have stayed in Paris see very little of each other – one becomes dreadfully self-centred. ... From day to day we're expecting a major offensive to break through the iron ring that surrounds us. We're really counting on the provinces because we can't send our little army off to be massacred. Those tricky Prussian bastards may well try to starve us out... I asked to be attached to General Vinoy's command and regret not having succeeded because it would have enabled me to follow all the operations...

EDOUARD MANET

The Siege of Paris, winter 1870

Paris, 7 November [1870]

TO SUZANNE MANET   The armistice has just been rejected, so the war will carry on worse than before – I've often regretted sending you away from Paris, but now I'm glad I did.

I'm joining the artillery and will be stationed at the Porte de Saint-Ouen; I'll be well off there. Eugène is in the volunteers in the National Guard. We're going to the funeral of our farmer Picard this morning.

EDOUARD MANET

*

Paris, 19 November [1870]

TO EVA GONZALÈS [in Dieppe]   Dear Mademoiselle Eva, a mutual lady friend who is also here under siege recently asked how I was putting up with your absence, since my admiration and friendship for you are common knowledge – I'll give you my reply directly: that of all the privations the siege is inflicting on us, that of not seeing you any more is certainly one of the hardest to bear . . . For the past two months I've had no news from my poor Suzanne who must be very anxious, though I write to her frequently. We're all soldiers here . . . Degas and I are in the artillery, as volunteer gunners. I'm looking forward to having you paint my portrait in my huge gunner's greatcoat when you're back – Tissot covered himself in glory in the action at La Jonchère – Jacquemart was there – Leroux was badly wounded and is a prisoner at Versailles – poor Cuvelier was killed – my brothers and Guillemet are in the National Guard battle units and are waiting to go into action . . . My paintbox and portable easel are stuffed into my military kitbag, so there's no excuse for wasting my time and I'm going to take advantage of the facilities available. A lot of cowards have left, among them, I'm afraid, our friends Zola, Fantin, etc . . . I don't think they'll be very well received on their return. We're beginning to feel the pinch here, horsemeat is a delicacy, donkey is exorbitantly expensive, there are butchers' shops for dogs, cats and rats – Paris is deathly sad, when will it all end – we've had more than enough . . .

EDOUARD MANET

*

Paris, 19 November [1870]

TO SUZANNE MANET   My dearest Suzanne, the time passes so slowly and it's cruel not to have had news of you all for so long. . . . Paris is deathly sad, there's beginning to be a shortage of gas which has been turned off in public buildings; food is becoming impossible . . . Smallpox is spreading fast and the peasant refugees are the most affected. We ourselves lead an active life which is very good for us. I'm on manoeuvres for two hours a day and everyone in my unit is very nice and polite with me . . .

There are cat, dog and rat butchers in Paris now, we eat nothing but horse when we can get it at all. I wish you could see me in my huge gunner's greatcoat . . . My soldier's kitbag also has everything I need for painting and I'll soon be starting to make studies out of doors (*114*) – they'll be worth a few francs as souvenirs. I'll be given every facility to do the most interesting things . . .

EDOUARD M.

Paris, 23 [postmark 22] November [1870]

So you didn't follow my instructions for sending your news – ten thousand telegrams arrived in Paris by pigeon recently but there was nothing for me... I long for the day when I can take a train to fetch you... You should take exercise, go for walks – practise the piano and above all don't worry, I'm not in any danger – Marie's big cat has been killed and we suspect someone in the house, it was for a meal of course, and Marie was in tears! She's taking very good care of us... One doesn't feel like seeing anyone, it's always the same conversations... the evenings go very slowly, the Café Guerbois is my only distraction and that's become pretty monotonous. ... I think of you all the time and have filled the bedroom with your portraits... Tell mother not to worry and to make the most of the good weather – We're having torrential rains here and I'm revelling in your wollen socks which come in very handy because we're up to our ankles in mud on the fortifications. Give my regards to the Viberts and to M. de Lailhacar who could probably do without them.

Goodbye my dear Suzanne, I embrace you lovingly and would give Alsace and Lorraine to be with you,

EDOUARD M.

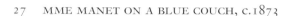

27   MME MANET ON A BLUE COUCH, C.1873

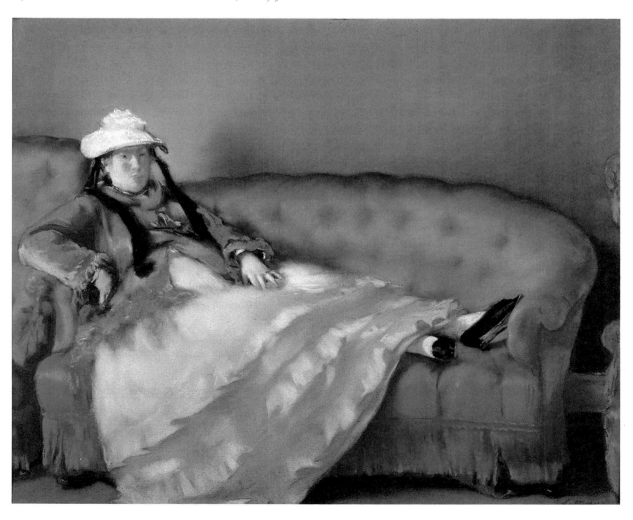

Paris, 24 November [1870]

To Suzanne Manet

I had just gone to bed yesterday evening when I heard the doorbell ring. It was a telegram from Oloron, and I opened it in a state of emotion. It's the first sign of life from you for over two months and will give me courage, which we can do with here. I've sent you a postal order. . . . As soon as you get it, send me a telegram with your news. If the letter with the order doesn't reach you, don't worry about it, it seems that three balloons have been captured by the Prussians . . .

*

2 December [1870]

Yesterday I was at the battle that was fought between Le Bourget and Champigny. What a din! One quickly gets used to it, with shells flying over one's head from all sides. . . . The Prussian prisoners are not being mistreated. It's the first time I've seen any; most of them are very young, like our militia, and they don't seem particularly sad at being captured. Of course, for them it means the end of the war. But when will it end for us? Tell Alexandre [Vibert] that I saw the Christian Doctrine brothers fetching the wounded under enemy fire, where the ambulance corps and infantrymen wouldn't go . . .

*

Paris, 7 December [1870]

I'm writing to you just as the news has reached Paris about the defeat of the army of the Loire. I think it was our last hope . . .
The artillery duties were too hard and I'm transferring to the general staff. . . .

With my love, Edouard Manet

. . . It's a great pity mother didn't want to lay in provisions. There's nothing to eat here.

*

Paris, 22 December [1870]

I want to send you our news as often as possible. . . . Eugène has been out with his batallion these last three days . . . Gustave was only kitted out today, and as for me, I'm so sore that I won't be able to ride for several days. It's freezing cold here. . . . There's no more coal, but fortunately I bought a thousand kilos a few weeks ago, which we keep for cooking – the laundresses won't be able to do any laundry for lack of fuel.
We have very little to eat, unrefined bread, occasionally a bit of meat. . . . If you're short of money which you must be, ask mother for some. Léon could probably do with some clothes. . . .
I don't know if the wind is in the right quarter for the balloons at the moment but I go on hoping that my letters are reaching you . . .

Paris, Sunday, 100th day of the siege [25 December 1870]

My dear Suzon [sic], although it's been so long, I still can't get used to coming back in the evening to this sad apartment. . . . What an end to the year! . . .

. . . Goodbye my dear Suzanne, your portraits are hanging in every corner of the bedroom, so I see you first and last thing . . .

Your husband, EDOUARD

*

[1 January? 1871]

. . . I think it's the first time since we've known each other that I haven't been able to give you a New Year's kiss . . .

Your loving husband, EDOUARD

*

Paris, 4 January 1871

. . . How I wish I knew that you are well, that you don't need anything, because I've always spoilt you and looked after you so much that you must miss me quite often, not to say constantly. I miss you too, I can promise you. Particularly since I've had to stay in my room for the last two days after riding gave me boils . . . I hope they won't last long, I get bored all alone in my room even though I'm surrounded by pictures of you. . . .

Eugène and Gustave are well. We went with Eugène to see the Morisot ladies – they're ill and are having difficulty coping with the hardships of the siege. . . .

*

Paris, 6 January 1871

To THÉODORE DURET

Your card has just arrived. I'm confined to my bedroom, having developed boils as a result of my new career as a cavalryman.

Yours ever, ED. MANET

*

Paris, 12 January 1871

To SUZANNE MANET

I was hoping for news of you all because a carrier pigeon arrived the other day with telegrams but sadly there was nothing for me . . . I've tried to persuade Eugène and Gustave to write a line but it's impossible to get them to do anything. . . . Give mother a kiss for me, I hope you're all getting on well together, you have the same interests and anxieties and I should be unhappy to think that there was anything less than perfect understanding between you. Farewell, my beloved, I embrace you and am for ever yours.

Your husband, EDOUARD

Paris, Sunday 15 January 1871

To Suzanne Manet ... time seems to pass so slowly and I would give anything to spend evenings at home with you now, with no thought of going out. You can't imagine how sad Paris is, there are hardly any carriages about. All the horses have been eaten ... No more gas, only black bread, and the cannon fire all day and all night long. ... Mother wouldn't have stood these conditions and you would certainly have fallen ill. There are many deaths in Paris. I hope you are pleased with Léon, he must take good care of you and mother. I sent him along to look after you and he should remember that, because lots of boys of his age are sent into battle here ...

Your husband, Edouard

*

Paris, 16 January 1871

I've got 'flu at the moment and am confined to bed. It's all very depressing, I can assure you ... The bombardment has been going on endlessly for several days now, the Faubourg Saint-Germain will be fairly smashed to pieces and yesterday a missile fell on the rue Hautefeuille. ...

I had a letter from Mme Morisot today to say that her son is well and a prisoner at Mainz. The poor things needed some good news; they were all very poorly when we went to see them on New Year's Day. I'm so glad, my dear love, that I sent you away. Besides the bad, not to say non-existent food, it's terribly cold here and there's no wood to make a fire. ...

17 January

Just a little goodnight before I go to sleep, my dear Suzanne. I can't get rid of this wretched 'flu ...

Although I hate being under military command, I'm looking forward to getting back to it. It's even worse being ill. This evening I amused myself by doing your portrait from a photograph on a little piece of ivory. I long to see you again, my poor Suzanne, and don't know what to do without you.

18 January

I'm again writing to you by the fireside, my sweet Suzanne, though my 'flu is getting better ... There were four thousand deaths from illness alone in Paris this week ... Eugène has been at Arcueil these last three days ... Gustave went off this morning with the 71st batallion. So I was having dinner alone when Jeanteaud arrived to share my extremely frugal meal.

19 January 1871

... Our bread ration is down to 300 grams now and what bread! Marie is going to keep a sample for you. ... Today the menu is rice pudding and jam. My 'flu is almost over and I'll be back on duty tomorrow. ...

... don't worry too much, look after yourselves, stock up with provisions for the return to Paris ... buy preserves, whatever you can lay hands on and do it right away. Believe me. People are going to starve to death in Paris after living through this siege, and everything will be exorbitantly expensive.

Your husband, Edouard

30 January [1871]

It's all over . . . There was no way we could have held out any longer. They are dying of hunger here and even now there is still great distress. We're all as thin as rakes, and I've been ill myself from exhaustion and bad food these last few days . . .

Unhappily, there have been many deaths here in Paris. Only we who have been through it can know what it's like. . . . You'll have to wait a little longer . . . I'll come and fetch you as soon as I can, and I'm longing for it.

*

Paris, 9 February [1871]

I'm coming to join you and hope to be with you by the beginning of next week. Sooner if I can. I can't wait to embrace you all. I've just heard that poor Bazille was killed at Beaune-la-Rolande on 28 November.

. . . Your husband, EDOUARD M.

*

Paris, 9 February 1871

To ÉMILE ZOLA [in Bordeaux]   I was pleased to have not just news but good news from you. You haven't been wasting your time. We've been having a hard time of it in Paris these last few months. I only heard yesterday of poor Bazille's death and am deeply upset about it. Unhappily, we've seen many people dying from all sorts of causes here. At one point your house was lived in by a family of refugees, on the ground floor at least. All the furniture was put in the upstairs rooms and I don't think there's too much damage for you to worry about. I'm leaving shortly to join my wife and mother who are at Oloron in the Basses-Pyrénées. I can't wait to see them again. I'll be passing through Bordeaux and may come and see you. I'll tell you what can't be written. . . .

EDOUARD MANET

*

Paris, Saturday 11 February [1871]

To SUZANNE MANET   I'll probably be leaving tomorrow to come and join you. . . . Eugène will be coming to join us a little later. Gustave wants to stay in Paris.

EDOUARD M.

*

28   HEAD OF A RECUMBENT MAN, c.1850–56

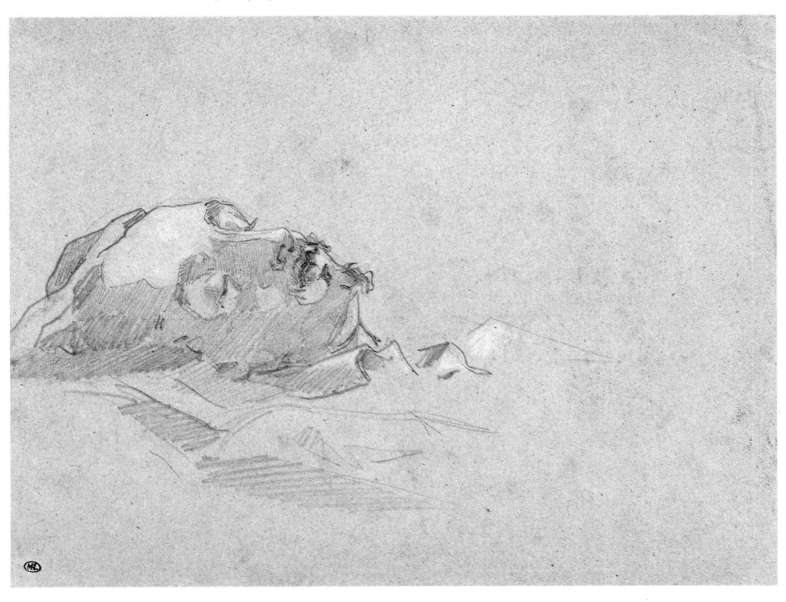

29   HEAD OF A BOY, c.1850–56

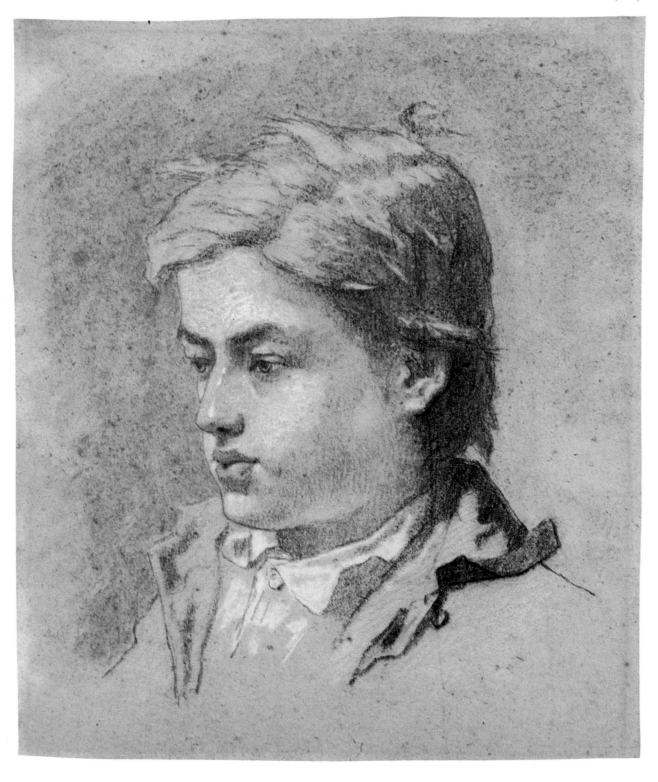

30   AFTER TINTORETTO'S SELF-PORTRAIT, C.1855

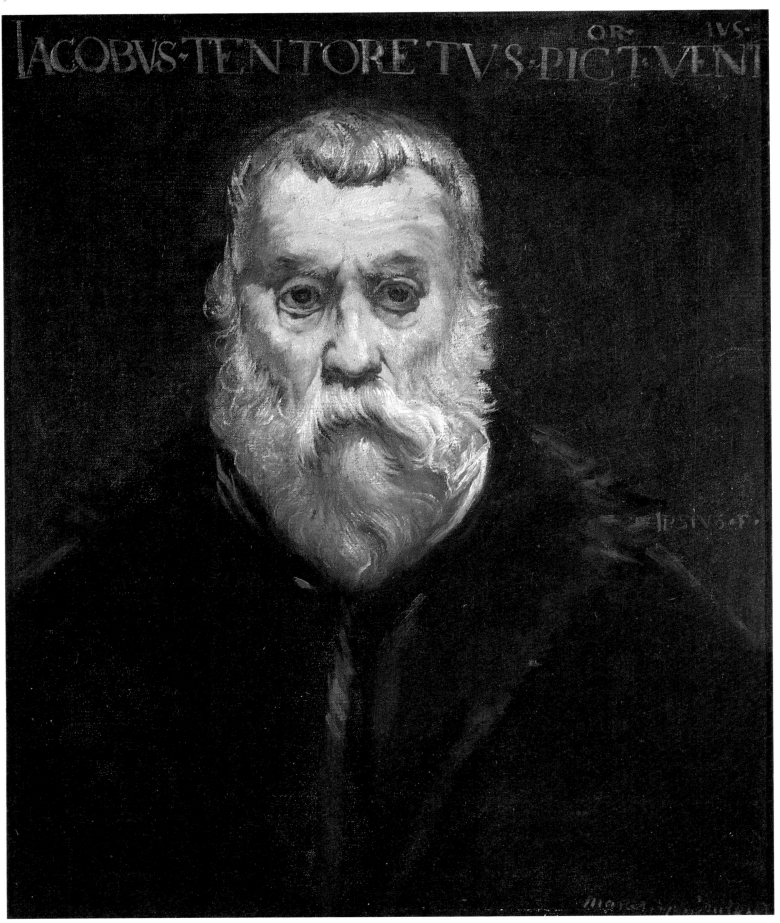

31   AFTER DELACROIX'S BARQUE OF DANTE, C.1858

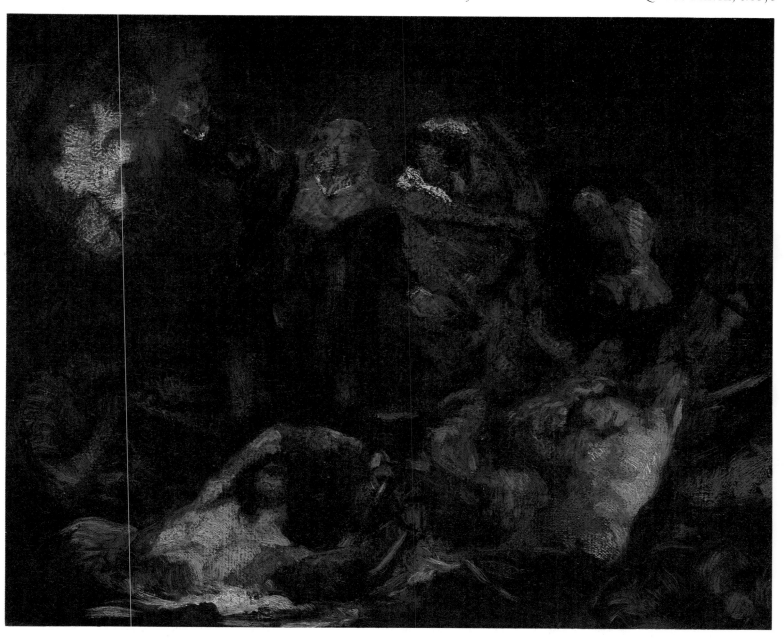

Study in Florence, 1857

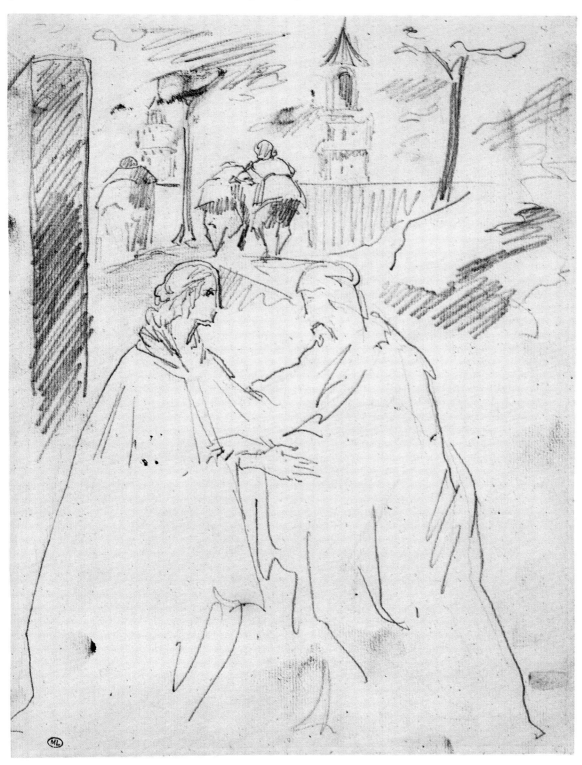

33　AFTER ANDREA DEL SARTO'S MADONNA DEL SACCO, 1857

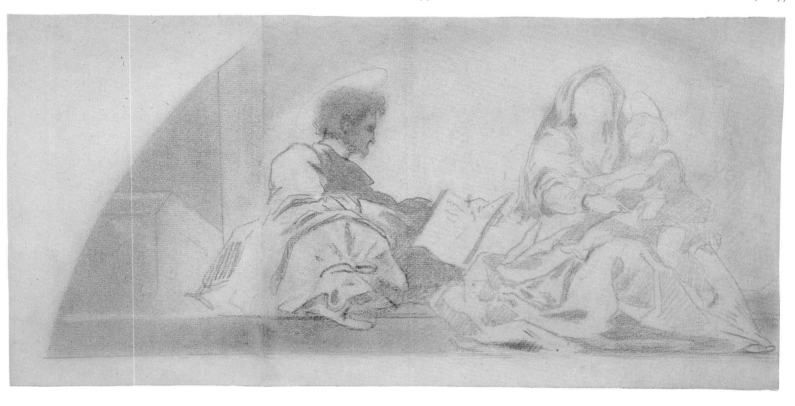

Study in Florence, 1857

34   AFTER BERNARDINO POCCETTI IN THE SS. ANNUNZIATA (DETAIL), 1857

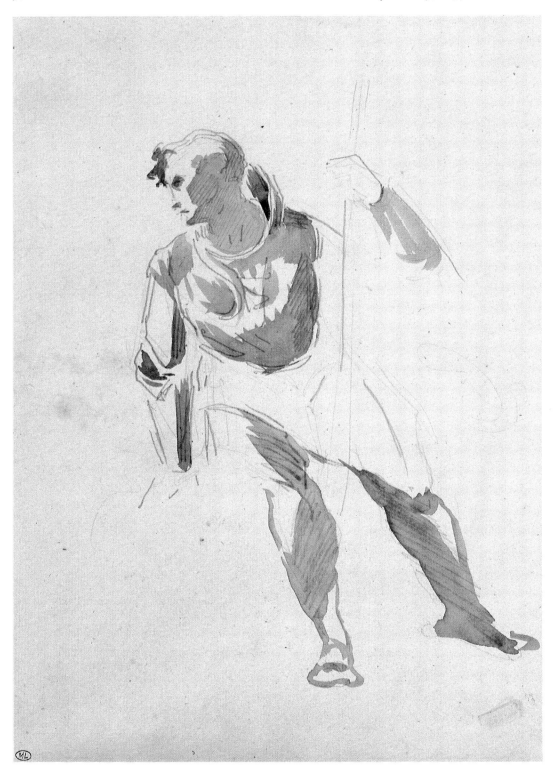

35   AFTER A DRAWING BY PARMIGIANINO, 1857

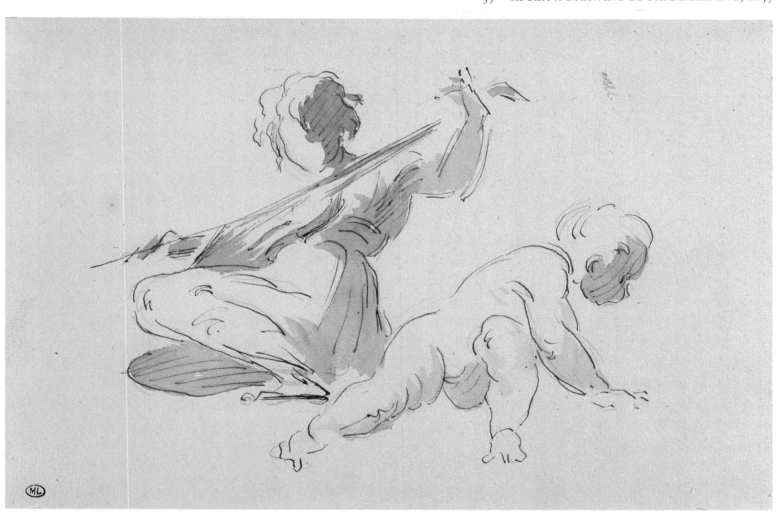
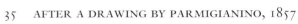

Study in Florence, 1857

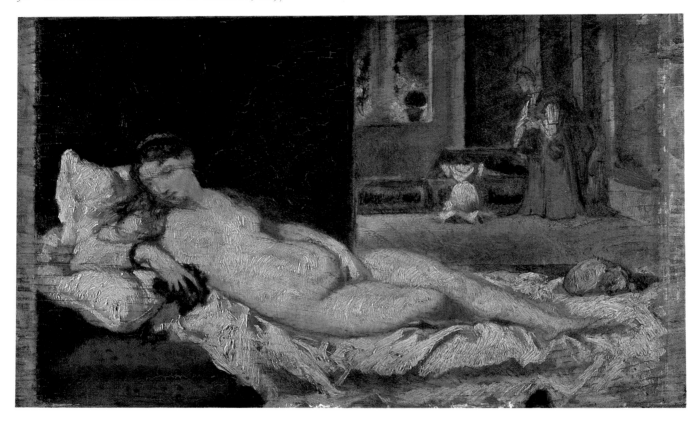

37   RECLINING NUDE, c.1858–60

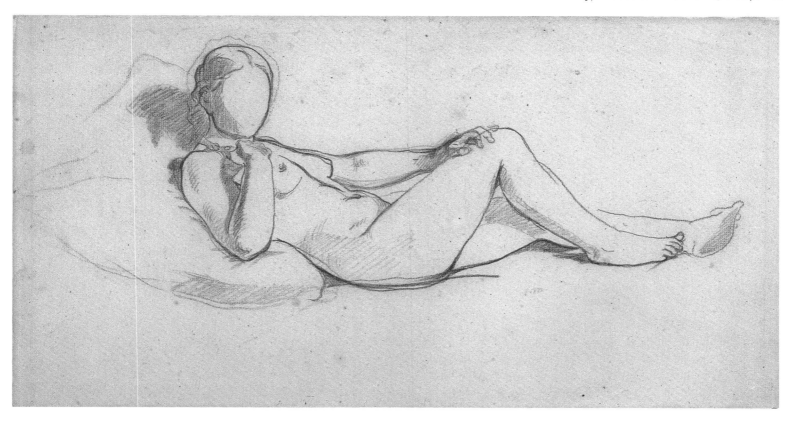

38   STUDY FOR A FINDING OF MOSES, c.1858–60

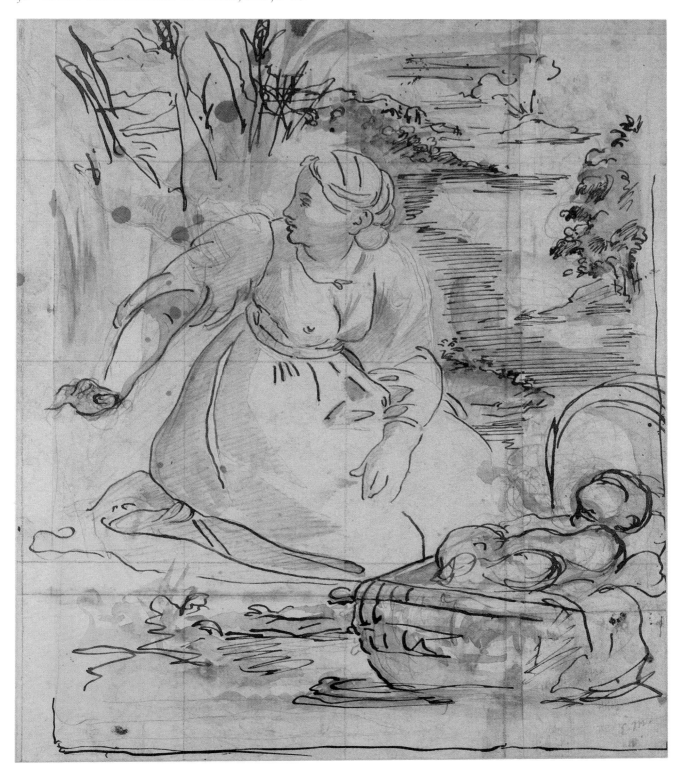

39   SEATED BATHER, C.1858–60

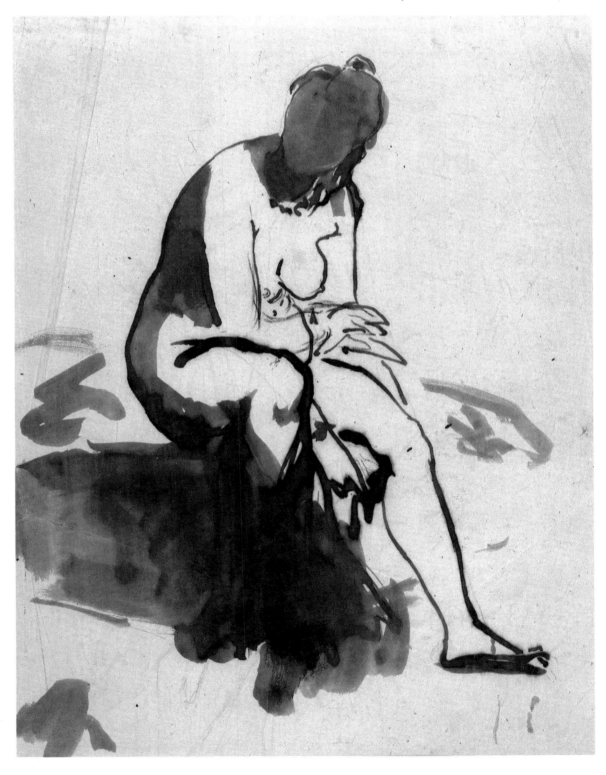

An early 'Salon composition', 1858–1860

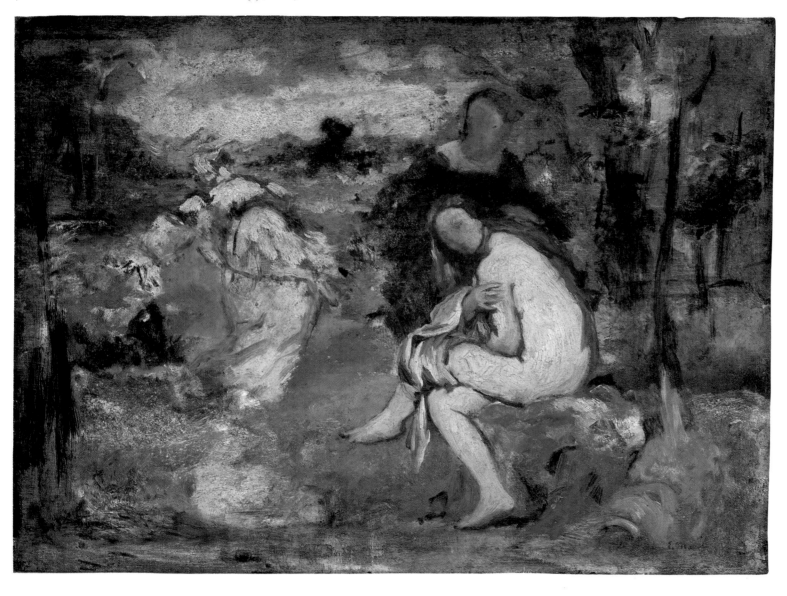

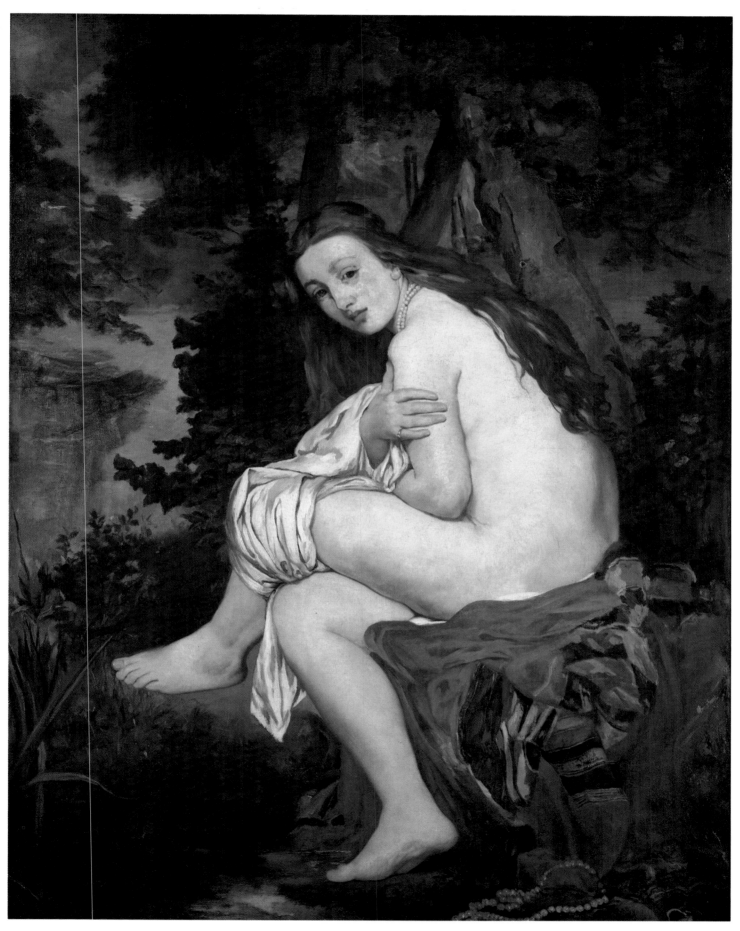

Suzanne Leenhoff as Manet's model

42   STUDY OF A HEAD IN PROFILE, c.1858–60

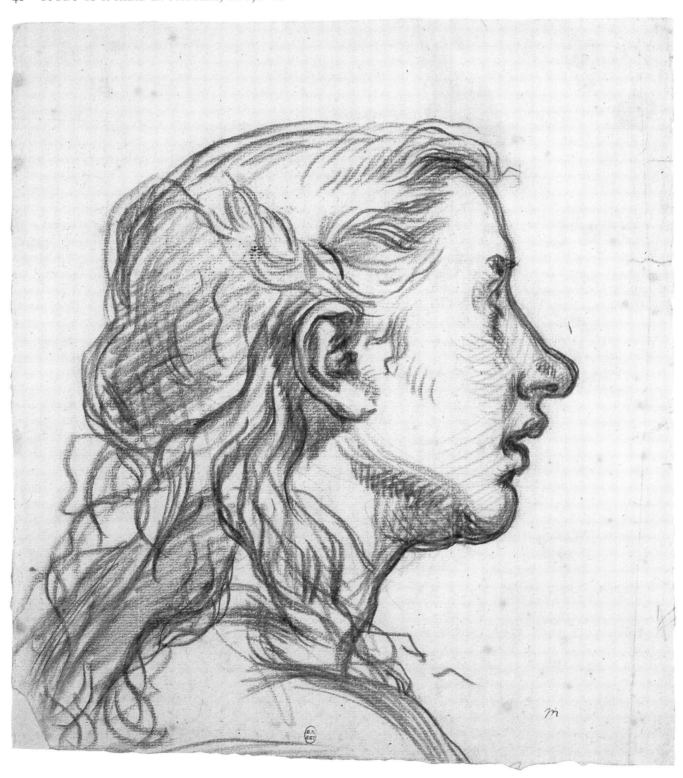

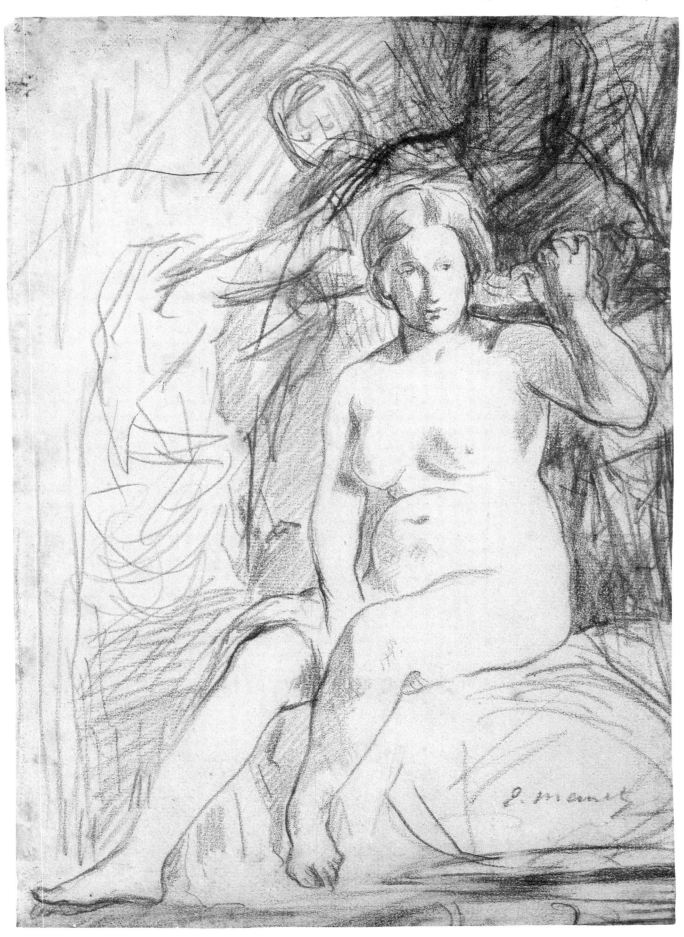

44 LA TOILETTE (WOMAN AT HER TOILET), C.1861–2

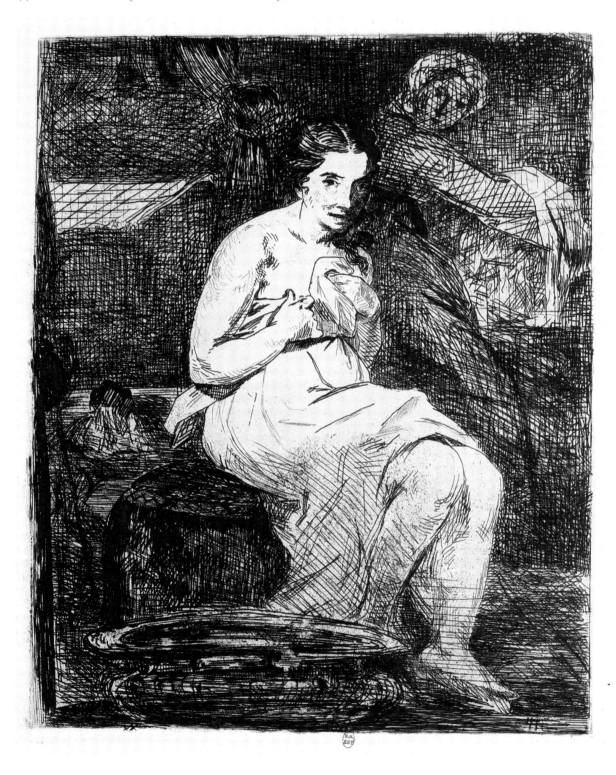

45 WOMAN POURING WATER / STUDY OF SUZANNE LEENHOFF, c.1858–60

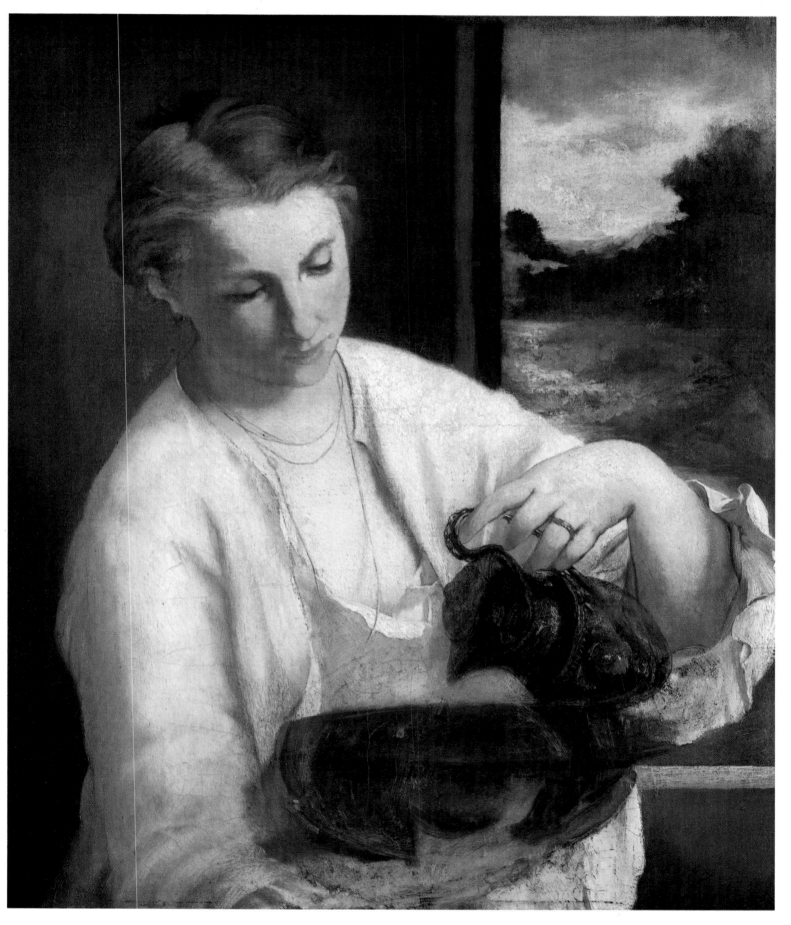

Manet's studio assistant, c.1858

46   BOY AND DOG, c.1862

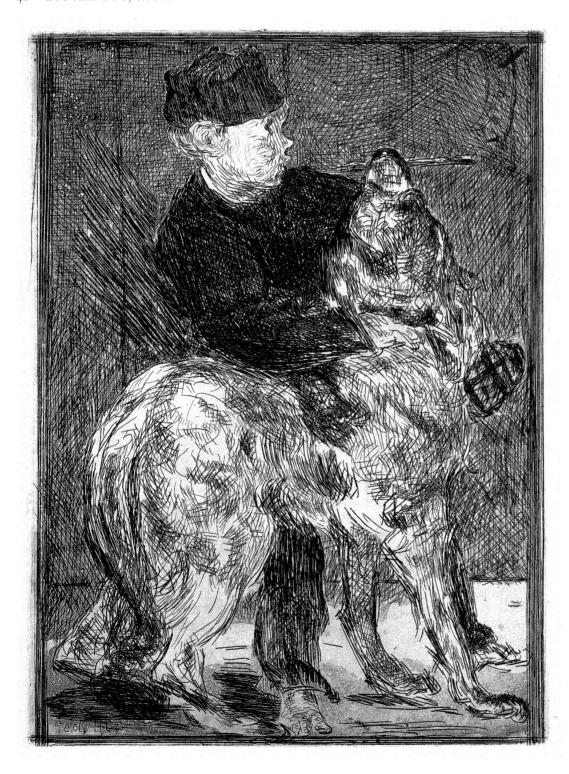

Manet's studio assistant, c.1858

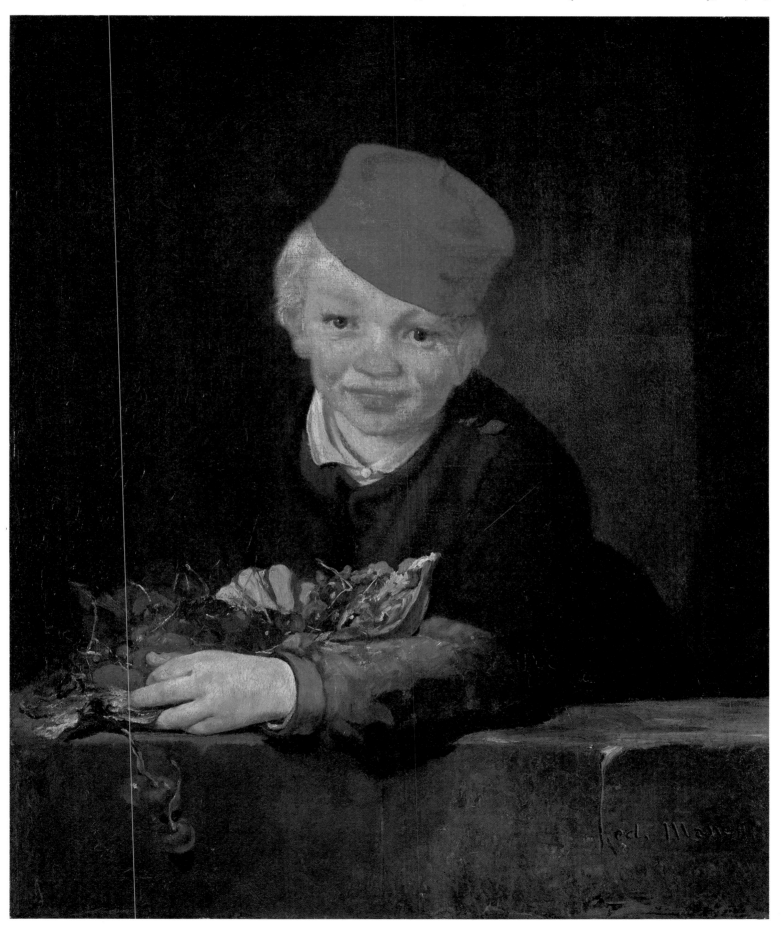

48   M. AND MME AUGUSTE MANET, d.1860

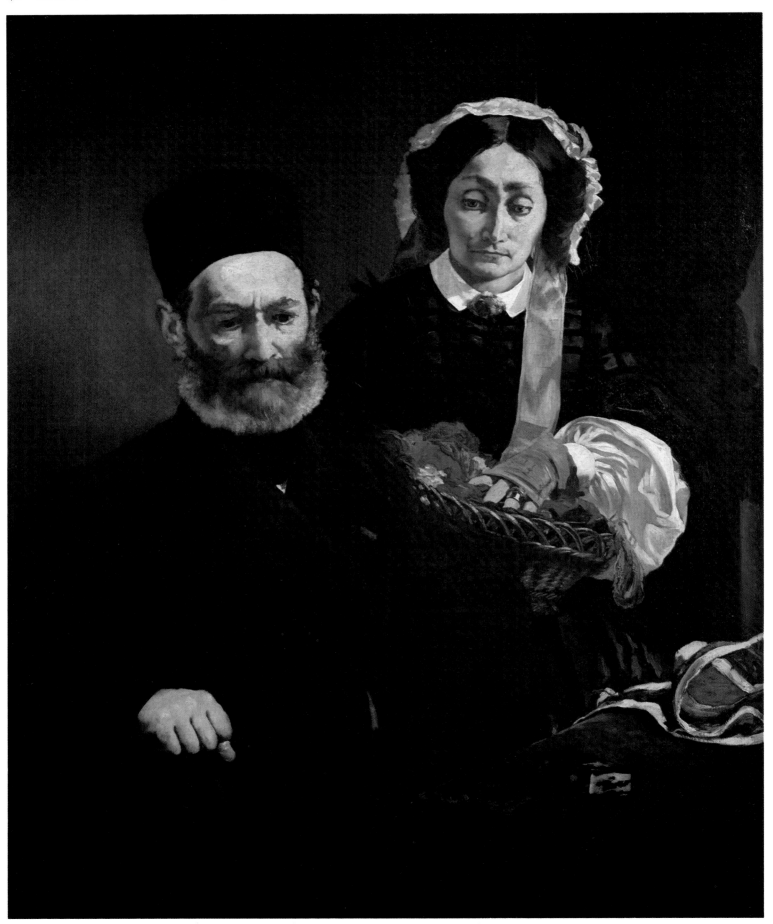

48   M. AND MME AUGUSTE MANET, d.1860

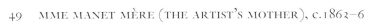

49   MME MANET MÈRE (THE ARTIST'S MOTHER), C.1862–6

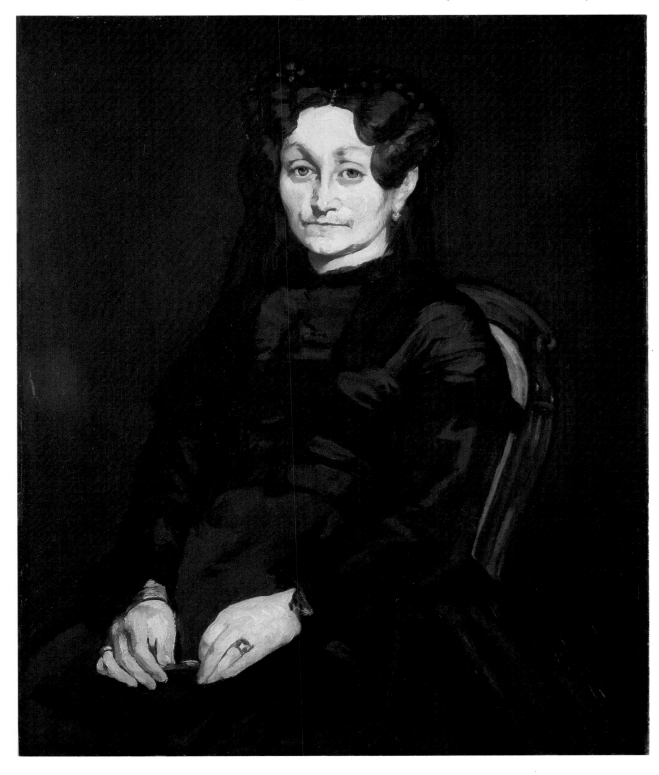

The first Salon refusal, 1859

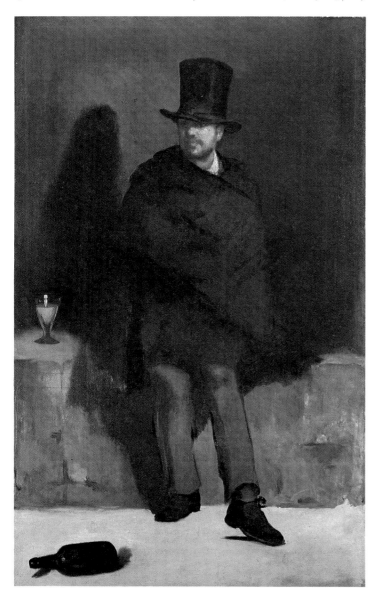

51 THE OLD MUSICIAN, d.1862

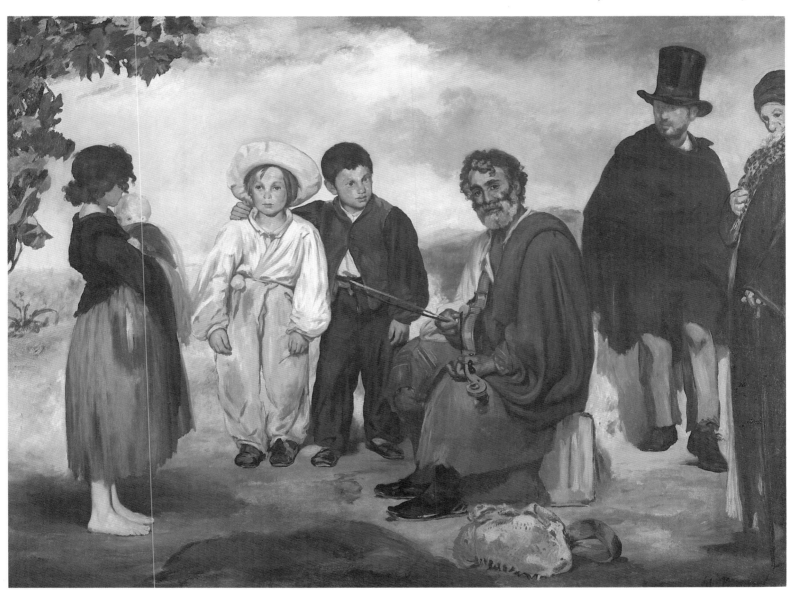

The Spanish influence

52   AFTER VELASQUEZ'S LITTLE CAVALIERS, C.1858–9

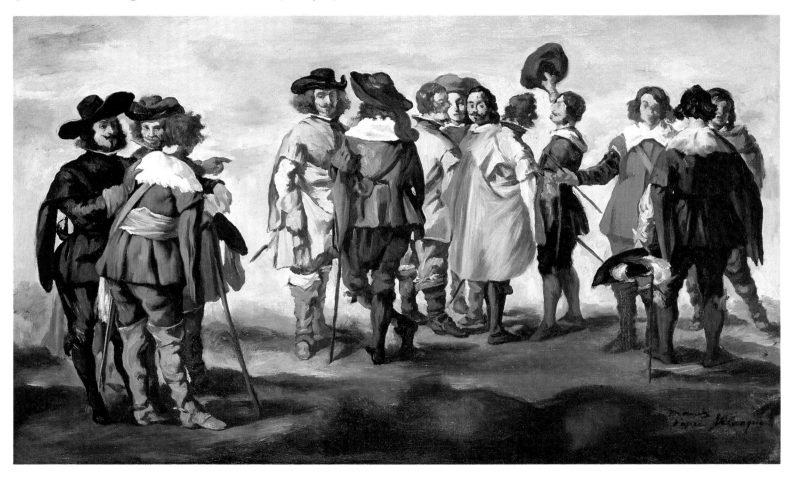

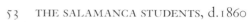

53   THE SALAMANCA STUDENTS, d.1860

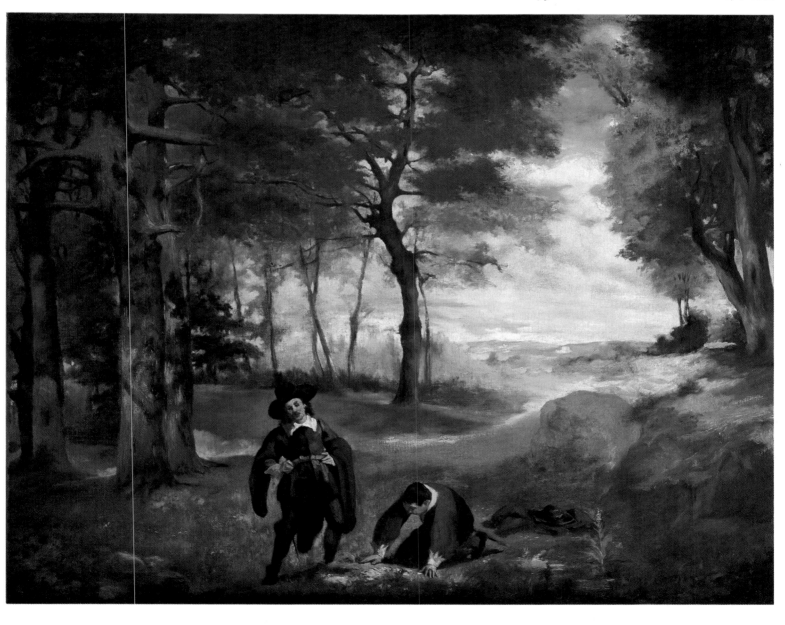

54   BOY WITH A SWORD (STUDY OF LÉON LEENHOFF), c.1860–61

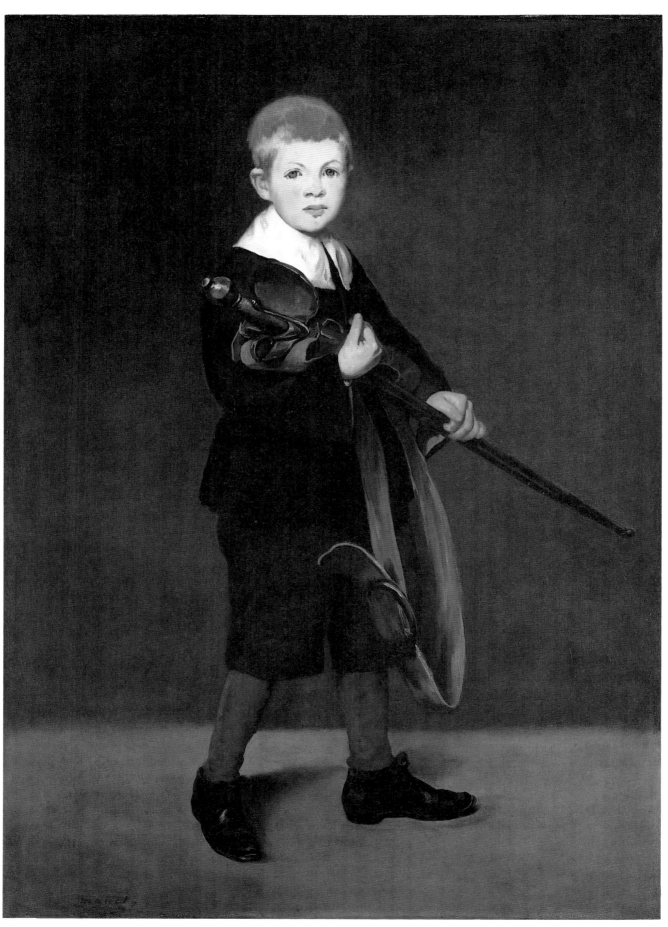

Léon Leenhoff as Manet's model, c.1860

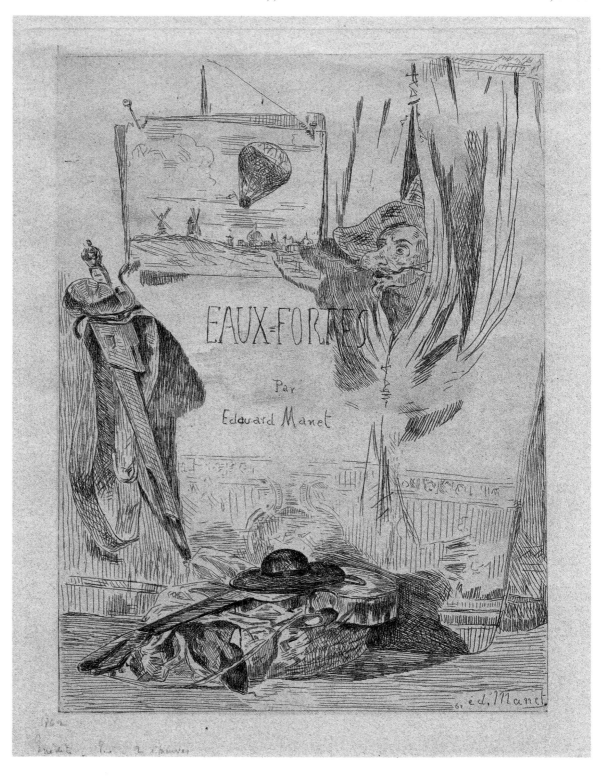

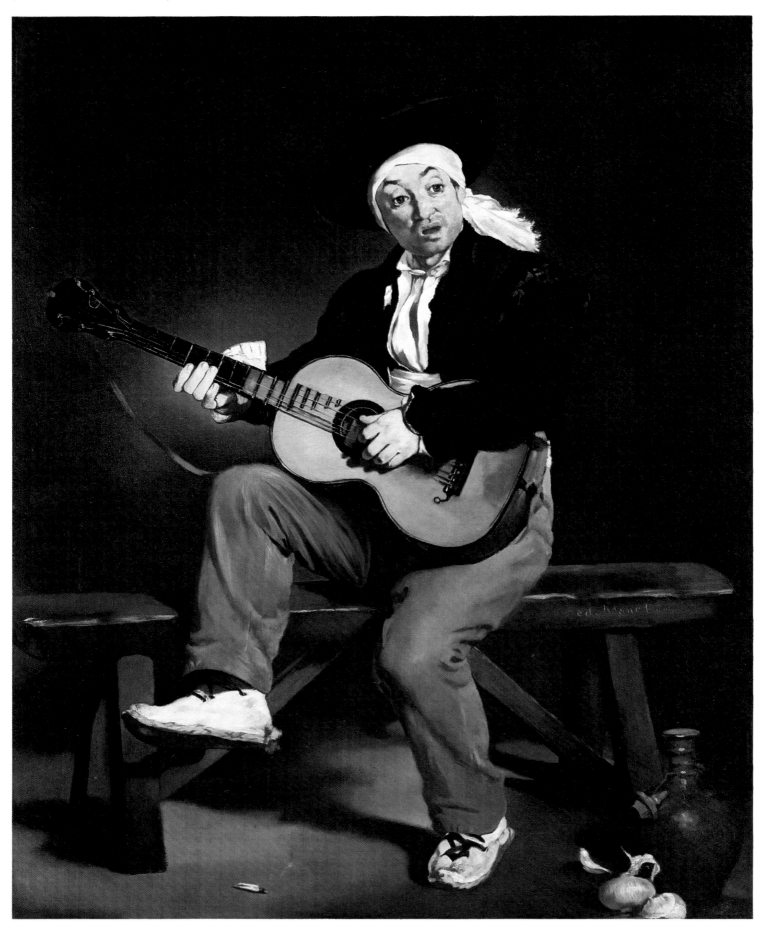

57   MLLE V... IN THE COSTUME OF AN ESPADA, d.1862

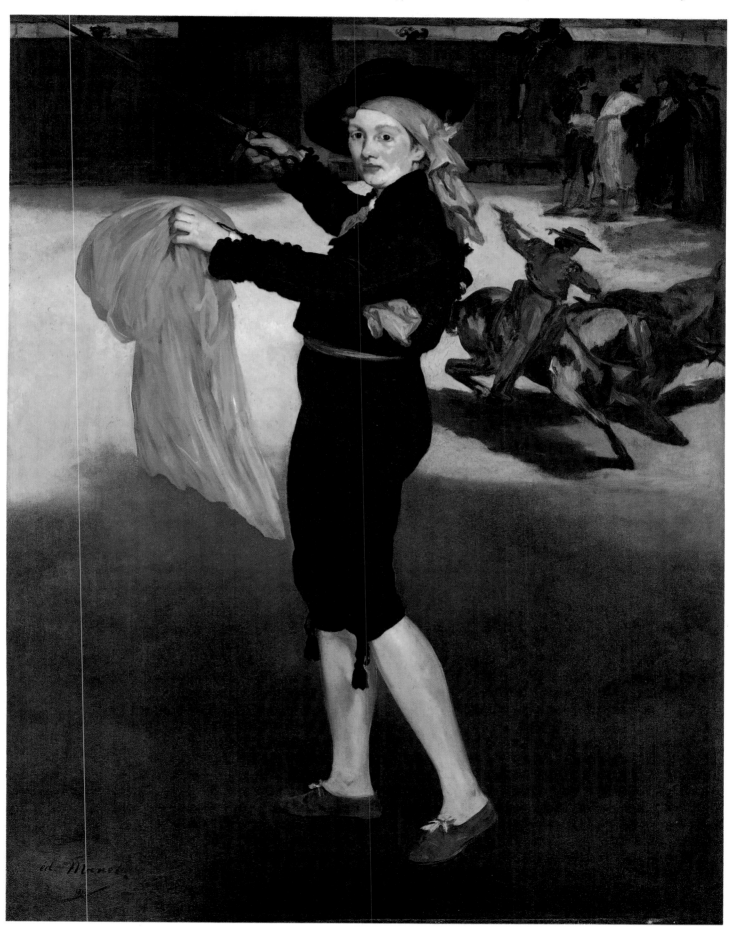

58   LE DÉJEUNER SUR L'HERBE (LUNCHEON ON THE GRASS), d.1863

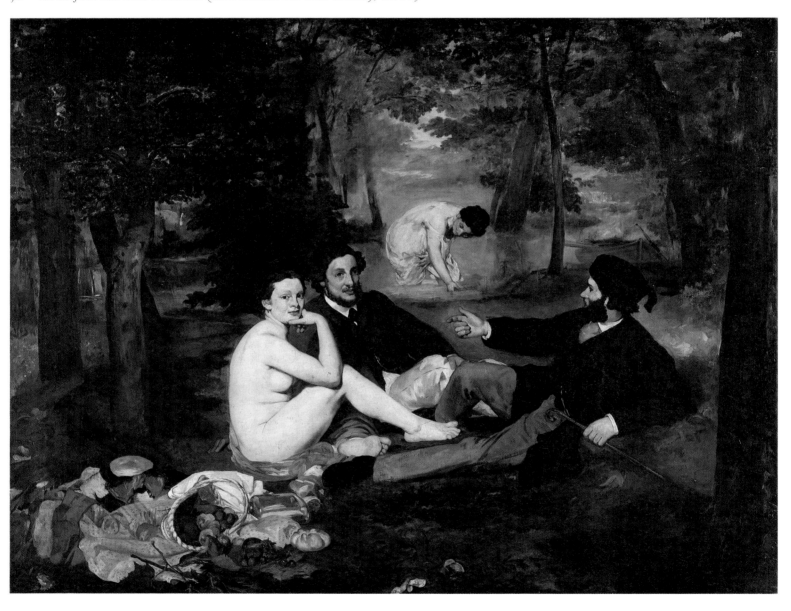

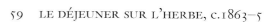

59   LE DÉJEUNER SUR L'HERBE, C.1863–5

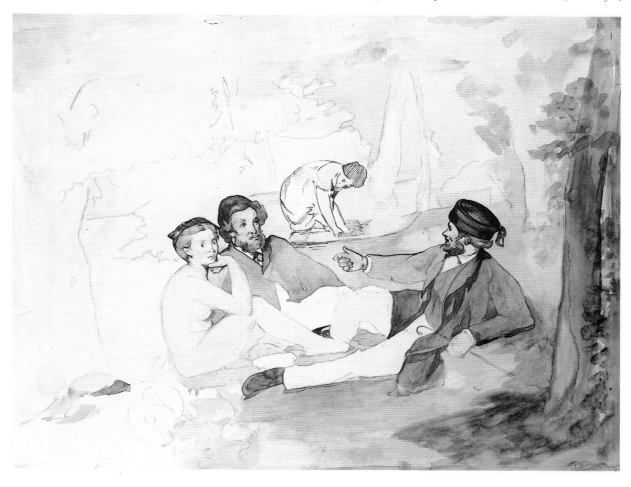

60   YOUNG MAN IN THE COSTUME OF A MAJO, d. 1862

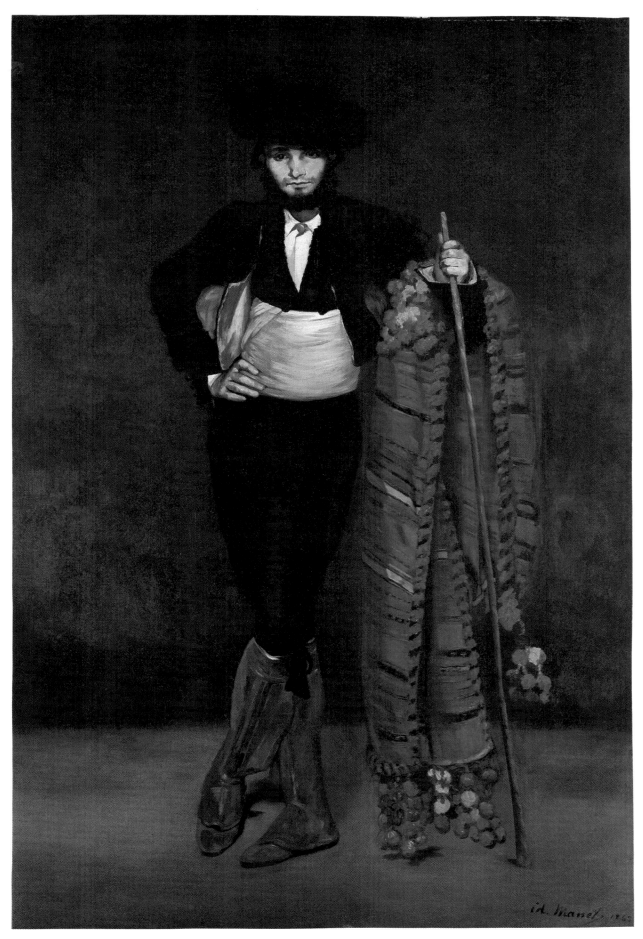

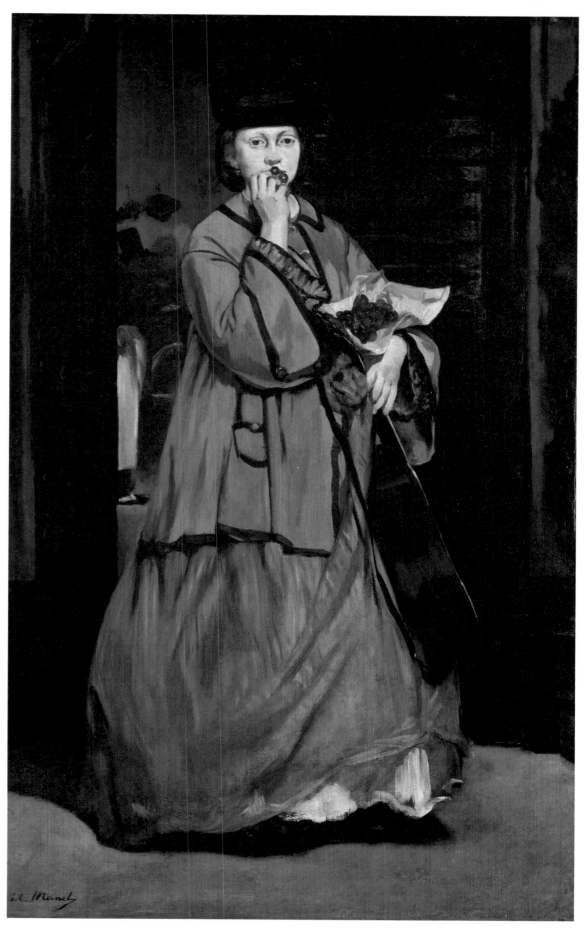

Plein air studies, 1861–1862

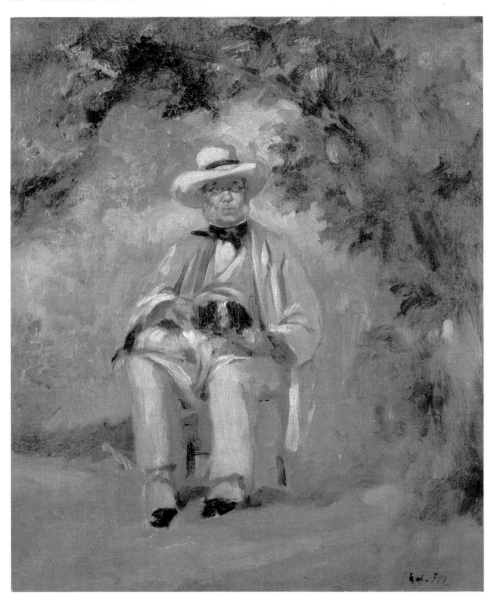

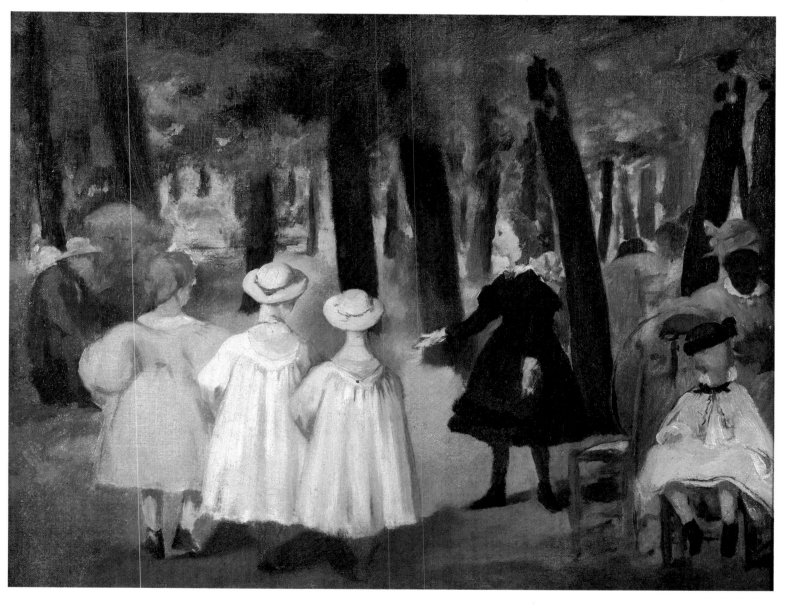

The influence of Baudelaire

64   BAUDELAIRE IN PROFILE, C.1862–5

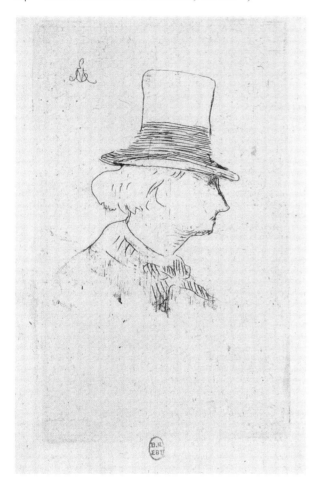

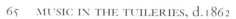

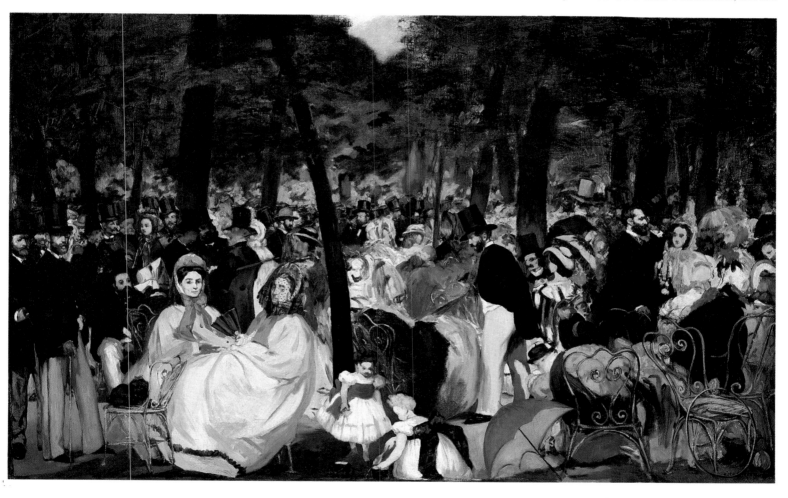

The influence of Baudelaire

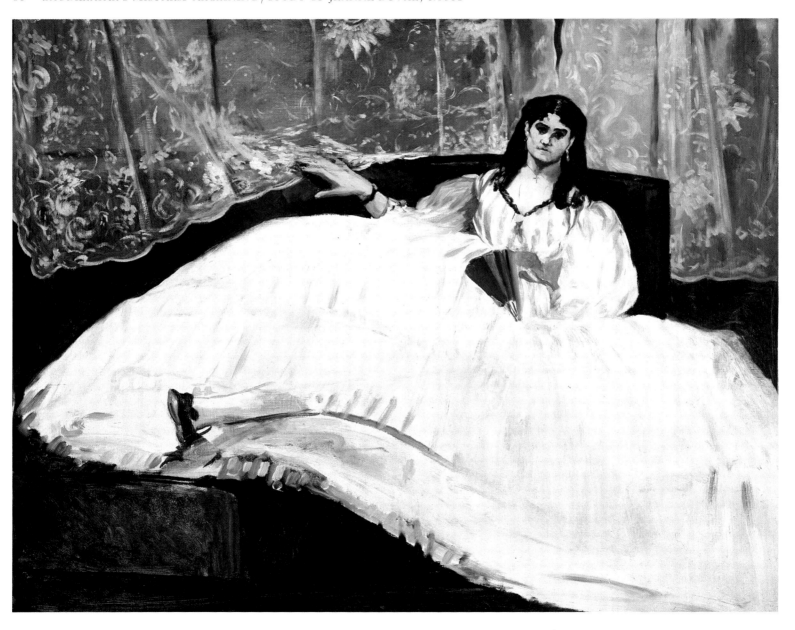

67   YOUNG WOMAN RECLINING IN SPANISH COSTUME, C.1862

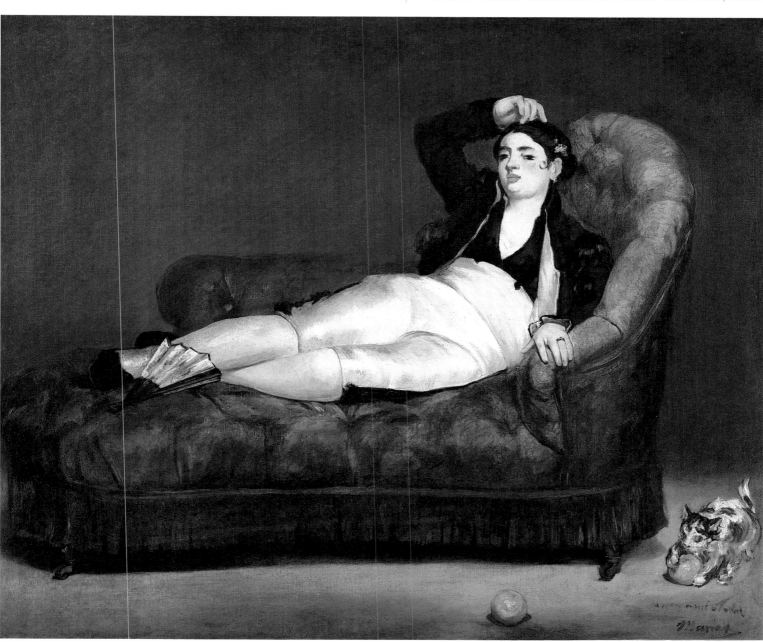

The Spanish ballet in Paris, winter 1862–1863

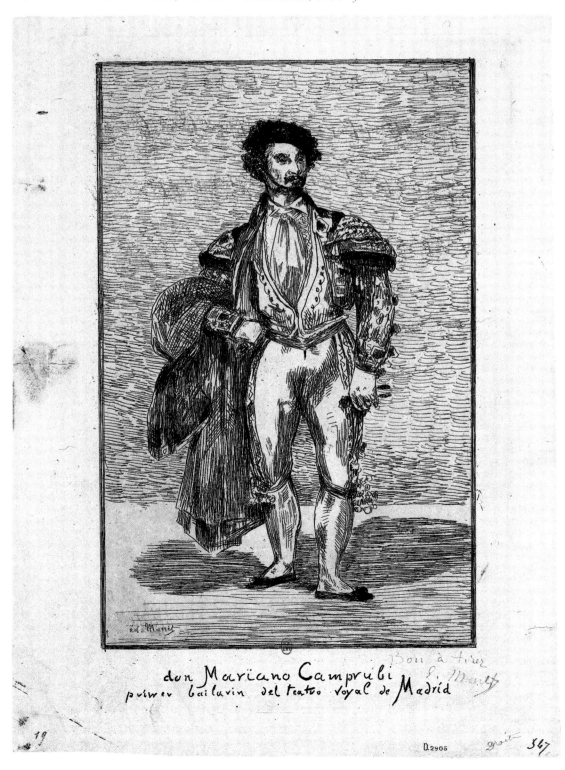

don Mariano Camprubi
primer bailarin del teatro royal de Madrid

69   LOLA DE VALENCE, COVER FOR A SONGSHEET, 1863

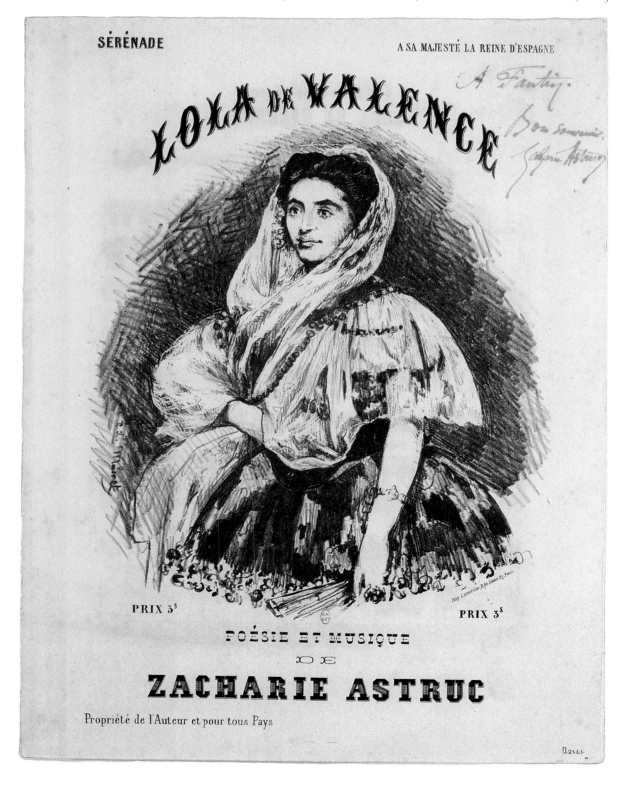

The Spanish ballet in Paris, winter 1862–1863

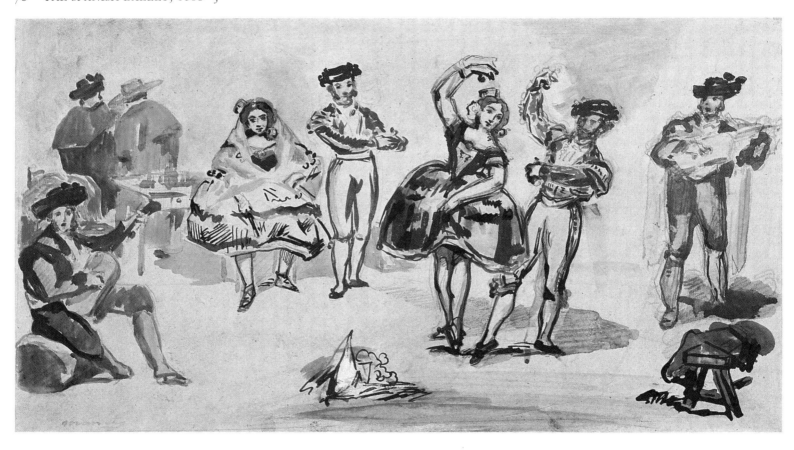

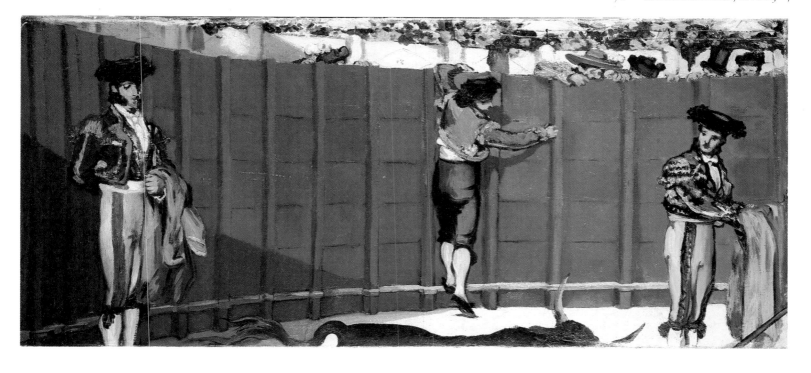

Fragment from the 1864 Salon *Bullfight*

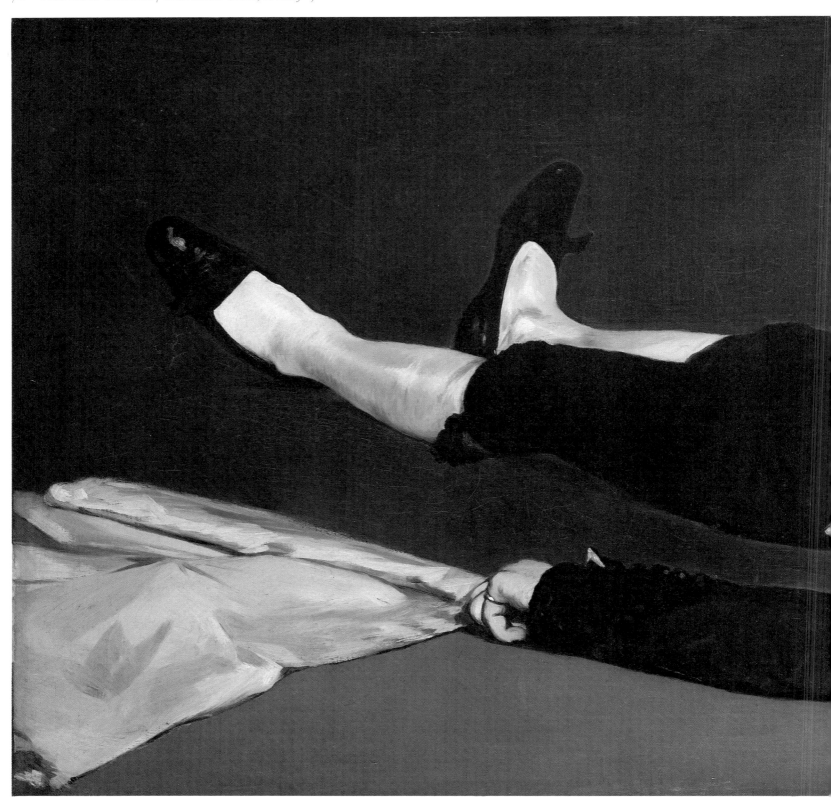

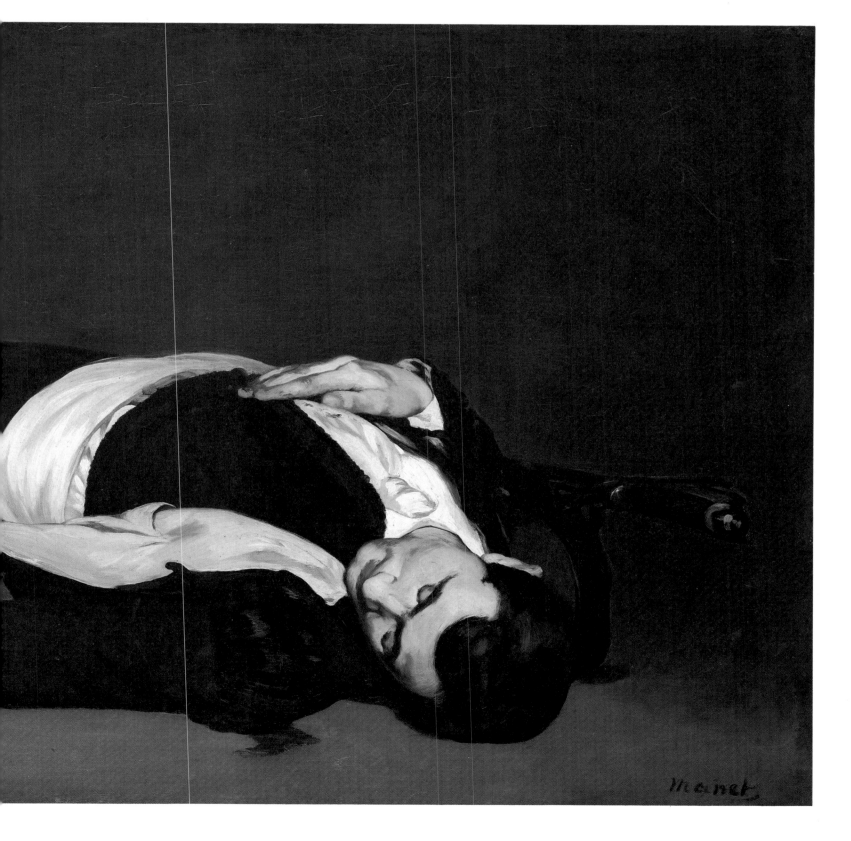

Summer at Boulogne, 1864

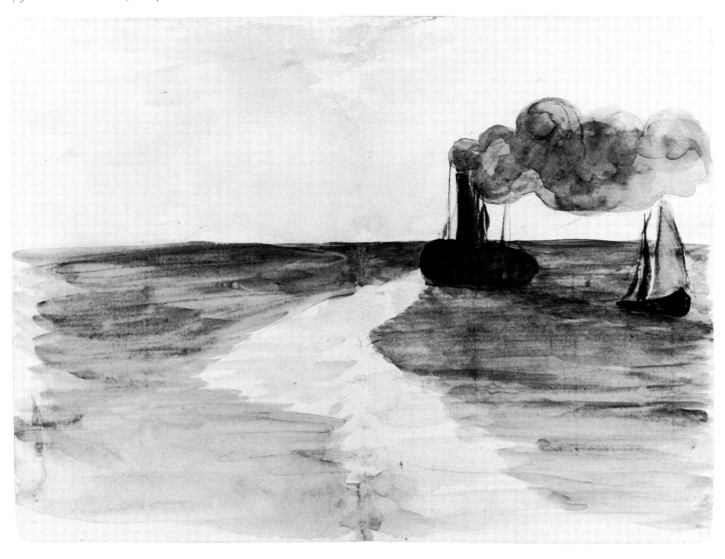

74   THE PORPOISES / SEASCAPE AT BOULOGNE, 1864

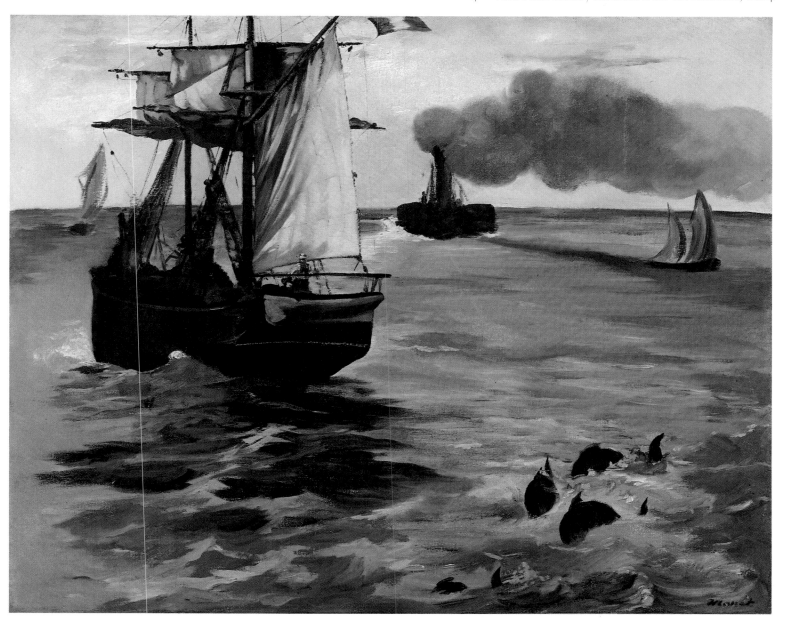

An American Civil War incident, 1864

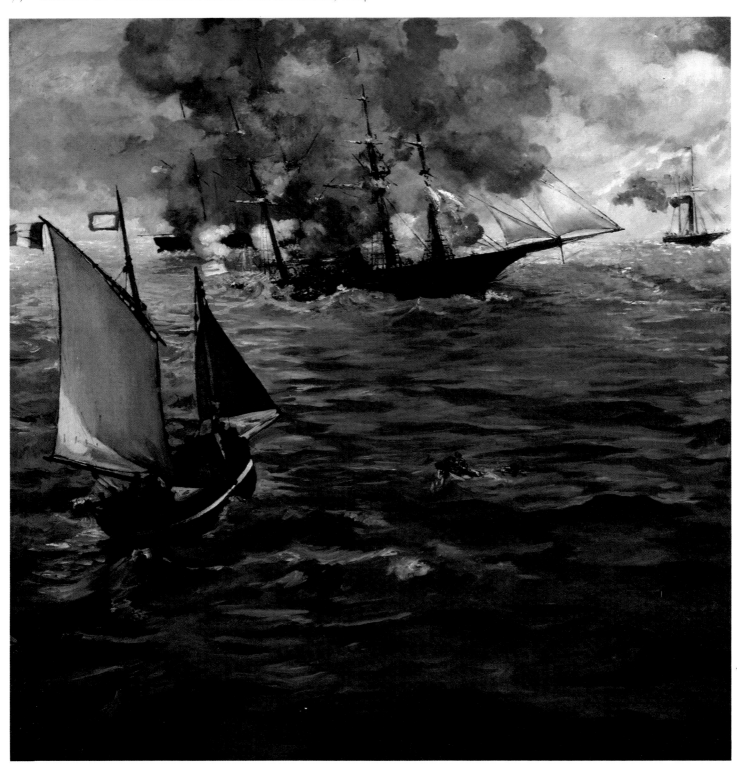

76   FISHING BOAT COMING IN BEFORE THE WIND / THE *KEARSARGE* AT BOULOGNE, 1864

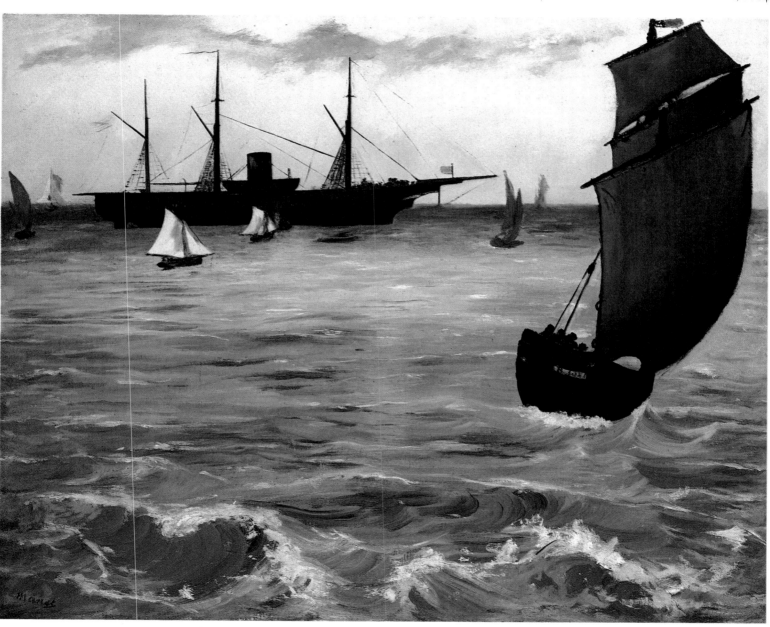

Still life, 1864–1865

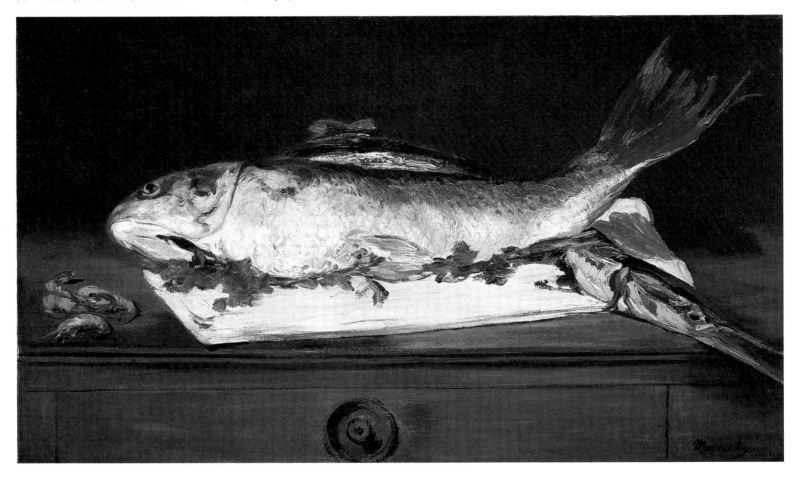

78   FRUIT ON A TABLECLOTH, 1864–5

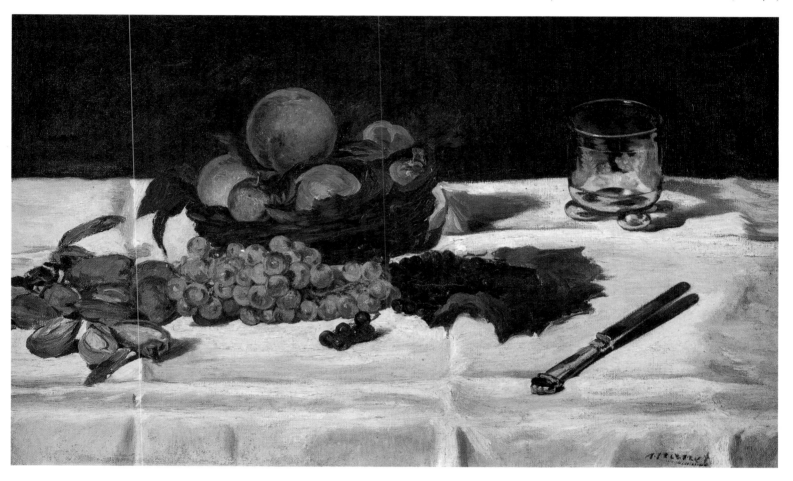

79   PEONIES IN A VASE ON A STAND, 1864

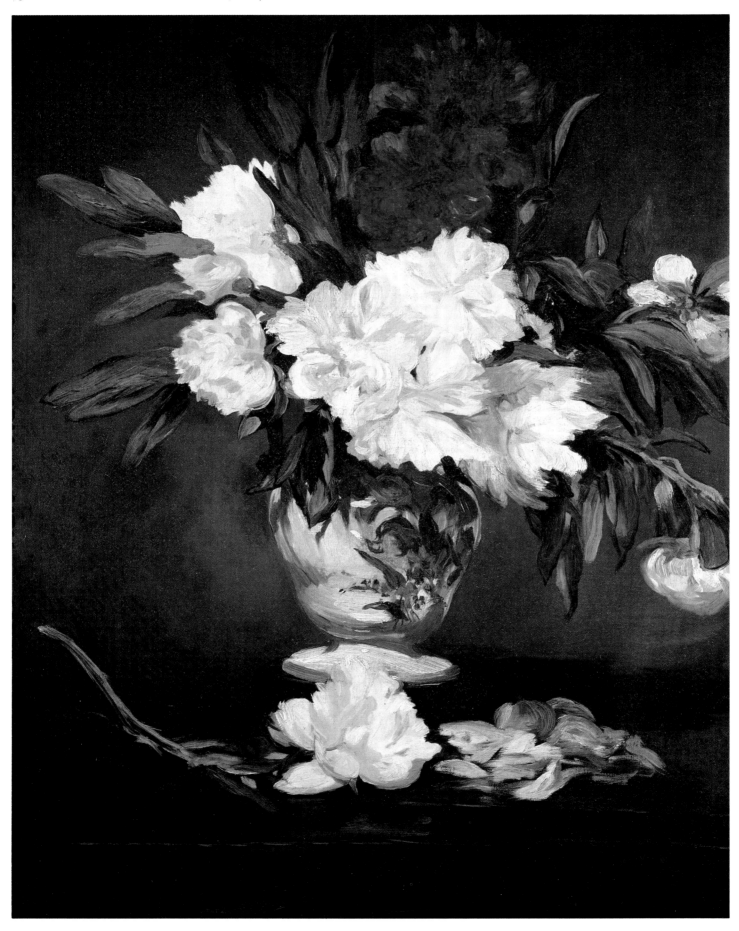

Still life, 1864–1865

80   BRANCH OF WHITE PEONIES WITH SECATEURS, 1864

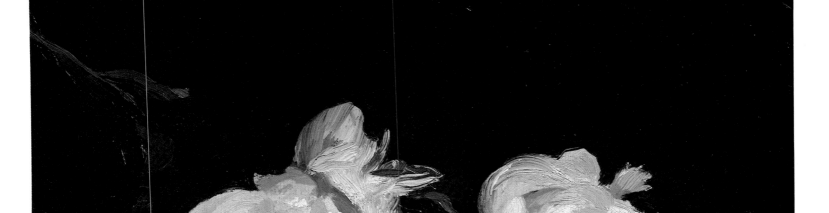

81   THE DEAD CHRIST AND THE ANGELS, 1864

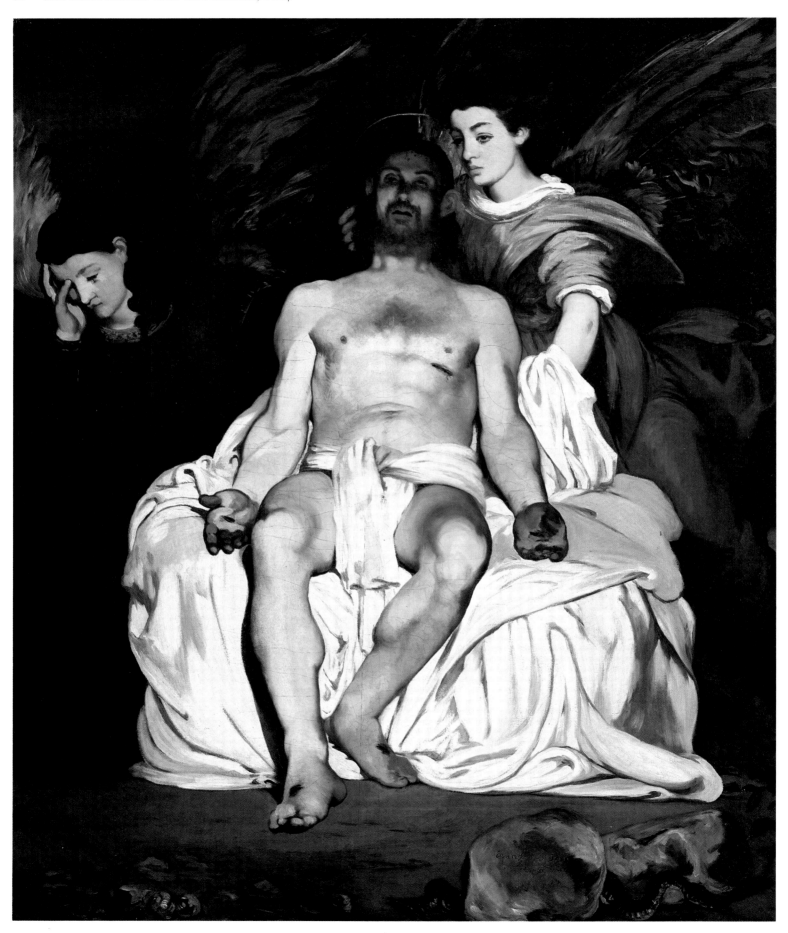

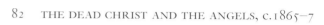

82   THE DEAD CHRIST AND THE ANGELS, c.1865–7

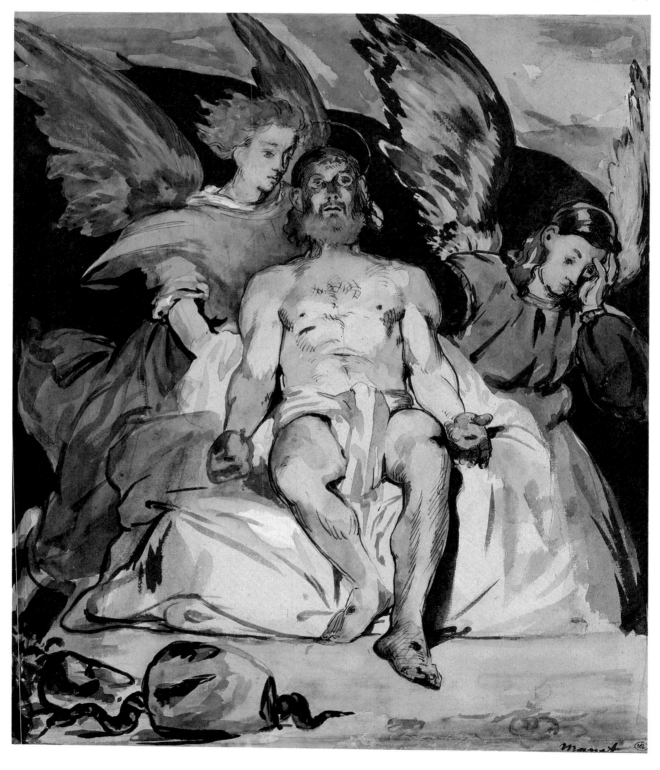

83   THE DEAD CHRIST AND THE ANGELS, c.1865–7

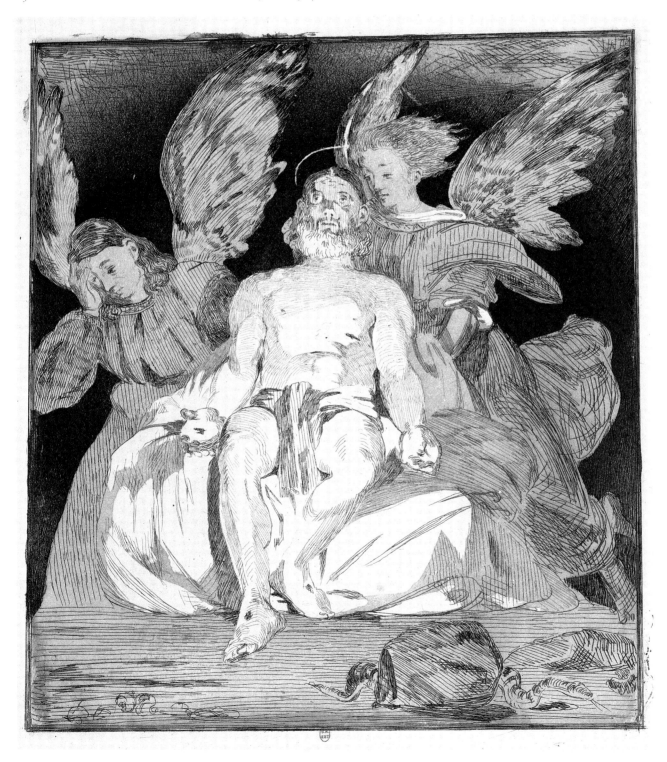

84 JESUS MOCKED BY THE SOLDIERS, d.1865

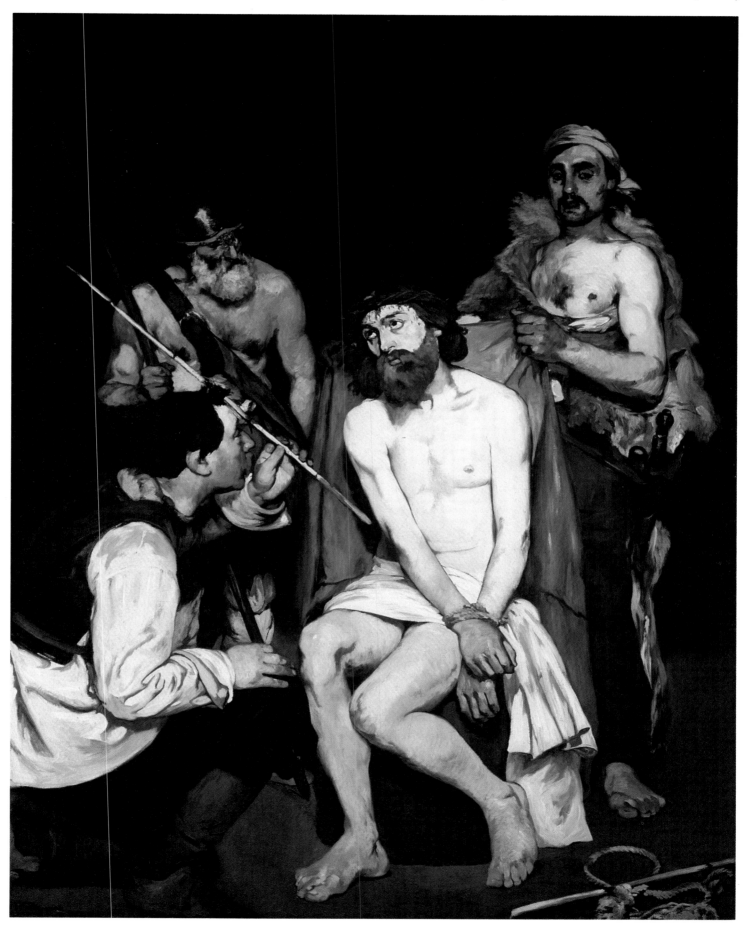

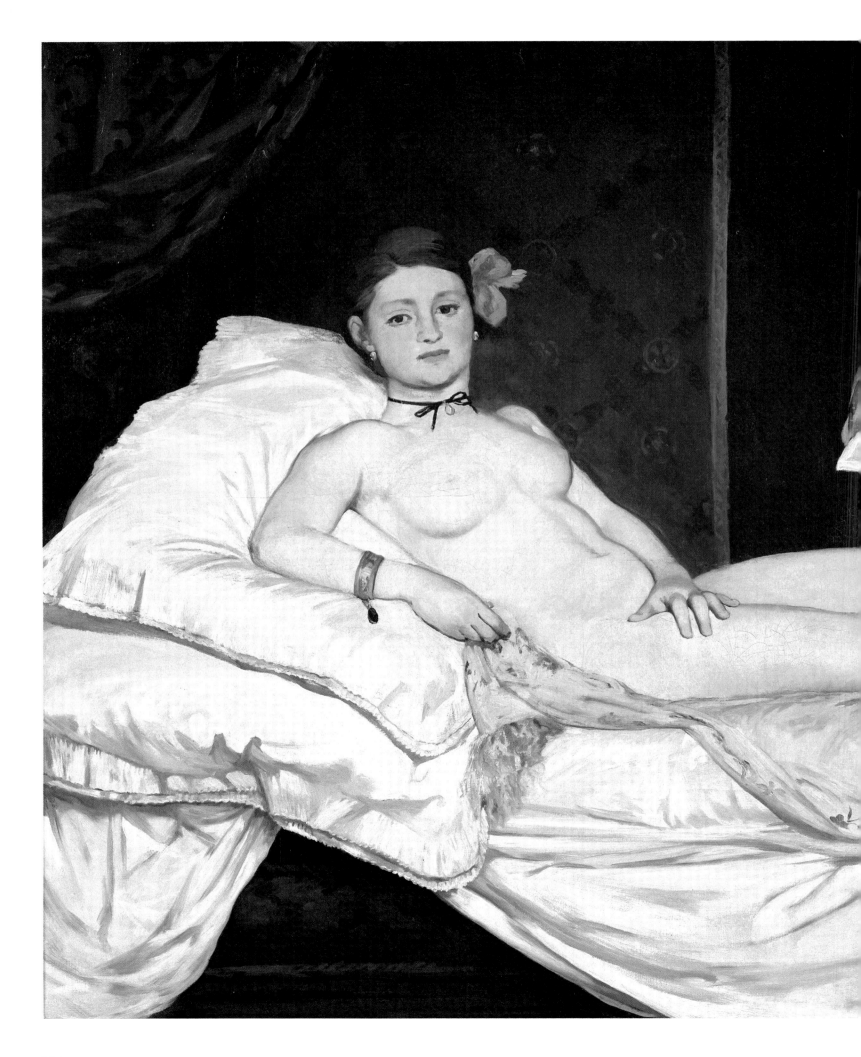

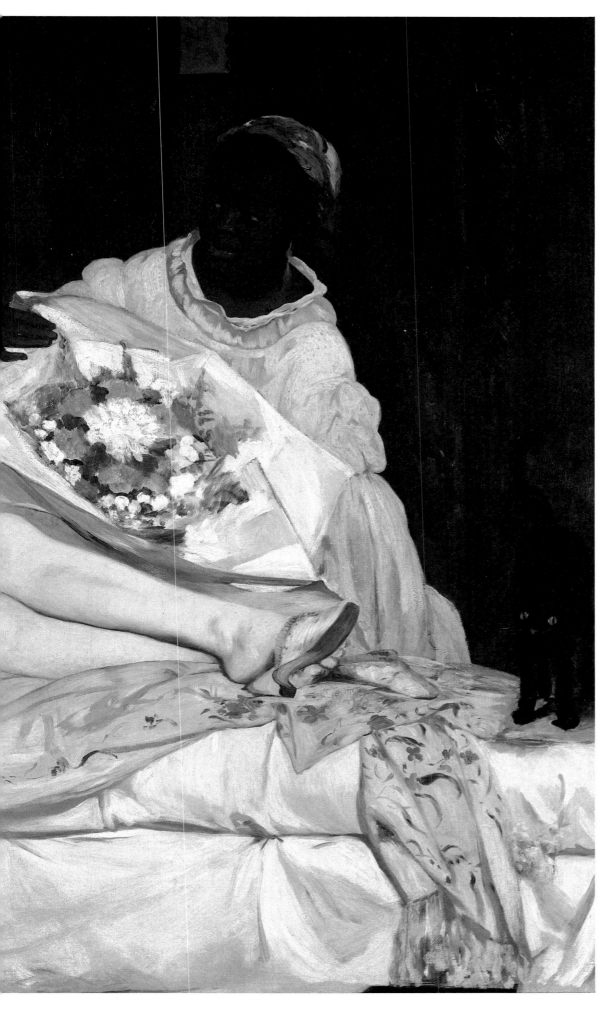

85   OLYMPIA, c.1860–65 / d.1863

After the visit to Spain, 1865

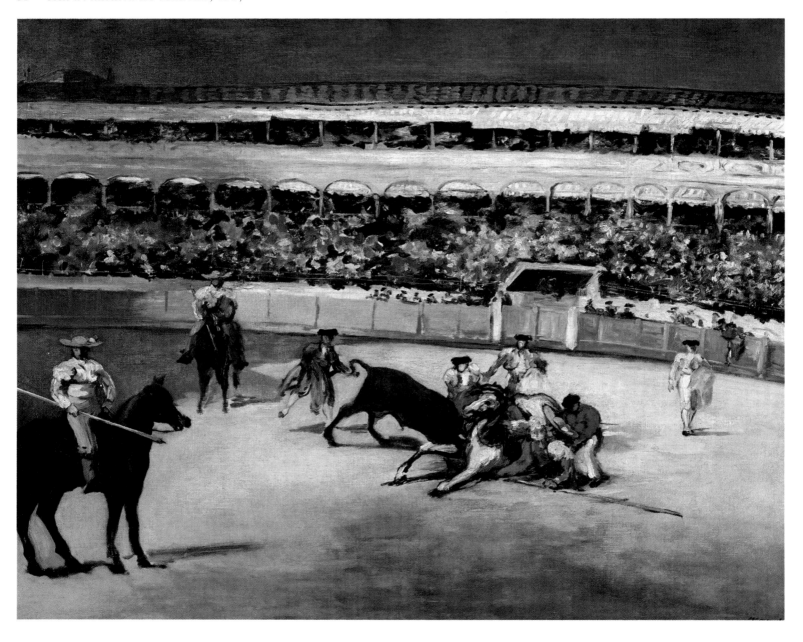

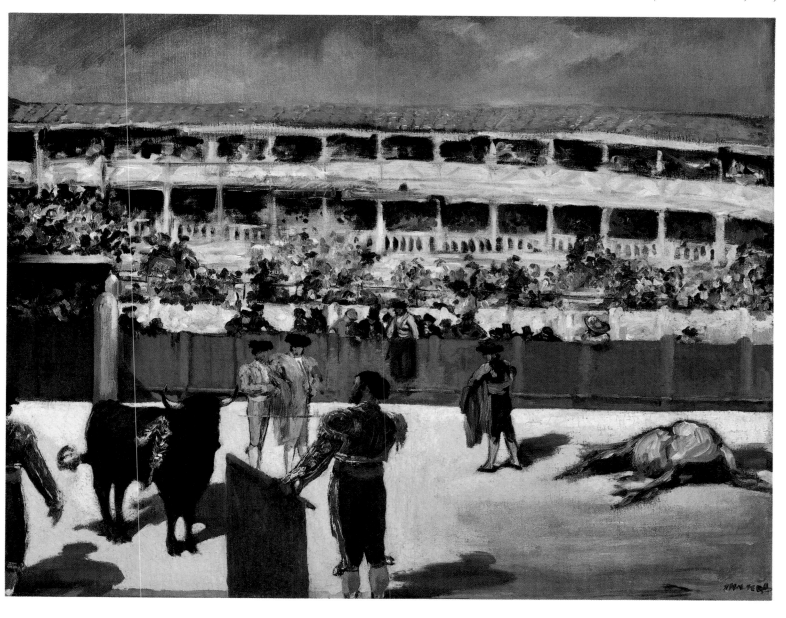

88   THE TRAGIC ACTOR / PHILIBERT ROUVIÈRE IN THE ROLE OF HAMLET, 1865–6

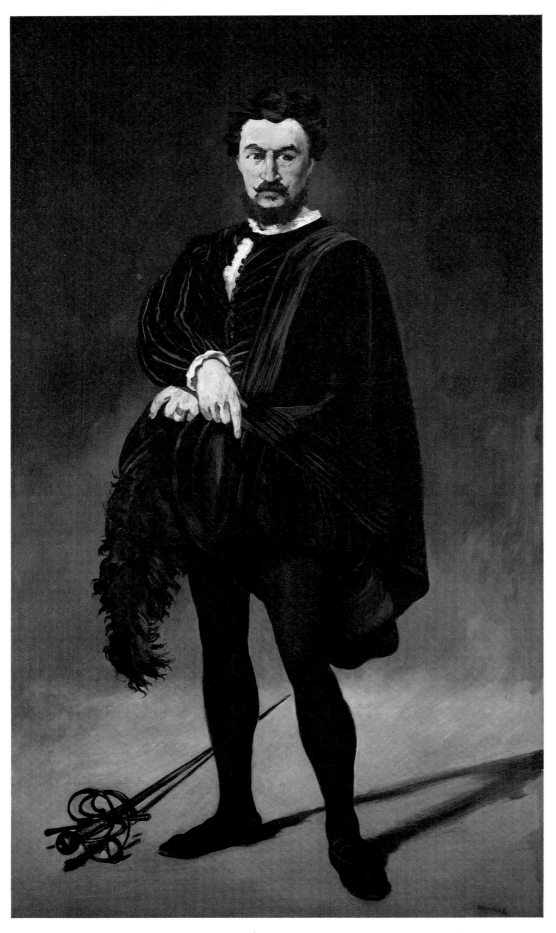

89   YOUNG LADY IN 1866 / WOMAN WITH A PARROT, 1866

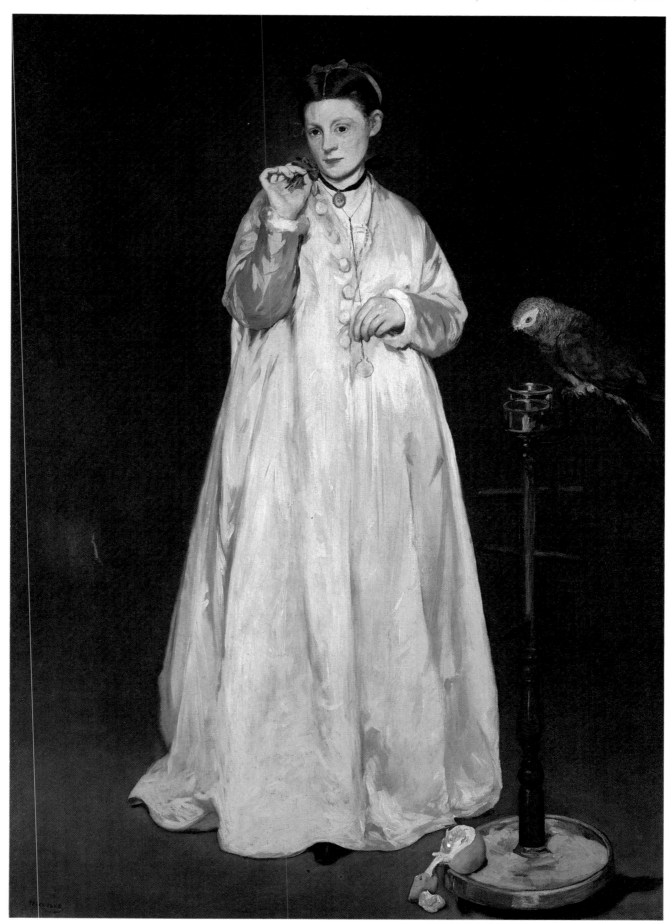

Portraits of friends

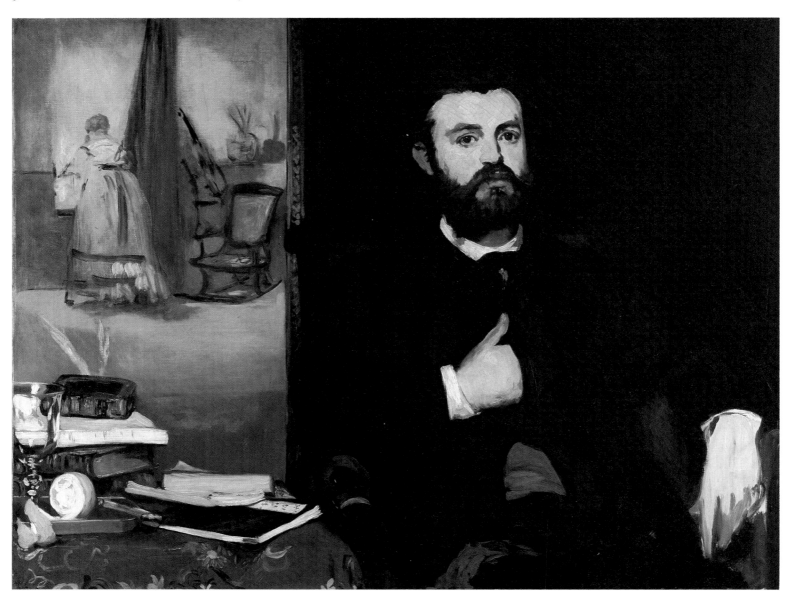

91   PORTRAIT OF ÉMILE ZOLA, 1868

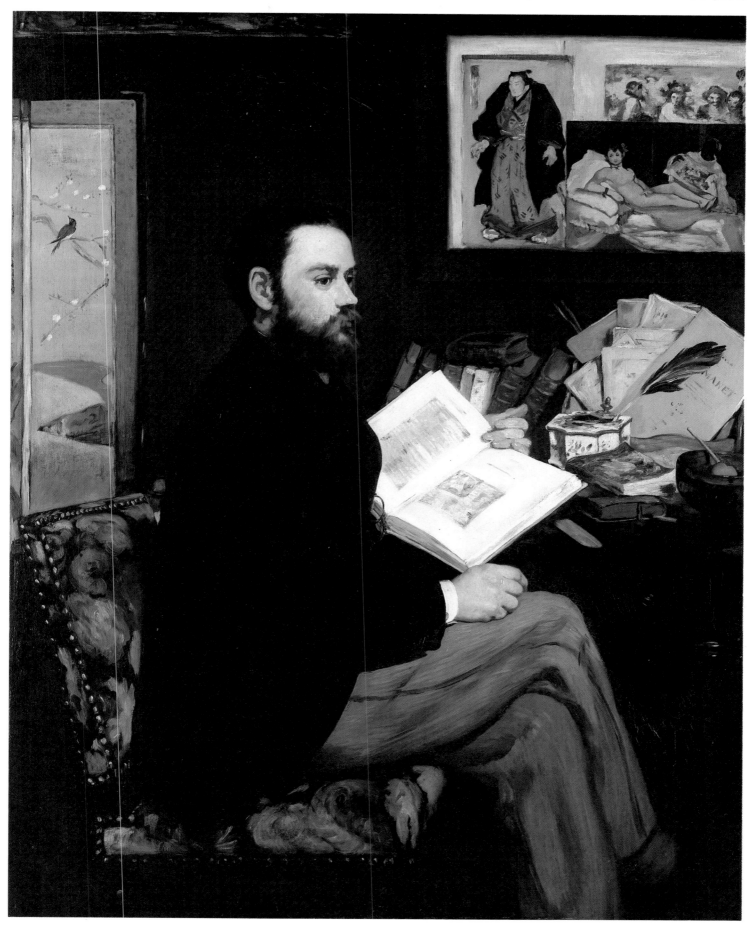

At the races, 1864–1867

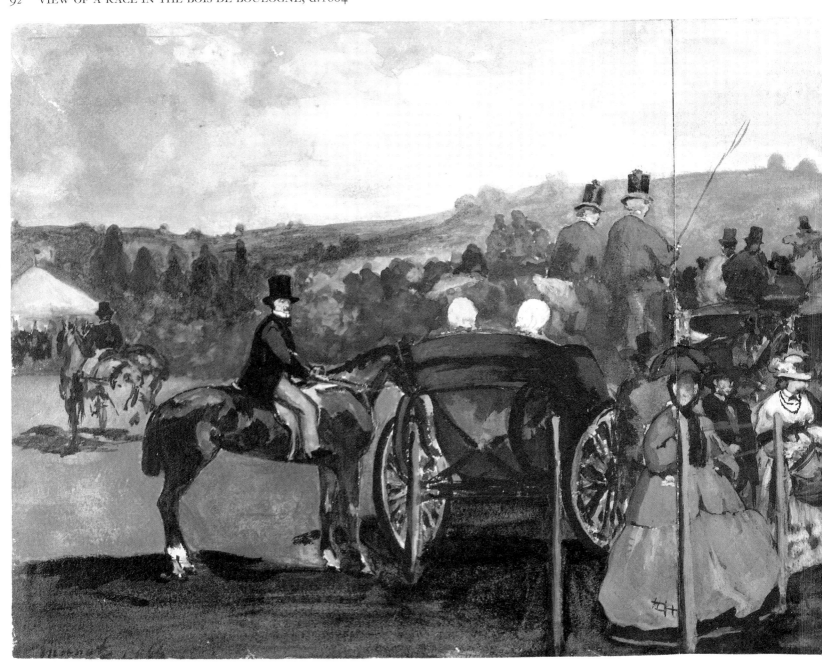

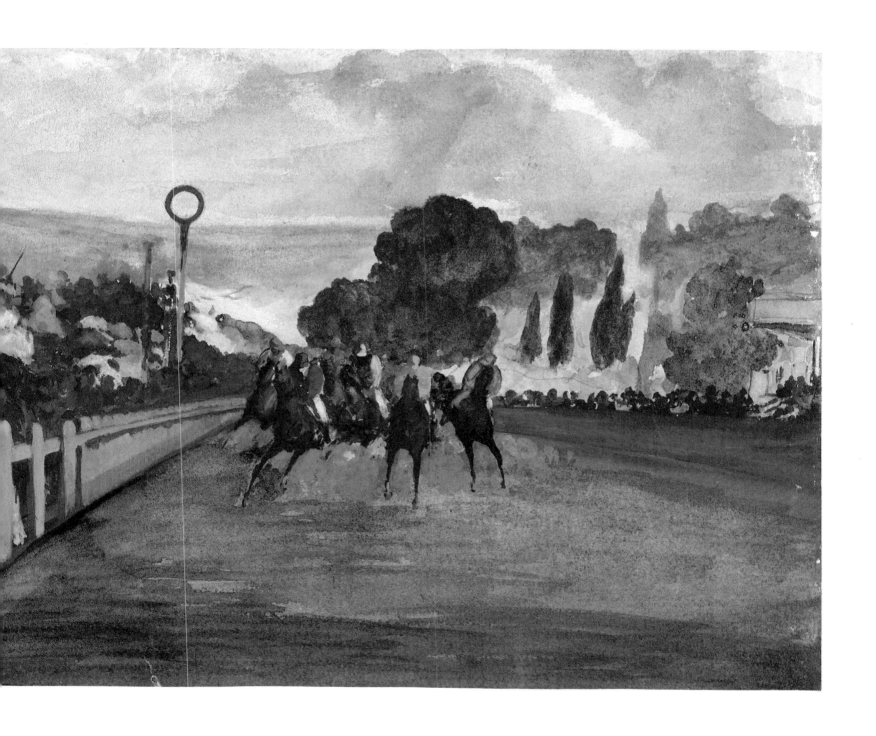

93   THE RACES, c.1865–7

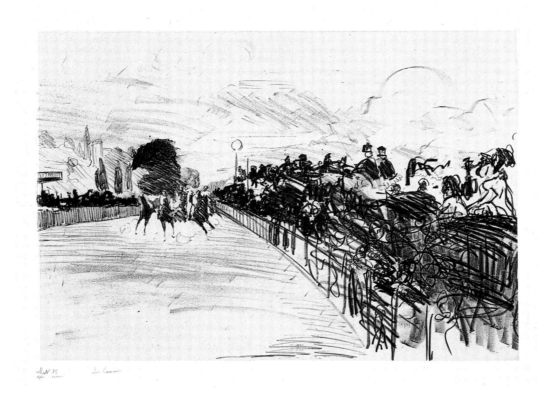

94   RACES AT LONGCHAMP IN THE BOIS DE BOULOGNE, d.186(7?)

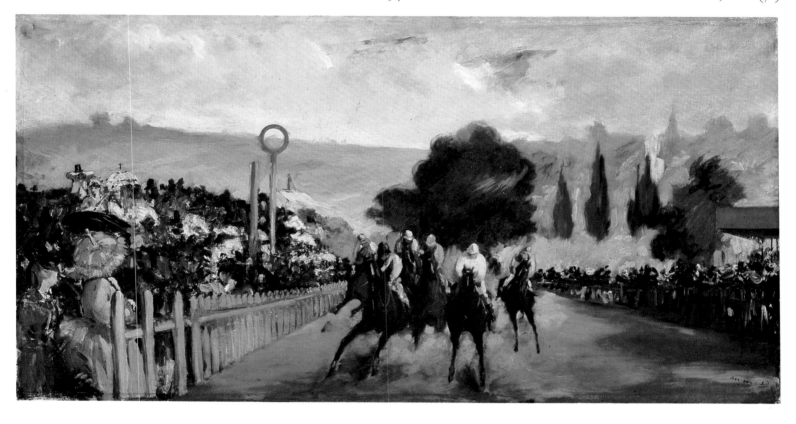

95   THE EXECUTION OF MAXIMILIAN (SKETCH), c.1867–9 / d.1867

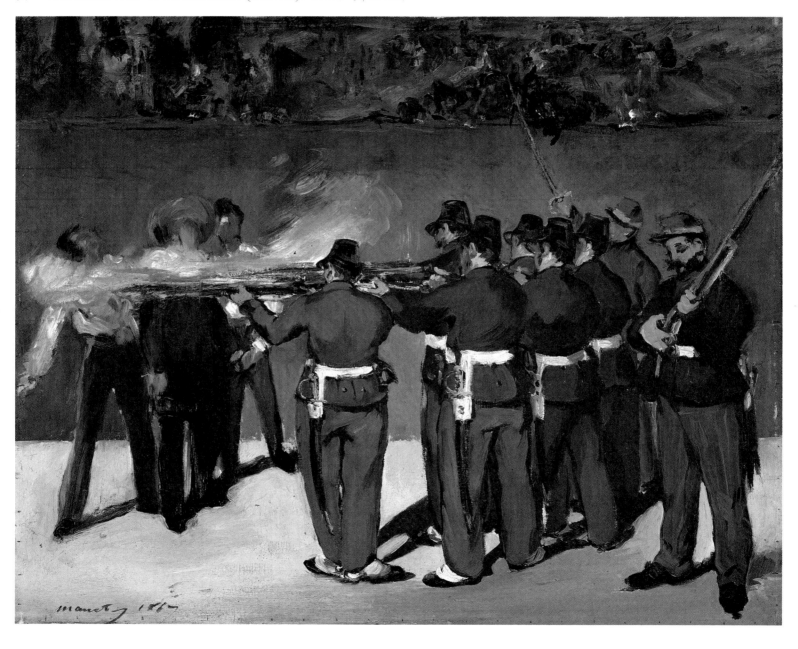

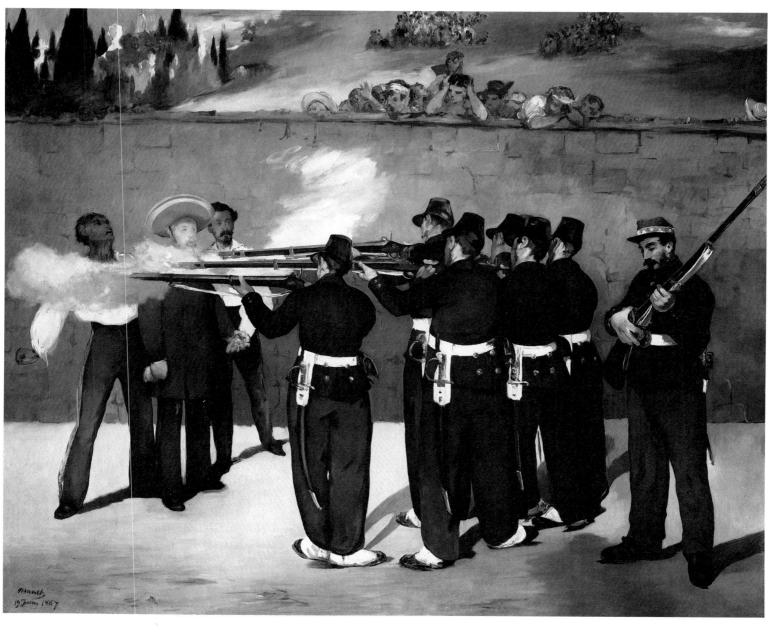

Summer at Boulogne, 1868

97 A MOONLIT SKY, 1868

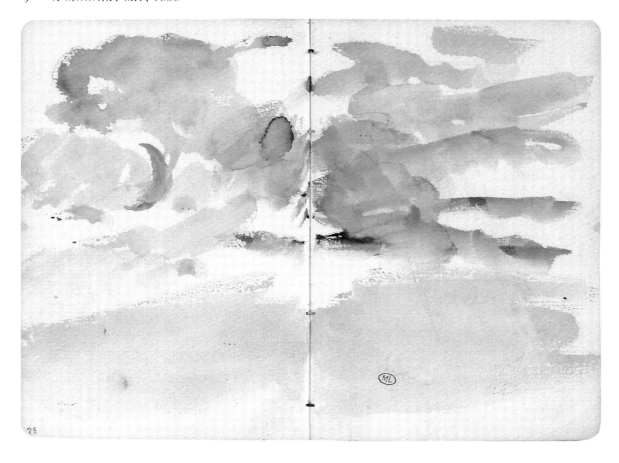

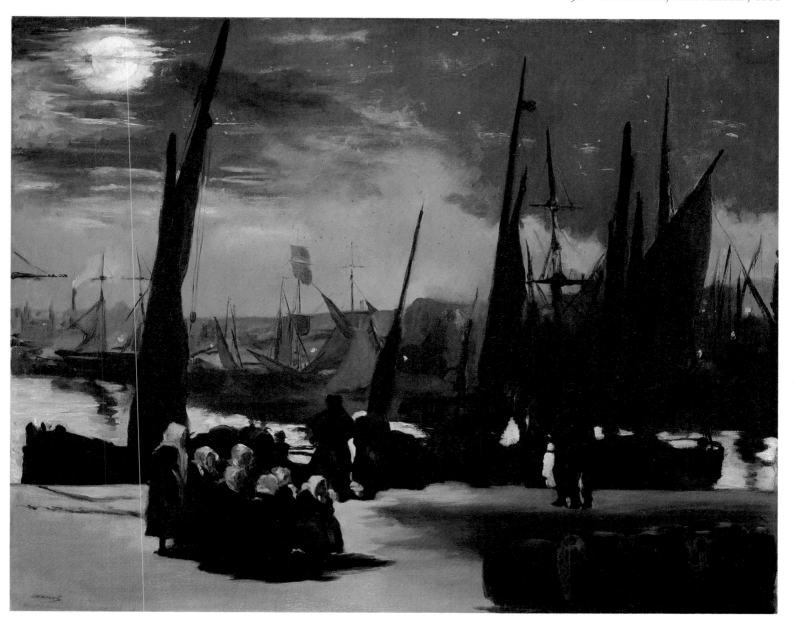

Summer at Boulogne, 1868

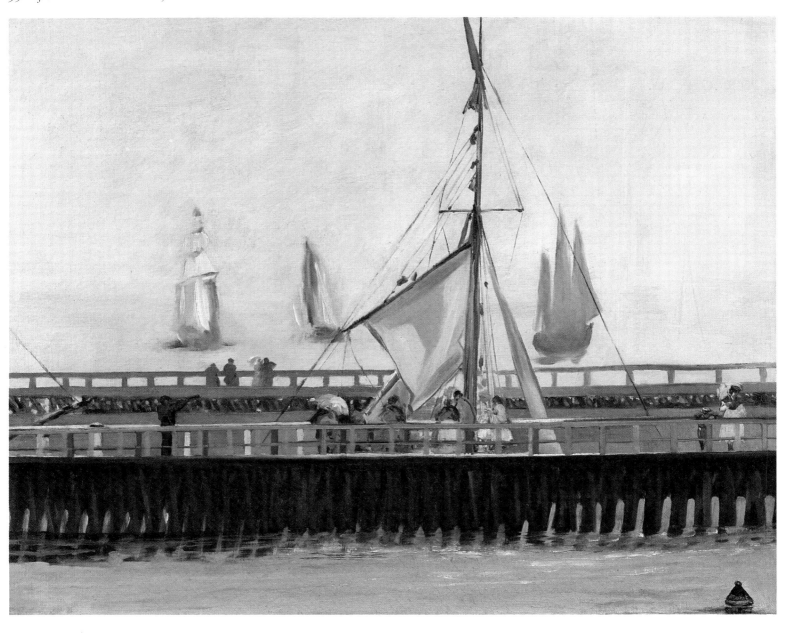

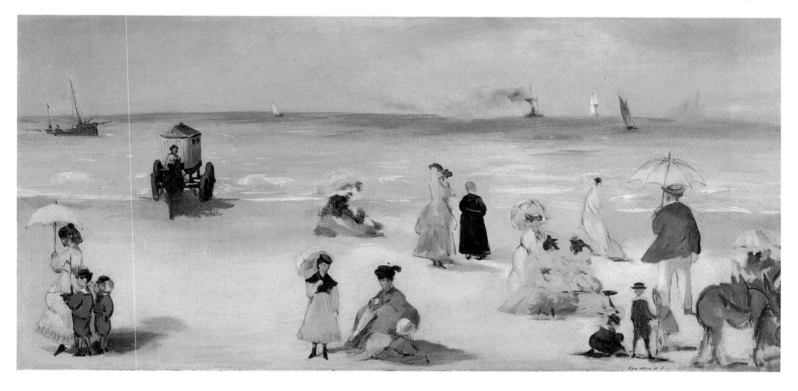

Study for a Salon picture

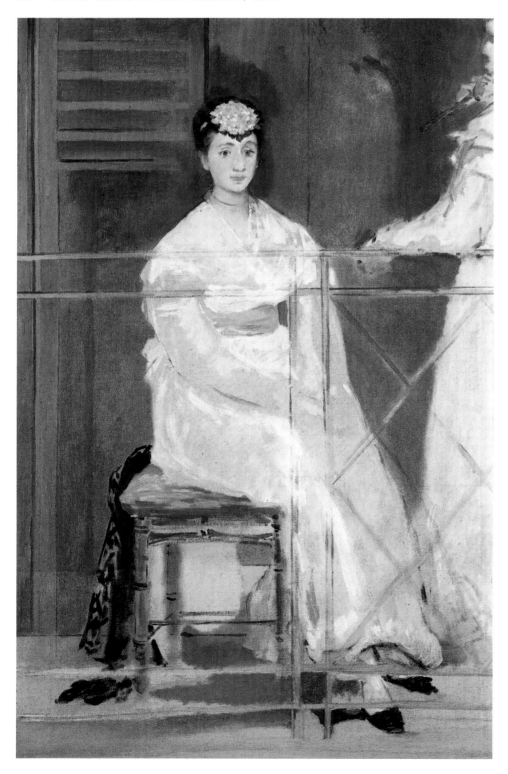

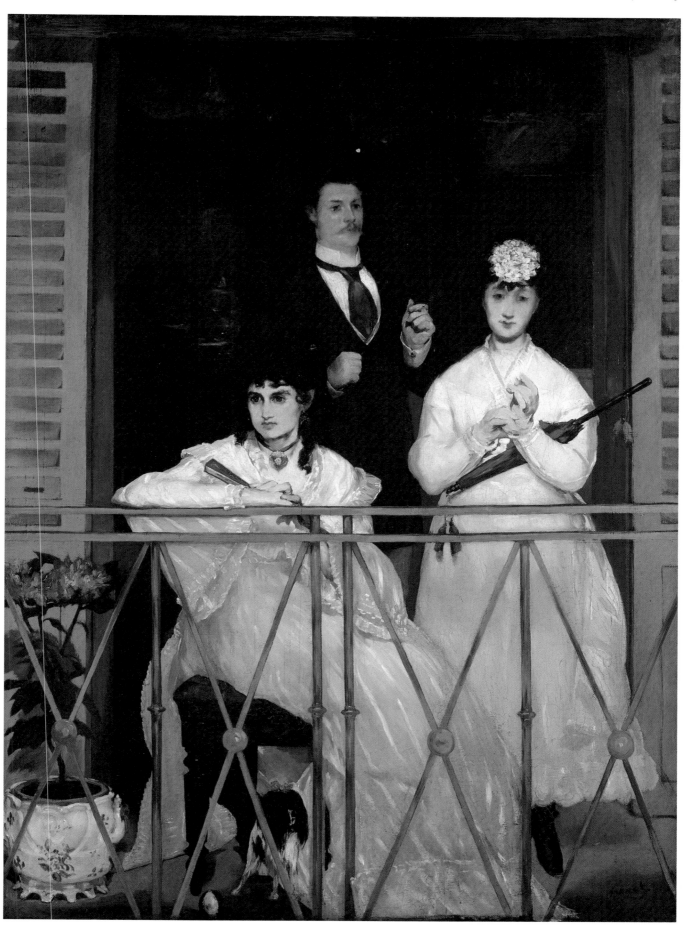

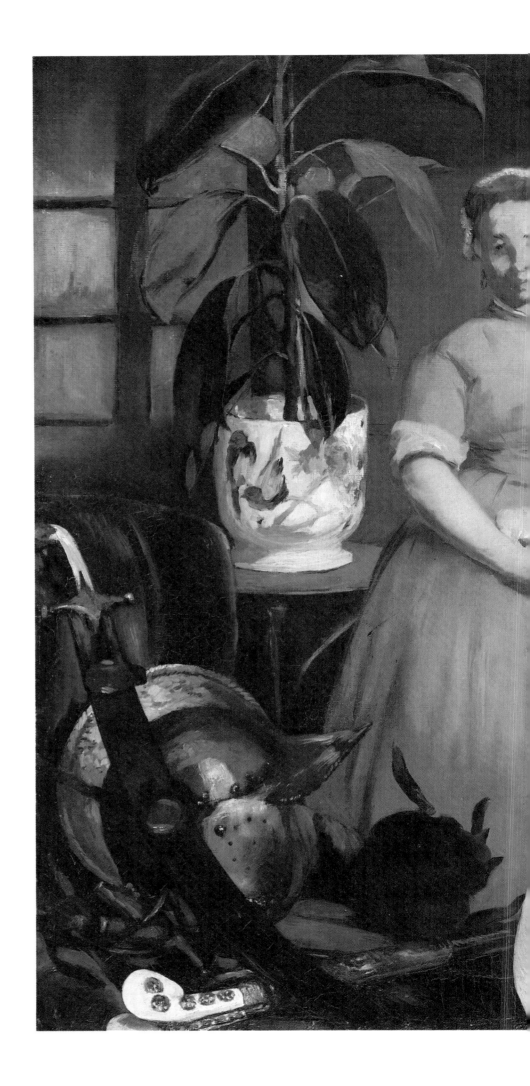

103   THE LUNCHEON, 1868–9

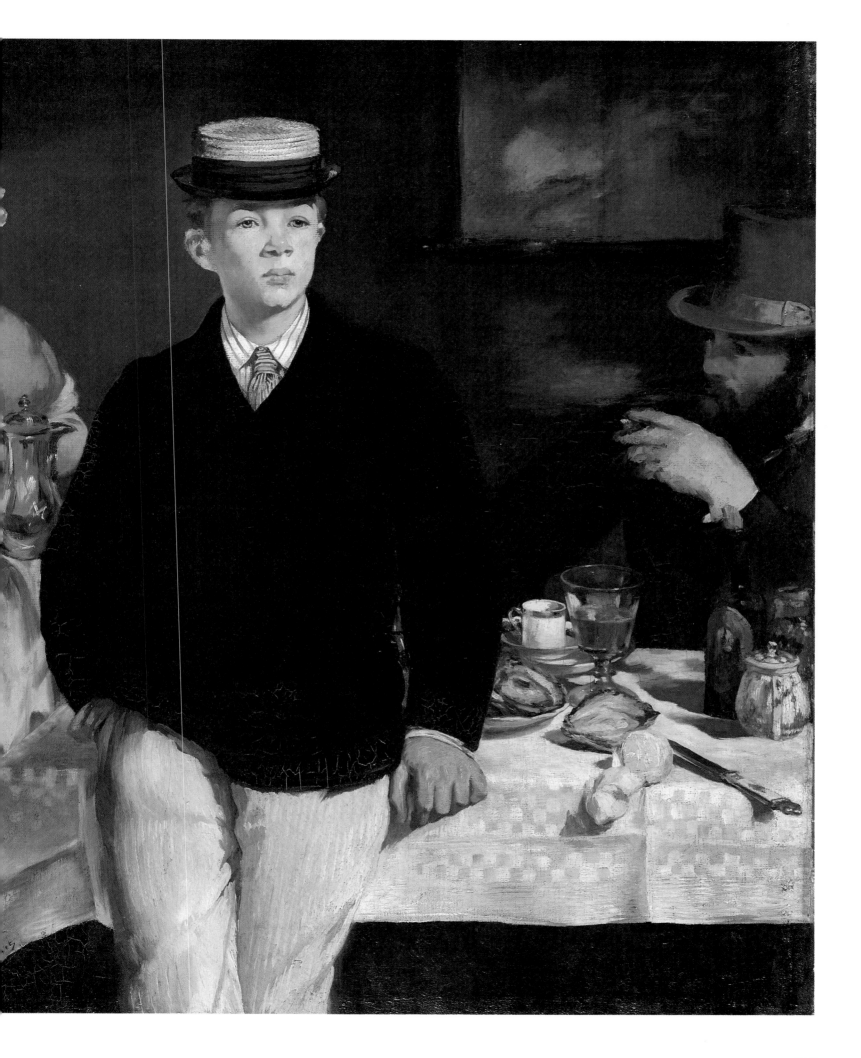

Still life, c.1868–1869

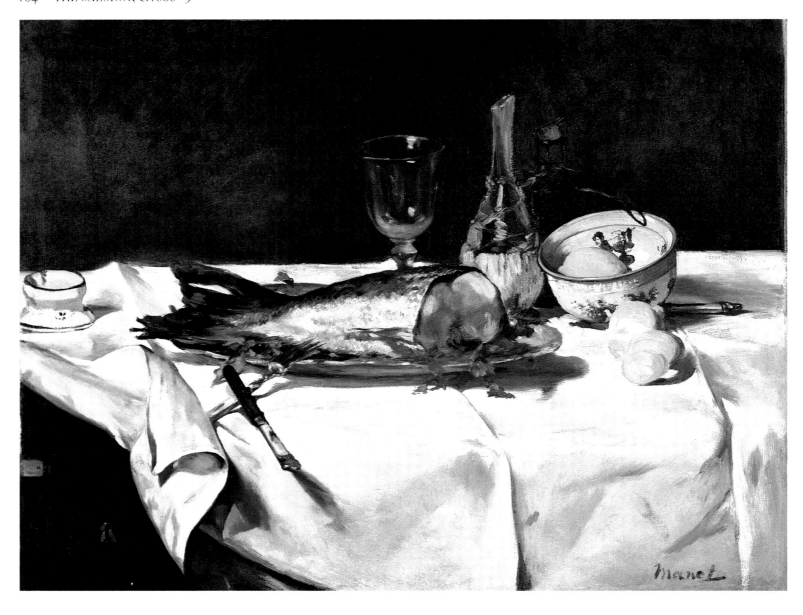

105   MELON, PEACHES AND GRAPES, c.1868–9

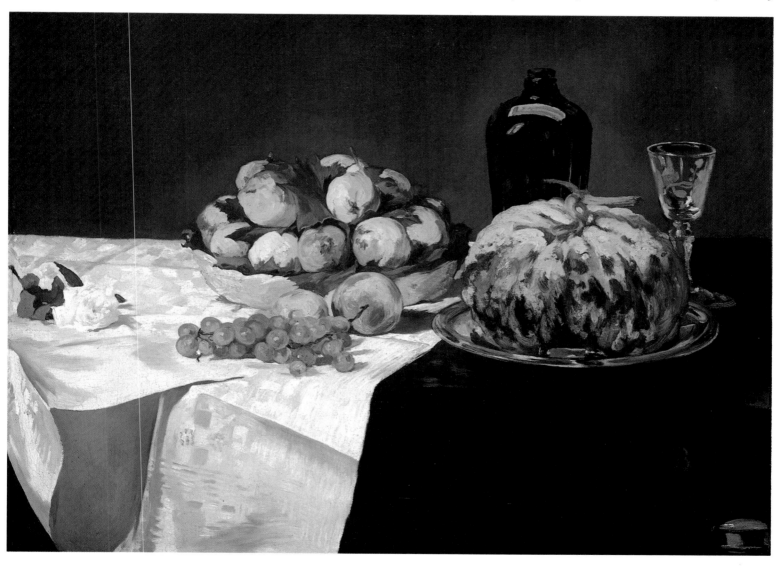

106 REPOSE / STUDY OF BERTHE MORISOT, 1869–70

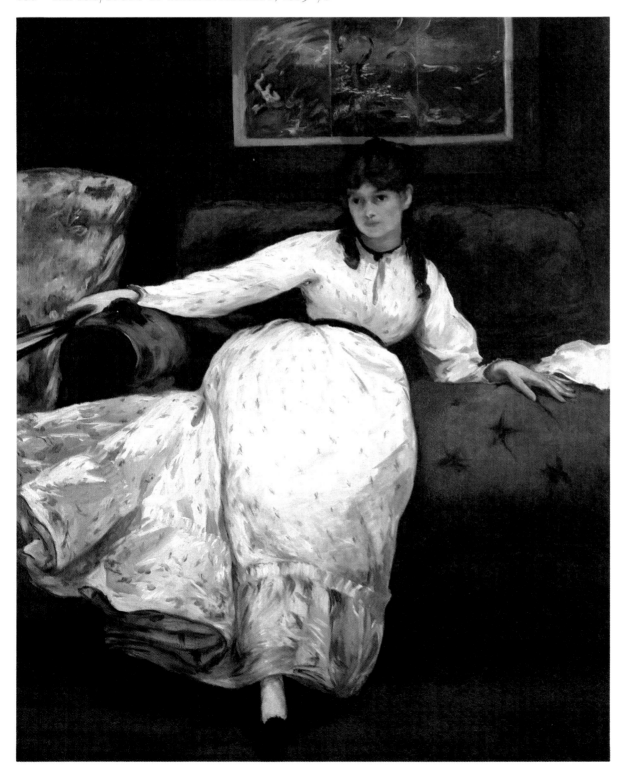

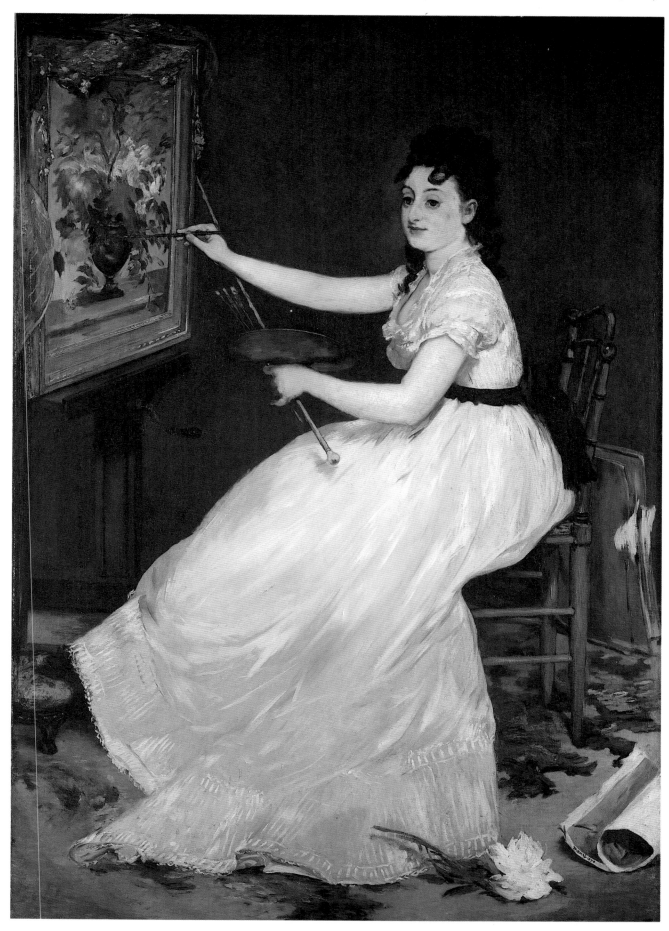

In the studio

108   EVA GONZALÈS IN MANET'S STUDIO, 1869–70

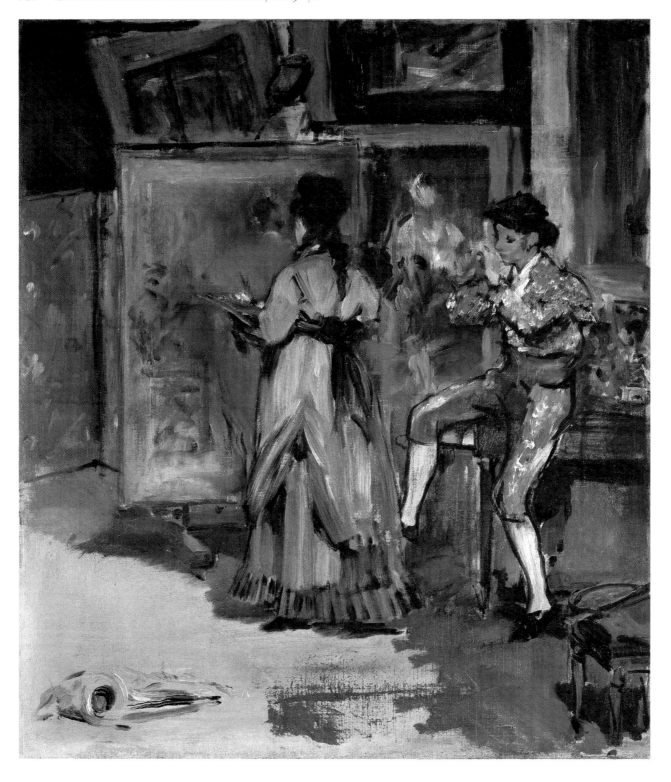

109　VELASQUEZ IN HIS STUDIO, PAINTING THE LITTLE CAVALIERS, c.1865–70

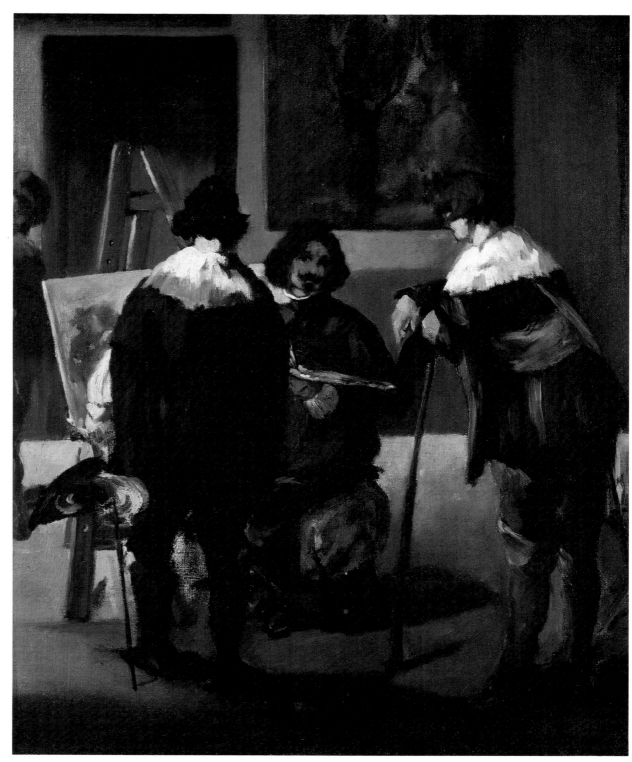

110   THE MUSIC LESSON, 1869–70

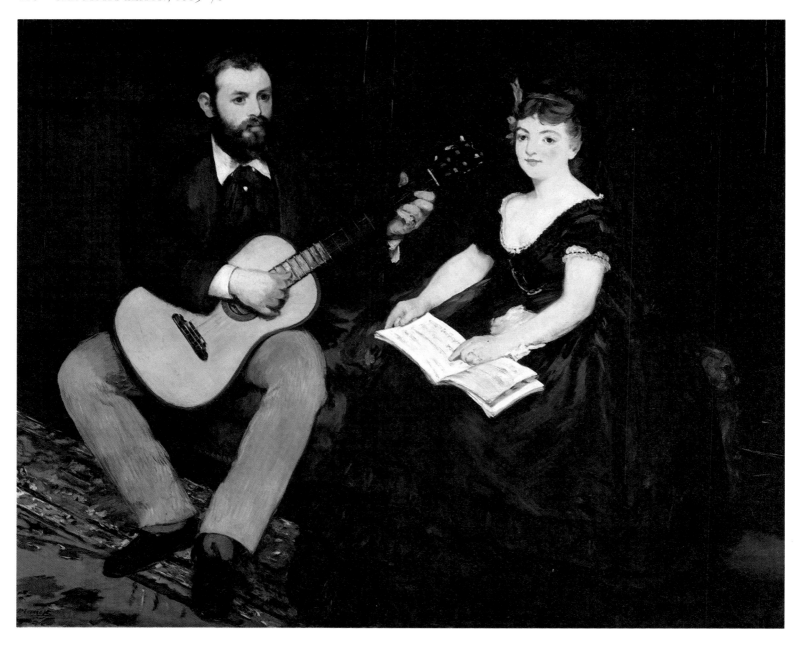

III   MME MANET AT THE PIANO, c.1867–70

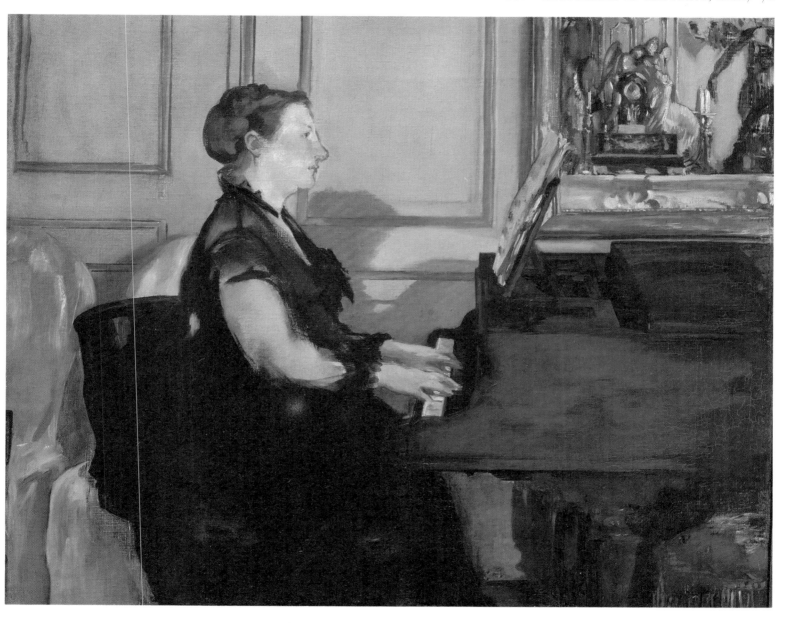

Friends and family

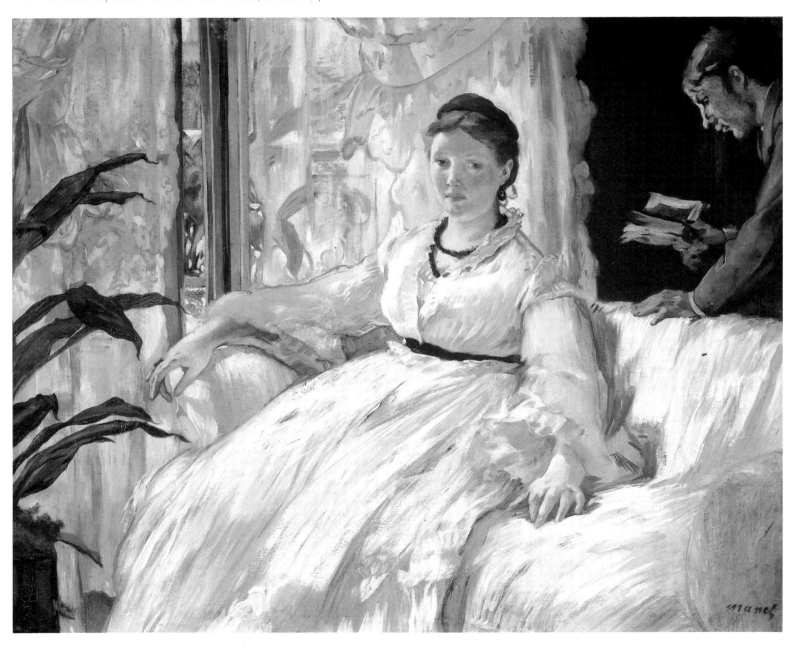

113   IN THE GARDEN, 1870

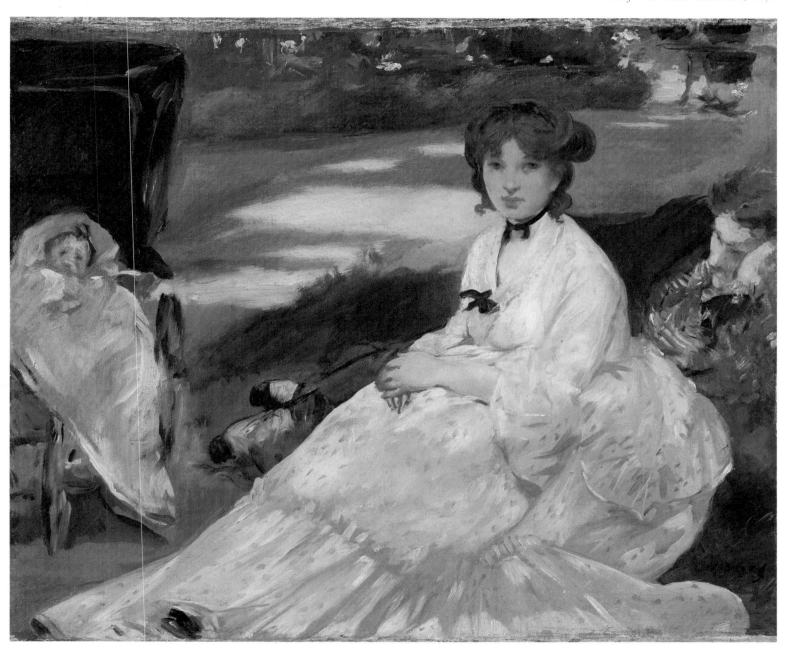

114   SNOW AT MONTROUGE, d.28 December 1870

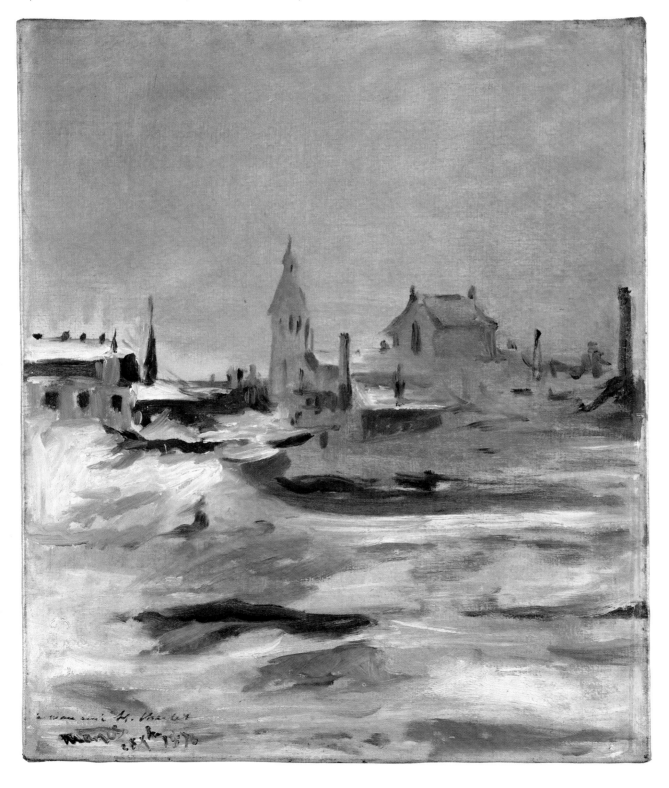

115   QUEUE AT THE BUTCHER'S SHOP, C.1871

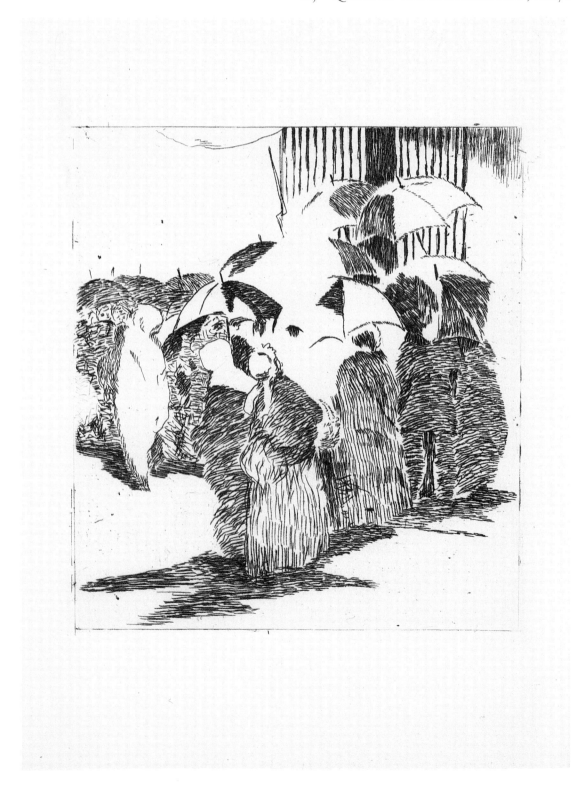

Soon after the surrender of Paris on 24 January 1871, Manet rejoined his family at Oloron-Sainte-Marie in the Pyrenees, moving on to Bordeaux where Zola was reporting on the new National Assembly's activities, and then to Arcachon on the Atlantic coast, where the family remained for a month. He started painting again as soon as he reached Oloron. Letters to friends and colleagues in Paris refer to money problems and plans to send pictures to exhibitions, as well as to his fears for the new Republic after the revolution of 18 March and the events of the Paris Commune. There is little information about Manet's activities after his return to Paris in the early summer of 1871, and although he is said to have gone to Boulogne he was still in Paris on 22 August, when he wrote to Duret in America. A painting of a game of Croquet (147) *is generally dated to this summer and the* Departure of the Folkestone Boat (148) *to 1869, but the pencil sketches for these pictures are on identical small sheets (146–7), suggesting that they were all done at the same time. In addition there is no proof that Manet was in Boulogne in 1869, so unless they were executed in 1868 (when Manet stayed there for some two months) all the sketches and paintings could have been made in 1871 or even 1872, a possible date in view of the purchase of* The Folkestone Boat *by the art dealer Durand-Ruel the following year.*

When Durand-Ruel first came to his studio in January 1872, Manet's fears of financial ruin turned to euphoria. His address book notes the agreement to buy a total of twenty-five paintings, to which the art dealer added the Combat of the Kearsarge and the Alabama (75), *lending it to the first post-war Salon held that year. Manet had been unable to complete a suitable new work, although he evidently planned a major history painting to record the executions of Paris Communards, as seen in a large gouache (142) based on his banned* Execution of Maximilian (96) *composition in reverse. Manet was also commissioned in 1872 to paint a racecourse (120) for a private patron, and came into contact with the celebrated opera singer Jean-Baptiste Faure (175), who was to remain a major client (although usually on very hard terms) for the rest of Manet's life. In post-war Paris things gradually returned to normal, and Manet's letters show him playing an active part in the cultural and social life of the city.*

In 1873, the year of his first unqualified success at the Salon with Le bon bock (151), *he met the poet Stéphane Mallarmé (129), probably in the circle of Nina de Callias (158, 159) and the poet and inventor Charles Cros. The following year, when the Salon jury rejected two out of the four works Manet submitted (123, 155, 157), Mallarmé came to his defence as Zola had done in 1866. The figure of* Polichinelle *or* Punch, *which carried politically sensitive connotations, appeared in two of these works (see 156, 157). In May Manet was trying to negotiate the sale of his* Polichinelle *lithograph to Eugène Montrosier, editor of a political review, when the watercoloured version appeared in the Salon. A first printing of the lithograph was evidently seized, suspected as a caricature of Marshal Mac-Mahon, the conservative French President, but it was finally allowed to appear in June. The print carries two lines by Théodore de Banville for whom Manet attempted to provide a frontispiece for a volume of poetry (126). Failing to complete the etching in time, Manet used the device on his notepaper* TOUT ARRIVE *– Anything can happen – as the first words of his apology. He also contributed illustrations for a review edited by Charles Cros and for a poem published at the end of the year. A little etched landscape (125) illustrating a poem by Cros is almost certainly a view*

of Argenteuil where Manet, Monet and Renoir were painting during the summer of 1874 (160, 161).
Charles Toché has left a long account of Manet's visit to Venice, now known to have taken place that winter
(164, 165), and it was during this period that Manet came closest to the Impressionism of his young friends.
His impressive study of a boating couple at Argenteuil *(162) was criticized and caricatured when the Salon*
opened in May 1875. A month later the folio edition of Edgar Allan Poe's poem The Raven *appeared with*
a prose translation by Mallarmé and large lithographic illustrations by Manet (127, 128).

In 1876 Mallarmé published L'Après-midi d'un faune *in a luxury edition with lively, impressionistic*
little woodcuts drawn by Manet who also hand-coloured the prints (130). The Salon jury that year rejected
both Manet's paintings (134, 169), and so he immediately decided to exhibit them by opening his studio to
the public and sending an invitation (131) to the Press. A terse letter to the critic Albert Wolff is Manet's
response to Wolff's statement that Manet had 'the eye but not the soul of an artist', although he was 'a
delightful and amusing young man'. The studio exhibition was a sensation and Manet was featured widely in
the Press. It also brought an introduction to Méry Laurent who was enthusiastic about Le linge *(134) and*
to whom Manet declared that he longed to paint women like her 'in green outdoor settings, among flowers . . .'
because he was 'not just an insensitive brute', a further response to other cutting statements in the review by
Wolff, of whom Manet left an unfinished and particularly unflattering portrait (135).

Mme Lecouvé as the simple, working-class mother doing her laundry in Le linge *and Marcellin*
Desboutin as The Artist *(169) marked a new preoccupation with urban life and its different types. 'Types'*
and 'portraits' became virtually interchangeable, for example in his depictions of Faure at the Opera (175),
Henriette Hauser as Nana *in her boudoir (171) or as the beauty at* The Skating Rink *(174), and Ellen*
Andrée as an elegant Parisienne *(170) or with friends in a lively café scene (186). When Manet sought*
a commission to decorate a chamber in the rebuilt Hôtel de Ville, he planned to include portraits of those
responsible for the city's greatness and prosperity, and was ironic about the banal and time-worn allegories
that the authorities preferred. Manet read Zola's naturalist novels, Le Ventre de Paris, L'Assommoir,
Nana *and the rest, and was also sensitive to Mallarmé's attitude to city life, his interest in its apparently*
frivolous and fashionable aspects as well as his dream, which he no doubt shared with the Republican Manet,
of a new art for the masses.

It was in the second half of the 1870s that Manet created the scenes of taverns and brasseries, cafés and
café-concerts (183–191) that were to find their fullest expression at the end of his career in A Bar at the
Folies-Bergère *(288). It was a period of intense experimentation as Manet cut, repainted and transformed*
his canvases, and when he wrote to the Ministry of Fine Arts in June 1879 in the hope that one of his
paintings would be purchased by the state, it was the more traditional image of Le bon bock *(151) that he*
proposed, rather than a recent composition. If 1879 was a year in which Manet felt he could address the
authorities directly, even if to no avail, in the hope of a civic commission or state purchase, it was also the year
in which it became clear that his health was gravely undermined, with the fatal effects of syphilis producing
terrible pains in his left leg and seriously affecting his mobility. His remaining three years were to be rich in
achievement but his strength was sapped and more and more of his time was spent with doctors and in clinics.

Chalet Servantie, 41 avenue Ste Marie, Arcachon, Monday 6 March [1871]

To Théodore Duret   It would be very kind if you could send me some money,
I thought I would have some coming in about now and would not have to ask before you
offered it – but there are a few commitments I must meet and I'm very short! We were sorry
not to see you at Arcachon, you could have spent a pleasant day here.

Edouard Manet

*

[Arcachon] 18 March [1871]

My gilder will call round one of these days to measure the
canvas (*Study of a young woman*) (*106*), I'm told there will be an exhibition on 20 May. He will
take it and put it in my place until the sending-in day, so you won't be disturbed. A little later
I may also relieve you of the *Balcony* (*102*) which I will be sending to London with the *Music
lesson* (*110*) if the letter of acceptance I have requested arrives.

Edouard Manet

*

Chalet Servanti, 41 avenue Sainte-Marie, Arcachon, 18 March 1871

To Félix Bracquemond   Many thanks, my dear Bracquemond, for sending me the
information. But you forgot to tell me the sending-in date and the final deadline, which is very
important. I saw in the papers that the French can still submit work to the International
Exhibition in London and that those who haven't received a letter of acceptance should ask for
one at the Hôtel de Cluny in Paris. I wrote off immediately. I simply have to raise some cash:
this dreadful war will have ruined me for years to come I'm afraid. What about you, will you
be sending something? You say nothing about your doings. Last week I went to Bordeaux.
I saw Balleroy and we talked of you, of course. He got me into the House – I never imagined
that France could be represented by such doddering old fools, not excepting that little twit
Thiers who I hope will drop dead one day in the middle of a speech and rid us of his wizened
little person . . .

How good it will be to get together again next winter. I feel confident that things will get
going again.

Ed. Manet

*

Arcachon, 21 March [1871]

We're living in an unhappy country where people are
only interested in overthrowing the government in order to join it. There just aren't any
disinterested people around, no great citizens, no true republicans. Only party hacks and the
ambitious, the Henrys of this world following on the heels of the Millières, the grotesque

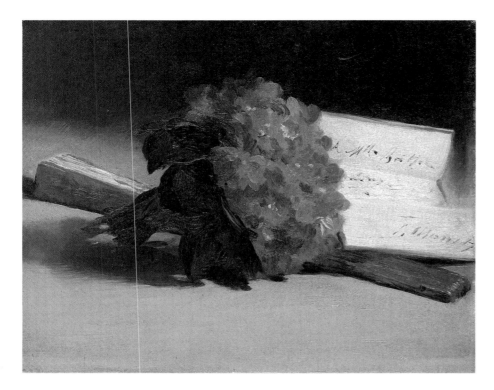

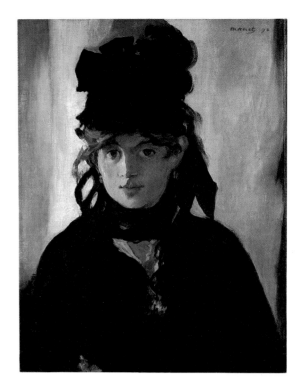

116   BUNCH OF VIOLETS AND FAN, 1872

117   BERTHE MORISOT WITH A BUNCH
      OF VIOLETS, d.1872

imitators of the Commune of 93, cowardly assassins who execute two generals, one because he was doing his duty at the time, the other because he was brave enough to criticize their cringing attitude to the enemy – these people are going to kill off, in the public mind, the sound idea that was beginning to gain ground, namely, that the only government for honest, peaceful, intelligent people is a republic, and that this form of government alone will enable us, in the eyes of Europe, to rise up from the appalling depths to which we have fallen. It is only in the provinces that you feel how much they hate Paris. It was a great mistake on the part of Thiers and the Assembly not to return to Paris immediately after the evacuation; the result was those dreadful riots that have brought despair and disgust to the hearts of all true Frenchmen.

What an encouragement all these bloodthirsty caperings are for the arts! But there is at least one consolation in our misfortunes: that we're not politicians and have no desire to be elected as deputies. I've had a letter from Fantin – he tells me he's emerged . . . What energy, I must say I wouldn't have had his courage, and I'm not looking forward to the return to Paris at all . . .

*

[10 June 1871]

To Berthe Morisot [in Cherbourg]   We came back to Paris a few days ago and the ladies send their affectionate good wishes to you and Mme Pontillon with whom you are no doubt staying.

What terrible events, and will we ever recover from them? Everyone blames his neighbour but the fact is that we're all responsible for what has happened. . . . we're all just about ruined and will have to work as hard as we can.

Eugène went to see you at Saint-Germain but you were not in that day. I was glad to hear that your house in Passy has been spared. I caught a glimpse today of poor Oudinot who has also had his moment of glory. But what a fall! I imagine, Mademoiselle, that you will not be staying long in Cherbourg. Everyone is returning to Paris, and the fact is it's impossible to live anywhere else.

[June–July 1871?]

To Théodore Duret   Here is the letter you've agreed to take with you [to America] – please don't forget it.

Would you be kind enough to leave me a note that will enable me to remove my pictures from your home if I need them while you are away.

Good luck, ED. MANET

*

Paris, 22 August [1871]

I've just received your draft order for 700 francs sent from New York on 9 August – it's come at the right moment. You can imagine I must have been in dire distress to put a knife to your throat like that, but there's no way of laying one's hands on anything here – there is just no money about these days – the provisional government seems not at all the right thing to get the country's finances back on their feet. I met Balleroy a few days ago, he had proposed the proclamation of a republic in a committee session but the left was absolutely against it on the grounds that the assembly cannot frame a constitution. I believe we're bound to see some *pronunciamentos* from the generals in the near future.

Your journey is going to be a most interesting one and will provide your inquiring and artistic nature with all sorts of pleasures. You mentioned Courbet. He behaved like a coward at his court-martial and doesn't deserve any further attention.

Martinet has announced a picture exhibition for October – he's rather good at these things – but you are one of the few really sound connoisseurs of our time, and you won't be there. Degas is making great progress and is bound to be successful in the very near future; he hopes to have something on your walls in the not too distant future. There was talk of your coming back soon, but the address you give in San Francisco suggests that you are following your original idea to go round the world – so *bon voyage* and good health to you, with my greetings . . .

Edouard Manet

*

[January 1872]

Recorded by Edmond Bazire   [To friends at the Café Guerbois]   Well! will you tell me who doesn't sell fifty thousand francs' worth of paintings a year?   [The friends: 'You!']

*

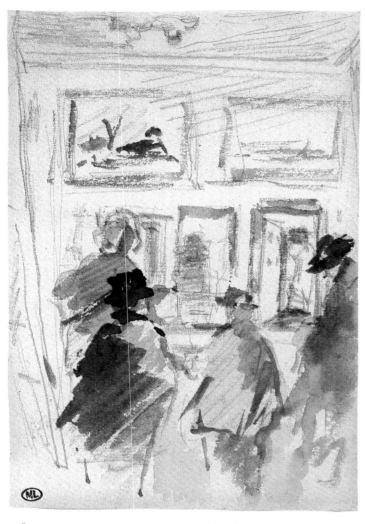

118   VISITORS IN THE STUDIO, c.1872/76?

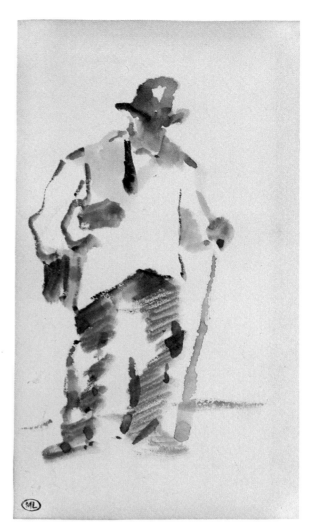

119   THE RAGPICKER / PHILOSOPHER, c.1871–2

MEMORANDUM OF PAINTINGS SOLD TO DURAND-RUEL

[January–February 1872]

DURAND-RUEL

4 philosophers (*50*), [see (*119*)]	6000 ×	sold to Fèvre [sic, name deleted]	
toreador – woman in majo costume (*57*)	4000 ×	boy with a sword (*54*)	1200
urchin [see (*18*)]	1500 ×		
fifer (*14*)	1500 ×		
Rouvière (*88*)	2000 ×	× guitar player (*56*)	3000
woman with parrot (*89*)	1500 ×	× dead man (*72*)	2000
street singer (*61*)	2000		
majo (*60*)	1500	price agreed 35,000 with	
Christ and the angels (*81*)	4000	Durand-Ruel for the	
repose B. M[orisot] (*106*)	3000	above pictures	
reader	1000		
the Spanish ballet [see (*70*)]	3000	12 January received 3000 frs	
bullfight (*87*)	500	× on account	
Bordeaux (*139*)	800		
beach (*100*)	600	18 January 2000 frs on account	
flowers (*79*)	600		
Boul[ogne] (*74?*)	600	15 February 1872 10,000 frs on	
Boulogne harbour – moonlight (*98*)	1000	account	
still life	600		

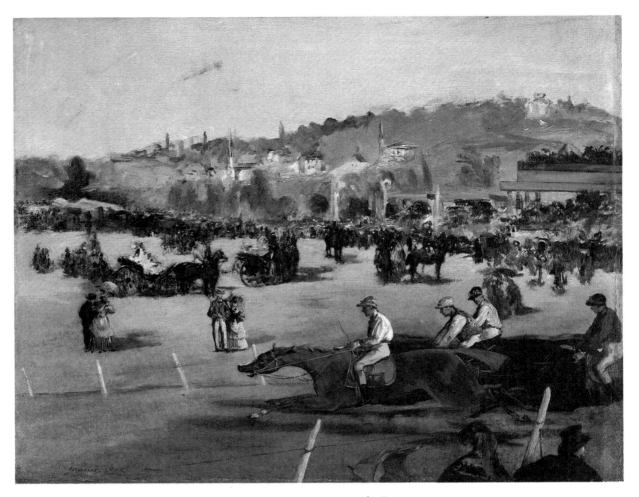

120   RACES AT LONGCHAMP IN THE BOIS DE BOULOGNE, d.1872

4 rue Saint Pétersbourg, 21 October [1872]

TO M. BARRET

Your picture is finished. I should be glad if you would come and see it one of these days.

Yours sincerely, ED. MANET

*

23 October 1872

Received from M. Barret the sum of three thousand francs in payment for my painting (*Races at Longchamp*) (*120*).

EDOUARD MANET

*

4 rue Saint Pétersbourg, 4 November [1872?]

TO THÉODORE DURET?

My dear friend, do send me Faure's address, so I can send him a proof of the *Guitarist* (*121*).

By the way, does he appreciate etchings and would it give him pleasure? For I don't like giving fine proofs to people who don't appreciate them – though I've every reason to believe and certainly hope that our celebrated baritone (*175*) is not one of those.

E. MANET

Monday [17 February 1873?]

TO MME GEORGES CHARPENTIER   Madame, You can count on Pagans next Friday – Bosch, however, is not free but would be delighted to oblige another time.

Yours sincerely, ED. MANET

*

[17 February 1873?]

TO ÉMILE ZOLA   Bosch is unable to go to the Charpentiers on Friday – he is dining out and has two evening receptions. He would be happy to go another time.

E. MANET

*

4 rue Saint Pétersbourg [1873?]

TO MME GEORGES CHARPENTIER   Madame, the guitarist Bosch asks me to convey his deep regrets but he is not free on the evening of the 11th.

Yours sincerely, ED. MANET

121   THE SPANISH SINGER / THE GUITARRERO, d.1861

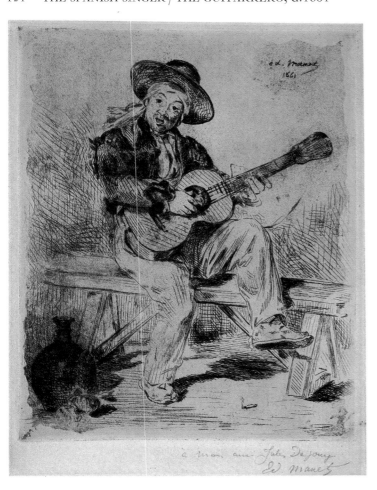

122   PLAINTE MORESQUE (MOORISH LAMENT), 1866

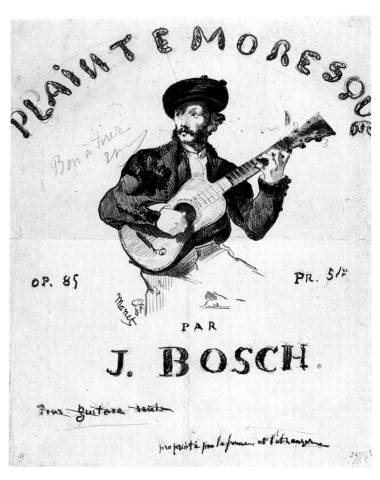

TOUT ARRIVE   Friday [late April 1873]

To Émile Zola   My wife had intended to call on Madame Zola yesterday
and convey our thanks for the *Ventre* [*Belly of Paris*], but was not feeling well. So I want to lose
no time in telling you that your latest book has arrived; it looks very good and extremely
promising. . . .

Best wishes to you all, Ed. Manet

*

Sunday [6 July 1873]

I'm leaving for Étaples at 6.30 tomorrow morning. I would
have liked to come and say goodbye to you this evening, but haven't yet finished packing.
Congratulations on your preface [to the play of *Thérèse Raquin*]. It's a masterly piece of writing.
I realized when your book arrived that you must still be in Paris, because on my return last
week after a short absence, my studio concierge told me that one of my gentlemen friends and
his *lady* had called and asked her to say that they were leaving for a spa. From her portrait of
the visitors I thought it must have been you. Otherwise I would have come to see you.

. . . my regards to Madame Zola, Edouard Manet

123   THE SWALLOWS (MANET'S MOTHER AND WIFE AT BERCK), 1873

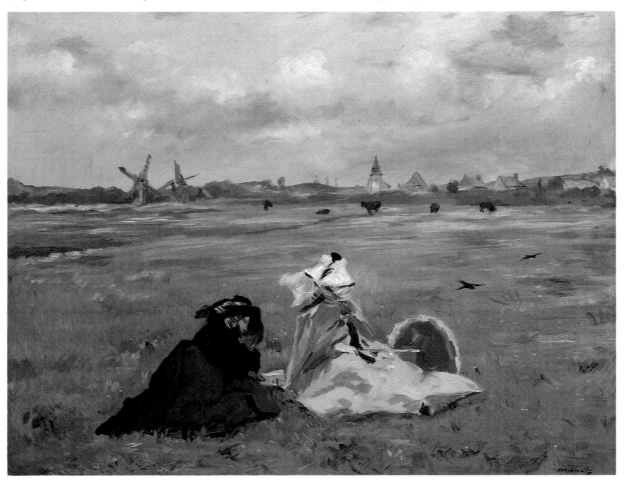

[1873]

RECORDED BY THÉODORE DURET   [To friends posing for the *Opera ball* *(157)*]   How do you put on your hat when you do it without thinking and feel completely at your ease? Well then, do it the same way when you're posing, without any affectation.

*

TOUT ARRIVE   Wednesday evening [8 April 1874 postmark]

TO EUGÈNE MONTROSIER   I very much appreciate your sympathy; I've had two paintings refused, the *Opera ball* *(157)* and a *Landscape with figures* *(123)*. They really are an ill-mannered lot, these artistic worthies! But if you are willing to help me a little, that's a great compensation.

Regards, EDOUARD MANET

*

TOUT ARRIVE   [12 April? 1874]

TO STÉPHANE MALLARMÉ   My dear friend, Thanks, if I had a few supporters like you, I wouldn't give a f... about the jury

Yours ever, ED. MANET

124   LETTER TO STÉPHANE MALLARMÉ

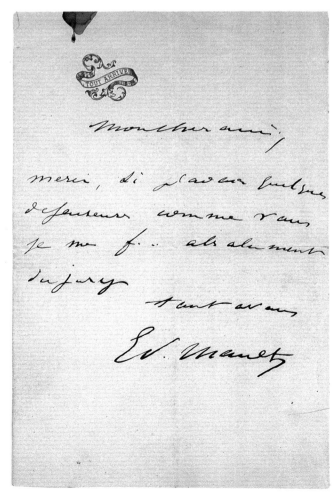

The Polichinelle affair

4 rue Saint Pétersbourg, Friday 13 [March? 1874]

To Lemercier & Co.   Dear Sir, Would you please get someone to attend to my *Polichinelle* stones (*156*). I want to send a proof to the [Salon] exhibition and am therefore in a great hurry. Let me know when we can do the proofing.

E. Manet

*

4 rue Saint Pétersbourg, 10 May [1874]

To Eugène Montrosier   Here is my final offer: I would let you have exclusive rights to my *Polichinelle* for the sum of two thousand francs. I would simply ask you to let me have two or three proofs.

I would be grateful . . . if you could reply as soon as possible because this is a good moment for me to go ahead with the printing of the lithograph.

Ed. Manet

*

4 rue Saint Pétersbourg, 14 May [1874]

Couldn't we reconsider the question of the *Polichinelle* – the price per proof is going to be so high, at 1 fr 60, that it will be very difficult to find an outlet. With the scheme for the 25 signed and numbered proofs on loose Japan paper that you will be able to sell to collectors for 50 francs, you are bound to make a profit – so make me, if you *want* to, an acceptable proposal. I've already taken Lemercier 30 sheets of the finest Japan paper for which I would not charge you. . . .

Ed. Manet

*

4 rue Saint Pétersbourg, Saturday 10 October [1874]

To Lemercier & Co.   Dear Sir, On your invoice of 18 June I note a charge for Hire and effacing of the 7 stones for the *Polichinelle*. But *I never instructed you to efface the stones*. If, as I hope, this has not been done, will you kindly let me know and put them aside because I think I have found a buyer.

Yours faithfully, Ed. M.

*

Thursday [2 April 1874?]

TO THÉODORE DURET
Here's the letter I've had from Monet. My rent has cleaned me out and I can't do anything to help him – can you give the hundred francs to the bearer of the picture?

ED. MANET

*

Monday [June–July 1874?]

I won't be there on Tuesday but if you can bring the money, leave it with the concierge. I'll be going to Argenteuil the following day, leaving at 7 in the morning.

Cordially, ED. MANET

*

[1874]

RECORDED BY THÉODORE DURET
Monet! his boat is his studio (*161*).

*

[1870s]

RECORDED BY ANTONIN PROUST
[To Jean Béraud, on Monet]   . . . Coquelin has a good eye, one day he will appreciate Claude Monet. There's not one of the school of 1830 who can set down a landscape like him. And when it comes to water – he's the Raphael of water. He knows all its movements, whether deep or shallow, at every time of day. I emphasize that last phrase, because of Courbet's magnificent remark to Daubigny who had complimented him on a seascape: 'It's not a seascape, it's a time of day.' That's what people don't fully understand yet, that one doesn't paint a landscape, a seascape, a figure; one paints the effect of a time of day on a landscape, a seascape, or a figure.

*

4 rue Saint Pétersbourg, Saturday 27 [June 1874?]

TO THÉODORE DURET
If you had an art enthusiast among your acquaintances whom you could point in my direction, I'm all prepared to make great concessions at the moment because I'm short of money.

ED. MANET

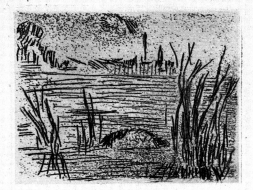

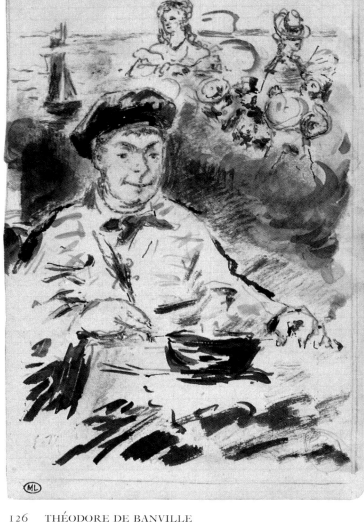

s'emplit de nénuphars, de joncs. Dans l'or fluide
du soir, les moucherons valsent.

Mais, rapprochés,
maintenant les coteaux s'élèvent. Des rochers
interrompent souvent les cultures en pente.
Tout le pays pierreux, où le Fleuve serpente,
nourrit, pauvre et moussu, la ronce et le bandit.
Le courant, étranglé dans les ravins, bondit
sur les roches, ou bien dort dans les trous qu'il creuse.

Mais l'eau n'interrompt pas sa course aventureuse,
malgré tant de travaux et de sommeils. Voici
la brèche ouverte sur l'horizon obscurci

125   RIVERBANK IN THE PLAIN
      ILLUSTRATION TO LE FLEUVE, 1874

126   THÉODORE DE BANVILLE
      PROJECT FOR A FRONTISPIECE, 1874

TO THÉODORE DURET   4 rue Saint Pétersbourg, Friday [June–July 1874?]

I can't let the *Woman's head* or the *Seascape* go for less than a
thousand francs each, it seems to me – He came to see me yesterday and at that price can't
decide whether to take that or an *esquisse* of horse racing. M. Quesnel also seemed to like the
'little water drinker' for which I'm asking two thousand francs – that's in fact the price I
quoted him some time ago. Regards and since there's nothing for it, let's leave the children to
their nannies and Ephrussi to Bonnat.

ED. MANET

*

4 rue Saint Pétersbourg, Friday [June–July 1874?]

If only M. Quesnel were convinced that he was getting a
real bargain in buying my picture for 600 francs, I wouldn't mind letting him have it because
M. [. .?] has decided on another one. In any case, my dear Duret, do whatever you think best –
your advice is usually sound.

ED. MANET

Frontispiece for Banville, 1874

TO THÉODORE DE BANVILLE

TOUT ARRIVE   Saturday [July 1874]

My dear Sir, I would like, for the book of Ballads, to do 'Banville, Conjuror of poetic images', showing him sitting at his table writing and smoking a cigarette with the principal themes in the book seen as little figures in the swirling spirals of smoke (*126*).

If you approve – I will come and sketch you at home at whatever time and date suit you.

With warm regards, ED. MANET

*

TOUT ARRIVE   2 August [1874]

(*Anything can happen*) even to botch the very etching one most wants to turn out well. – I'm very sorry and ashamed but am obliged to leave in the next few days and it would be impossible for me to be ready by September. So for the time being I must deprive myself of the pride and pleasure it would have given me to do something for one of your books.

ED. MANET

*

After the summer holidays, 1874

TO EUGÈNE MONTROSIER

4 rue Saint Pétersbourg, Tuesday 6 October [1874]

My dear Montrosier, I'm back, so do come round to the studio – I have some pictures to show you and we can have a talk.

Regards, E. MANET

*

RECORDED BY JACQUES DE BIEZ

[October 1874?]

I like what you have written about me. There have already been favourable responses from quite a number of people. But I feel that they don't have a very clear view of my underlying intentions. They don't really understand my innermost thoughts, or at least what I am trying to show. Their writing shows courage as well as goodwill, and for that I am very grateful. But some of them set about it in the wrong way. Look at X . . ., for example, who has just praised me to the skies. But so clumsily. He writes as one would about a young tearaway. But how can I tell him so? Besides, it would be ungrateful of me to hold it against him. One can't be angry with him, but he is an imbecile.

[Venice, winter 1874–5]

RECORDED BY CHARLES TOCHÉ   [On the encounter with Toché at the Café Florian]   I can see you're a Frenchman . . . Heavens, how boring it is here!

[On a motif for a picture near the Salute]   I'll put in a gondola with a gondolier wearing a pink shirt and an orange scarf, one of those handsome fellows, as dark as a Moor (*164, 165*).

. . . It's the most difficult thing, to give the impression that a hat is sitting properly on the model's head, or that a boat has been constructed from planks cut and fitted according to the rules of geometry.

[On planning a picture of the regatta at Mestre]   When faced with such a distractingly complicated scene, I must first of all choose a typical incident and define my picture, as if I could already see it framed. In this case, the most striking features are the masts with their fluttering, multicoloured banners, the red-white-and-green Italian flag, the dark, swaying line of boats crowded with spectators, and the gondolas like black and white arrows shooting away from the horizon; then, at the top of the picture, the watery horizon, the marked target and the islands in the distant haze.

I would first try to work out logically the different values, in their nearer or more distant relationships, according to spatial and aerial perspective.

The lagoon mirrors the sky, and at the same time acts as a great stage for the boats and their passengers, the masts, the banners, etc. It has its own particular colour, the nuances it borrows from the sky, the clouds, from crowds, from objects reflected in the water. There can be no sharp definition, no linear structure in something that is all movement; only tonal values which, if correctly observed, will constitute its true volume, its essential, underlying design.

The gondolas and other boats, with their generally dark colours and reflections, provide a base on which to set my watery stage. The figures, seated or in action, dressed in dark colours or brilliantly vivid materials, with their parasols, handkerchiefs and hats, appear as crenellated forms of differing tonal values, providing the necessary *repoussoir* and defining the specific character of the areas of water and gondolas that I can see through them.

Crowds, rowers, flags and masts must be sketched in with a mosaic of coloured tones, in an attempt to convey the fleeting quality of gestures, the fluttering flags, the swaying masts.

On the horizon, right at the top, are the islands. There should be no more than a suggestion of the most distant planes, veiled in the subtlest, most accurately observed tints.

Finally the sky should cover and envelop the whole scene, like an immense, shining canopy whose light plays over all the figures and objects.

The brushstrokes must be spontaneous and direct. No tricks, you just have to pray to the God of all good, honest artists to come to your aid!

[On painters and schools]   Spain is so simple, so grandiose, so dramatic, with its bone-dry stones and green-dark trees! Venice, when all's said and done, is just a decor. . . .

[On Veronese's *Triumph of Venice* in the Palazzo Ducale]   It leaves me cold! Such wasted effort, such empty expanses! No emotion whatsoever! I love the Carpaccios with their naïve charm like illuminated books of hours. And . . . the Titians and Tintorettos in the Scuola di San Rocco are incomparable . . . But in the end, you see, I always come back to Velasquez and Goya!

[On Tiepolo]   They're so boring, these Italians, with their allegories, their characters from *Jerusalem delivered* and *Orlando furioso*, with all that showy bric-à-brac. An artist can say everything with fruit or flowers, or simply with clouds. . . .

Wednesday [late 1874–early 1875]

TO STÉPHANE MALLARMÉ

We've missed the boat with Bachelin – so please go and get the manuscript back. I've just seen Lesclide this afternoon and mentioned it to him without giving your views – don't tell him you've shown it to Bachelin and make whatever arrangements you wish, he will probably be at Mendès's this evening.

Regards, MANET

*

Sunday [March–May? 1875]

TO RICHARD LESCLIDE

I'm much alarmed by the black silk you're intending to put on the spine of the portfolio – it will look like a funeral announcement. Parchment, or a soft green or yellow paper similar to the colour of the cover, that's what we need.

I've been round to Lefman's – now it's up to you.

ED. MANET

*

4 rue Saint Pétersbourg, Thursday [May–June 1875]

None of the drawings for *Le Corbeau* (*127, 128*) must be reproduced – as for the press copies I'll sort it out with Mallarmé and you can add your names to our list.

ED. MANET

127   POSTER FOR LE CORBEAU (THE RAVEN), 1875

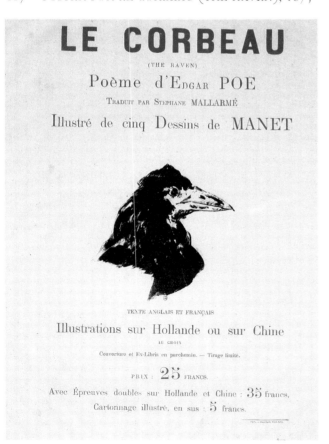

128   AT THE WINDOW, FROM LE CORBEAU, 1875

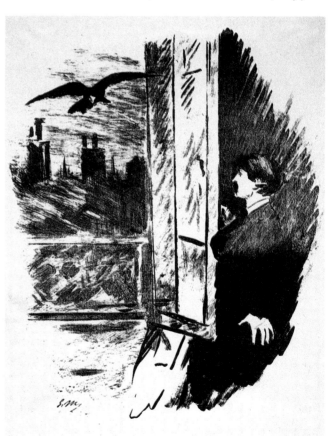

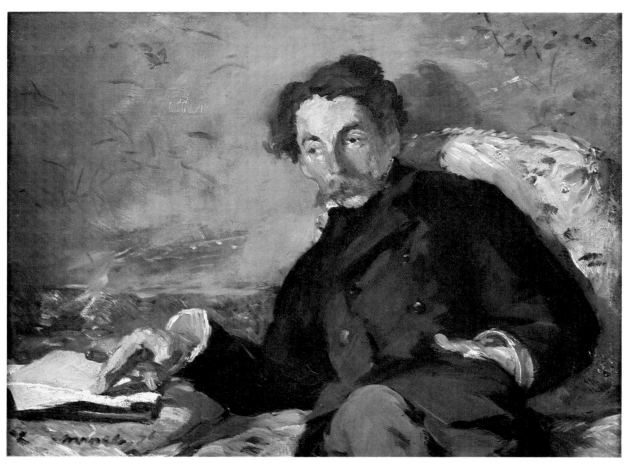

129   PORTRAIT OF STÉPHANE MALLARMÉ, d.1876

TO STÉPHANE MALLARMÉ   Wednesday [June–July? 1875]

I thought I would be seeing you any day now. I haven't sent Lefman any Japan paper because I don't have enough for a set of the drawings – my own proofs can be used for V[ictor] H[ugo]'s copy.

E. MANET

*

Paris, 9 September [1875]

[Addressed to Equihen]   It's a pity you're not in Paris right now. We've just had a letter from Mr Widdleton in New-Yorck [sic], who publishes and has the rights to the works of Poe, asking us how much we would charge for an edition of 500 to 1000 copies of *Le Corbeau* – he wanted an immediate reply; Lesclide and I decided to ask 15 francs per copy for 500, 10 francs for 1000. It's a business deal which could be of the greatest importance for us – we must sort things out with Lesclide and have a much more serious arrangement with him. This year we'll be bringing out the *City in the Sea* [see (204)], next year another poem – this American publisher could be a goose that lays golden eggs for us. What we must decide is whether we should deal directly with him in future or go through Lesclide – so I haven't mentioned our new publishing projects to him. If my letter reaches you, write and tell me what you think about all this and if you can find some unknown thing by Poe to work on.

ED. MANET

Paris, Sunday [19, postmark 20 September 1875]

Your first letter which you had addressed 'in town' went all over Boulogne before finally reaching me this morning at rue St Pétersbourg – the next delivery brought your note of the 17th. Lesclide hasn't told me about the new proposals, he's so tactless, but let's forget about it, I've got major plans to tell you when you're back.

The weather is being kind to me and I'm working non-stop every morning, hoping it will stay fine till the end of September; Mme Lecouvé is being very cooperative [see (*134*)]. The rich patron in question hasn't reappeared. I'm still expecting him, but if he doesn't come that's the end of my trip to Italy. I've had nothing recently in the way of articles on *Le Corbeau*, let's wait before thanking the man with the crook [Léon Cladel?].

I suggest you make a trip to Berck. The place is worth a visit. As for you, I hope the work goes well and you have a very good time at Equilen [sic]. If there's any news, I'll write to you.

ED. MANET

If the deal came off, the Auvergnat in the passage Choiseul [Alphonse Lemerre] would be livid – it occurred to me right away.

A deal for Monet

Wednesday [summer 1875?]

TO THÉODORE DURET I went to see Monet yesterday and found him in despair and absolutely broke.

He asked me to find someone who would take between ten and twenty pictures *of their choice* for 100 francs apiece. Shall we do the deal ourselves, putting up 500 francs each?

Of course no one, and least of all he, should know that we're in on this. I thought of trying to find a dealer or collector but suspect they might refuse.

Unfortunately, it takes people as knowledgeable as we are to do a good piece of business, in spite of the repugnance we may feel, in order to help out a talented artist. Send me an answer as soon as possible or suggest a rendezvous.

E. MANET

*

Friday [summer 1875?]

TO EUGÈNE MANET I've seen Monet recently and he's absolutely broke; he wants to get hold of a thousand-franc bill and for that he's offering 10 pictures *of one's choice*. If you have 500 francs at your disposal we could do the deal together – as far as I'm concerned, I know that with 5 paintings that I could dispose of for a profit of at least 100 francs, we would recover our outlay almost immediately – If you're game, send me a cheque for 500 francs and I'll go and collect the canvases from him. Obviously he mustn't know that we are the ones doing the deal – but I've tried other people and no one dares take the risk – it's just absurd.

EDOUARD

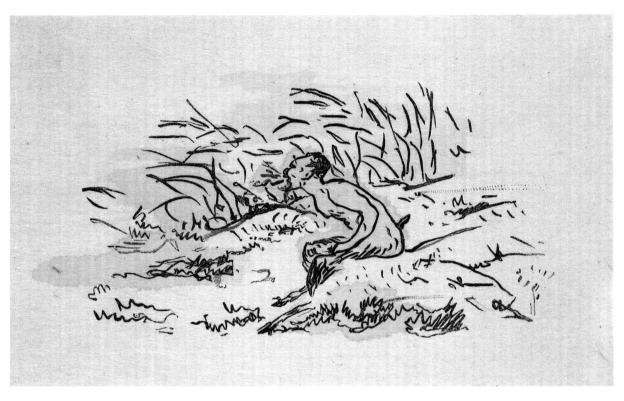

130   THE FAUN — FRONTISPIECE, 1876

[August–October 1875?]

TO STÉPHANE MALLARMÉ   I've written to Mendès and taken the letter round myself;
let's make a date for Monday at 11.30 if you can sort things out with Mendès.

E. MANET

*

Wednesday [late 1875–early 1876]

I just don't know what Bracquemond was thinking of, this
M. Bouvy is an industrial engraver who doesn't do burin work, so we'll have to find another
engraver. I called on Burty yesterday but he wasn't in.

E. MANET

*

[early 1876]

We can't possibly go ahead with the tinting (*130*), the cost
would be appalling – I'm quite prepared to take it on myself; it will take me a day.

MANET

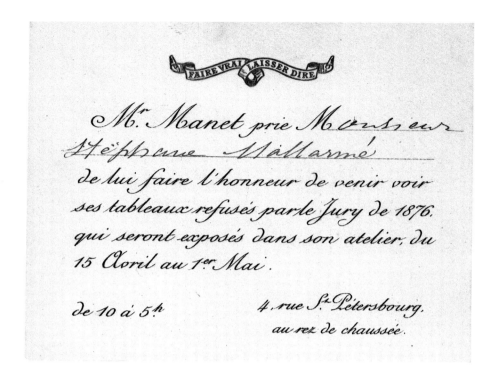

131   MANET'S
        INVITATION
        TO MALLARMÉ

BE TRUE COME WHAT MAY

M. Manet begs Monsieur
Stéphane Mallarmé
to do him the honour of coming to see
his pictures rejected by the Jury of 1876,
which will be on exhibition in his studio, from
15 April to 1 May.

from 10 to 5 o'clock   4, rue St Pétersbourg
                                                              ground floor

*

4 rue Saint Pétersbourg, 18 April [1876]

TO ALBERT WOLFF

So that's it, I have an artist's eye and So-and-so has his soul.
I am comforted by the fact that you always express your sympathy for me personally.

Regards, ED. MANET

*

4 rue Saint Pétersbourg, 21[?] April [1876]

TO JULES NORIAC

Thank you for writing about me so sympathetically in your
article in Le Monde illustré [22 April] yesterday – I appreciate it all the more since it comes from
a writer whose talent I have often had occasion to admire since our days in the 101st regiment.

I have had the pleasure of meeting you, Sir, on many occasions and hope that at the next
opportunity you will let me come and shake hands with you as I would with an old friend.

With my warm respects, ED. MANET

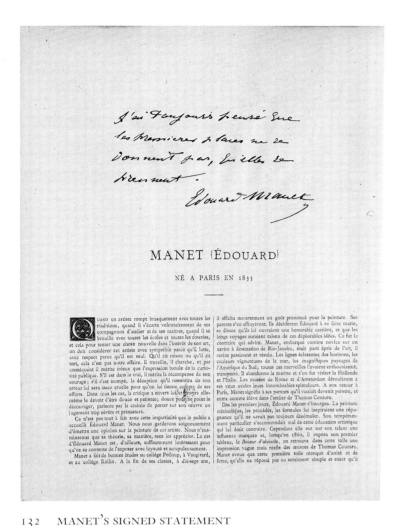

132   MANET'S SIGNED STATEMENT
       LA GALERIE CONTEMPORAINE, APRIL 1876

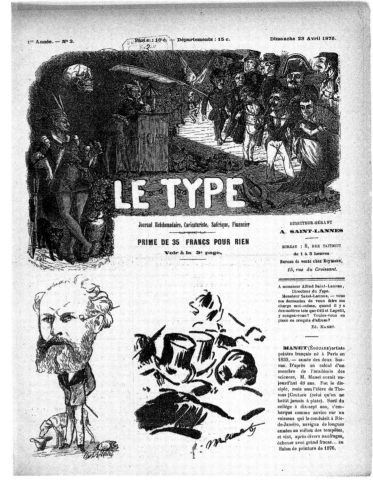

133   MANET'S LETTER, SKETCH AND CARICATURE
       LE TYPE, 23 APRIL 1876

[Published April 1876]

TO THE READERS OF *LA GALERIE CONTEMPORAINE*   I have always believed that the prime positions are not given away, they have to be fought for (*132*).

EDOUARD MANET

*

[Published 23 April 1876]

TO ALFRED SAINT-LANNES, DIRECTOR OF *LE TYPE*   Are you asking me to do a caricature of myself when there are specialists like Gill and Lepetit, can you be serious? Wouldn't you like this album sketch instead (*133*)?

ED. MANET

*

4 rue Saint Pétersbourg, Sunday [7 May 1876 postmark]

TO JULES CASTAGNARY   Thank you for having defended me so valiantly and authoritatively [in *Le Siècle*] and please accept my warmest regards.

ED. MANET

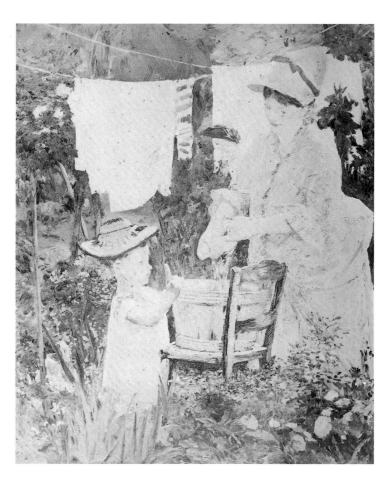

134 PHOTOGRAPH BY GODET OF *LE LINGE*
(THE LAUNDRY, d.1875), c.1875–6

[1876]

RECORDED BY ANTONIN PROUST [On hearing Méry Laurent say of *Le linge* (*134*) 'But that's very good indeed'] Who are you, Madame, to like what everyone else dislikes?... You see, this is as close to truth as one can get. You can feel the air around this woman and child....

... What I've always longed to do would be to place women like you in green outdoor settings, among flowers, on beaches, where contours are eaten away in the open air, and everything melts and mingles in the bright light of day, because I can assure you I'm not just an insensitive brute....

Only a fool could think that I'm out to create a sensation. Have I ever attempted to assassinate the duc de Guise? Do I try and bring Napoleon back from the grave?

I interpret what I see as straightforwardly as possible. *Olympia* (*85*) is a case in point, what could be more naïve? People have objected to the hard contours, but they were there. I saw them. I painted what I saw. And the *Women on the jetty at Boulogne* (*98*), I can't think of a less conventional, more honest, more directly observed work than that!

It would have been so easy to add to those two pictures the little touches so dear to M. Wolff's heart! People fight each other for the things that critic likes, as if they were pieces of the true Cross. In ten years' time they won't fetch tuppence.

If I had painted the Empress Josephine washing her dirty linen rather than Jeanne Lorgnon doing her laundry, what a triumph that could have been, my dears! There wouldn't have been enough engravers to reproduce such a masterpiece, or enough critics to sing its praises.

But there you are, I didn't know the Empress Josephine personally. Meissonier knew her; he knew Napoleon I, too. I would have liked to meet Napoleon III, but luck was never on my side... So I don't know Napoleon III and he doesn't know me.

Rottembourg, Montgeron (Seine et Oise), Tuesday [July 1876]

To Eva Gonzalès   Your letter has reached us in the country and Suzanne...
has handed me the pen to reply...

There are far too many distractions here for me to be able to get down to serious work;
I've started lots of things that I probably won't be able to finish – a portrait of the master of
the house [Ernest Hoschedé] and his daughter (*176*), but I can never get him to sit for it, he's
always in Paris. A portrait of Carolus Duran (*177*) who is our neighbour in the country. I'm
going to get down to it seriously in the next few days and make a real effort because we don't
want to prolong our stay – I have things to do in Paris and we'll probably be back there early
next week. I came to the country for a rest and have never been so exhausted.

ED. MANET

*

[late July–August 1876]

To Émile Zola [in Brittany]   I've just heard that you had a nearly fatal accident but also
that you all came out of it as well as possible – Thank goodness. You'll be getting a letter from
Flor who came and asked to be introduced to you. Too late, you had just gone off. He's in
charge of a very handsome publication [*La Galerie contemporaine*, see (*132*)]. Give him all the
information they need. My best wishes to you and your wife and remember me to your
charming companions the Charpentiers. On Friday I'm to start a portrait of Mlle Isabelle
[Lemonnier, see (*210*)].

ED. MANET

I've just read the latest instalment of L'Assommoir in *La République des lettres* – marvellous!

*

Tuesday [15 August 1876 postmark]

To Stéphane Mallarmé   I went this very morning to see my photographer [Godet]
who will be writing to you today. He'll have to make a new negative and I'll send him the
picture (*134?*). We're not leaving for Fécamp until Thursday. No news here. We're knocked out
by this tropical heatwave.

ED. MANET

*

Sunday [October 1876]

I'm lunching in town and may arrive a little late. Please take
the key – I should have let you know, but I forgot – so while you are waiting you might
compose a poem entitled 'A forgetful friend', lambasting me as much as you praised me in the
article in the English review [*Art Monthly*].

E. MANET

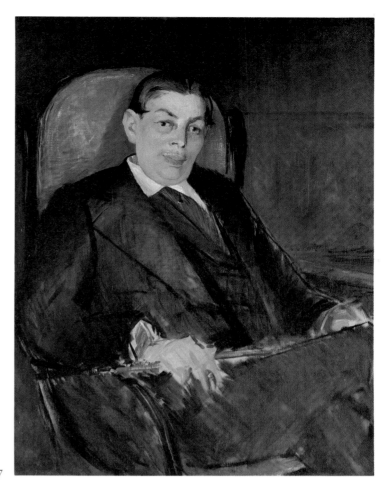

135   PORTRAIT OF ALBERT WOLFF, 1877

19 March [1877]

To Albert Wolff   My friends Messrs Monet, Sisley, Renoir and Mme Berthe
Morisot are going to hold an exhibition and sale at the Salle Drouot. One of these gentlemen
will bring you a catalogue and invitation, and has asked me for this letter of introduction.

You may not care for this kind of painting yet, but some day you will. Meanwhile it would
be nice of you to say something about it in *Le Figaro*.

I haven't yet asked you to come and see my portrait of Faure [see (*175*)], because it's not yet
finished. Between ourselves, I've been given extra time....

Ed. Manet

*

Monday [1877]

Would you wear your blue frock coat with the velvet collar
and your brown trousers tomorrow? It will look a bit jollier.

E. Manet

*

[1877]

Recorded by Antonin Proust   That creature [Albert Wolff] gives me the creeps... They
say he's a wit. Some wit. It's like a penny bazaar. When there's none left, there's more on the
way. Wit? Well, it would be a disgrace if he didn't have any, since that's his stock in trade...
[After another adverse review]   Did I ask the impossible? – I asked him to stay neutral.

Tuesday 31 [April 1877]

TO ÉMILE ZOLA   I understand you have almost if not quite finished your
move. Would you like me to call and collect your portrait (*91*) to get it cleaned? You would be
well advised to send the frame to Nivard for repair. Drop me a line.

ED. MANET

*

[1877–8]

RECORDED BY CHARLES TOCHÉ   [On Faure's portrait at the Salon]   . . . at least my tailor
appreciates me. And so does Faure. How they jeered at my portrait of him as Hamlet (*175*)!
With the left leg they said was too short! When someone is rushing forward, how could his legs
be like those of an infantryman standing to attention? And the sloping floor? Good grief! I'd
like to see our academic drawing masters attempting to convey the illusion of Hamlet running
towards the spectator . . .

*

[September–October? 1878]

TO THÉODORE DURET [in England]   All your friends will regret your forced absence but it's in
such a good cause.

I met several Impressionists yesterday and your great expectations have filled them with
fond hope which they can certainly do with because the press is still undecided. Monet arrived
yesterday with many excellent canvases – though it's not the best moment to try and sell
them.

Zola has building work going on and is still in the country [at Médan]. I met some people
who had been to see him; he read them the first two chapters of *Nana* which sounds wonderful
and way ahead of everything else in its realism – another triumph, no doubt.

I've been working hard this summer and hope to have some good things in the next
exhibition, and today Proust asked me to do his portrait for the next Salon (*212*).

As for you, you will no doubt be able to finish your study in spite of your new activities.
I was rereading your latest book recently and I am convinced that that is the only way to
write history.

In any event, your prolonged stay over there won't do your political ambitions any harm.

EDOUARD MANET

*

Monday [9 December 1878]

TO ÉMILE ZOLA [at Médan]   Bergerat wants me to do two drawings for his publication
[*La Vie Moderne*], to illustrate a story of yours entitled 'Jean-Louis'. I find it impossible to
draw peasants here in Paris, in the winter. Mightn't you have a little something set in Paris?
It would be more in keeping with my resources and the season.

ED. MANET

*

RECORDED BY ANTONIN PROUST   [On Burty's criticism]   You think it's not bad. Well, you're not hard to please. Like Mme Mansion at the Fualdès trial, Burty says neither yes nor no. While he was sorting out my etchings the other day, he told me I ought to let public opinion get used to me and lead it along gently. The strange fellow! When he's writing about Jean-Paul Laurens's picture of *The Austrian High Command*... he adopts a different tone. Then he's as accommodating as he is for Gérôme's *Eminence Grise*. How grey an Eminence! How very grey! He should say what he thinks or not say anything at all. Théodore Duret does not mince his words. Not to mention Zola!

[On visiting the Fine Arts section of the *Exposition universelle*]   Well!... those people! How they can laugh at the work of Degas, Monet and Pissarro, crack jokes about Berthe Morisot and Mary Cassatt, and double up with laughter in front of Caillebotte, Renoir, Gauguin and Cézanne, when they produce painting like that! I do my best to find something I like. I just can't. And there are things that really upset me. Look at Gustave Moreau. I've a great deal of sympathy for him, but he's going in the wrong direction... [and] will have a deplorable influence on our times. He favours a return to the incomprehensible whereas we want everything to be understood. No doubt about it. It is he who sets the tone nowadays, so much so that what is admired in Corot's work is not the clear definition of the studies from nature but the vagueness of the studio pictures.

[On a visit from foreign members of the *Exposition* jury]   Sir Frederick Leighton, the president of the Royal Academy of Art in London... was here yesterday with Henri Hecht who had introduced me to him a few days earlier. I was busy painting Madame Guillemet (*207*). Léon had gone out, and the famous painter was in my way. He wandered about the studio and stopped in front of the *Skating rink* (*174*), saying: 'It's very good but, Monsieur Manet, don't you think that the outlines are not well enough defined and that the figures dance a bit too much?' I replied 'They're not dancing, they're skating; but you're right, they do move and when people are moving, I can't freeze them on the canvas. As a matter of fact, sir, I have been told that the outlines of *Olympia* (*85*) are too well defined, so that makes up for it.' He realized he was annoying me and went away....

[On portraiture]   ... no one has tackled the woman of the Second Empire, although she typified a particular period, just as Papa Bertin characterized the bourgeoisie of 1825 to 1850. What a masterpiece the portrait of Bertin is.... Dry? [in reply to Arsène Houssaye] Dry? Come along! M. Ingres chose Bertin to typify an epoch; he represents him as a Buddha of the prosperous, well-fed, triumphant bourgeoisie. Anyone who destroys that will be as much of a vandal as M. Ingres who destroyed paintings by Gleyre, whose presence near his own work displeased him.

You were talking about women. I didn't do the women of the Second Empire but I did those who came afterwards. Mme de Callias (*158*), Fanny Bergolle, Léontine Massin, Henriette Hauser (*171*), Countess Cabalesti, Ellen Andrée (*170*, *186*) and quite a few others who have their own particular character.

One study, though not of a woman, fascinated me, and that was my *Desboutin* (*169*). I didn't claim to have summed up an epoch, but to have painted the most extraordinary character in a neighbourhood. I painted Desboutin with as much passion as Baudelaire [see (*17*)]....

[On a plea not to rework a portrait of Isabelle Lemonnier]   That's good advice... all the

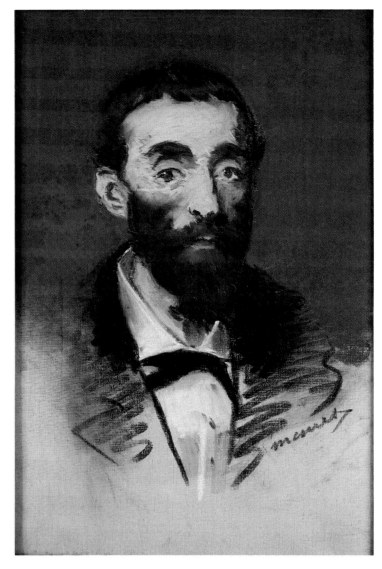

136 PORTRAIT OF CABANER, c.1880–81

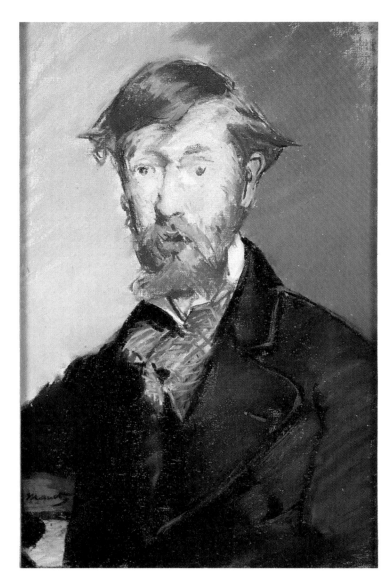

137 PORTRAIT OF GEORGE MOORE, c.1878–9

more so since I may well be forced to leave it at that, as so often happens when the model doesn't come back. That's always been my principal concern, to make sure of getting regular sittings. Whenever I start something, I'm always afraid the model will let me down . . . They come, they pose, then away they go, telling themselves that he can finish it off on his own. Well no, one can't finish anything on one's own, particularly since one only finishes on the day one starts, and that means starting often and having plenty of days available. On the other hand, some of them come back without being asked, wanting me to do some retouching, which I always refuse to do. Look at that portrait of the poet [George] Moore (*137*). As far as I was concerned, it was all finished in a single sitting, but he didn't see it that way. He came back and annoyed me by asking for a change here, something different there. I won't change a thing in his portrait. Is it my fault if Moore looks like squashed egg yolk and if his face is all lopsided? Anyway, the same applies to everybody's face and this passion for symmetry is the plague of our time. There's no symmetry in nature. One eye is never exactly the same as the other, there's always a difference. We all have a more or less crooked nose and an irregular mouth. But you can't tell that to the geometry buffs. Cabaner, the composer, was the perfect model (*136*) . . . . He was the most unlikely, the most bizarre character I've ever met, and full of talent too.

To the Prefect of the Seine Department
and the President of the Municipal Council   Sir, I have the honour to submit for your esteemed consideration the following project for the decoration of the municipal Council chamber in the new Paris Hôtel de Ville:

A series of painted compositions representing 'the Belly of Paris', to use the current phrase that seems appropriate to express my ideas: the various corporations would be shown in their appropriate settings, representing the public and commercial life of our times. I would show the Paris Markets, Railways, River Port, Subterranean systems, Parks and Racecourses.

On the ceiling would be painted a gallery, and walking around it in appropriate groupings and poses, all those eminent citizens who have contributed or are contributing to the grandeur and wealth of Paris.

I am, Sir, etc., EDOUARD MANET

Artist, born in Paris, 77 rue d'Amsterdam

*

[1879]

Recorded by Antonin Proust   [On the Hôtel de Ville project]   . . . I have no intention of criticizing Viollet-le-Duc . . . On the contrary I am very grateful for the way he received me when he was directing operations at the Hôtel de Ville. I asked him at that time to allow me to decorate one of the rooms. Unfortunately, after agreeing to my request, he sent me to see M. Ballu. But M. Ballu, my dear Proust, treated me as if I were a dog about to lift his leg against a municipal wall!

If the city life of Paris is to be depicted in the Paris town hall, then what we obviously need is allegory. The wines of France, for example: Burgundy wine symbolized by a brunette, Bordeaux by a redhead, Champagne by a blond. Or we could have Mercury and his magic wand and suchlike nonsense. Then the history of Paris, its ancient history of course. A kind of Old Testament. As for the New, nothing doing! But just think how interesting it would be later on to have portraits of the men who are currently running the affairs of the city. Why are we so struck by [Hals's] painting of the Regents in Amsterdam? Because it conveys such a truthful impression of something actually seen. Today, however, monuments are expected to reconstitute antediluvian history, and Cuvier has the last word.

But our eyes are meant to see with. Can you think of anything livelier than Carpeaux's dance group on the façade of the Opera? How its modernity resounds in the midst of everything round it and how one longs to do away with everything behind it . . . Above all Baudry's paintings. Baudry is unhappy because the foyer of the Opera is dark and his paintings are invisible. He'd be unhappier still if they were visible. He's too intelligent not to realize that they are out of place . . .

The fact is, Degas should have decorated the foyer of the Opera. Post-*Semiramis* Degas, that is. He would have created a series of absolute masterpieces, on one condition, that M. Charles Garnier would have seen fit to let in some light. Our modern architects are wonderful in some ways but they're so afraid of strong daylight. They're all for little bays, for little openings. . . .

To come back to M. Ballu, he took leave of me with a wonderful remark: 'Your proposals are very interesting,' he told me, 'but I'm not in charge at the Hôtel de Ville. Write to the Prefect of the Seine Department.' I did, but I never received a reply.

Thursday 17 April [1879]

To ALPHONSE PORTIER   Monsieur, when the [Fourth Impressionist] exhibition ends, would you please send Mlle Cassatt's *Woman Reading* to M. Antonin Proust, Deputy, at 32 Boulevard Haussmann, where the sum of 300 francs will be paid as agreed.

Yours faithfully, E. MANET

*

Thursday [8 May 1879 postmark]

To STÉPHANE MALLARMÉ   Do try and persuade Rothschild [the publisher] – I'm afraid that the way I'm hung in the Salon (*163, 207*) will leave me as poor as before, and I'm in need of money.

E. MANET

*

77 rue d'Amsterdam, 6 June 1879

To EDMOND TURQUET   Mr Under-Secretary of State, I had the honour to be received in audience by you around the middle of last May and without giving me any great hopes concerning the purchase of one of my Salon pictures (*163, 207*), you were kind enough to promise that you would reconsider the matter and give me your personal answer as soon as you had done so. I am therefore taking the liberty, Mr Under-Secretary, of reminding you of your further statement that you would also consider the acquisition for the Luxembourg of one of my works from a private picture gallery, such as the *Bon bock* (*151*), or any other that has received the consecration of the Salon. . . . trusting in your promise, I remain, Mr Under-Secretary of State,

Yours faithfully, EDOUARD MANET

[Stamped *Ministry of Fine Arts, Office of the Under-Secretary of State, 17 June 1879* and *Fine Arts Administration, Promotion Division*; annotated 'Lafenestre' and 'Discuss this with Mr Under-Secretary of State'; marked in blue pencil 'File'.]

*

Monday [28 July 1879]

To ÉMILE ZOLA [at Médan]   Your letter is more than welcome and I hope you will agree that it seems a good idea to ask to have it published in *Le Figaro*.

I must confess that I feld sadly disillusioned when I read the article [in *Le Figaro*, 26 July] and was deeply hurt by it.

ED. MANET

[1879]

RECORDED BY ANTONIN PROUST   ... I have good news for you, I've sold one of my café-concert pictures [(*187*), later exchanged for (*186*)] to a M. Etienne Barroil. Méry got him to buy the picture and since M. Etienne Barroil is a gentleman he sent me a crate of mandarins from Marseilles, a taste of his sunshine. When I go out, I take lots of mandarins, I fill my pockets with them and give them to the local children who come begging. They'd probably prefer money, but I prefer to give them a share in something I enjoy. The pleasures of this world! Well, they're made of things that mean little to some people but a lot to others.

*

[1878–9]

[On the abandoned portrait of Gambetta]   There's another one who will end up with Bonnat! ... He'll be persuaded by Burty and his kind. Though Gambetta is different. He's more open-minded than the rest of his party – it's strange how reactionary republicans can be when it comes to art.

It's so much easier to trot out the clichés, to pay homage to a so-called ideal beauty. How can you talk of ideal beauty, beauty defined for all time, when everything is in a state of flux? They should drop those hoary old notions. When I say that beauty is in a state of flux, that's not exactly what I mean. I mean that beauty is relative. What would one think of an artist who studied the character of the head of a man like Gambetta and analysed the particular characteristics that develop in such a man of action, only to go off to the Louvre and copy the *Discus Thrower* on the grounds that that alone is beautiful. But it's exactly what we're advised to do. Charles Blanc is one exponent of this belief, and there are plenty of others. The truth is that our only obligation should be to distil what we can from our our epoch, though without belittling what earlier periods have achieved. But to try and mix them into what barmen call a cocktail is plain stupid. I must say, I would have liked to leave an image of Gambetta as I see him. But there's no hope of that now.

*

[14 July 1879]

[On the fête given by Gambetta at the Palais Bourbon, and Méry Laurent's maid Elisa]   It was wonderful, but there was candle-wax dripping all over the place. Fortunately, Elisa got it all off me. Elisa is such a good girl! There really are good people, you see, there are lots of them, lots more than one thinks. Now, I don't claim to be more democratic than the next man. In fact I'm decidedly aristocratic. But when I meet someone like Elisa, I love and admire the whole human race.

*

Oloron-Sainte-Marie, February 1871

138   LÉON ON THE BALCONY, OLORON-SAINTE-MARIE, 1871

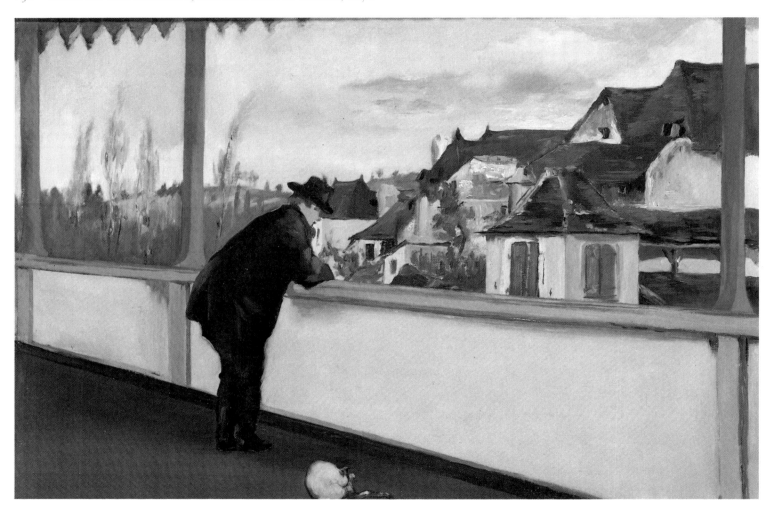

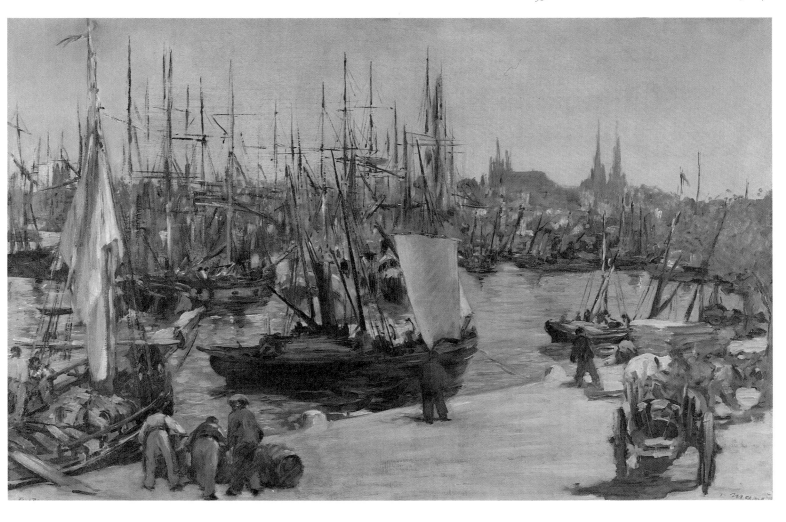

Arcachon, March 1871

140   THE BAY AT ARCACHON, 1871

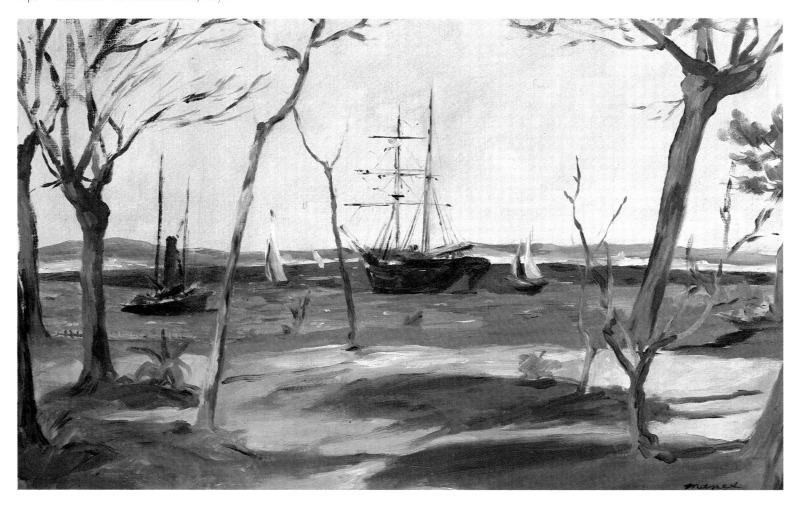

141   INTERIOR AT ARCACHON, MME MANET AND LÉON, 1871

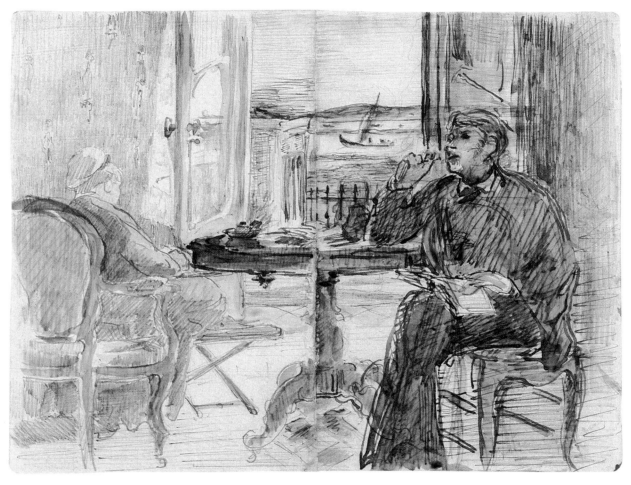

142   THE BARRICADE, 1871

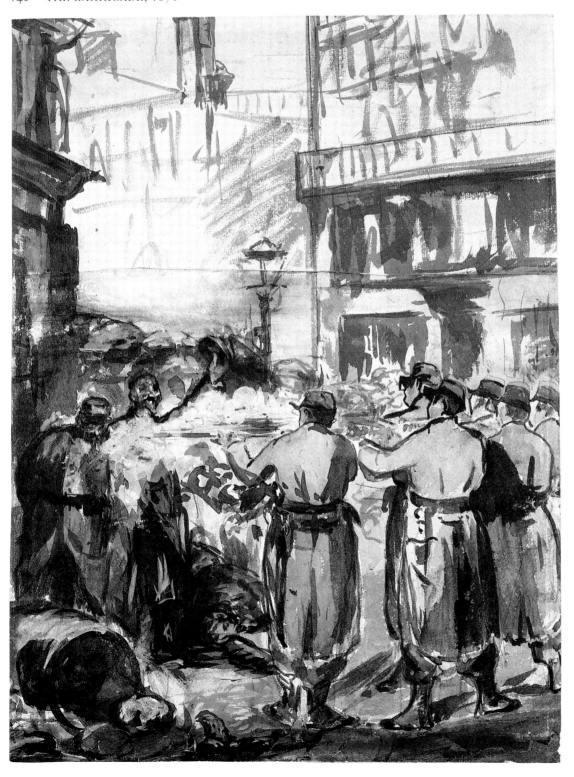

143   GUERRE CIVILE (CIVIL WAR), d.1871

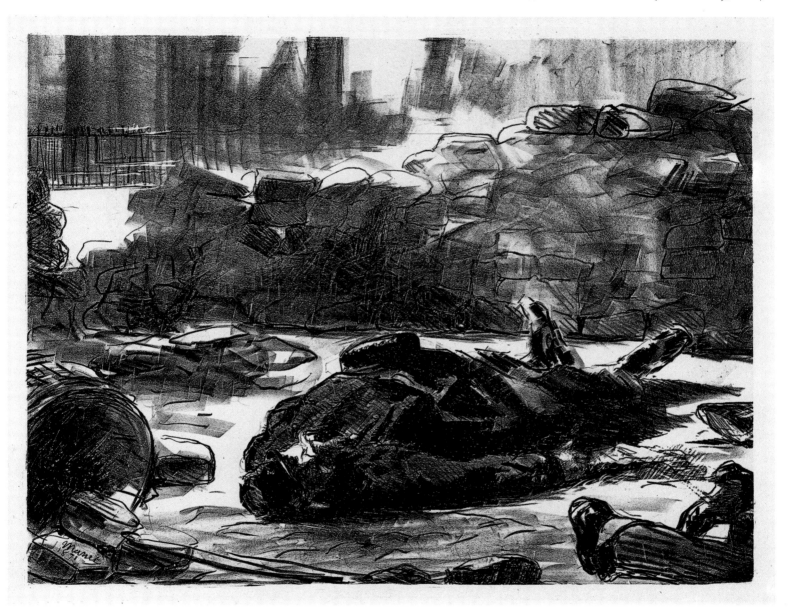

Aftermath of war

144 THE TRIAL OF MARSHAL BAZAINE BEFORE THE COUNCIL OF WAR AT VERSAILLES, 1873

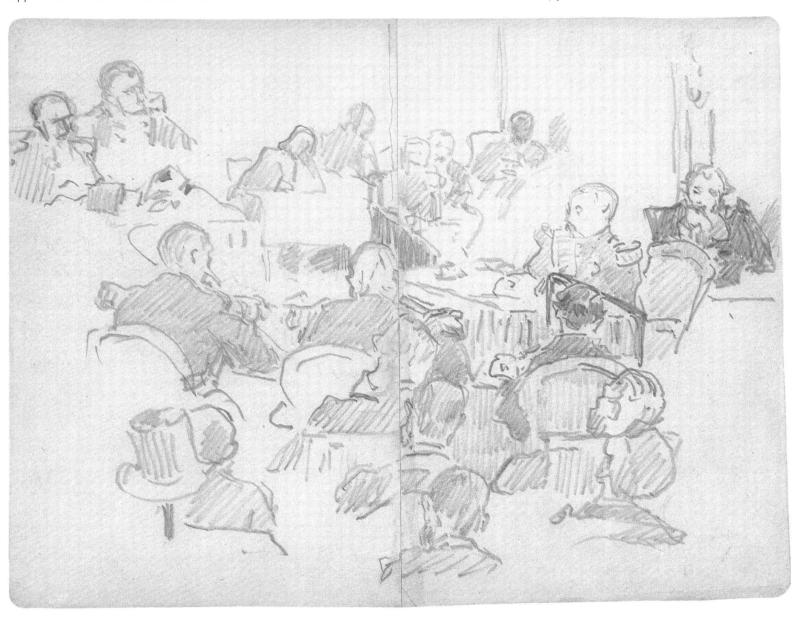

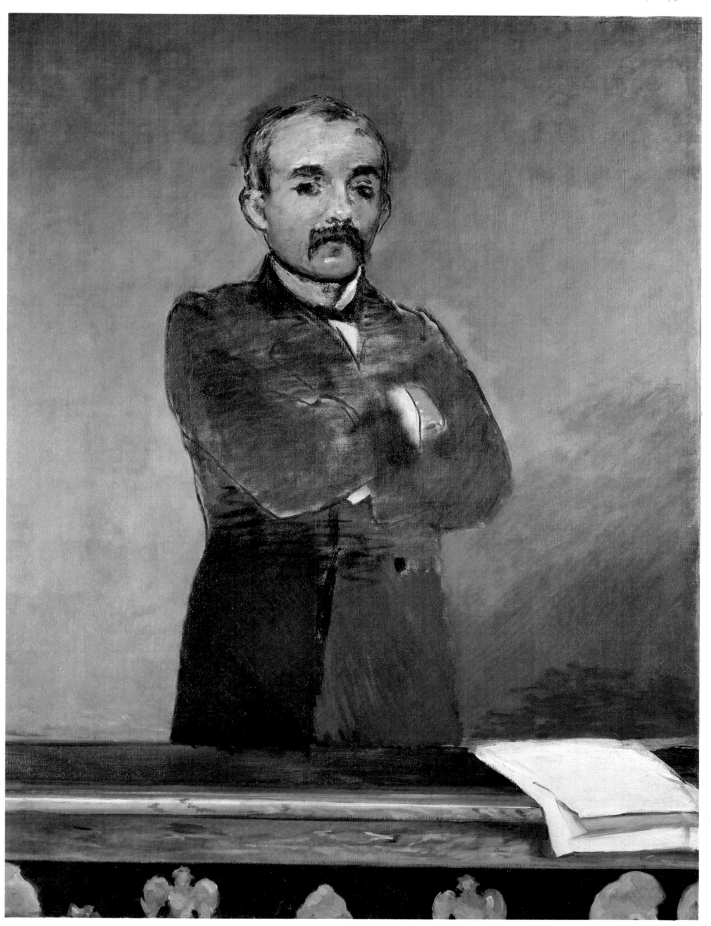

146   SKETCHES OF A GAME OF CROQUET, 1868 / 71?

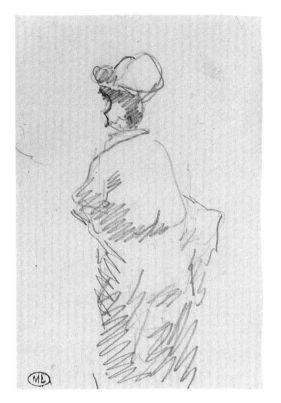

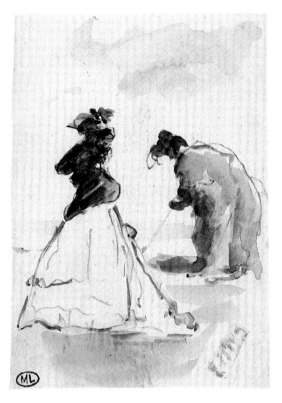

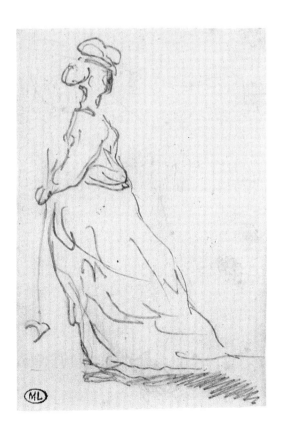

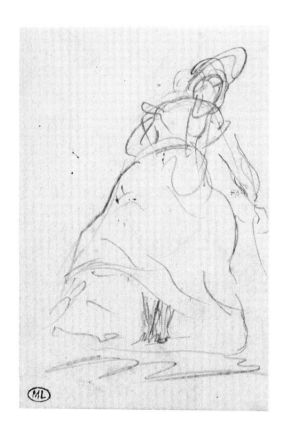

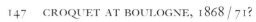

147   CROQUET AT BOULOGNE, 1868/71?

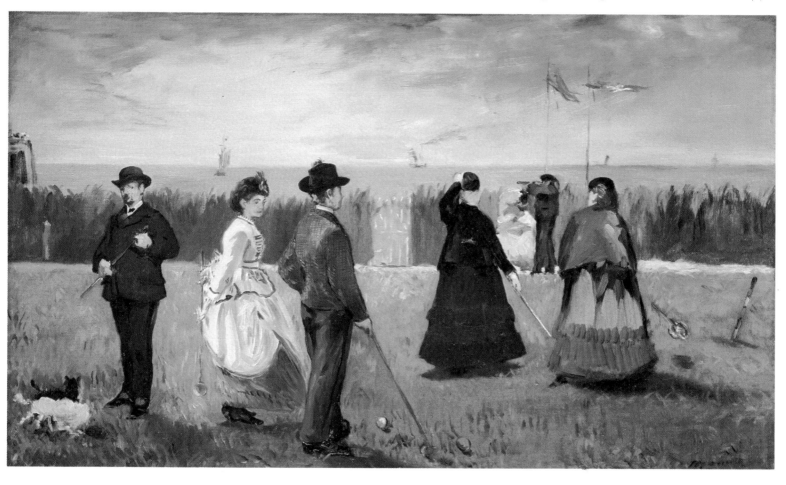

Summer at Boulogne, 1868/1871?

148   THE DEPARTURE OF THE FOLKESTONE BOAT, 1868/71?

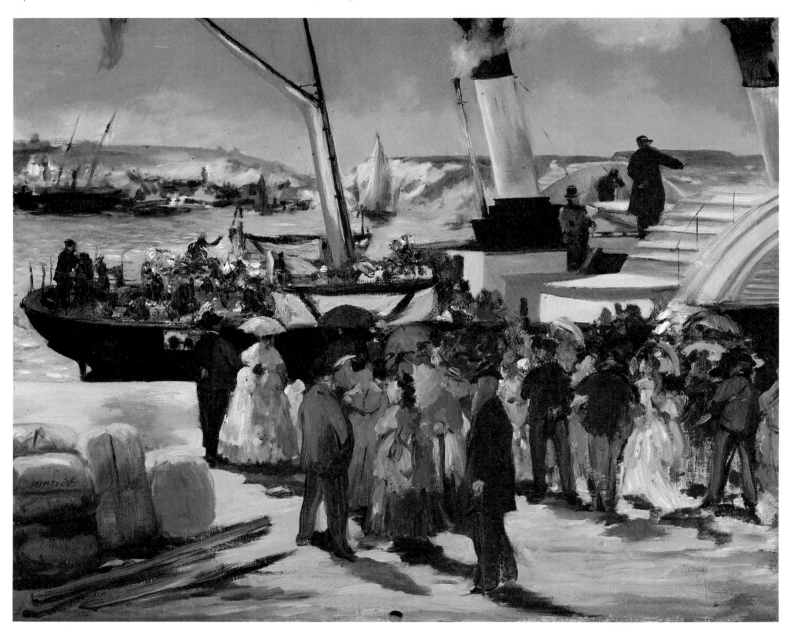

149   SKETCHES OF FIGURES ON THE HARBOUR AT BOULOGNE, 1868/71?

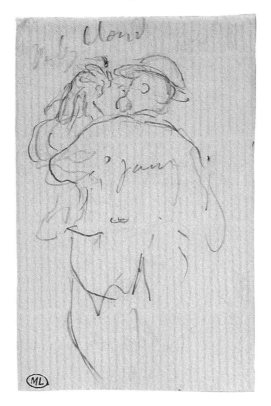
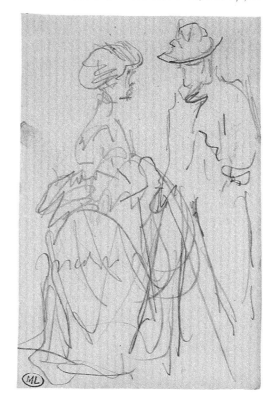

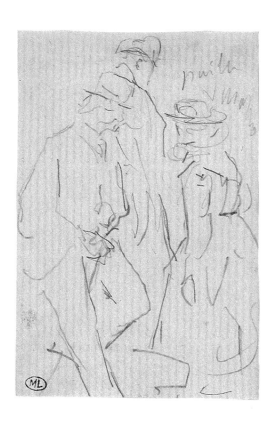
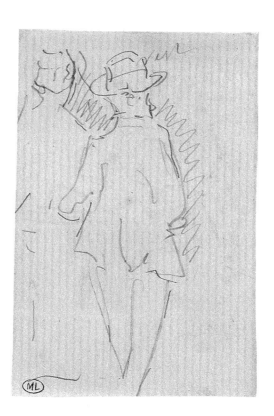

Visit to Holland, 1872

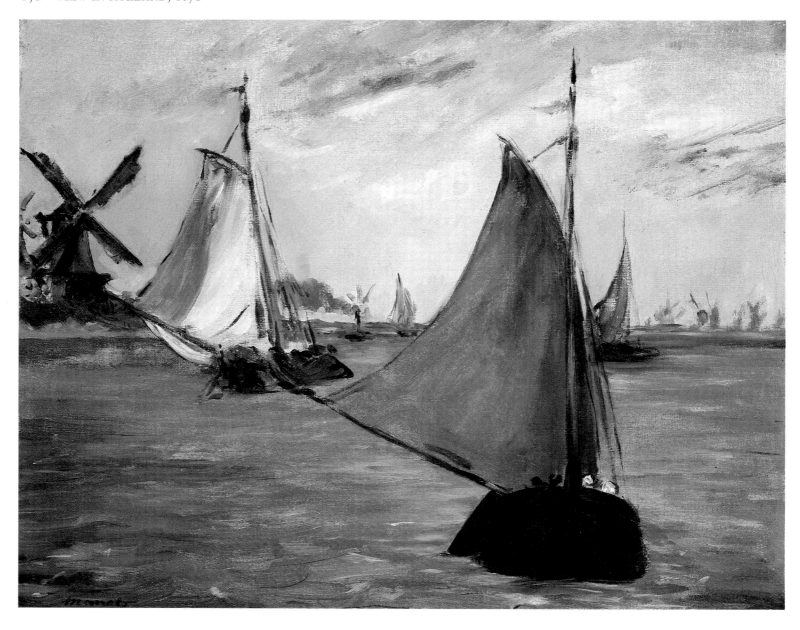

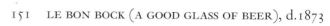

151   LE BON BOCK (A GOOD GLASS OF BEER), d.1873

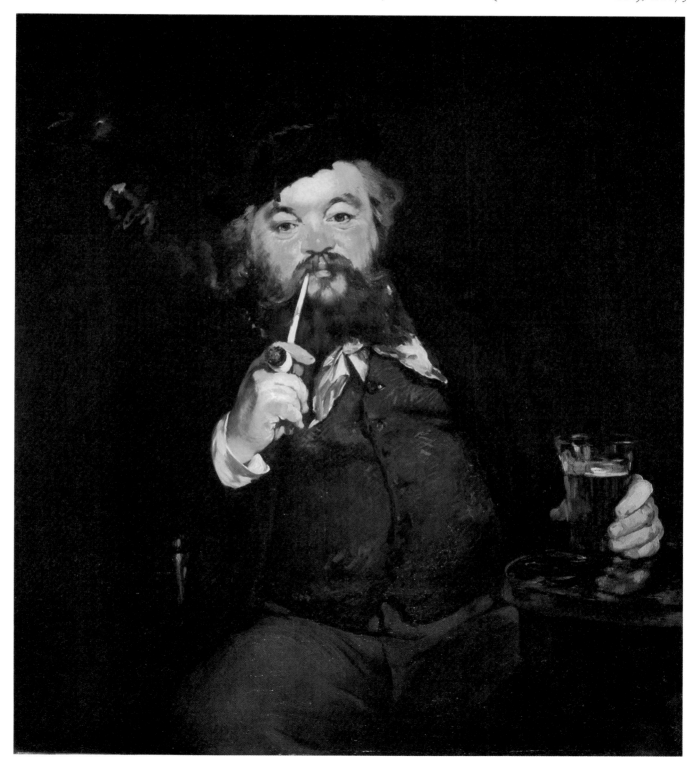

Summer at Berck, 1873

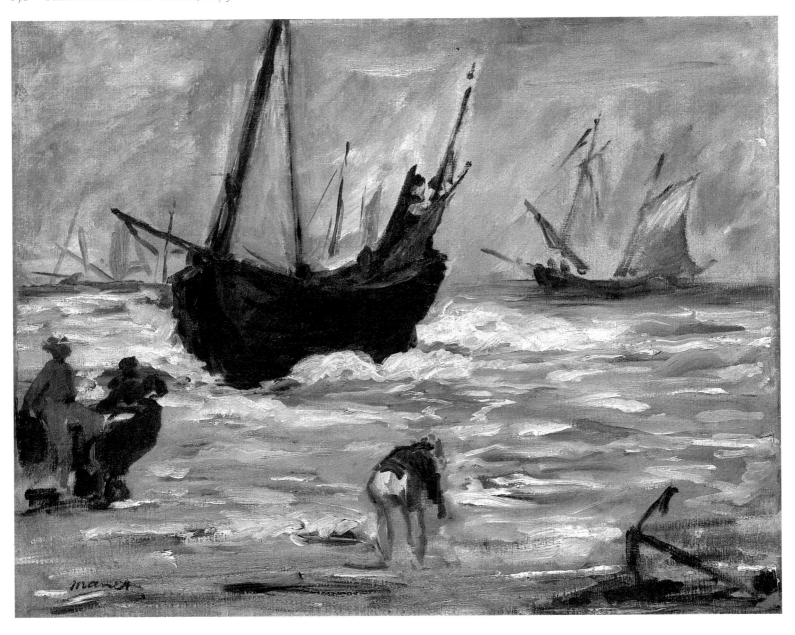

153   ON THE BEACH (MME MANET AND EUGÈNE AT BERCK), 1873

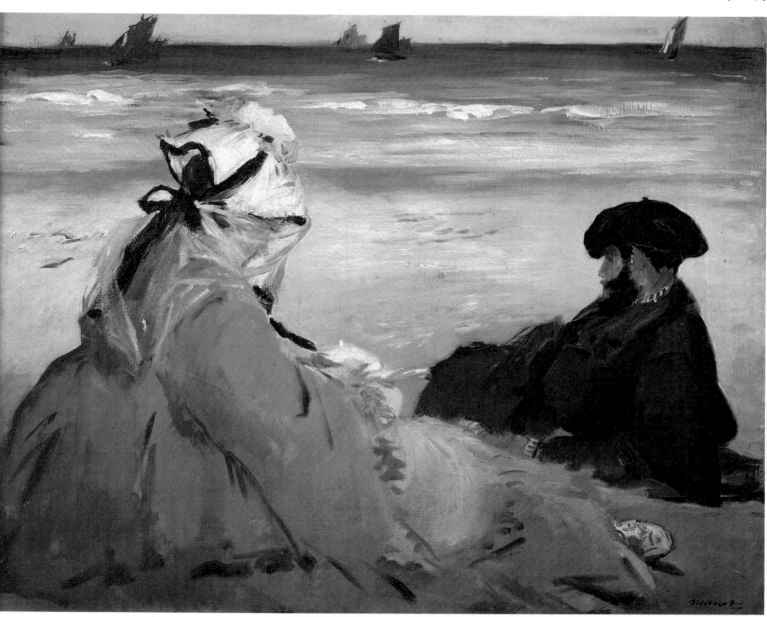

Sketch for a Salon composition

154   THE RAILWAY LINES AT THE PONT DE L'EUROPE, 1873

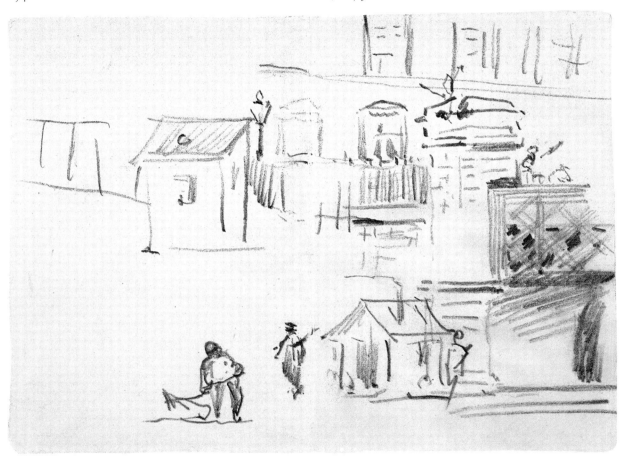

155   LE CHEMIN DE FER (THE RAILROAD), d.1873

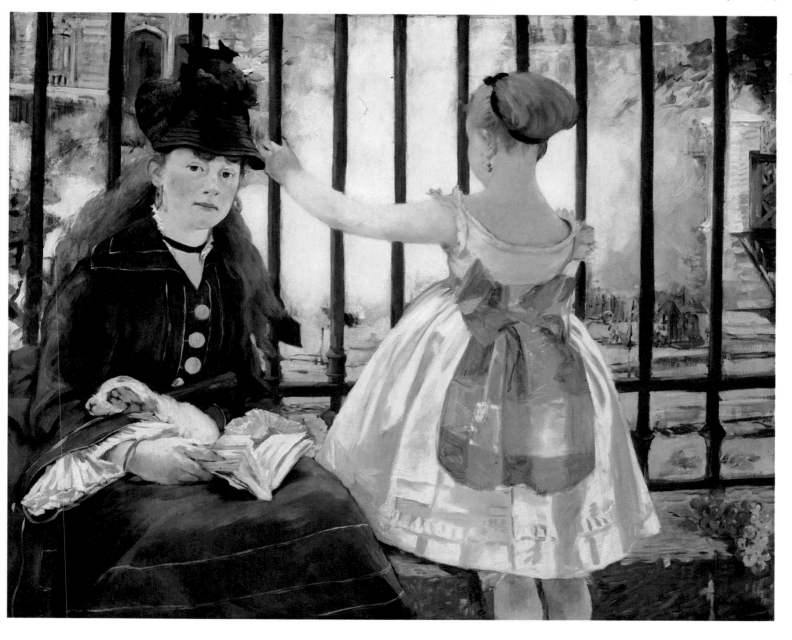

156   POLICHINELLE, 1874

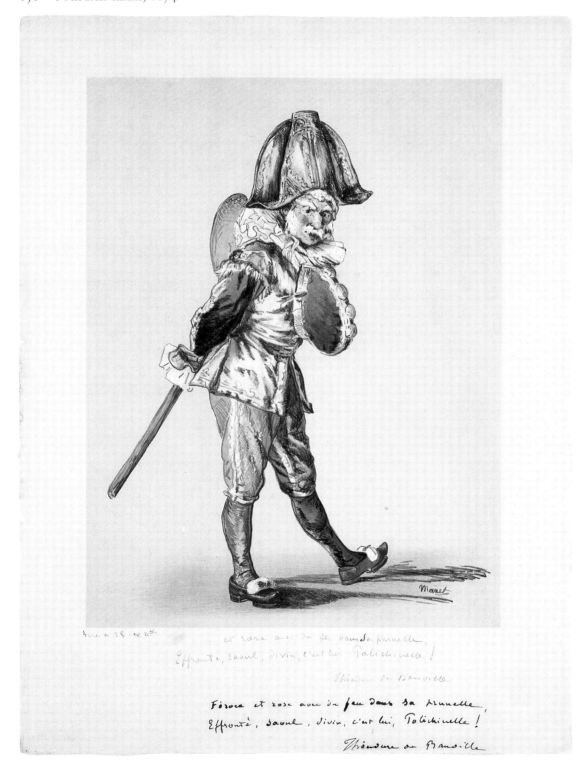

157   MASKED BALL AT THE OPERA, 1873–4

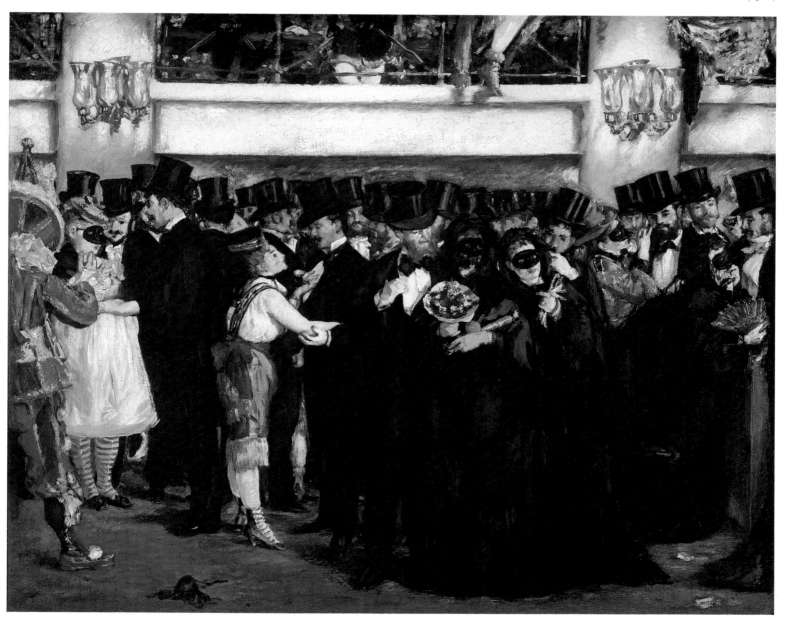

A modern muse, 1873–1874

158   LADY WITH FANS / PORTRAIT OF NINA DE CALLIAS, 1873–4

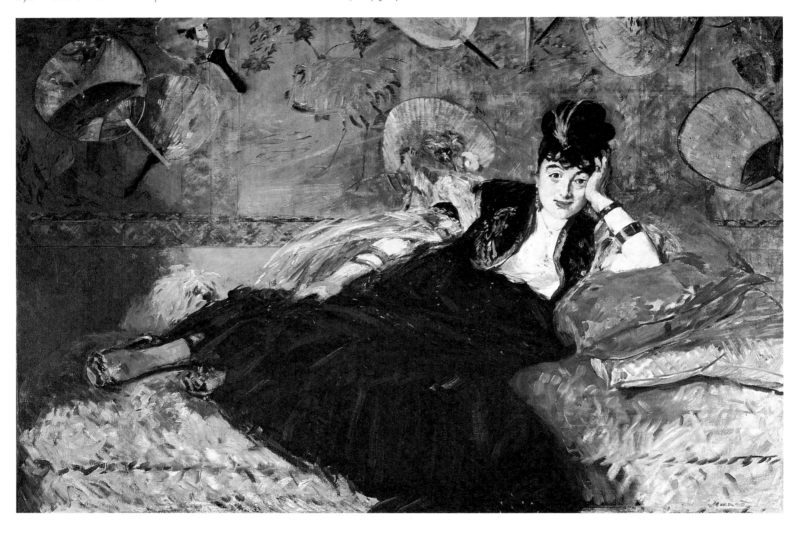

159　THE PARISIENNE / NINA DE CALLIAS, 1873

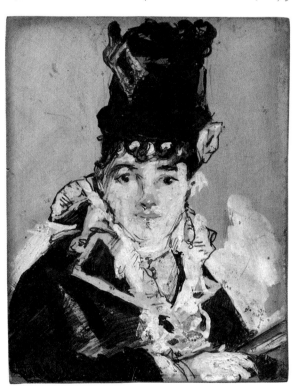

With Monet at Argenteuil, 1874

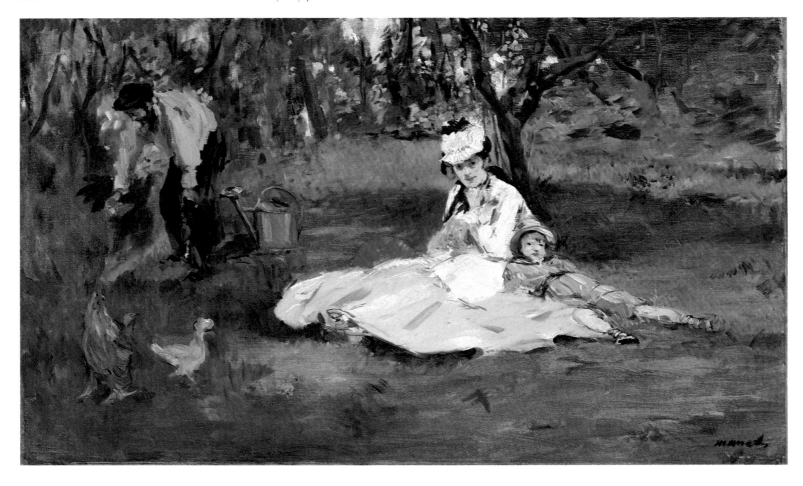

161 MONET IN HIS STUDIO BOAT, 1874

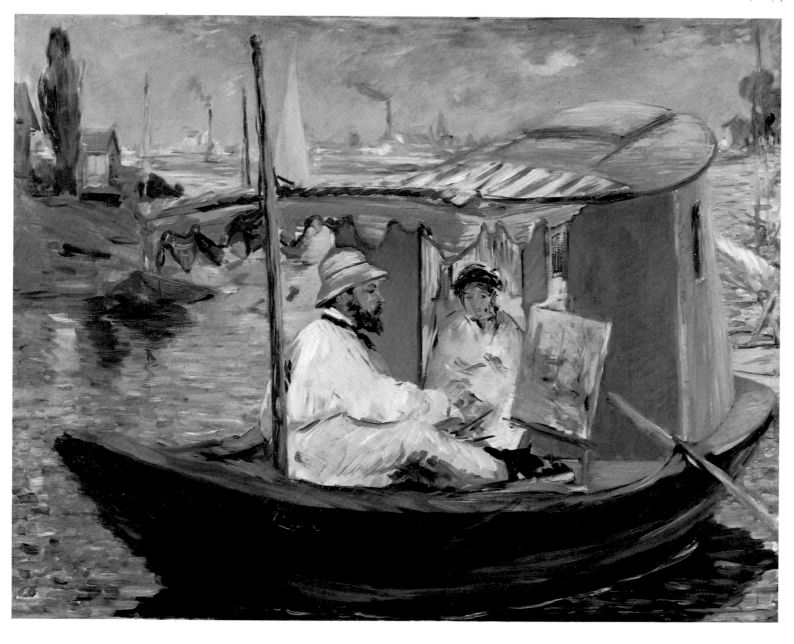

162   ARGENTEUIL, d.1874

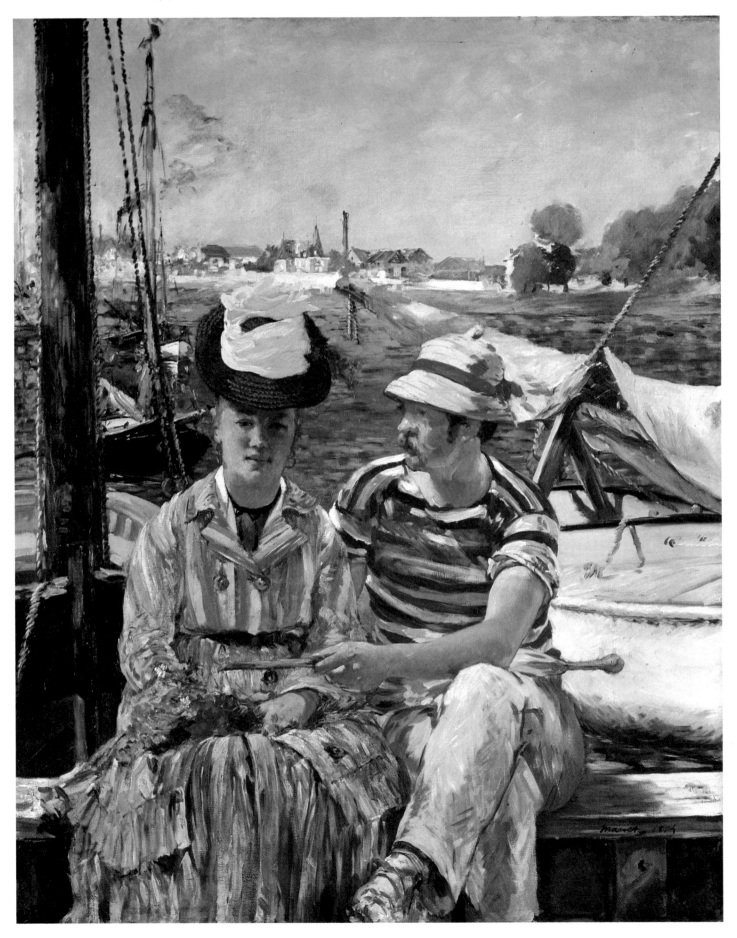

163   BOATING, 1874–6

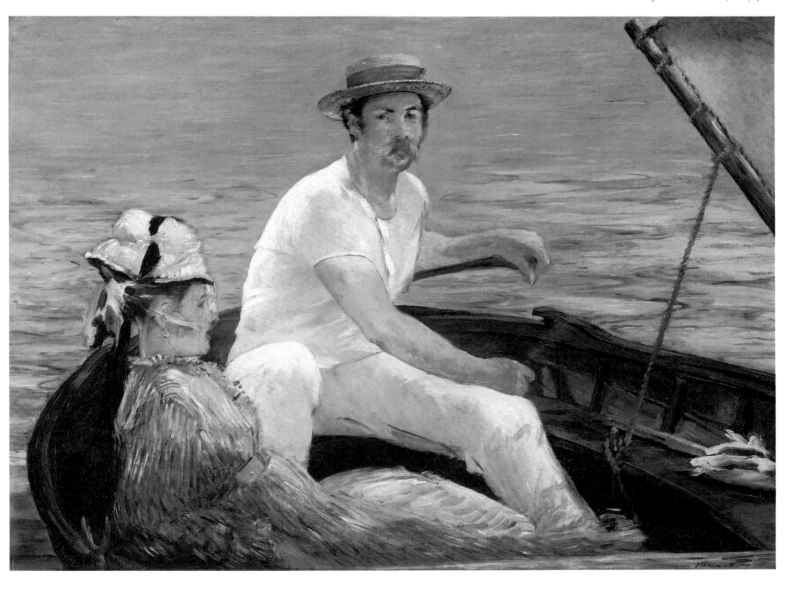

Venice in winter, 1874–1875

164 VENICE, THE GRAND CANAL / BLUE VENICE, 1874

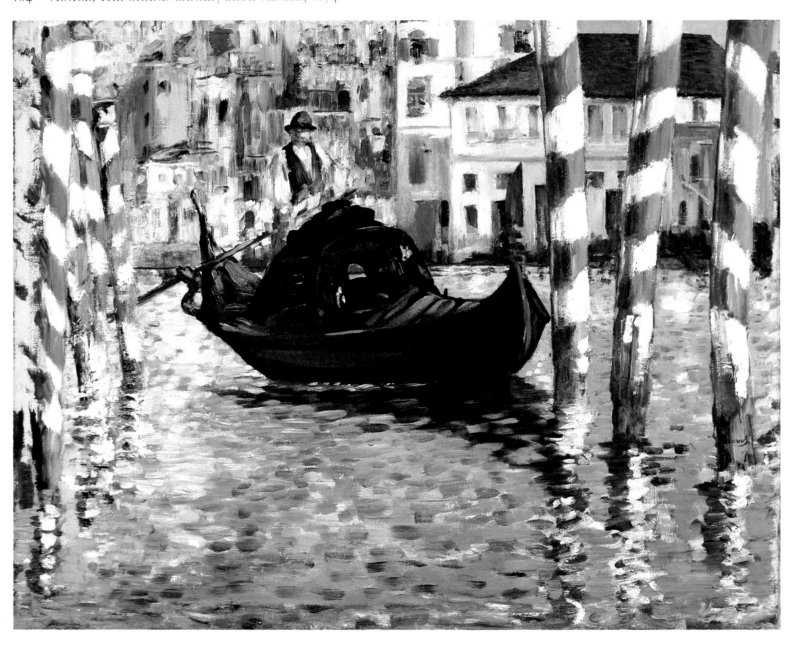

165   VIEW IN VENICE / THE GRAND CANAL, 1874

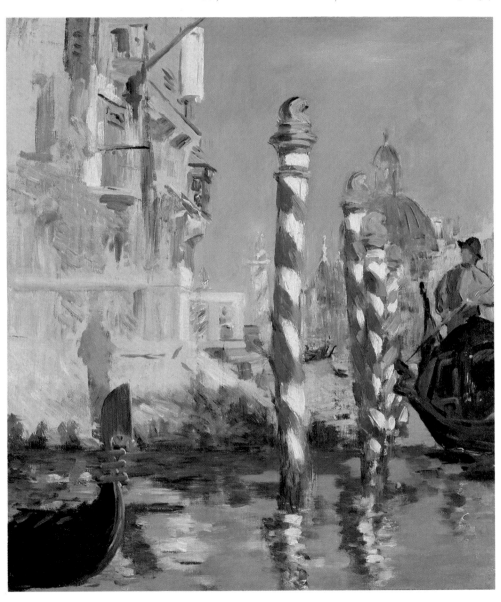

166   TAMA, A JAPANESE DOG, 1875

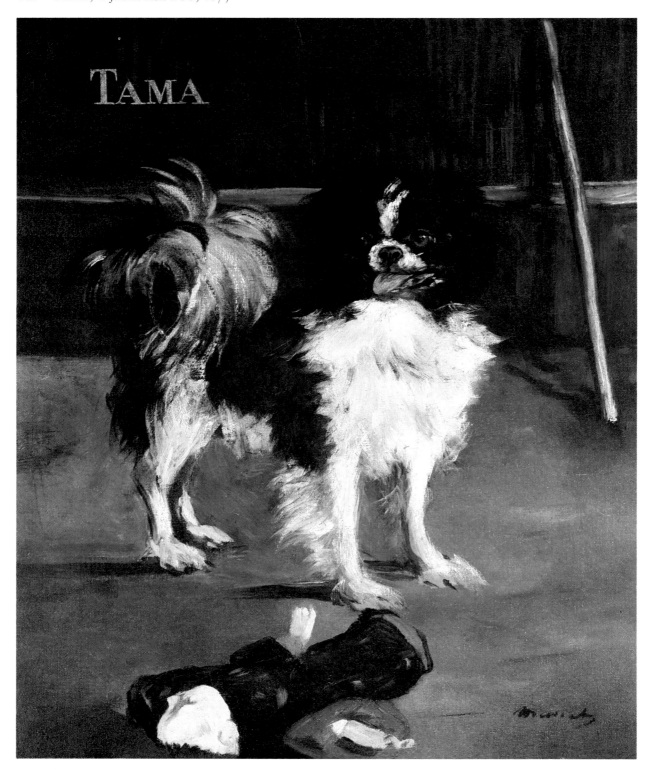

167   SKETCHES OF TAMA, 1875

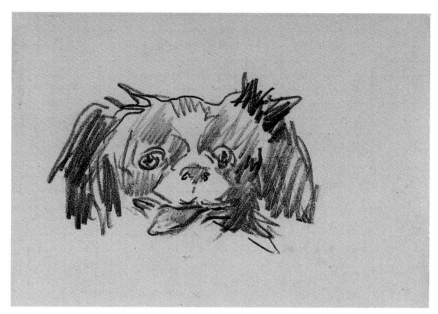

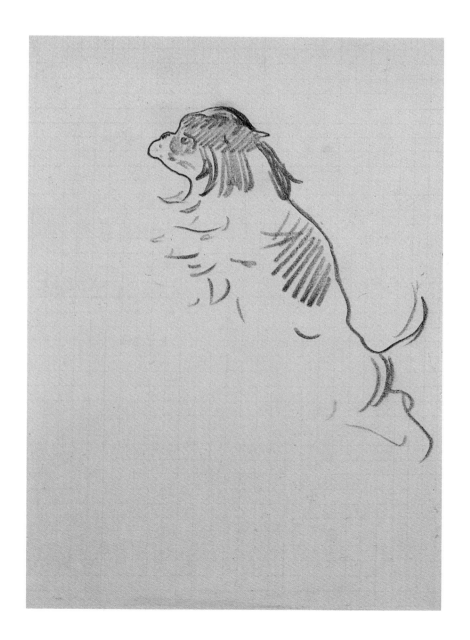

Study of Desboutin

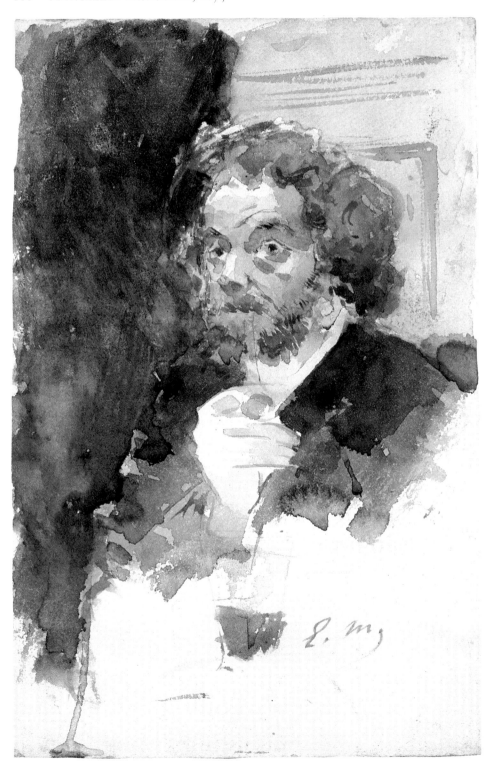

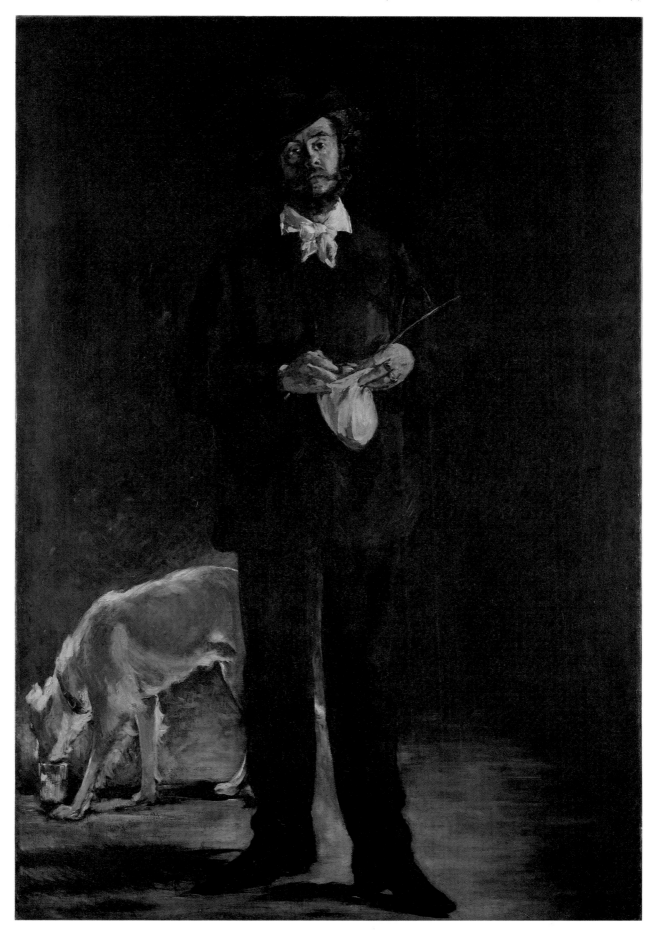

Women of the Third Republic

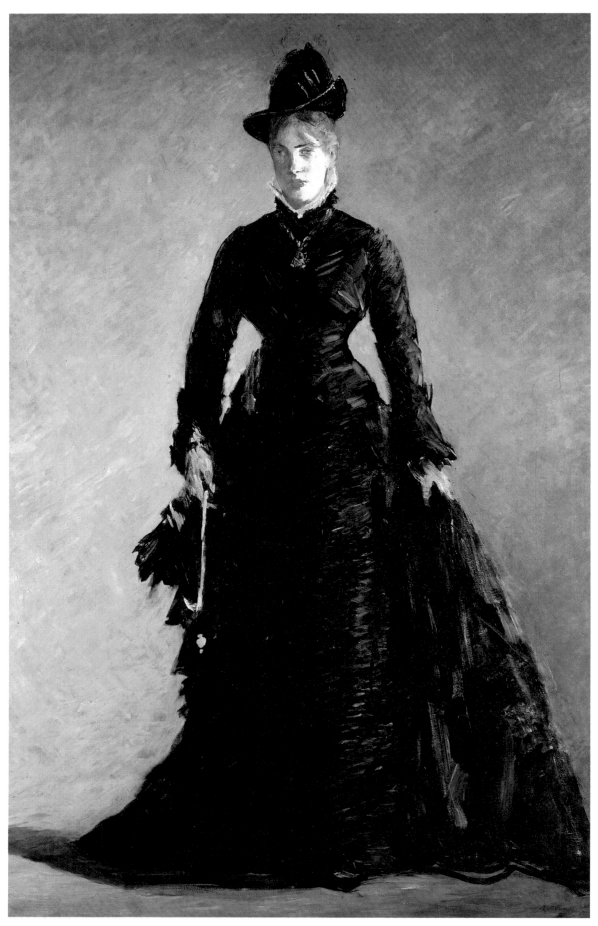

170   THE PARISIENNE / STUDY OF ELLEN ANDRÉE, 1874–5

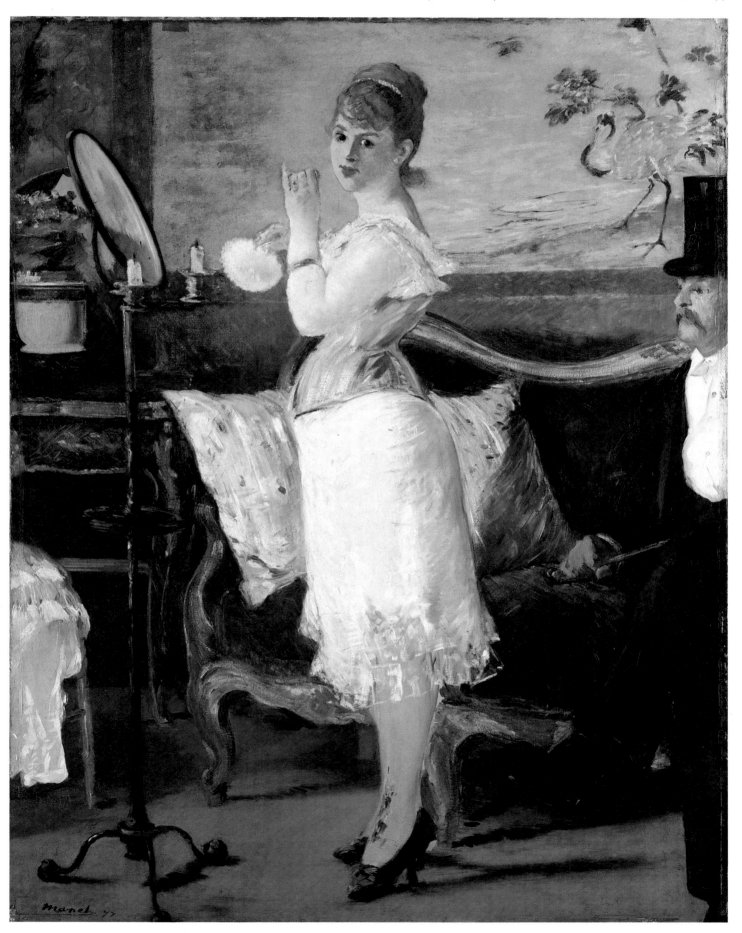

172   BEFORE THE MIRROR, c.1876–9

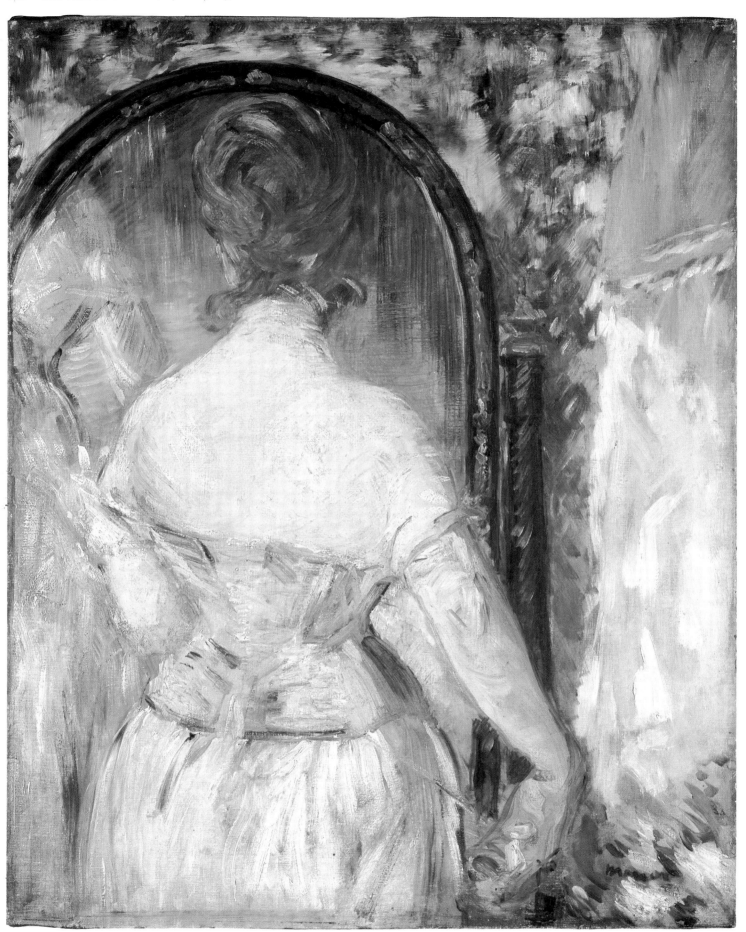

173   LA TOILETTE (WOMAN AT HER TOILET), c.1876–9

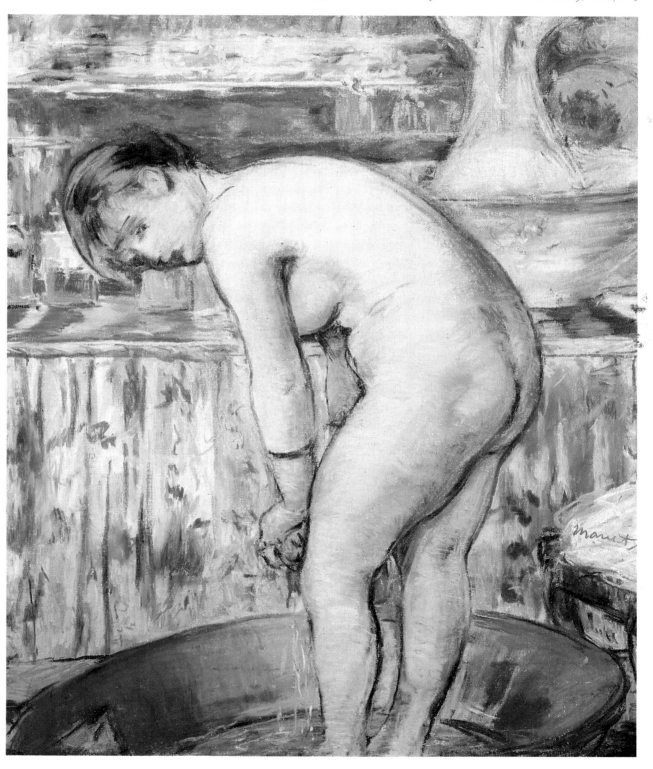

Parisian entertainments

174   THE SKATING RINK, 1877

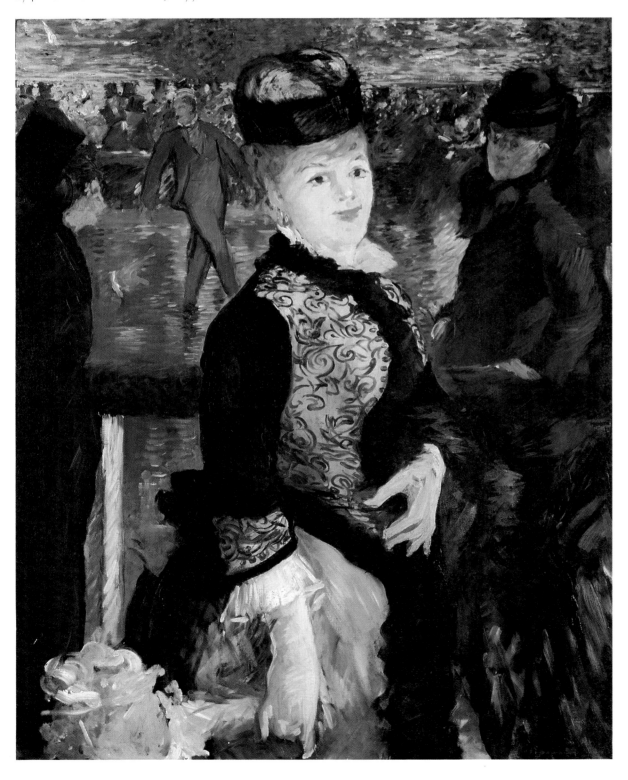

175   PORTRAIT OF FAURE IN THE ROLE OF HAMLET AT THE OPERA, 1877

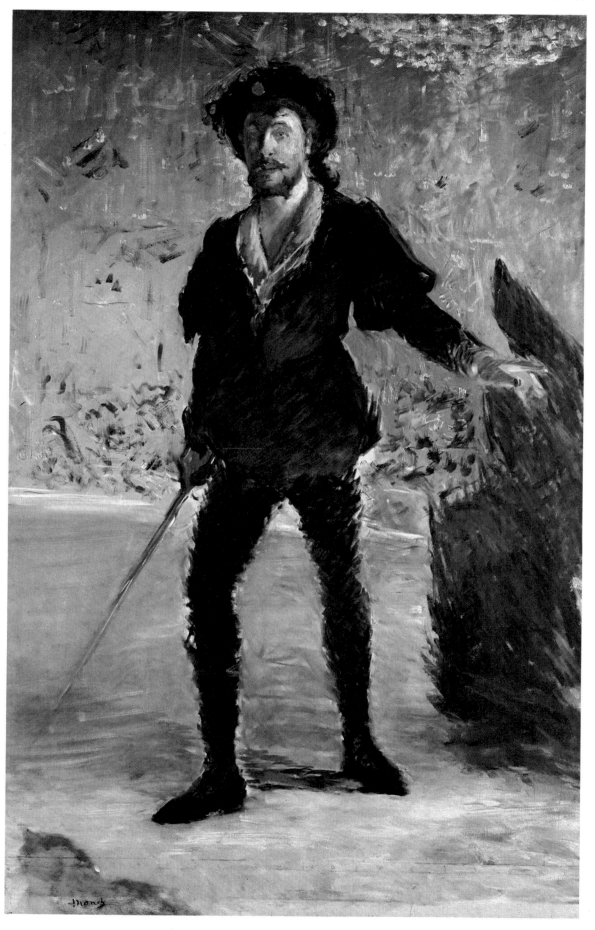

Visit to Montgeron, 1876

176 ERNEST HOSCHEDÉ AND HIS DAUGHTER MARTHE AT MONTGERON, 1876

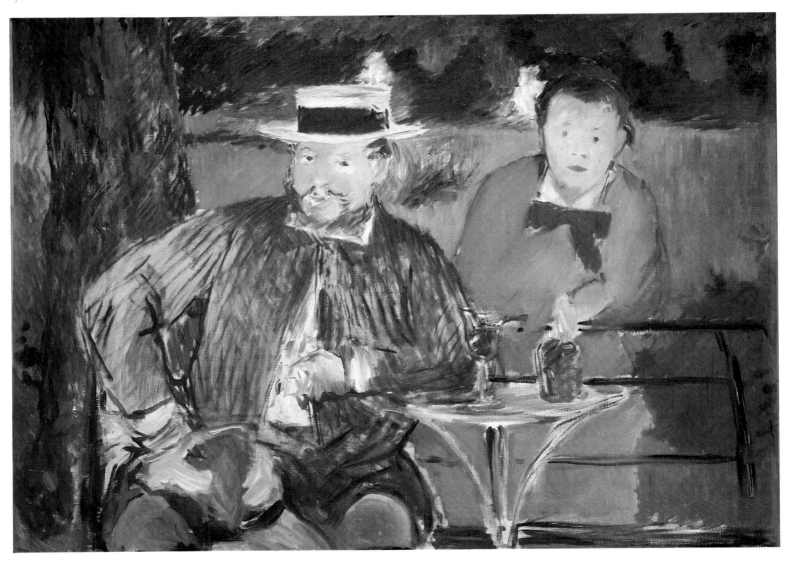

177 CAROLUS DURAN AT MONTGERON, 1876

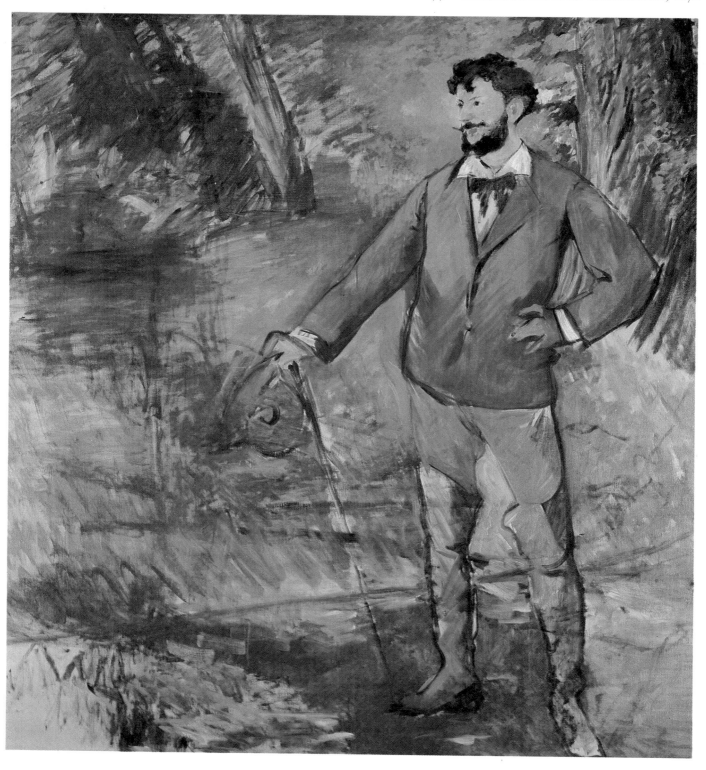

The view from Manet's studio, summer 1878

178 THE RUE MOSNIER WITH PAVERS, 1878

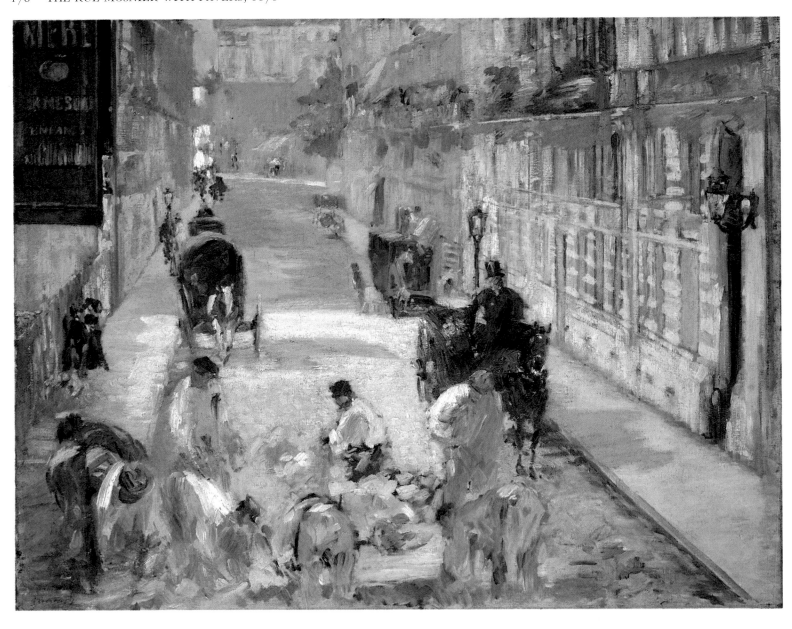

179   THE RUE MOSNIER, 1878

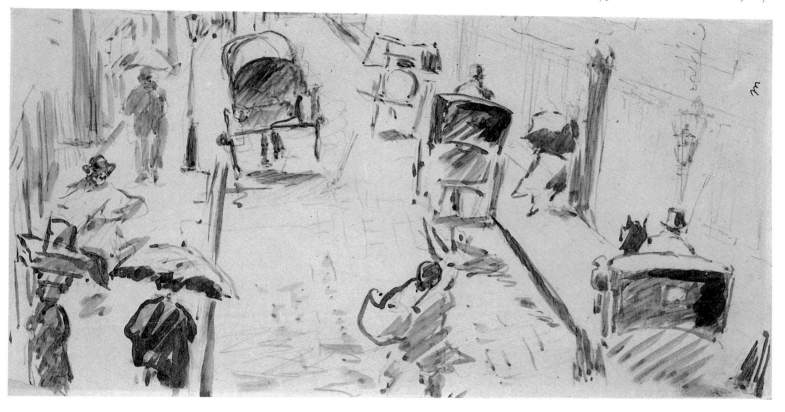

No Fête for the poor, 1878

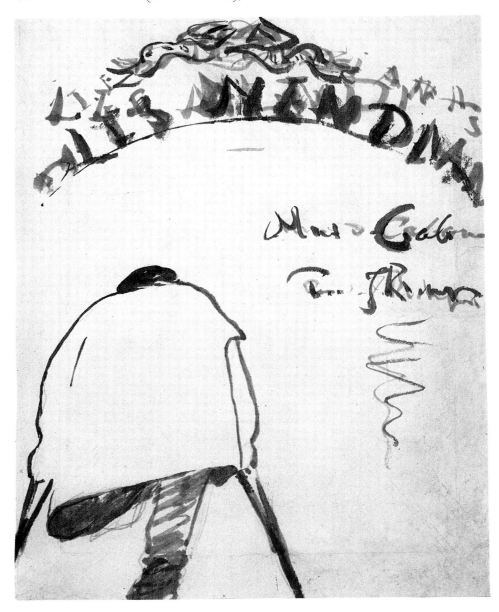

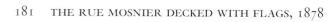

181   THE RUE MOSNIER DECKED WITH FLAGS, 1878

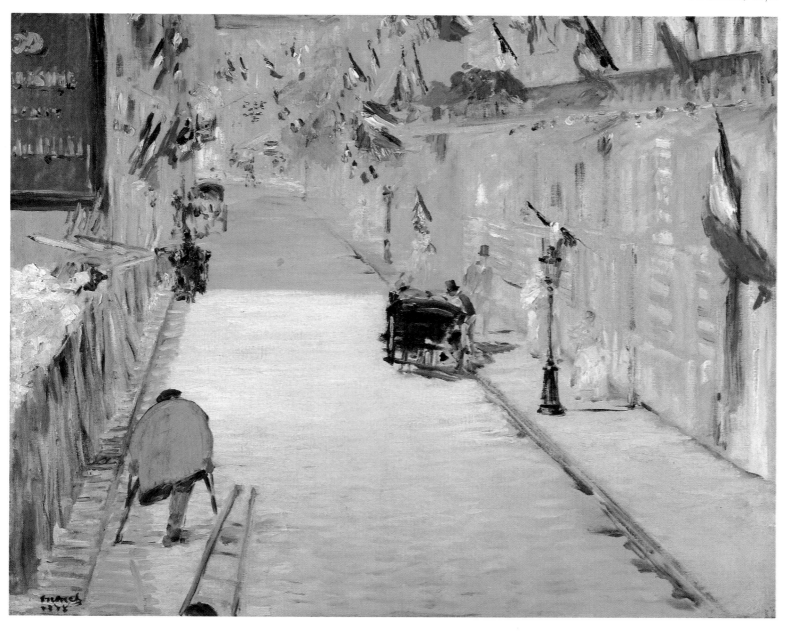

City scenes

182 VIEW FROM THE PLACE CLICHY, c.1878

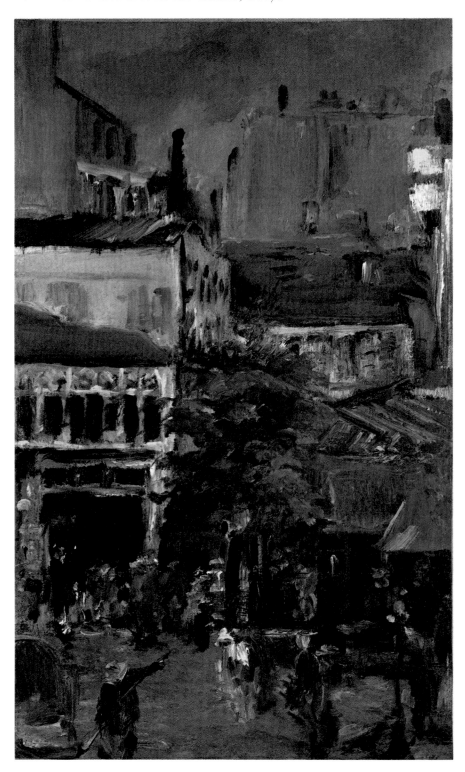

183 THE TAVERN / AT THE BARRIÈRE DE CLICHY, c.1878

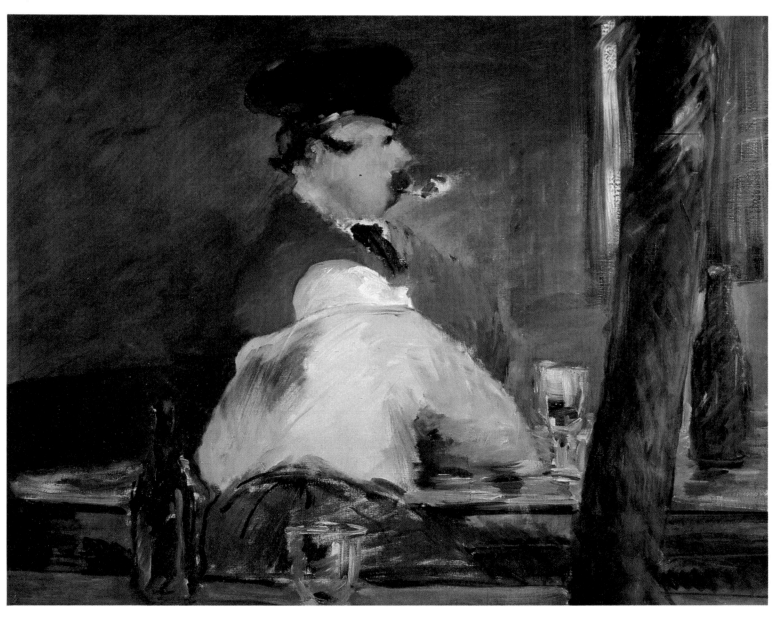

184   WOMAN WRITING, c.1878

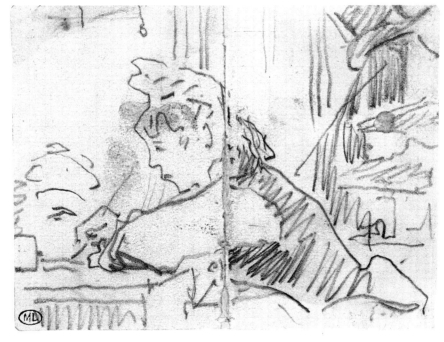

185   MAN WRITING IN A CAFÉ / 'CHEZ TORTONI', C.1878

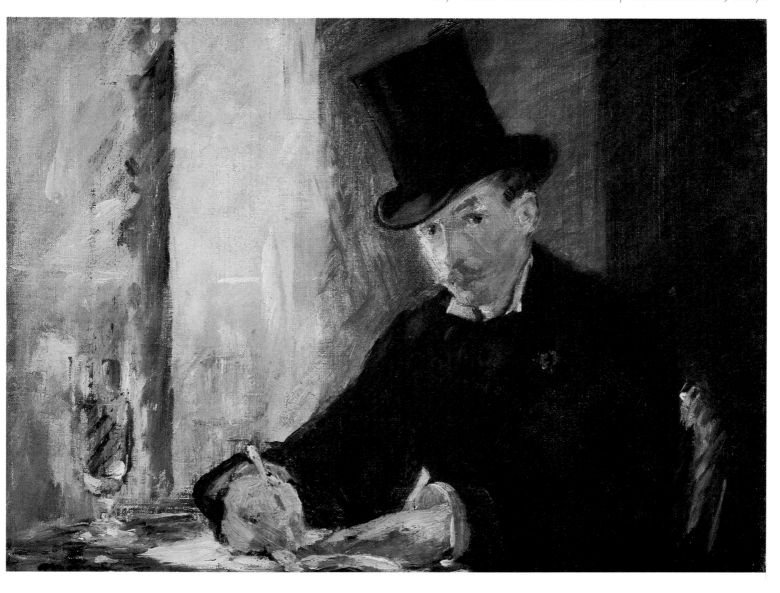

Café scenes

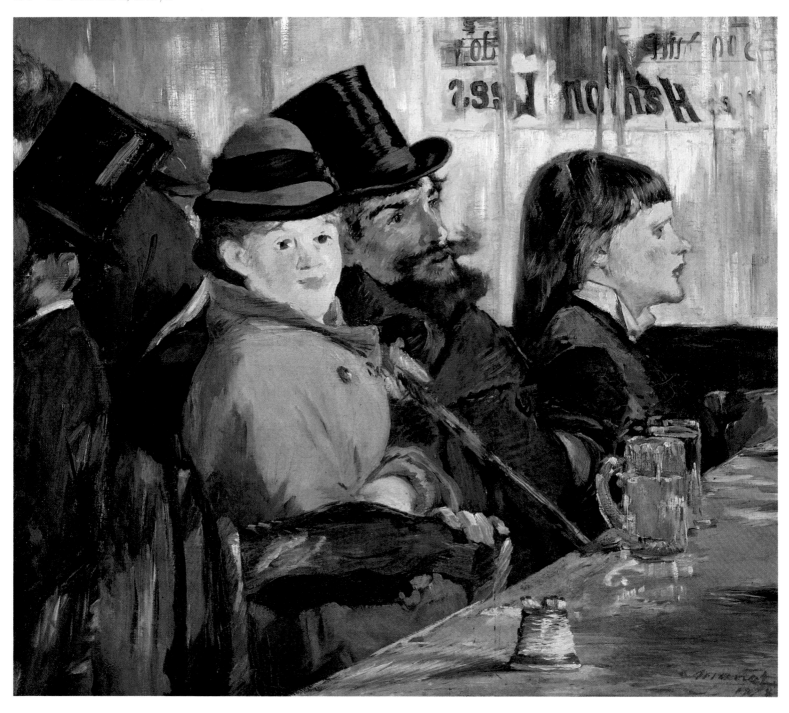

187   CORNER OF A CAFÉ-CONCERT, 1878–80 / d.187[8?]

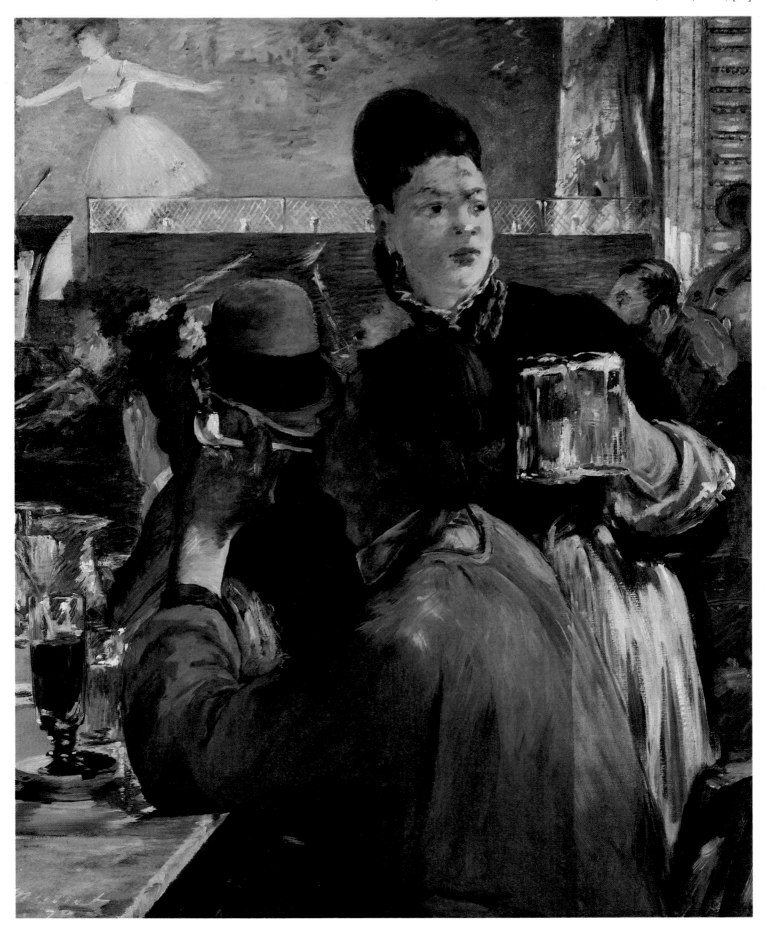

Café scenes

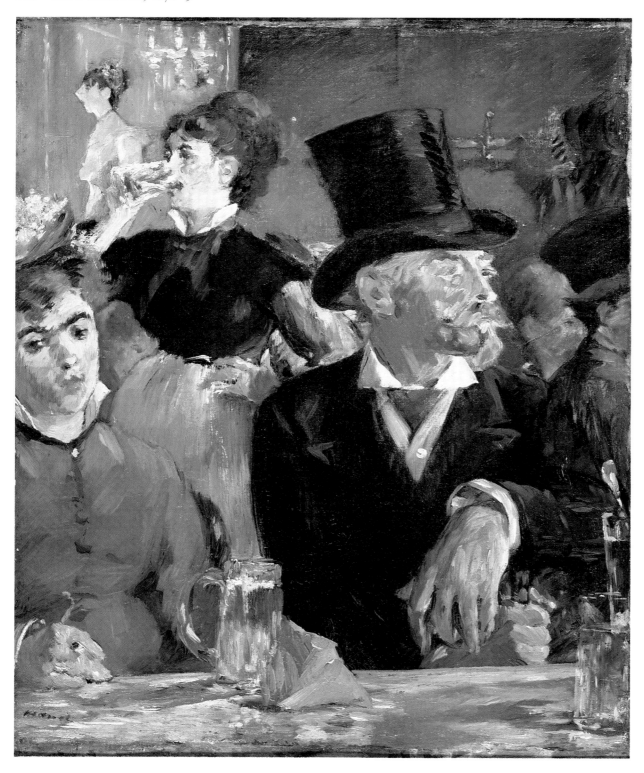

189 THE BEER DRINKERS, c.1878–9

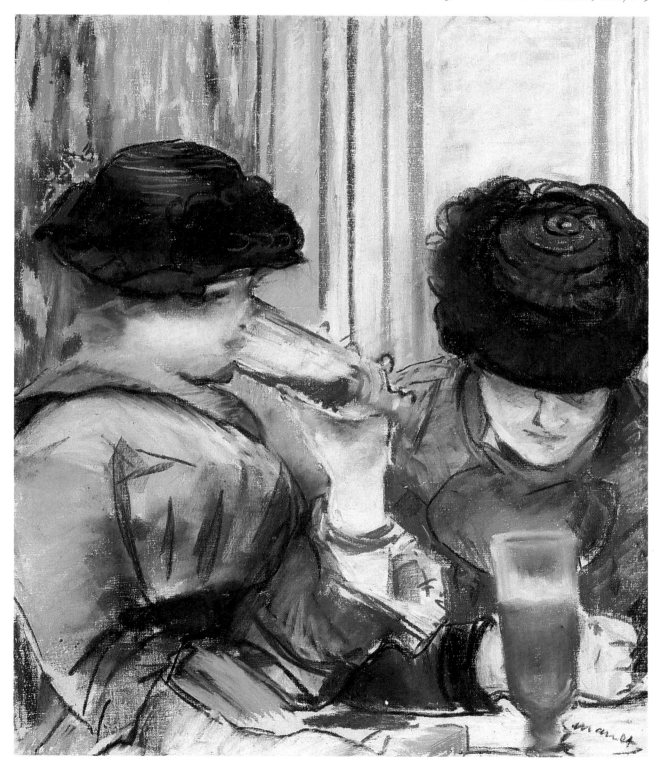

Café scenes

190   A CAFÉ ON THE PLACE DU THÉÂTRE FRANÇAIS, c.1876–8

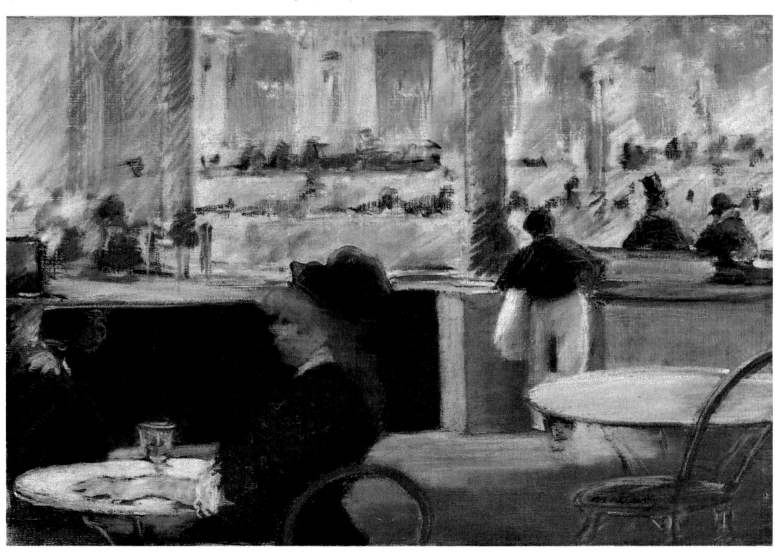

191   LA PRUNE (THE PLUM BRANDY), c.1876–8

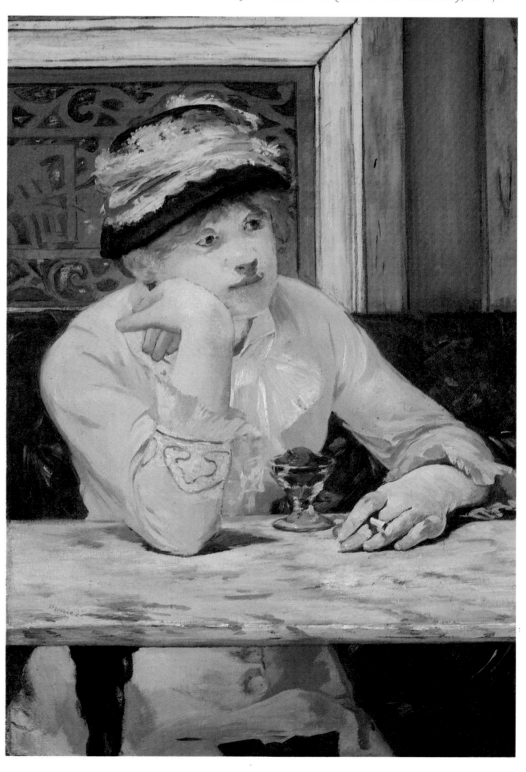

In the spring of 1880 the editor of the fashionable magazine La Vie moderne *invited Manet to provide the first one-man exhibition to be held in its galleries on the boulevard des Italiens. Manet assembled the best of his recent works, borrowing a pastel portrait from Mme Zola (192) to whom he apologized for not making the request in person since he was no longer allowed to climb stairs. He put together a dazzling show of twenty-five paintings and pastels (193), including the* Skating Rink *(174) and many of his recent café scenes, the study of Monet in his studio boat (161) from 1874, portraits and several intimate studies of women. The following month Manet's portrait of Antonin Proust (212) was shown at the Salon, together with a scene of a couple flirting in a well-known restaurant garden (208). Remarks to Proust about the religious connotations of the portrait and his desire to paint a crucifixion suggest sombre intimations of mortality and add poignancy to his lovers in a garden.*

Manet's condition was deteriorating fast and giving cause for serious concern. His doctor had prescribed hydrotherapy in a Paris clinic, and he also spent nearly half the year – five long months from the beginning of June until early November – at Bellevue to the west of Paris, following a similar course of treatment, though in much less comfortable circumstances. Proust confused the dates, placing Manet's stay at Bellevue in 1882, while Tabarant stated without proof that Manet was already there in 1879, returning the following year. However, the many dated letters sent from a rented villa at 41 route des Gardes at Bellevue in the summer of 1880 suggest that this stay there in 1880 was the first. With bad weather to prevent him working and bored away from Paris, Manet amused himself by writing to his friends, and soon took to decorating his missives with ink or watercolour sketches (196–8, 214, 215). The self-styled 'lonely exile' wrote letters, many of them to Mlle Isabelle Lemonnier (210), that are witty, tender or plaintive; he threatens or cajoles by turns, soliciting replies and visits, looking forward to the diversion of the 14 July fête, which he celebrates both for the fête nationale and for the amnesty, playing a fugue and variations on Mme Guillemet's pretty boots and shoes (215) and planning to paint her young sister Marguerite. His friends come and go during the holiday season; Mlle Lemonnier is pictured in a bathing suit (197) and interrogated at Luc-sur-mer. He drums up support for exhibition plans and describes to several correspondents the portrait he was painting that September of Emilie Ambre (226), the prima donna *opera singer who owned a house nearby and had toured the* Execution of Maximilian *(96) in America the previous year. Besides the dated or datable letters a certain rhythm can be imposed on the remainder, although the precise dates of, for example, Mlle Lemonnier's illness, her move to a new apartment and visit to Luc-sur-mer, or of Henri and Eva Guérard's holiday at Honfleur, remain uncertain.*

The amnesty of 14 July 1880, to which one of Manet's illustrated letters refers, enabled those who had supported the Paris Commune to return to France. Among them was the radical politician and journalist Henri Rochefort, who had been deported to a penal colony in New Caledonia. After a sensational escape in 1874 he had settled in Geneva, and was now able to make a triumphal return to Paris. Manet decided to paint Rochefort's portrait and to recreate the scene of his escape as a dramatic modern history painting for the Salon of 1881. Rochefort gave him details of the escape of which Manet painted two versions (225), but in the end it was the portrait (224) that he sent to the Salon. It was shown there with a very large portrait study of *Eugène Pertuiset*, and although the works were not to the jury's taste on political or aesthetic grounds, Manet was at long last awarded a medal which put him hors concours *in respect of future Salons.* Pertuiset, a celebrated lion hunter, was a friend and patron of Manet in his later years and acquired many of his still-life pictures of fruit, flowers and a splendid ham *(221)*. Manet made a drawing of the portrait *(201)* for reproduction in a review of the Salon in the journal L'Art.

Following his relative success at the Salon, Manet again left Paris to spend several months in the country, this time at Versailles. He probably went there in June or early July, and on 30 July commented gloomily on his health in a letter to Mallarmé. He told Eva Gonzalès on 23 September, 'it's been raining here for a good month and a half', and looked forward to being back in Paris at the beginning of October. His ill-health and the unfavourable weather left him inactive and depressed. He was finally persuaded to do some drawings to illustrate Mallarmé's translation of the Poems of Edgar Poe *(203, 204)*, but painted little more than a view of his garden *(217)*, which he described as 'quite the most hideous of gardens', and some still-life studies. He dreamed, however, of painting far more inspiring subjects, referring to his ride on a locomotive on the Versailles line beside the train driver and fireman whom he called 'the real heroes of our time', and hoping for good weather in Paris in October so that he could start a painting for the next Salon.

In November Antonin Proust was nominated Minister of Fine Arts in Léon Gambetta's short-lived government, and Manet was immediately made a chevalier of the Legion of Honour, in spite of protests from the President of the Republic. The award delighted Manet but left him bitter about the 'twenty lost years' that he might have been spared if official encouragment and recognition had come earlier. In spite of ill-health he was able to complete A Bar at the Folies-Bergère *(288)* for the Salon of 1882, as well as a study of the actress Jeanne Demarsy as Spring *(229)*. They were his final triumph. Asked to reproduce both of them, he made a drawing of Spring but had trouble in completing to his satisfaction an etching of his picture *(205)*.

For the third year running Manet spent the summer months from July to the end of September in the Paris suburbs, this time at Rueil. The papers began to circulate rumours about his illness, to which he attempted to put a halt with a blatant lie. He announced to Méry Laurent and Mallarmé that he intended to stay at Rueil until the end of October but returned to Paris on 27 September, dating his will three days later. At Rueil he was able to paint a number of views of the house and garden *(232)* and sketch out a study of Bibi, Berthe Morisot's little daughter Julie *(231)*. Back in Paris, he struggled to lay in his canvases for the following year's Salon, but had to abandon them unfinished *(233, 234)*. His last written documents *(apart from an unverifiable letter said to date from after the operation on his leg, the following April)* are notes in his account book recording the repayment of several debts in January 1883 and sales of pictures, notably an important group of works to Faure and the belated payment by Proust for Jeanne or Spring *(229)*. The last item is dated 21 February. His family noted that his last picture, a vase of flowers *(238)*, was painted on 1 March. On 9 March Berthe Morisot wrote to her brother that she had seen Manet, desperately ill, at his home. The inexorable advance of gangrene led to amputation of the lower part of his left leg, and Manet died ten days later, on 30 April 1883.

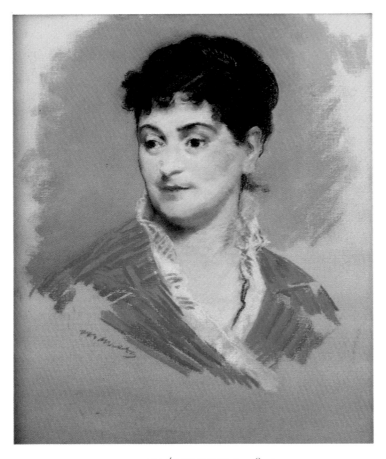

192   PORTRAIT OF MME ÉMILE ZOLA, 1879

Monday [before April 1880]

TO MME ÉMILE ZOLA   Dear Madame, Would you be kind enough to lend me your
pastel (*192*) and allow me to exhibit it along with others at *La Vie moderne*? Forgive me for not
coming to make this request myself but I am not allowed to climb stairs.

My regards to Zola and my best respects to you, Madame,   E. MANET

*

[March–April? 1880]

TO ÉMILE BERGERAT   I think my friend Fantin would be prepared to do a drawing
after his portrait of me [for *La Vie moderne*] – Do ask him. I will send him a photograph of the
portrait, since I don't think he has a print of it, and a word in support of your request.

E. MANET

*

[April–May? 1880]

Bellio has sent someone round here to pay for the pastel
which he bought for 500 francs. I'm sending you 75 francs on this amount.

E. MANET

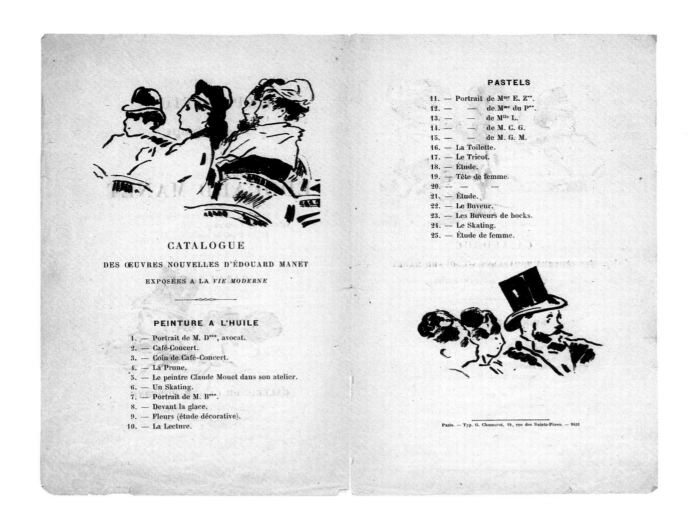

193 CATALOGUE
OF RECENT WORKS BY EDOUARD MANET
EXHIBITED AT *LA VIE MODERNE*
APRIL 1880

OIL PAINTINGS

1. Portrait of M. D[ejouy], lawyer
2. Café-Concert (*188*)
3. Corner of a Café-Concert (*187*)
4. The Plum Brandy (*191*)
5. The artist Claude Monet in his studio (*161*)
6. A Skating Rink (*174*)
7. Portrait of M. B[run]
8. Before the mirror (*172*)
9. Flowers (decorative study)
10. Reading (*112?*)

PASTELS

11. Portrait of Mme E. Z[ola] (*192*)
12. — of Mme du P[aty] (*209*)
13. — of Mlle L[emonnier] (*210*)
14. — of M. C. G[uys]
15. — of M. G. M[oore] (*137*)
16. La Toilette (*173?*)
17. Knitting
18. Study
19. Head of a woman
20. — —
21. Study
22. The Drinker
23. The Beer Drinkers (*189*)
24. The Skating Rink
25. Study of a woman

*

[After 8 May? 1880]

To Émile Bergerat

I haven't had the drawing [of *Café-concert* (*188*)] back from *La Vie moderne*, but I can do another. If it's for you it's *free* – if it's for someone else, three hundred francs.

E. Manet

RECORDED BY ANTONIN PROUST   [On Proust's portrait (*212*)]   It needs a frame . . . without a frame, the painting loses one hundred per cent. Well, we've got it this time; what a suggestion of depth in the background! I'll finish it tomorrow. There's only the barest indication of the hand in the glove, but just two or three brushstrokes will be enough to suggest it.

[On the painting of *Chez le père Lathuile* (*208*)]   Look at that . . . I'm going to have a really good Salon next year, a really effective Salon. I hoped Ellen Andrée would pose for the woman in the Père Lathuile picture. We did actually start it. And then she stopped coming. I hope those navel-worshippers [the Salon jury] won't throw me out or, if they let me in, that they don't hoist me up to the ceiling!

*

[1879–80]

RECORDED BY LOUIS GAUTHIER-LATHUILE   [To M. Lathuile Senior on seeing his son in uniform] That gives me an idea. I'll paint your son as a Dragoon.

[To Louis Gauthier-Lathuile, on posing with Ellen Andrée for *Chez le père Lathuile* (*208*)] I'll get you to pose together . . . You, you're a volunteer flirting with a pretty woman. Place yourselves like this and like that and chat with each other while I'm working. . . .

[On posing with Mlle Judith French]   Take off your tunic . . . Put on my jacket! . . .

*

[May 1880]

TO ANTONIN PROUST   Your portrait (*212*) has been at the Salon for three weeks now, my dear Proust, unflatteringly displayed on a slanting panel near a door and getting a still more unflattering reception. But it's my lot to be abused and I take it philosophically. No one realizes, though . . . how difficult it is to place a figure on canvas and concentrate all the attention on this single figure without losing its lively, full-blooded character. Compared with that, it's child's play to bring off two figures whose attraction lies in their contrasting personalities. Oh yes, the portrait in a hat, in which everything is blue, so they said! Well, I'm ready for them. I myself won't be there to see it. But when I'm gone they'll recognize the rightness of my vision and my ideas. Your portrait is an absolutely honest work. I can remember as if it were yesterday the quick way I sketched in the glove belonging to the bare hand. At that very moment you said, 'Please, not another brushstroke', and I felt we were in such perfect agreement that I couldn't resist the impulse to embrace you. Well! I hope no one takes it into his head later on to stick the portrait in a public collection! I've always been horrified by the mania for piling up works of art without leaving any space between the frames, as if they were the latest fancy goods on the shelves of a fashionable shop. But time will tell. It's in the lap of the gods.

ED. MANET

RECORDED BY ANTONIN PROUST   There's one thing I've always wanted to do. I would like to paint a Crucifixion. You're the only one who could pose for my interpretation of the subject. I was thinking about it the whole time I was painting your portrait (*212*). It was an obsession. I painted you as Christ wearing a hat, in your frock coat with a rose in the buttonhole – as Christ on his way to visit Mary Magdalene. But Christ on the cross. What a symbol! Even if you searched for ever, you would never find anything to equal it. Minerva is a fine subject, Venus too. But the heroic image and the image of love must for ever be surpassed by the image of sorrow. It lies at the root of the whole human condition and is its poetry.

But that's enough now . . . I'm getting morbid. It's Siredey's fault; doctors always remind me of undertakers. Though I feel a lot better this evening.

*

Saturday [29 (postmark 30) May 1880]

TO STÉPHANE MALLARMÉ   I'm leaving for Bellevue tomorrow – and won't have seen you to say goodbye. I hope you are out of bed now and if I haven't been to see you, you know it's because I'm not allowed to climb stairs. Anyway, let's wish each other good health and good luck.

E. MANET

*

[1880]

RECORDED BY ANTONIN PROUST   [On walking at Bellevue]   It would be easier for me to follow the slope down than to climb . . . but it's better to clamber up than go tumbling down. Let's go on to the terrace at Meudon.

[On meeting a little girl selling flowers]   You can't imagine how infuriating it is to be in this state. If I were well, I'd have raced back home to fetch my paintbox.

. . . How strange . . . the contrast between the awkwardness of a child and the self-assurance of a young girl. But not to have the strength to convey it now. Still, it's a vision that has made me forget my illness for a moment. That's something.

*

41 route des Gardes, Bellevue [June? 1880]

TO MME MÉRY LAURENT   I'm doing penance, my dear Méry, as never before in all my life. Still, if the end result is good, there'll be no regrets. I find the water treatment here absolute torture, and they don't make one nearly as comfortable as at Béni-Barde's [clinic in Paris]. One of these days I'll go for a ride. I hope, my dear Méry, that you will write and send me your news. Don't leave the Barroil business [the exchange sale of the *Café* scenes (*186, 187*)] hanging fire because I really need the money. Everything is more expensive here than in Paris and there is no reduced rate for the water treatment. I'm waiting impatiently for fine weather so that I can start work.

Regards, with love, ED. MANET

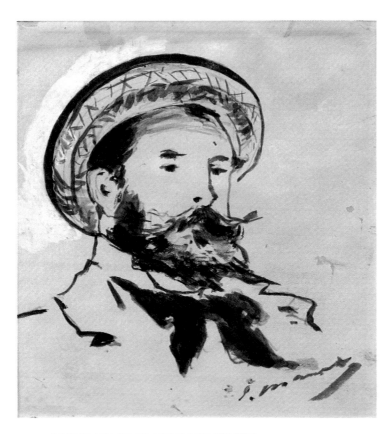

194   PORTRAIT OF CLAUDE MONET FOR
HIS EXHIBITION CATALOGUE, 1880

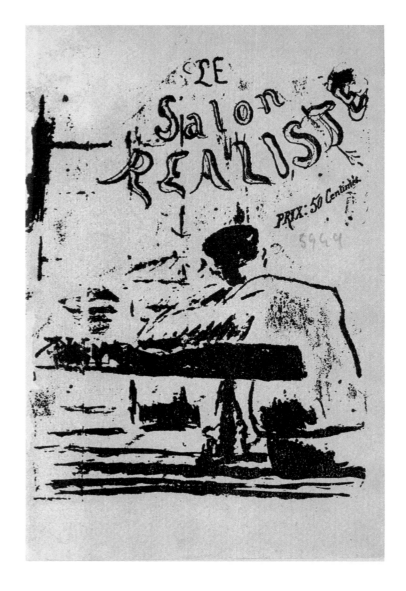

195   COVER OF LE SALON RÉALISTE, 1880

Bellevue [before 7 June 1880]

TO THÉODORE DURET   I've just received the little Monet booklet [see *(194)*] – I
hope the public launch goes well and wish you luck with it. I'll probably come to Paris one of
these days to see Taipert at *La Vie moderne*.

I think the fresh air is already making me feel better and after gulping it down for three or
four months I hope to be fighting fit.

E. MANET

*

Bellevue [19 June 1880 postmark]

TO STÉPHANE MALLARMÉ   It's a long time since I had any news from you so get your
pen at once and tell me what's going on in your part of the world.

Bellevue and its excellent air are doing me good and I hope to improve after three or four
months here. To tell the truth, I'd put up with anything to get my health back. The bad
weather has so far prevented me from getting down to serious work and I'm looking forward
impatiently to starting something substantial.

E. MANET

[Bellevue,] Wednesday [23 June 1880 postmark]

I was stunned, my dear Mallarmé, when your letter came yesterday – so all the time I was thinking enviously of you trotting off to your college late as usual, you were in fact ill in bed. Anyway, you're convalescing now, though this awful weather doesn't help one to recover – I'm longing for some lasting sunshine.

Have you read Zola's articles in *Le Voltaire* on 'Naturalism at the Salon'? If so, let me know what you think. If you don't have them, I'll send them and you can tell me what impression they have made on you and what impression you think they might make on the public.

E. MANET

*

Bellevue [after 23 June? 1880]

TO THÉODORE DURET

It seems I was mistaken but I didn't judge Zola's article from a personal point of view and it seemed to me a bit too eclectic. We are so much in need of support that I thought a little radicalism would not have been out of place.

Please tell me what you think, and throw my first letter in the fire. I've just had a letter about all this from someone in whose opinion I have the greatest confidence and who is sorry that the article was not more widely noticed.

E. MANET

*

[Bellevue, Summer 1880]

TO A FRIEND IN BRUSSELS

. . . I've decided to send my Salon picture (*208*) to Ghent; just as a matter of form. I don't expect any more success there than in Paris, because people behave like sheep the world over. . . .

*

Bellevue [Summer 1880]

TO LOUIS MARTINET

Done for 600 francs, times are hard, please give the money to my brother-in-law who will bring you this note.

E. MANET

*

41 route des Gardes, Bellevue [Summer 1880]

TO ZACHARIE ASTRUC

Tell me what you're up to, is your health all right now? It would do me good to have a chat with you. Still, I'm much better and hope my stay here will do me a world of good. I'm living here like a shellfish. Tell me what's going on.

E. MANET

41 route des Gardes, Bellevue, Monday [5 July 1880]

TO ZACHARIE ASTRUC   You know, my dear Zacharie, how much I love my old friends and how much I care about everything that concerns them. So I was delighted to get your letter with all its information about your work and your expectations.

As you so rightly say, time is a great healer – and I am putting a good deal of trust in it. I'm living like a shellfish in the sun, when there is any, and as much as possible in the open air, but when all's said and done the countryside only has charms for those who are not obliged to stay there.

Go and see [Antonin] Proust; he knows how much I admire your mind and your outstanding talent, but a recommendation does not necessarily secure a job on a paper – you must know it's like a shop where they stock whatever goods they think will please the customers; but go and chat him up, you've got a silver tongue.

Hoschedé came to lunch in Bellevue yesterday, he is hope incarnate – he deserves to succeed and actually tries his best, but he started by getting a Belgian to do his first *Paris fashion* plate. Will he never learn?

. . . good luck and good health, my dear Zacharie, that's still the main thing.

ED. MANET

*

Bellevue, 7 July [1880]

TO MME EVA GUÉRARD-GONZALÈS   Dear Madame, the papers have been singing your praises every day, and since you have occasionally asked my advice, I should like to share in the rejoicing. It seems that the well-earned success you have been enjoying for some time has been consolidated this year [with her pastel in the Salon]. What a pity you didn't identify yourself as a pupil of some Bonnat or Cabanel [instead of 'MM. Chaplin and Manet'], you've shown too much courage and that, like virtue, usually goes unrewarded.

Léon tells me you have started work, have you found some pretty models? Our one and only etcher [her husband, Henri Guérard] is the one for that – he knows them all and how to get hold of them.

I hope you will come and see us again at Bellevue when the [14 July] fête is on, we'll at least have some entertainment to offer. . . .

ED. MANET

*

Bellevue, 9 July [1880]

TO MLLE ISABELLE LEMONNIER   Just a quick 'good morning', I wish the morning post would bring me one every day. I fear you are not as fond of your friends as I am. Léon is counting on you for the fête. Take care not to tire yourself out with the preparations for your move.

M

*

41 route des Gardes, Bellevue, 13 July [1880]

TO THÉODORE DURET? My dear friend, You took someone to my studio recently. Isn't there some way of turning that to financial advantage? It would be more than welcome at the moment and seeing that I can't do anything for myself I would appreciate it if my friends could find buyers for my work. I've sold enough pictures for other people. It would be just the right moment to do the same for me. I'm counting on you and Luquet.

ED. MANET

*

Bellevue, Sunday morning [11 or 18 July 1880]

TO MLLE ISABELLE LEMONNIER It's no good at all from memory – if only I had the model [sketch of Isabelle (196)] in front of me. Post the letters you write me like the last one, so I get them in the morning. Now that I have your permission, I shall write to you often, it gives me pleasure. Yesterday we had a visit from Mad. Loubens and we're expecting Mme Guillemet some time today.

This Zizi [sketch of Mme Manet's cat] is no good, I'll do you a better one next time. And send me your photograph so I can be sure of getting a better likeness when I sketch you.

EM

196 LETTER TO ISABELLE LEMONNIER, 11 or 18 July 1880

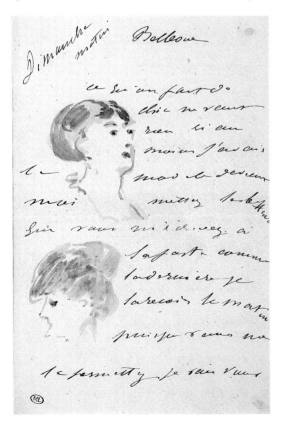

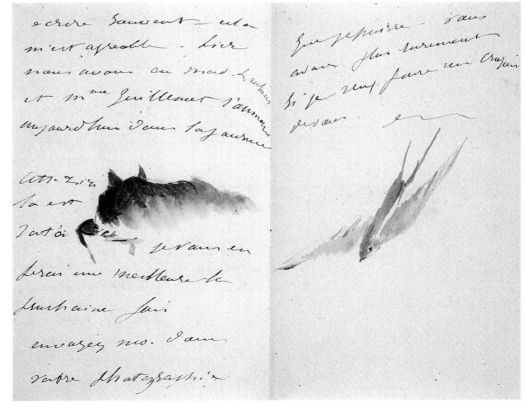

Bellevue [before 14 July 1880]

To Mlle Marguerite   It's all arranged, dear Mademoiselle, my mother asks me to say that we are counting on you while your brother-in-law is at Saint-Aubin. Bring your needle-work and the light-coloured summer dress you told me about, and if you have a pretty garden hat don't leave it behind [see (*216*)]. The Bellevue fête will take place while you're here.

E. Manet

*

Bellevue [before 14 July 1880]

To Mlle Isabelle Lemonnier   I'm sure you're dreaming Banners and storming of the Bastille – It seems we're very well placed to see the fireworks.

A Sunday visit from the Guillemets, the young wife has asked me to make her peace with you, the [enclosed] note is just a formality of course, she's counting on your bringing her lots of customers – so much for that.

Don't let devotion to the Republic allow you to wear yourself out at the fête, it's just as important to save your strength as to exert yourself for *la Patrie*. Let me know if your corsage was returned in good condition, and send me whatever news there is.

EM

*

Bellevue, 14 July 1880

To an Unknown Correspondent   Long live the Republic   Ed. Manet

*

Bellevue, 14 July 1880

To Mlle Isabelle Lemonnier   Long live the amnesty   Ed. Manet

I shan't write any more – you never answer.

*

Bellevue [after 14 July 1880]

I'm waiting, dear mademoiselle, for you account of the fête – you were seen taking a walk that evening – with whom? Your fireworks and the illumination of your garden were written up in the papers, let me know something of what was said and what you did. I can't understand your silence.

EM

*

Bellevue, Tuesday [July–August? 1880]

What's become of you, it must be your move that keeps you from thinking of your friends. We'll soon have news of you, won't we, or better still a visit.

E. Manet

Bellevue, Thursday [July–August? 1880]

TO MME JULES GUILLEMET   Nonsense if you will, dear Madame, but such sweet
nonsense [sketches of her skirts and boots (*215*)] which enables me to spend my time very
pleasantly. I'm getting better and better, and a letter from you now and then would help my
cure along – so don't be too economical with them.

I haven't seen Mlle L[emonnier], her mother is very ill and she is moving. Still, I'm surprised
to have had no news from her. I hope you won't find my letters a bore, you'll tell me, won't
you, and send me your news soon . . .

E. MANET

*

Bellevue [July–August? 1880]

TO MLLE ISABELLE LEMONNIER   You're really not being very nice to us – you are either very
busy or very unkind. But one hasn't the heart to hold it against you

M

*

41 route des Gardes, Bellevue, Tuesday [July–August 1880]

TO MME GEORGES CHARPENTIER   We heard yesterday evening that Mlle Isabelle is ill and
there are fears she may have an eruptive fever. Knowing our concern and affection for her,
please send news of her as soon as possible and reassure the lonely Bellevue exiles.

ED. MANET

*

41 route des Gardes, Bellevue, Friday [July–August 1880]

TO GEORGES CHARPENTIER   Could you arrange to send me C.O.D. the 4 or 5 volumes of
the Goncourts on the 18th century, in the Charpentier edition.

I'm aware of all your troubles with illness. My regards to you and Mme Charpentier.

ED. MANET

*

Bellevue, Thursday [July–August 1880]

TO MLLE ISABELLE LEMONNIER   Dear little mademoiselle, everything seems to be happening
to you at once; Léon gave us news of you last night. Don't tire yourself too much, you're a
convalescent. I *don't want* Charpentier to send me the books *I've got them*.

Regards, I'd give you a kiss if I dared, EM

*

Bellevue, Sunday [25 July 1880]

TO MME JULES GUILLEMET   I won't be able to go to Paris tomorrow. Something that
required my presence has been put off until early August and they won't give me leave to run
off without an excuse. O liberty! thou art but a word. *It will be no great loss to you*, blissfully
busy as you are with all the preparations for your departure. Enjoy yourselves, and don't forget
the lonely Bellevue exiles, tell Jules not to lose track of the Pigeonnier business.

E. MANET

*

Bellevue [August 1880]

TO MLLE ISABELLE LEMONNIER [at Luc-sur-mer]   It's not my fault if the peaches [sketched] in Bellevue are
unattractive, even the prettiest girl can only give what she's got. Tell me what's happening on
the beach at Luc and in the surrounding country, nothing shocks me, everything amuses me.
It's a long while since we saw Mme L[oubens?], just the odd visitor to Bellevue and that's all.
I've been working a little and if it weren't for the almost constantly thundery weather, which
doesn't suit me, I'd be feeling all right.
    You're probably getting in some bathing (*197*), tell me about all that and more.
    Regards to Madame Charpentier, to you and our dear publisher . . .

ED. MANET

*

Bellevue [August 1880]

TO NADAR   Thanks for thinking of me, dear Nadar, *L'Hôtel des
Coquecigrues* has arrived and finds me recuperating in the country at Bellevue. I read it through
from cover to cover, which tells how much I enjoyed it.
    It's plum time and I'm sending you a few [sketched] from my garden.

ED. MANET

*

Bellevue, 20 August [1880]

TO ANTONIN PROUST   Would you please recommend me warmly to M. Oudet, the
senator from the Doubs department. There's an exhibition in Besançon to which I'm sending
two rather important pictures, but if you don't have a senator or a deputy up your sleeve, you
can stuff yourself, to use a vulgar expression. M. Oudet looks after artistic affairs down there.
The Bellevue air is doing me a power of good and I'm making the most of it.

E. MANET

*

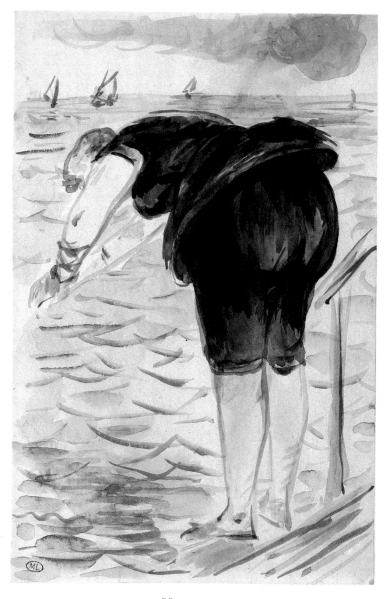

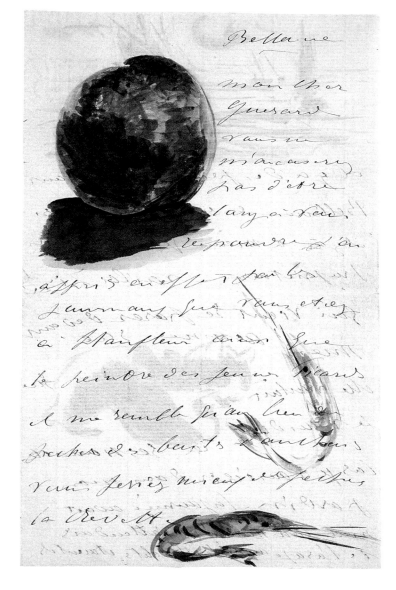

197   ISABELLE DIVING, 1880   198   LETTER TO HENRI GUÉRARD, SUMMER 1880

Bellevue [August–September 1880]

To Henri Guérard [at Honfleur]   You won't have to forgive me for being slow to reply. The
fact is, I've learnt from the papers that you have been seen in Honfleur with the painter of the
young Picards. It strikes me that you would be better off shrimping rather than fishing for tins
of anchovies (*198*).

There are painters everywhere, Bellevue is overrun with them too, some are even property
owners – now here's Zizi come to pose in front of me [sketch (*214*)] as if she wanted me to send
you news of her – you see, I'm writing to you in the garden. The day got off to a bad start,
I was expecting a storm and the easels were stored away.

Yesterday we had a visit from the Guillemets back from the seaside. I've begun painting the
young sister [Mlle Marguerite (*216*)] but don't know if I'll have time to finish.

My mother and my wife [sketches (*214*)] send the ladies their best wishes. Léon is still
making his daily trips and rather enjoys it, he sometimes brings me interesting news from Paris.
I don't know why I'm suddenly reminded of Desboutin [sketch, see (*168*)], perhaps because
I had a visit from Liardo recently.

. . . best regards, a letter from Madame Guérard would give me great pleasure,   E. Manet

Bellevue, September 1880

To Mme Méry Laurent   If I hadn't had news of you yesterday from a Béni-Bardeuse, I should think you had gone off to the East Indies or some such place, but there must be more going on in Paris than in Bellevue –

*

Bellevue [late September? 1880]

To Mlle Isabelle Lemonnier   If you are coming to see us as I very much hope, it would be better to come on a Sunday. I'm doing a portrait of my neighbour, Countess Emilie Ambre (*226*), and I leave every day after lunch for Les Montalais. It's true that she will be going to America on 8 October and we'll be staying here till the end of the month.

E. Manet

Bellevue [27 September 1880 postmark]

To Mme Eva Guérard-Gonzalès [at Honfleur]   I was hoping for a sketch both of you and by you, dear Madame Eva [sketch], and won't let you forget it. I've made rather a mess of your Henry [sketch] but neither of you will hold it against me. I could easily improve it by making it a better likeness. I see you're spending your time agreeably. As for me, I'm working again. At the moment I'm doing a portrait of Mlle Emilie Ambre (*226*), a landowning *prima donna* neighbour. I go and work on it every day because she's leaving for America on 8 October. We intend to stay on at Bellevue until the end of the month. I'm much better and am beginning to feel really hopeful.

With regards from all of us to all of you . . ., Ed. Manet

*

Bellevue [September? 1880]

To Mme Méry Laurent   It wouldn't be so bad if I could see the rue de Rome from my window but no, it's always that wretched Panthéon – what a thing to have to look at. This silence, my dear Méry, is it laziness? Even that would be better than indifference. Has the most sensitive of hearts succumbed to some new passion? Quickly, tell me the latest about the life I hold so dear. My health continues to improve, apart from occasional bouts of depression . . . True, the life I'm leading is not exactly varied. I don't even have much inclination to work and hope that will suddenly change.

It would be sweet of you to send a box of Evans [tooth] powder round to the concierge at the rue d'Amsterdam. My brother-in-law [Léon] will be going to collect something from the studio in the next few days and will be able to pick it up at the same time . . .

EM

*

Bellevue, 28 September [1880]

I really don't understand your letter, my dear Méry.
Extending my stay in Bellevue doesn't mean that my health is worse, on the contrary, I'm getting better and better but I expect October to be fine and I'm going to stay out in the fresh air. I should have lunched at Les Montalais yesterday with *la belle* Valtesse but the party had to be postponed since the lady of the manor at Ville d'Avray [Valtesse de la Bigne] already had someone coming to lunch with her.

E. MANET

*

Bellevue, 10 October 1880

TO MLLE MARTHE HOSCHEDÉ   Dear little mademoiselle Marthe, I for my part collect autographs of the people I like best, so you can imagine how welcome you letter is [see (*199*)].
I'll send you what you want when I'm back in Paris; I have only two letters here that are good enough for the album, I'll put them in an envelope for you.
We'll be at Bellevue till the end of October; the stay has done me so much good I'm sorry to be going back to town.
Give your mama my good wishes. I was unlucky enough to miss her by a quarter of an hour last week at *L'Art de la mode* where I called on its friendly director [Ernest Hoschedé] for news.

ED. MANET

*

Bellevue, 15 October [1880]

TO ÉMILE ZOLA [at Médan]   Thanks, my dear Zola, for sending your book.
The feathers have certainly been flying recently, and your holiday this year can hardly count as a rest. Still, you have broad shoulders and a ready pen.
The air of Bellevue has done me a world of good and I'm going to take advantage of it for another fortnight. But I'm afraid that naturalist painting is more out of favour than ever . . .

ED. MANET

*

Bellevue, 20 October [1880]

TO FÉLIX BRACQUEMOND [see (*200*)]   Let's put off the visit to [Edmond de] Goncourt if you don't mind, the weather is dreadful and I've got a cold. I'll come and see you one morning. I expect to be leaving Bellevue at the end of the month.

E. MANET

*

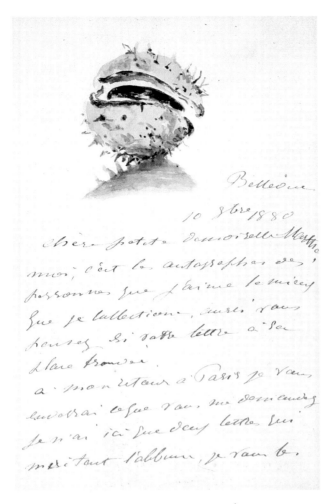

199   LETTER TO MARTHE HOSCHEDÉ,
       10 October 1880

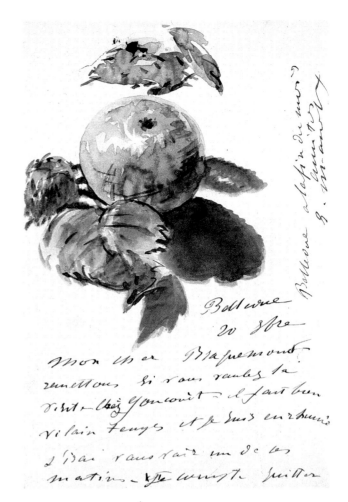

200   LETTER TO FÉLIX BRACQUEMOND,
       20 October 1880

Bellevue, 20 October [1880]

To Mlle Isabelle Lemonnier

You promised to invite yourself to lunch with us before our return – have you forgotten? Won't you afford us this pleasure? I know it's a lot to ask so late in the year. We'll be back on 3 November.

E. Manet

*

To Théodore Duret and   Paris, 22 November [1880]
James McNeill Whistler [in London]

My dear Duret,   Here is the letter for Whistler.
    I've been back in Paris since early this month, and am well enough to be thinking of doing a picture for the Salon. The picture will be entitled the *Escape* (*225*). When you're in Paris I'll hope to be able to say hello to you.

    My dear Whistler,   Since you are a great painter and my friend Théodore Duret is a great connoisseur, I am introducing him to you. He very much wants to tell you in person how much he admires your work – and you will soon see how good his judgment is.

Regards, Ed. Manet

Saturday [4 December 1880 postmark]

To Stéphane Mallarmé   I saw Rochefort (*224*) yesterday. The craft they used was a
whaleboat – the colour was dark grey – six people – two oars (*225*). I'm very anxious to see
you . . .

E. Manet

*

28 December [1880]

To Berthe Morisot   Don't be surprised at the arrival of a new type of easel
which is very useful for pastels. It's my modest New Year's gift.

Ed. Manet

*

[1880–81]

Recorded by Antonin Proust   [On being offered a chair at Mme Virot's hat shop]   I don't
need a chair . . . I'm not a cripple. . . .
How could she be so tactless? Trying to make me look like a helpless cripple in front of all
those women! Talking of women, I saw a really beautiful one on the Pont de l'Europe
yesterday. She had that typically Parisian way of walking, but with a bit of extra flair. I'll do
her from memory, more or less of course, some things stay engraved on my mind. For example,
I could etch a plate of the fête given by Gambetta at the Palais Bourbon.
[On doing a pastel of a woman from memory]   That's not right . . . It's just impossible to
do anything without a model . . . a landscape perhaps, but a figure from memory, never!
Speaking of figures, I'm going to do one when I've finished *Spring* (*229*). I'll paint Méry Laurent
as *Autumn* (*230*). Yes, she's agreed to sit for her portrait. I discussed it with her yesterday.
She's had a fur-trimmed coat made by Worth. And what a coat! It's fawn-brown with an old-
gold lining and I was in raptures over it . . . As I was leaving, I told Méry Laurent that when
her coat was worn out, she should let me have it. She promised she would. It'll make a
wonderful background for the things I'm planning to do.

*

Paris, 17 March [1881]

To Théodore Duret [in London]   . . . I'm sending the portraits of Rochefort (*224*) and
Pertuiset [see (*201*)] to the Salon. The *Rochefort* seems to be meeting with the sort of success
the *Bon bock* (*151*) had in its day. We'll have to wait for the Salon. Ephrussi, who often comes
to see me, has bought a pastel and a small picture – Deudon has also purchased a pastel. You
seem to be extending your stay in London and apparently you've made good use of your time
quite apart from your business activities.

Best wishes to Whistler and you, Ed. Manet

Monet must be doing reasonably well now because he brought me some money the other day.

[16 April 1881 postmark]

TO STÉPHANE MALLARMÉ   A new paper is being launched and I have been asked for names of friends. If you are interested in the book section, go and see Hoschedé or M. Oudart, at *L'Art de la mode*, not far from the Magasins de l'Eau de Vichy on the Boulevard Montmartre. Give them my card.

ED. MANET

*

77 rue d'Amsterdam, Thursday 21 April [1881]

TO THE EDITOR OF *L'ART*   Dear Sir, With reference to your letter of 19 April, I have the honour to reply that I shall be sending you a pen drawing of one of my Salon entries (*201*).

Yours faithfully, E. MANET

201   AFTER MANET'S SALON PICTURE
       PERTUISET THE LION HUNTER, 1881

202   LETTER TO ÉMILE ZOLA, 1881

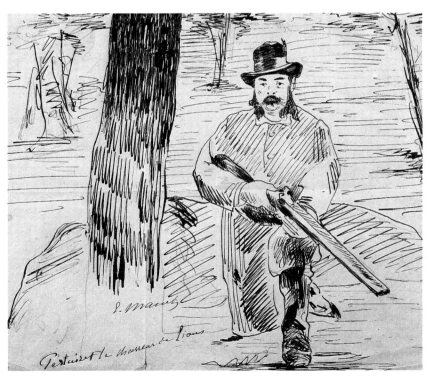

20 avenue Villeneuve-l'Étang, Versailles, Saturday [Summer 1881]

TO THÉODORE DURET   If you are prepared to come out to Versailles, we would be delighted. Come for lunch at twelve.

E. MANET

*

[Versailles,] 29 July 1881

TO LOUIS GAUTHIER-LATHUILE   Sold to M. Gauthier Lathuile [sic] a seascape for the price of one thousand [francs] to be taken in goods and a picture (*Oloron Sainte-Marie*) (*138*) for the price of two hundred francs paid cash.

ED. MANET

*

Versailles, 25 August [1881]

TO CHARLES EPHRUSSI [c/o M. Alexandre Dumas at Puys] It's now Thursday and I still haven't heard from you. You are evidently enthralled by your host's wit and have forgotten your friends at Versailles – I can understand that, but it's hard all the same. Come on, take up your very best pen and get on with it.

I had lunch yesterday with Ignace... Are you having a good time? When you are at Béraud's please remember me to him and his wife.

Warm regards, ED. MANET

*

[Versailles,] Monday morning [August–September 1881]

TO ÉMILE ZOLA [see (*202*)]   I was waiting impatiently for this morning's article and hope to be among the first to congratulate you. Throughout this campaign [in *Le Figaro*, against political opportunism], you have shown yourself to be the forthright, frank and honourable man I have long admired.

ED. MANET

*

[1881]

RECORDED BY GEORGES JEANNIOT   Colour is a matter of taste and sensibility. Above all, you must have something to say; otherwise, forget it. You're not a painter unless you love painting more than anything else. And a grasp of technique is not enough, there has to be an emotional impulse. Science is one thing but for an artist, imagination is more important... One day, on my way back from Versailles, I climbed into the locomotive, beside the driver and the fireman. Those two men were a magnificent sight, so calm and collected, so staunch! It's an appalling job and they and men like them are the real heroes of our time. When I'm better, I'll do a painting of them...

*

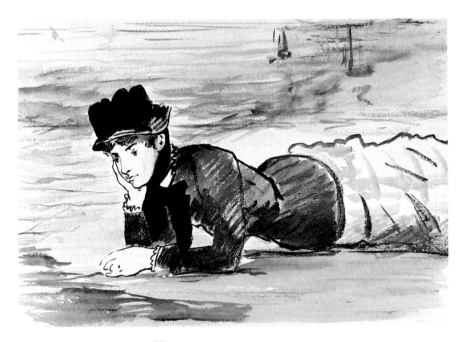

203   ANNABEL LEE, 1881

Versailles, 30 July [1881]

TO STÉPHANE MALLARMÉ [at Valvins]   My dear Captain, You know how happy I am to embark
on any kind of project with you, but just now what you ask would be too much for me.
I don't feel capable of making a decent job of it, I have no models and above all no imagination.
I wouldn't do anything worthwhile so you must excuse me.

I haven't been too happy about my health since I came to Versailles. I don't know if it's the
change of air or fluctuations in the temperature but I seem to be worse than I was in Paris –
I may get over it.

ED. MANET

I'm returning the sheets [of drawing paper] you sent me which might be of use to someone
more intelligent than me.

*

Versailles [after 30 July 1881]

I feel very guilty and am afraid you may be a bit cross with
me, because I've been thinking, after all, it's selfish of me not to have accepted the work you
proposed – but it's also true that some of the things you suggested seemed impossible, such as
the woman lying in bed, seen through a window. You are a terrible lot, you poets, and it's
often impossible to visualize the things you imagine. Also, I wasn't feeling very well and was
afraid of not being able to finish in time. If it's possible to take up the idea again when I'm back
in Paris, I'll try and do justice to both poet and translator, and I'll have you on hand, to keep
my spirits up. You must have had some big storms but no shipwrecks [on the Seine], I hope,
and it would be nice to have news of you.

E. MANET

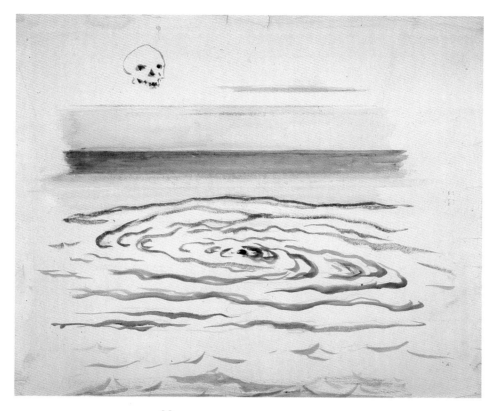

204   CITY IN THE SEA, 1881

I'm sending my dreadful drawings (*203, 204*) together with an autograph for Mlle Mallarmé. It is appropriate and will be a nice addition to her collection.

E. MANET

*

Versailles, 23 September [1881]

TO MME EVA GUÉRARD-GONZALÈS [at Dieppe]   ... we've had to put up with dreadful weather just like you, unfortunately, I think it's been raining here for a good month and a half. Having intended to do studies in the park designed by Le Nôtre, I was reduced to painting my own garden which is quite the most hideous of gardens (*217*), and a few still lifes (*218, 219*), and that's all I shall be bringing back. I find the constant rain rather hard to bear and regret that we have been unable to take advantage of all the overtures of our delightful neighbours. The energetic Guérard has all the luck, he has encountered both Guillemet and Renoir ... As for you, dear Madame, you seem to have taken advantage of the bad weather to do nothing – though you could perfectly well have done a few of your fine pastels on a rainy day at home ... I read in this morning's *Figaro* that Emmanuel Gonzalès was back in Paris – as we shall be on Saturday week, it's time to go home. I hope the weather will be fine enough in October for me to start something for the next [Salon] exhibition ...

Goodbye, dear Madame, our regards to you all, ED. MANET

*

The Legion of Honour, New Year 1882

[1880]

RECORDED BY GIUSEPPE DE NITTIS [To de Nittis on Degas' disdain for the Legion of Honour]
All that contempt, dear boy, it's a lot of nonsense. You've got it, that's the thing . . .

My dear [Degas], if these honours didn't exist, I wouldn't invent them; but they do. And you must, when you can, go for everything that can set you apart from others. It's one more hurdle passed; one more weapon. We can never be too well armed for the endless battles we have to fight in this miserable life. I've not been decorated. But that's not my fault, and I promise you I will be if I can. I'll do everything in my power to bring it about.

*

[December 1881–January 1882]

TO ERNEST CHESNEAU Thank you, my dear Chesneau, for your kind letter. We hope Madame Chesneau is better and my wife and I send her our best regards.

When you write to Nieuwerkerque [sic], tell him that I appreciate his good wishes but that he could have been the one to decorate me. He would have made my fortune and now it's too late to compensate for twenty lost years. But what about you, my dear Chesneau, how are you? I sympathize all the more with the state of your health since I'm not too well myself.

E. MANET

*

29 December 1881

TO BERTHE MORISOT [in Nice] Since I prefer to send you nothing rather than a shabby present, I'll confine myself for the time being to good wishes. I'm sure of finding a way to make up for it later in the year . . . Will you be taking a little trip to Italy? I wish you would go to Venice and do some pictures there in your own very personal style. . . .

The year isn't ending too well as far as my health is concerned. However, Potain's diagnosis leaves room for hope, so I'm following his orders to the letter.

. . . Today dear old Fantin called to congratulate me, and then Faure called, radiant because he's on the New Year's Honours List and he has even commissioned me to do his portrait. . . .

*

[February–March 1882]

I've just had a visit from that terrible Pissarro who discussed your coming exhibition. These gentlemen all seem to be at sixes and sevens . . . Gauguin is playing the dictator. Sisley whom I also saw wants to know what Monet should do, and as for Renoir, he's not yet back in Paris.

I'm surprised Eugène didn't remember how cold it can be in Florence. We spent two freezing months there years ago.

In future, it would be better not to worry my mother too much about Bibi's [Julie's] health; she gets into a frightful state over it . . . As for me, I've been better these last two days and have stopped using my stick, which is something. . . .

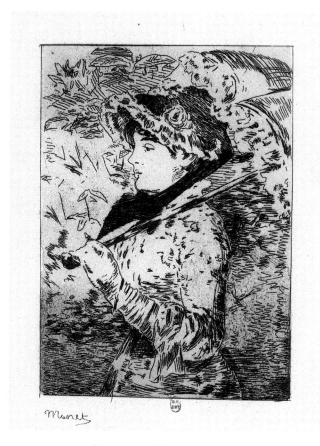

205 JEANNE / SPRING, 1882

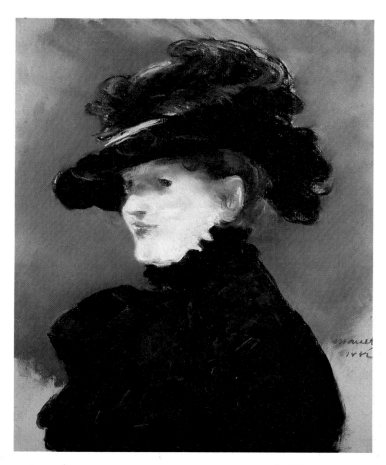

206 MÉRY LAURENT WITH A BLACK HAT, d.1882

29 April [1882]

To GUSTAVE GOETSCHY   It's impossible to do a drawing of the *Bar* (*228*) with a
process that doesn't reproduce half-tones – I'll do the other picture, *Jeanne* (*229*). If that's all
right, drop me a line.

E. MANET

*

Monday [1 May 1882]

To ALBERT WOLFF   My dear Wolff, I haven't given up hope that you may one
day write the splendid article that I've been looking forward to for so long and that you are
quite capable of doing when you want to – but I would prefer if possible that it should be in
my lifetime – and I must warn you that I'm getting on in my career. Meanwhile, thanks for
yesterday's piece [his Salon review in *Le Figaro*] and regards

E. MANET

*

2 May 1882

To HENRI GUÉRARD   Thanks, my dear Guérard – obviously, etching is no longer
for me, so score the plate (*205*) with a good strong burin stroke, and regards

ED. MANET

[Rueil, 8 July 1882]

To 'Sphinx' at *L'Événement*   Dear Sphinx, I see in this morning's 'Echoes' a report about my health which, however well meant, is inaccurate. I am not in the least ill. I simply sprained my foot before leaving Paris. Would you be so kind as to reassure *my numerous friends*, as you call them, as soon as possible.

Cordially, E. Manet

*

18 rue du Château, Rueil [mid-July 1882]

To Mme Méry Laurent   We're not exactly spoilt by fine weather, my dear Méry. Still, perhaps the new moon will bring some sunshine. I take advantage of the fine intervals to walk about my garden (*232*), but to feel really well and happy, I have to be able to work. I don't know who played me the nasty trick last week of publishing a deplorable bulletin about my health in *L'Événement*, which was reprinted in all the papers. I hope you've quite recovered, send me news of yourself and the world. I'm sorry about my bad handwriting, but I've got a terrible pen and I want to get this off this evening.

E. Manet

*

18 rue du Château, Rueil, Monday [August–September 1882]

I was about to write when your letter came. I've been really lazy and it takes all my old affection for you to make me get down to writing. What an awful month, all this rain and wind are not exactly calculated to make the countryside attractive, especially to an invalid. My only pleasures are carriage rides and reading, for I've been able to do hardly any work out of doors. You say you have heaps of things to tell me but why not do it in your next letter? If you wait till I'm back in Paris, I shall have to be very patient, as I may extend the stay here till the end of October. I want to get back in rather better shape and these last two months have really done me good.

Goodbye, my dear Méry, . . . write me a long letter full of news. I'm quite out of touch here and eager to know about all our friends

E. Manet

*

Rueil [16 September 1882 postmark]

To Stéphane Mallarmé [at Valvins]   No, indeed, I wasn't very well when I got to Rueil but am feeling better now. What awful weather – I've begun a few outdoor studies (*231*, *232*) and I'm afraid I may not be able to finish them.

But I do want to find the courage to stay on here until the end of October, despite the monotony.

I've just read *Rocambole* by Ponson du Terrail, it's quite remarkable, and that, with a few carriage rides, is all the entertainment I've had. You are lucky, my dear friend, to be in good health. . . .

Ed. Manet

Rueil, 25 September [1882]

TO EUGÈNE PERTUISET   A sum of money just received will enable me to manage without your help. So thank you for your willingness to oblige and I hope to see you soon. I'll be back in Paris on Wednesday [27 September].

Regards, E. MANET

*

30 September 1882

TO HIS EXECUTORS AND HEIRS   This is my will.

I appoint Suzanne Leenhoff, my lawful wife, as my universal legatee. In her last will, she will leave everything that I have left to her to Léon Koella, called Leenhoff, who has given me the most devoted care; I believe that my brothers will find these arrangements perfectly natural.

The pictures, sketches and drawings remaining in my studio after my death are to be sold at auction. I should like my friend Théodore Duret to take charge of this sale, trusting entirely in his taste, and in the friendship he has always shown me, to decide what should be put up for auction and what should be destroyed. I should like him to choose from my work a picture to remember me by.

From the proceeds of the sale of my pictures, the sum of fifty thousand francs shall be taken and given to Léon Koella, called Leenhoff. The remainder shall revert to Suzanne Leenhoff, my wife. I wish my cousin Jules Dejouy to act as my testamentary executor, and entrust him especially with the interests of my wife. I ask him to accept, in memory of me, a gold snuff-box that belonged to my grandfather.

If I die before the sale of my properties at Gennevilliers goes through, I would like my wife to continue to live with my mother.

I charge my wife to give to my brothers and my friends whatever mementos of me she considers appropriate.

Made in Paris and written entirely in my own hand on 30 September 1882.

EDOUARD MANET

It is clearly understood that Suzanne Leenhoff, my wife, will leave in her will to Léon Koella, called Leenhoff, the fortune I have left to her.

*

[January–February 1883]

MANET'S FINAL SALES MEMORANDA

1 January	Faure	The Conservatory (*207*) Rochefort (*224*) 1 Landscape at Rueil (*232*) Les Tuileries (*65*) Boy peeling a pear	11000 fr
2	Proust	Jeanne (*229*)	3000 fr
21 February	Bérend	Cabaner pastel (*136*)	1000 fr

207   IN THE CONSERVATORY / STUDY OF M. AND MME JULES GUILLEMET, d.1879

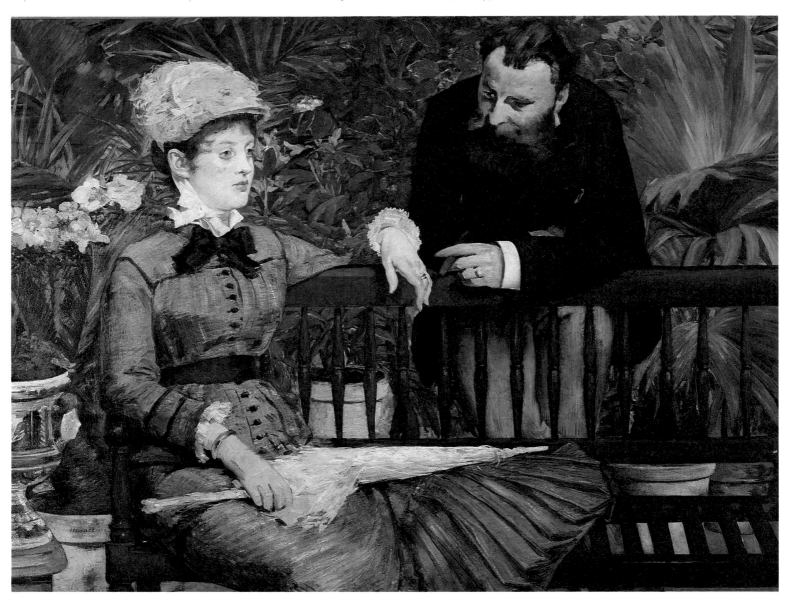

208 CHEZ LE PÈRE LATHUILE, d.1879

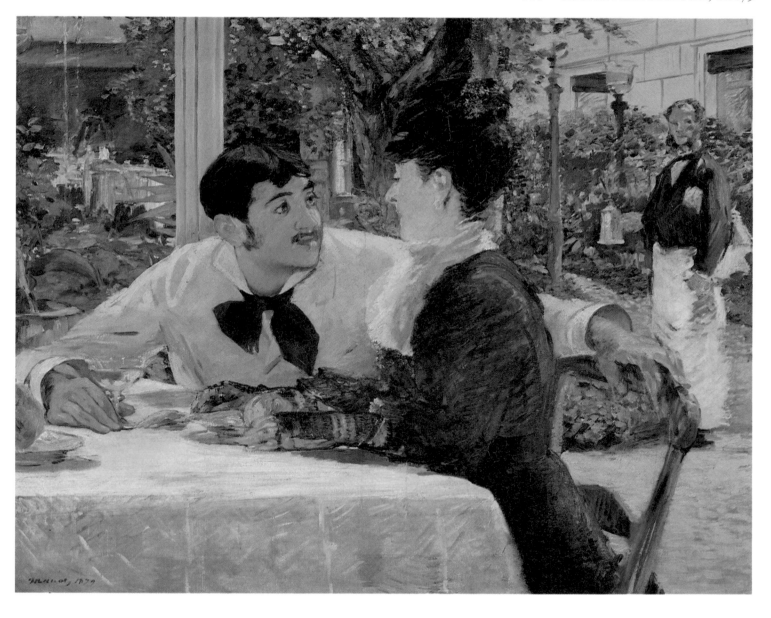

209 PORTRAIT OF MME DU PATY, c.1878–80

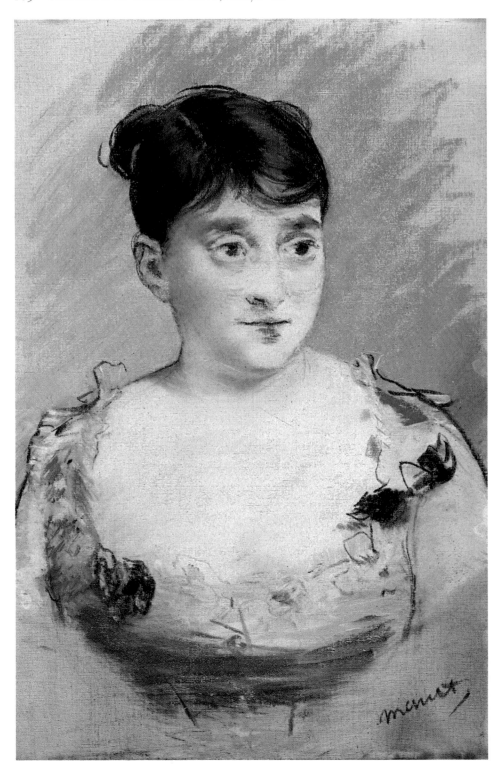

210   PORTRAIT OF MLLE ISABELLE LEMONNIER, c.1878–80

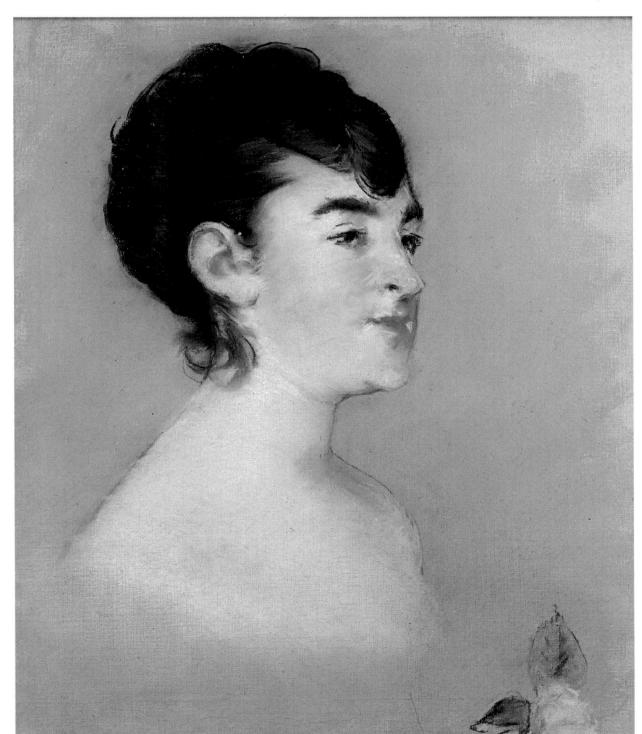

Last portraits

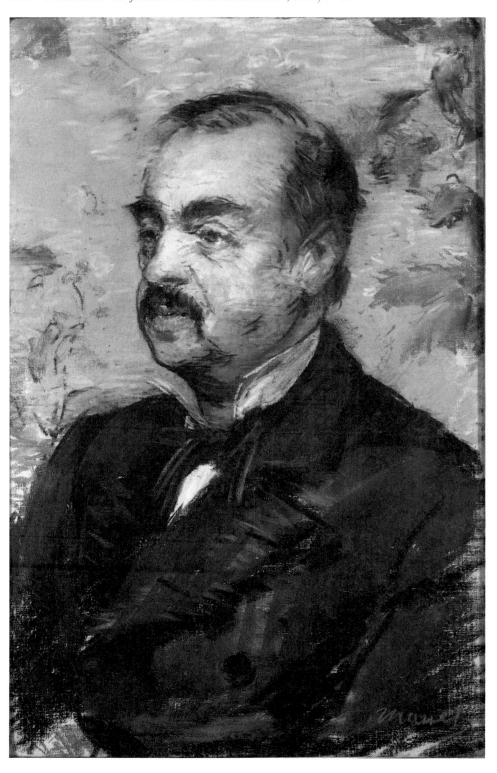

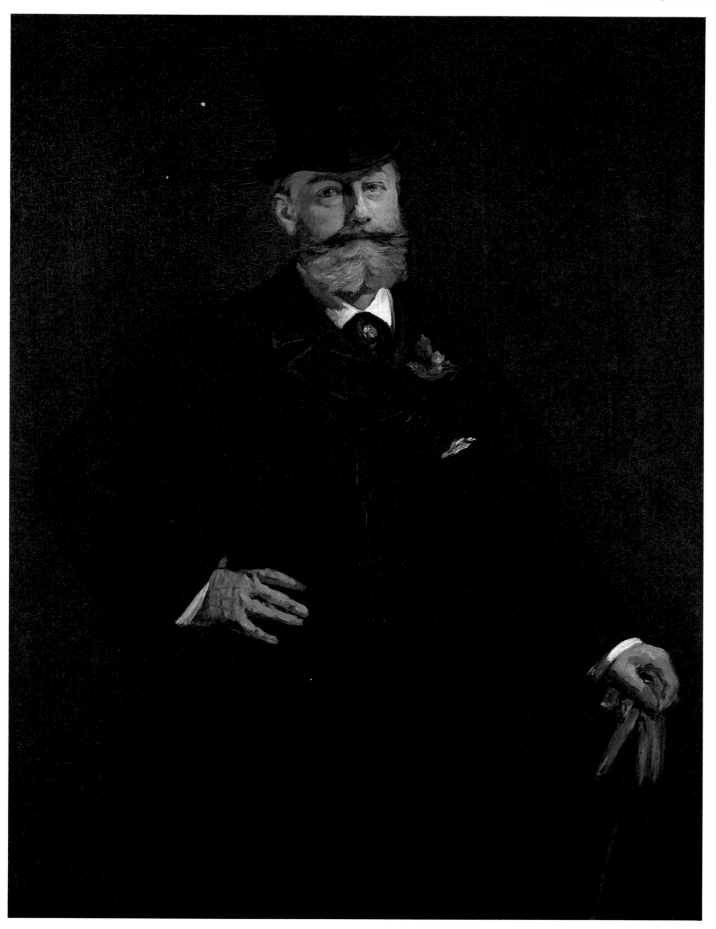

213 MME MANET WITH HER CAT, c.1880–82

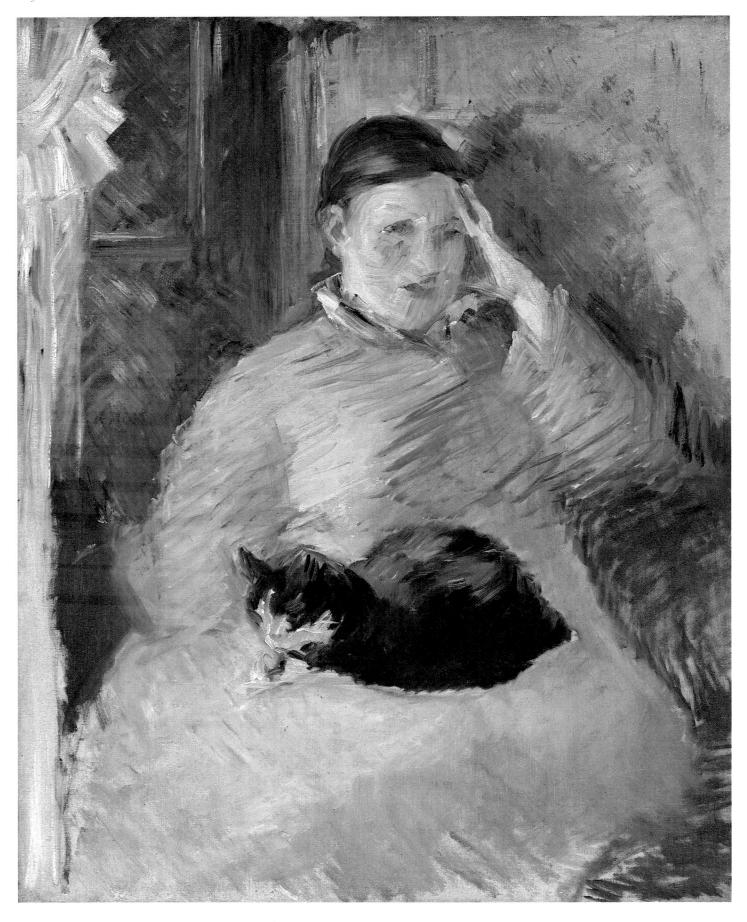

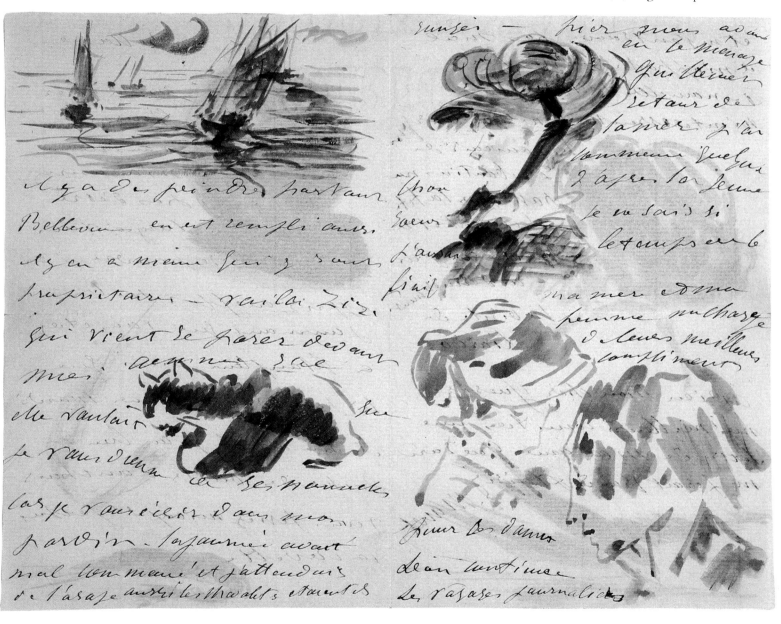

Letters from Bellevue, 1880

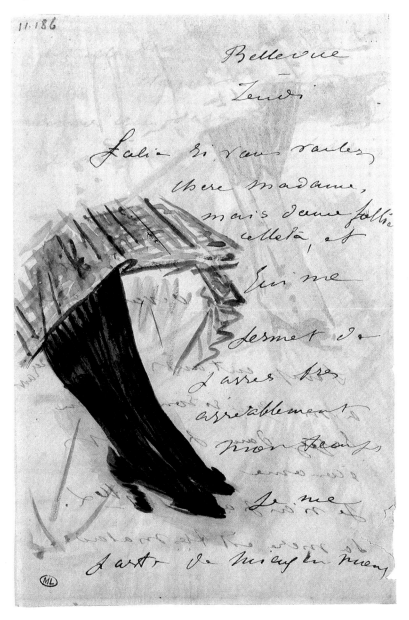

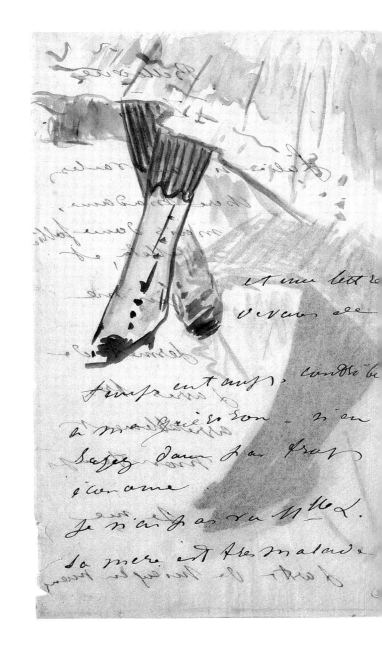

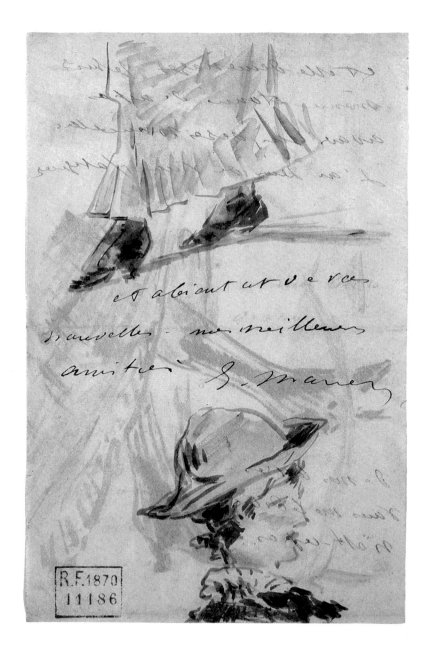

216   MLLE MARGUERITE IN THE GARDEN AT BELLEVUE, 1880

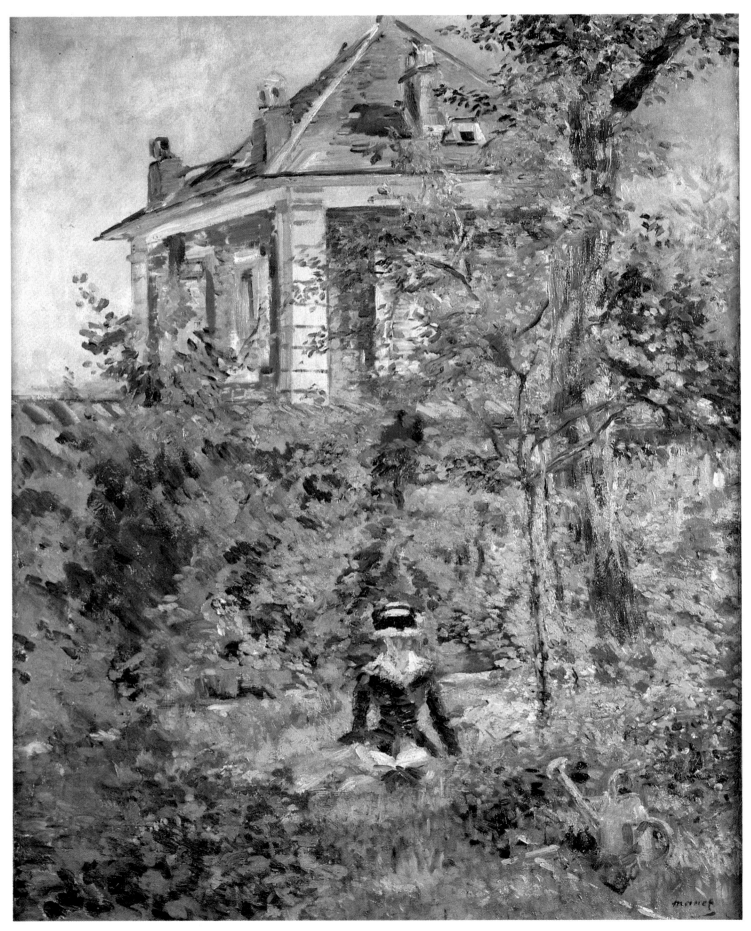

217 'MY GARDEN' AT VERSAILLES, 1881

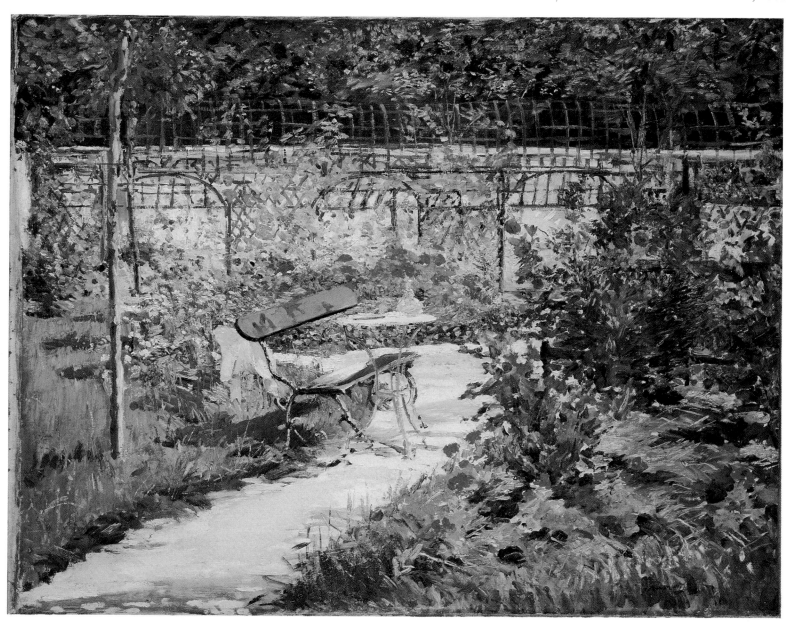

218   THE GREAT HORNED OWL, 1881

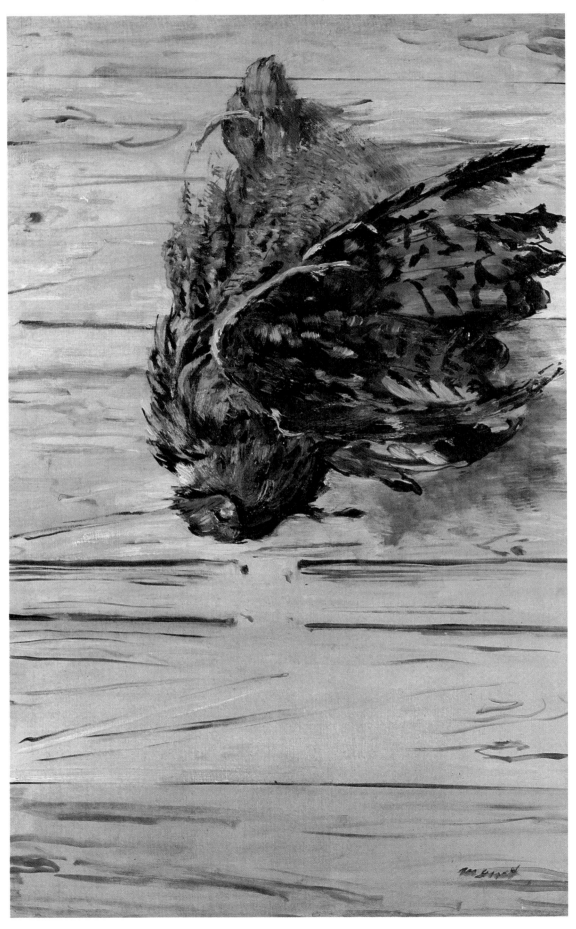

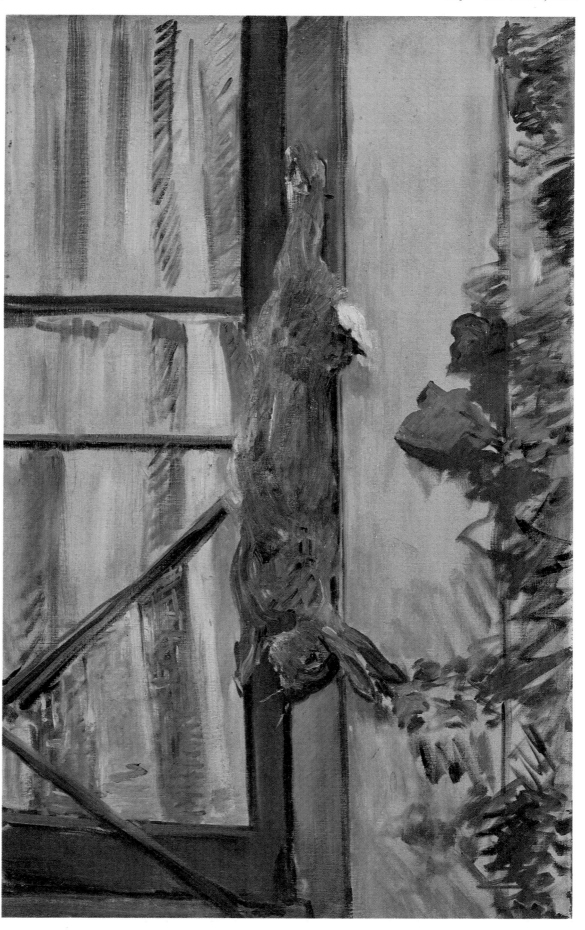

220   BUNCH OF ASPARAGUS, 1880

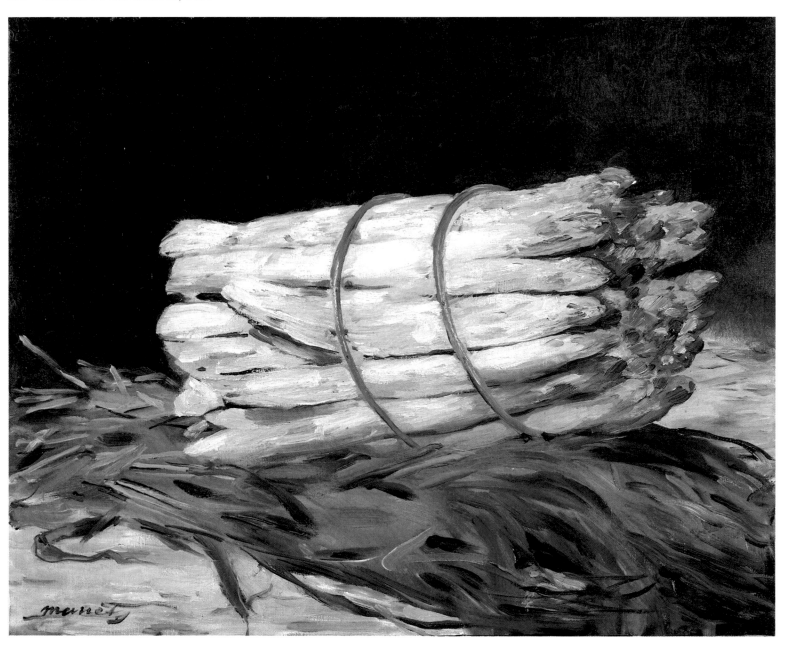

221   THE HAM, c.1877–80

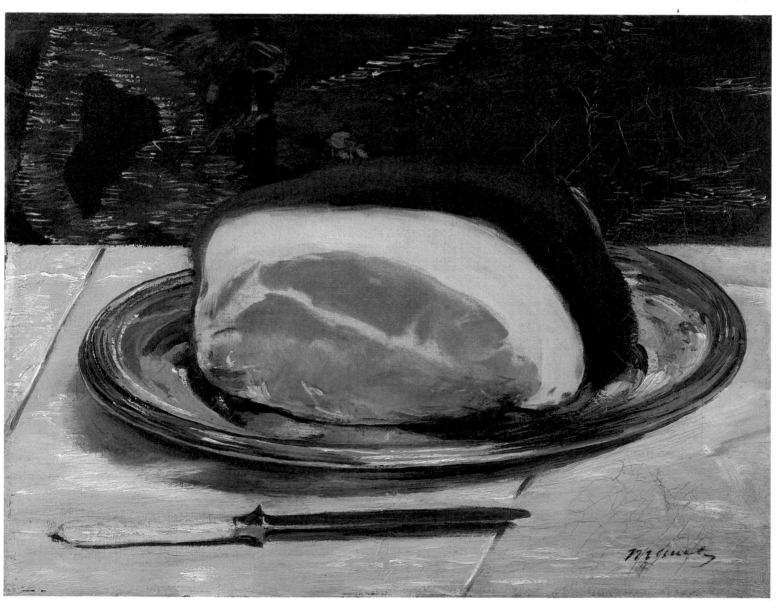

222   BRIOCHE WITH CAT AND PEARS, c.1879–80

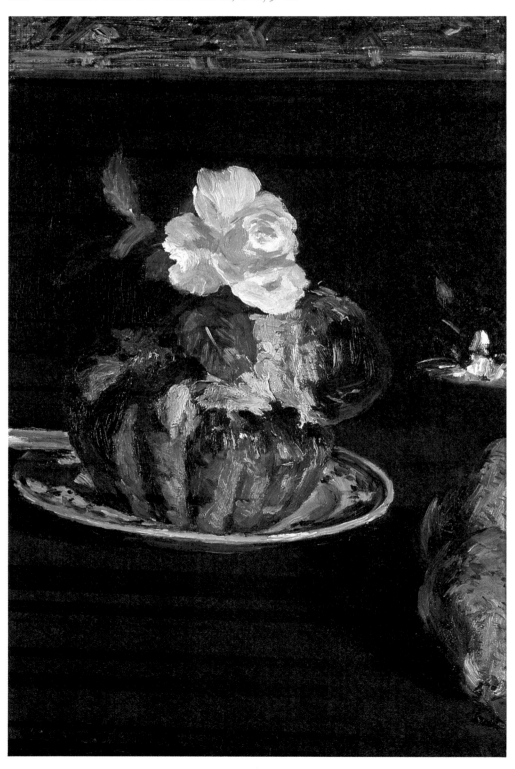

223   THREE APPLES, C.1881

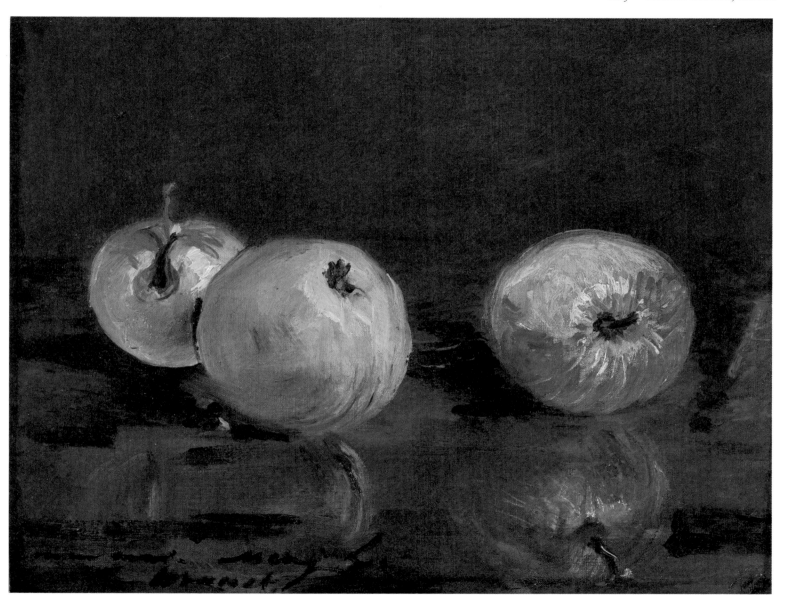

224   PORTRAIT OF HENRI ROCHEFORT, d.1881

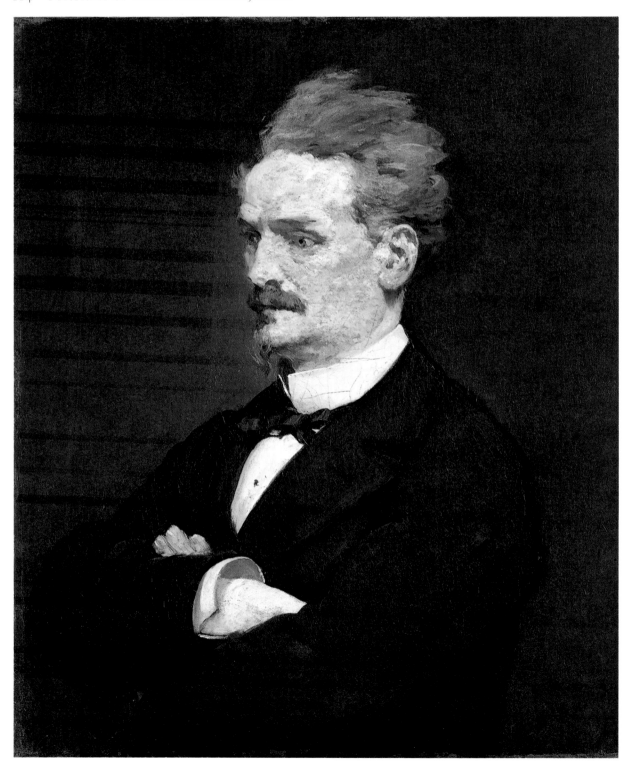

225 THE ESCAPE OF ROCHEFORT, 1880–81

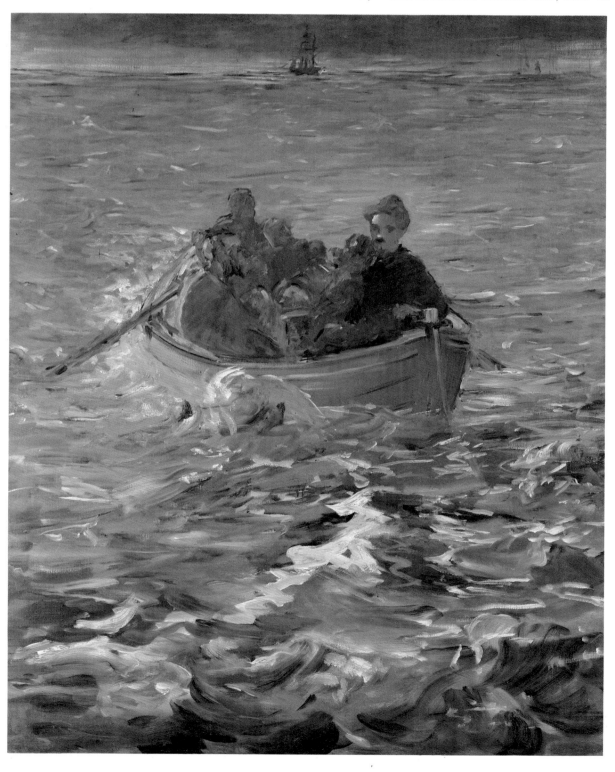

226   PORTRAIT OF ÉMILIE AMBRE IN THE ROLE OF CARMEN, 1880

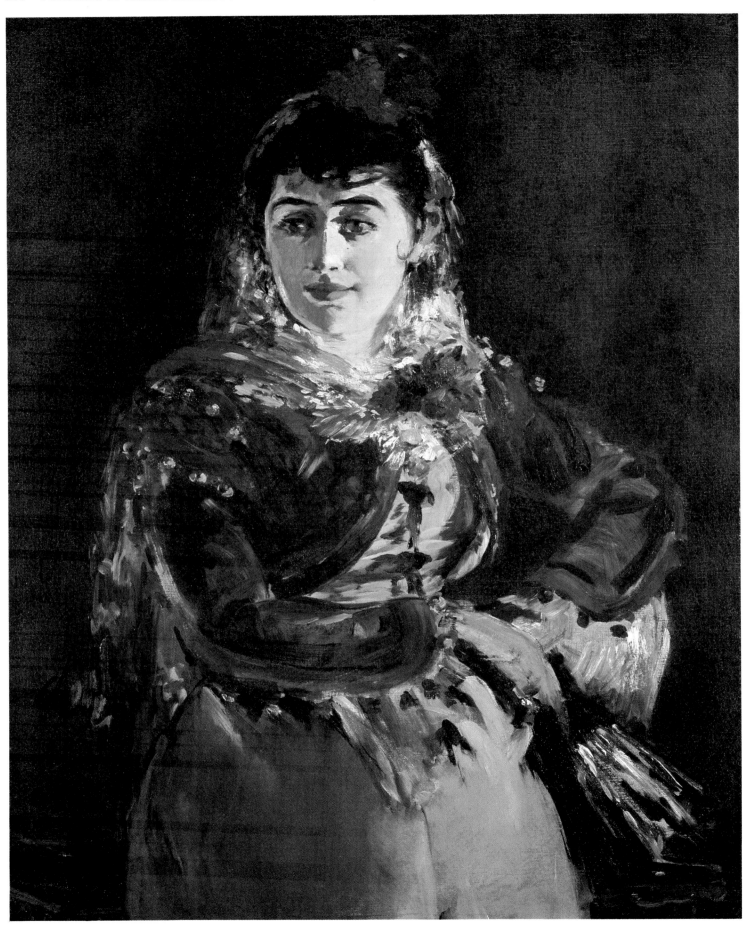

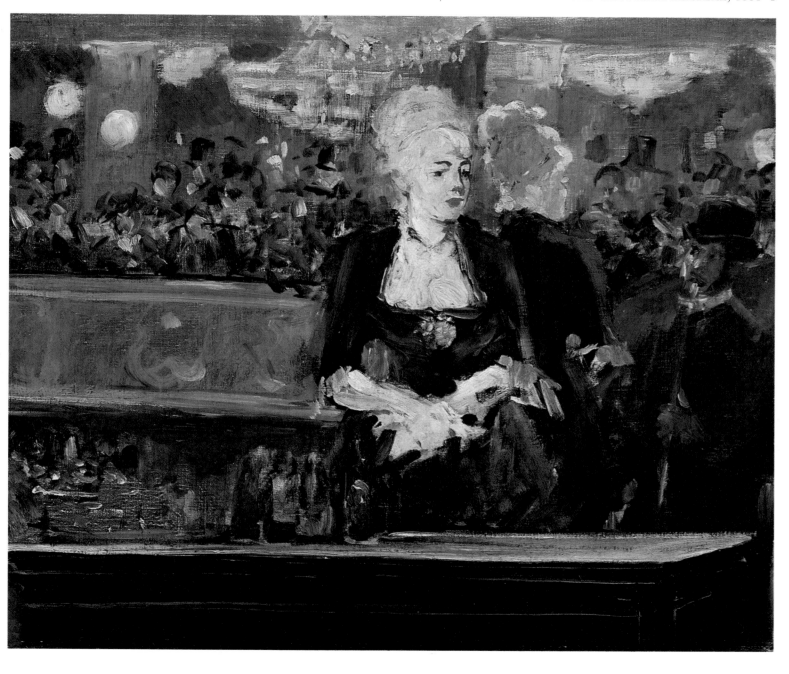

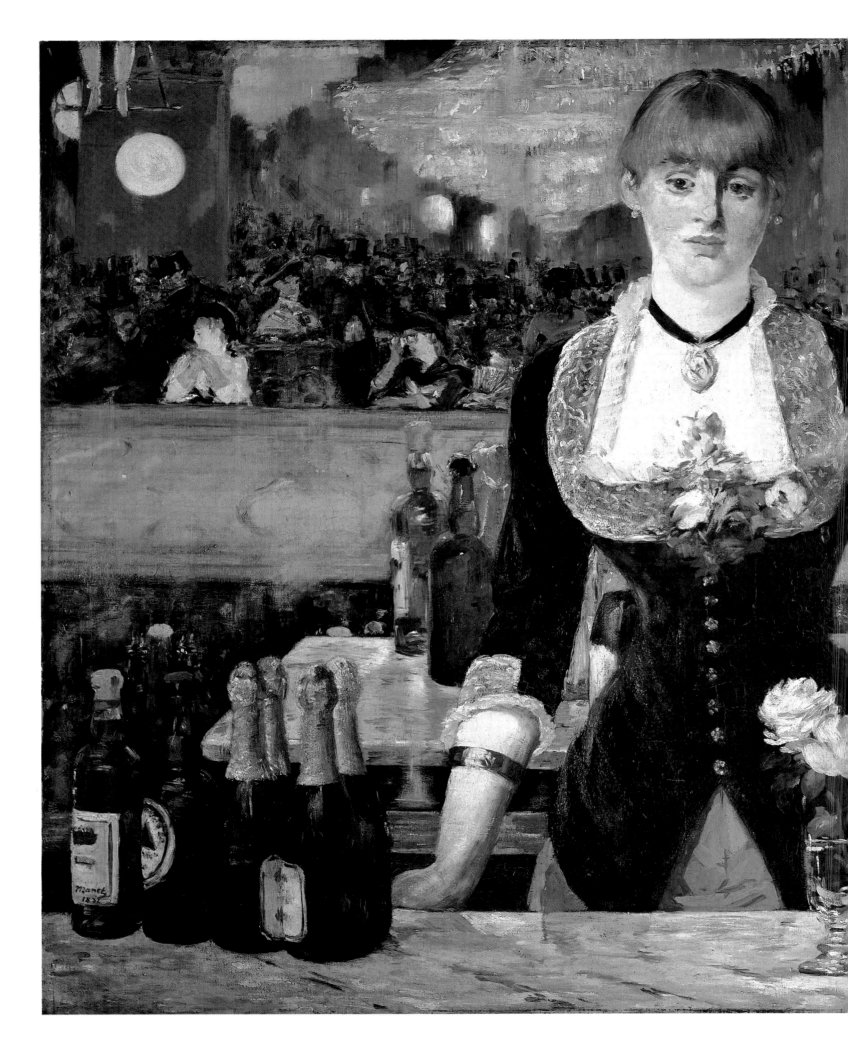

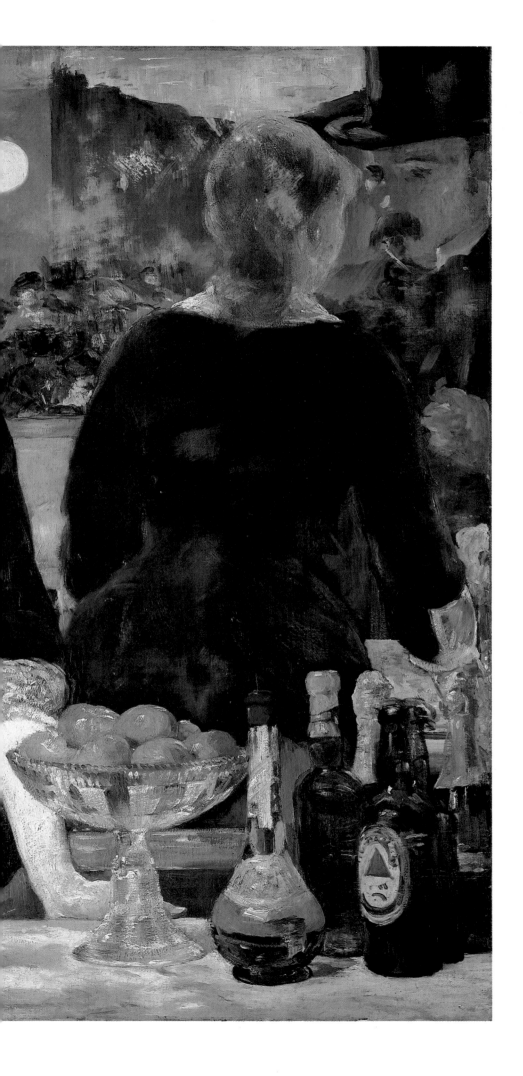

228   A BAR AT THE FOLIES-BERGÈRE, d.1882

229 SPRING / STUDY OF JEANNE DEMARSY, d.1881

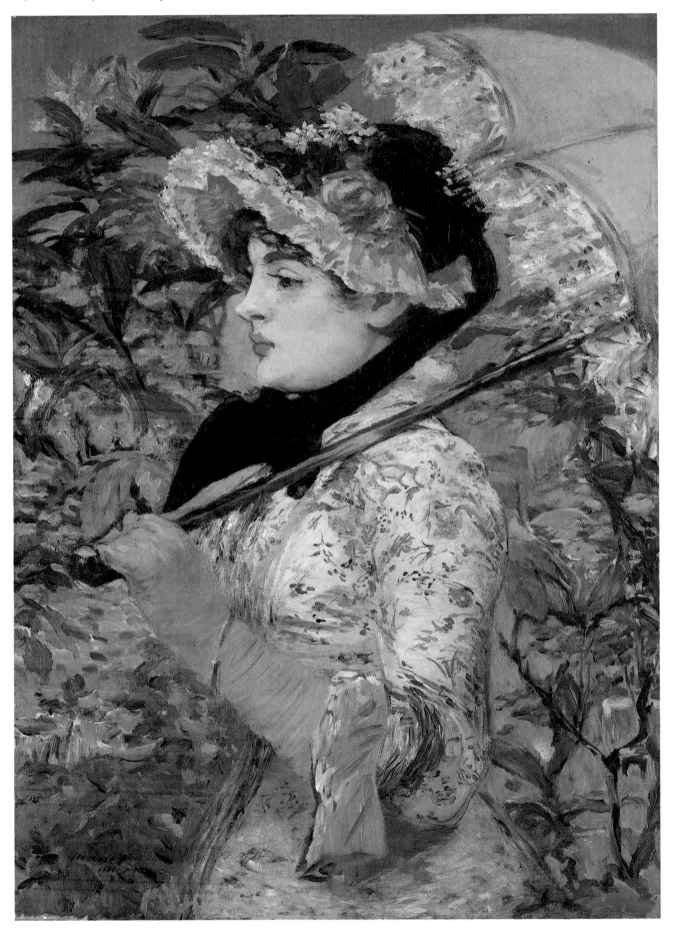

230 AUTUMN / STUDY OF MÉRY LAURENT, 1882.

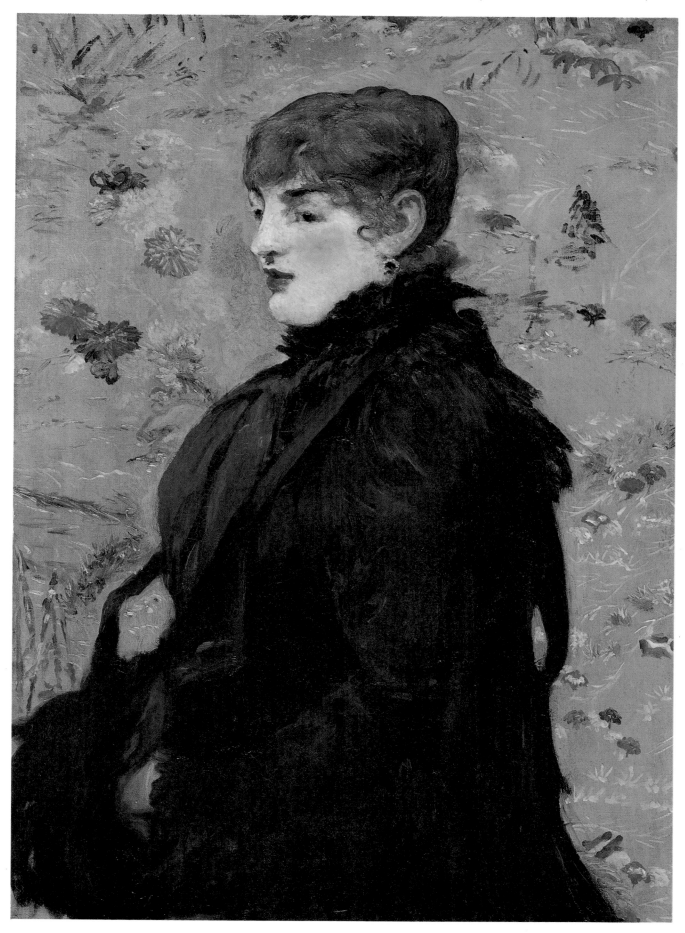

Last summer at Rueil, 1882

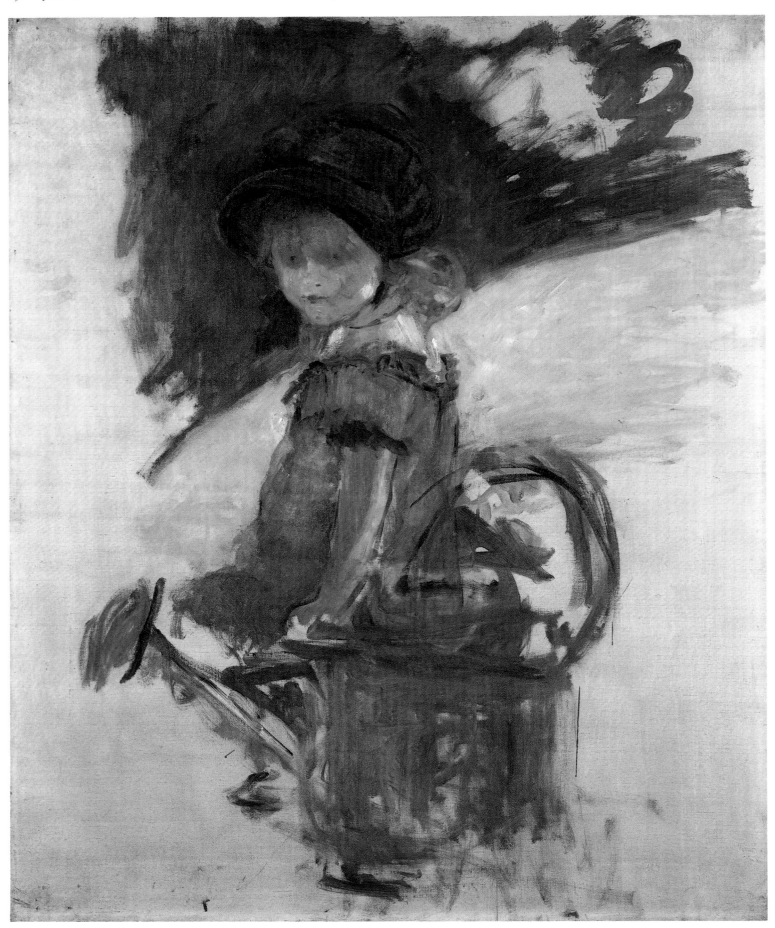

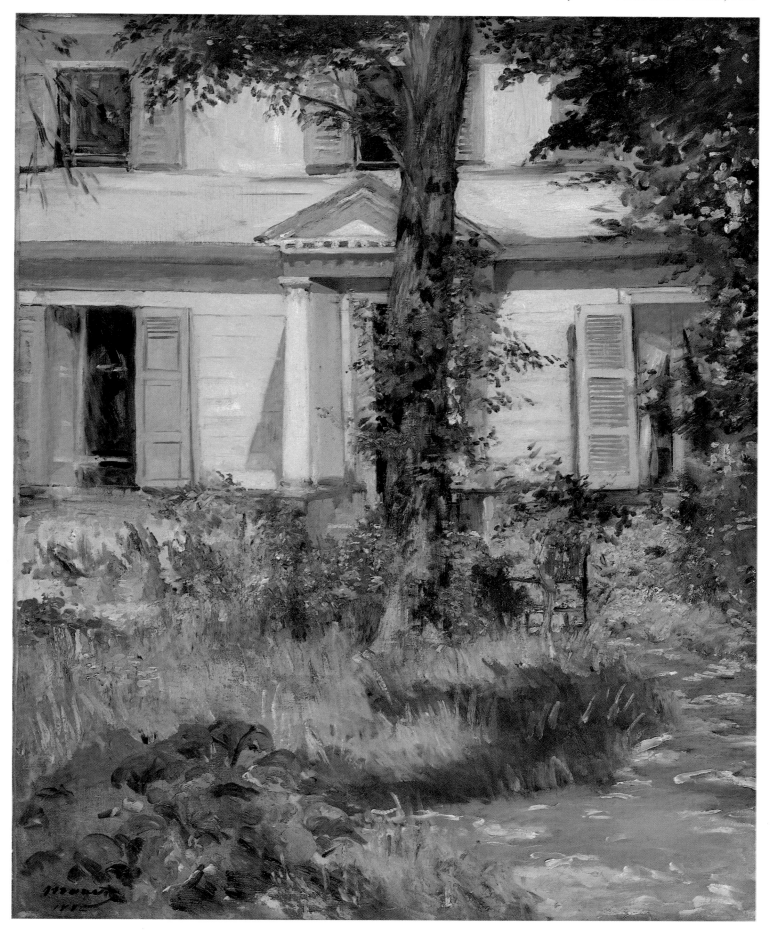

233   THE AMAZON (THE HORSEWOMAN), 1882–3

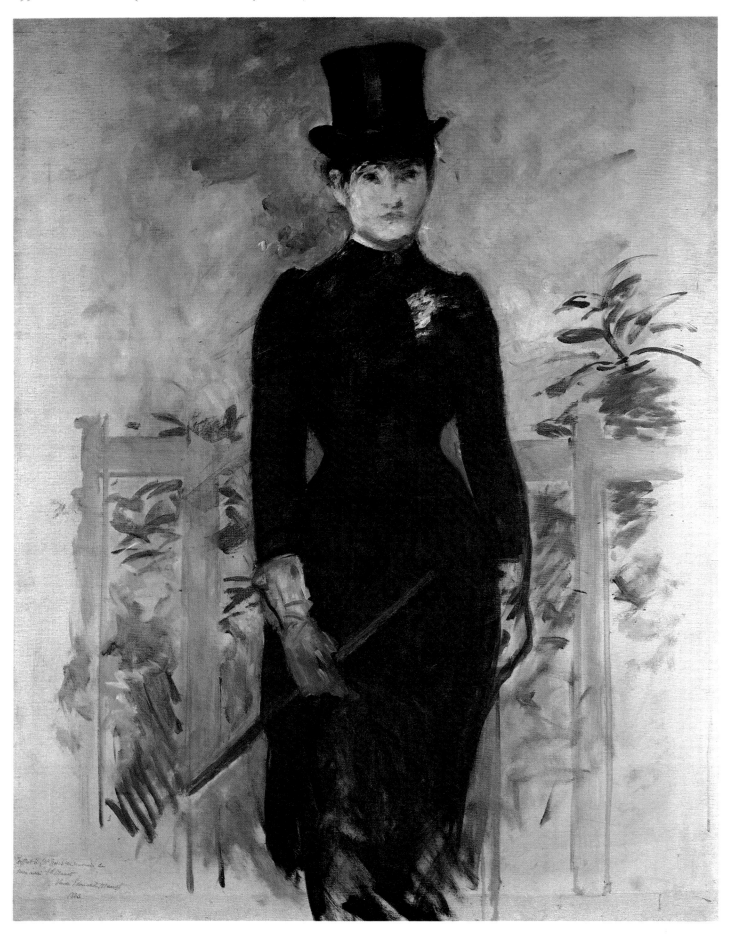

234 THE BUGLER, 1882–3

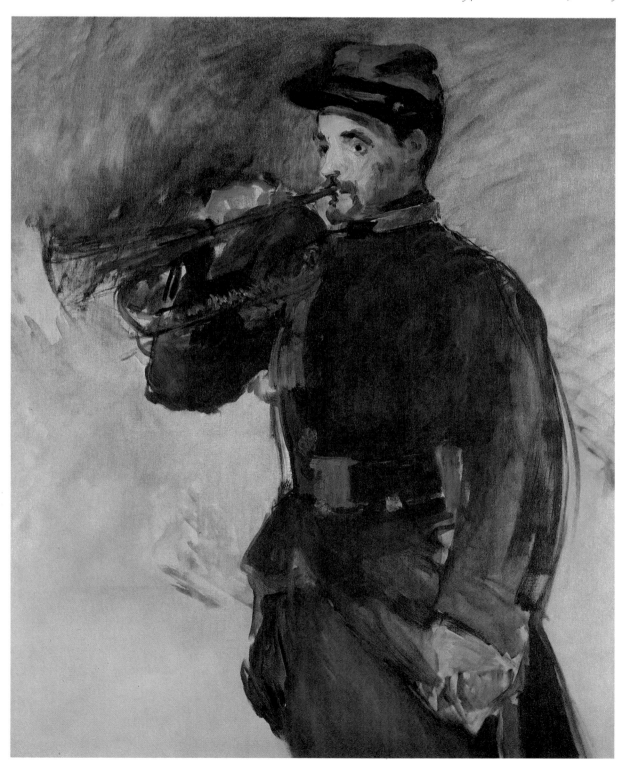

Last flower paintings, 1882–1883

235   LILAC AND ROSES IN A LITTLE GLASS VASE, c.1882

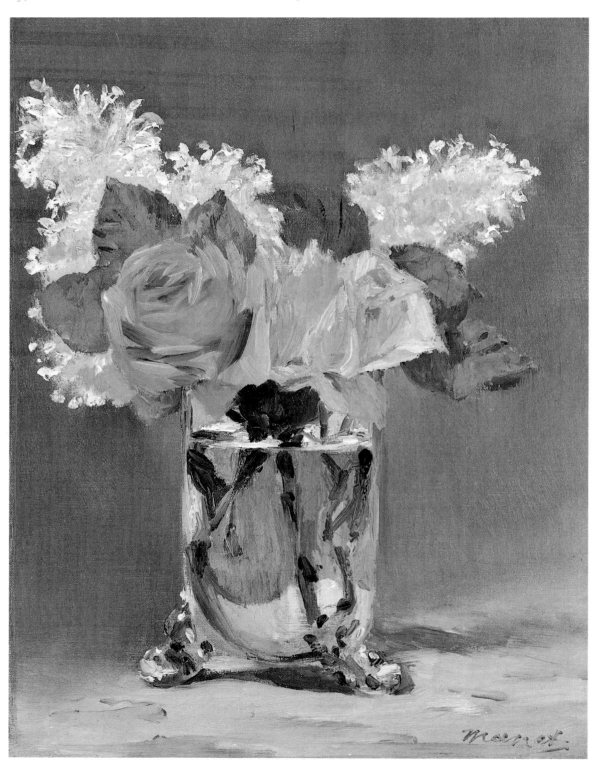

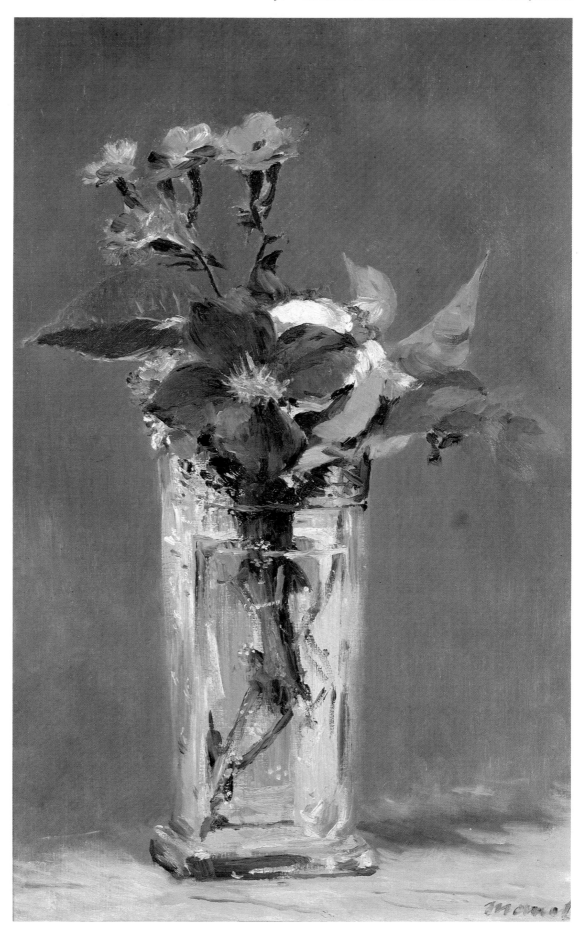

237 WHITE LILAC IN A GLASS VASE, 1882–3

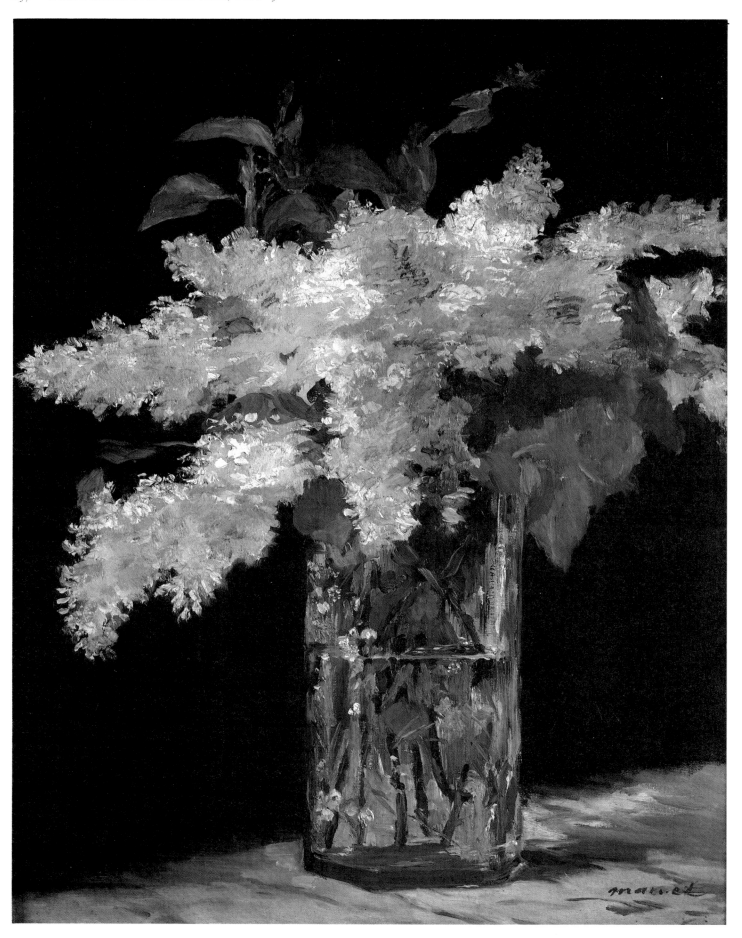

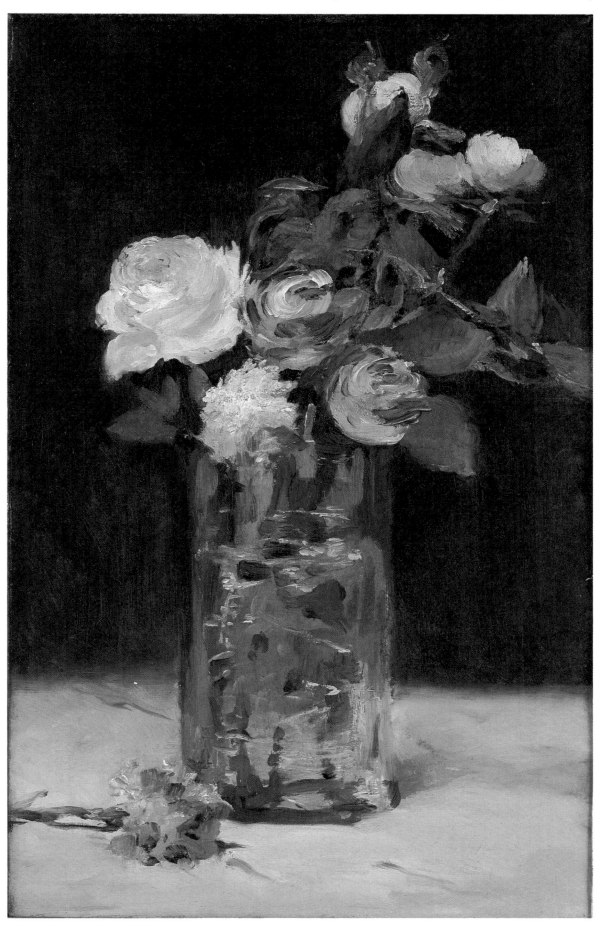

Manet on Art

[Undated]

RECORDED BY ANTONIN PROUST   We're on the wrong track. Who was it who said that drawing in the transcription of form? The truth is, art should be the transcription of life. In other words, at the École des Beaux-Arts, they do fine work but a lousy job. . . .

An artist must be a 'spontaneist'. That's the proper term. But in order to achieve spontaneity, you must master your art. Trial and error won't get you anywhere. You must translate what you feel, but your translation must be instantaneous, so to speak. One talks of *l'esprit de l'escalier*, or taking a belated step with a witty retort. No one has ever talked of *l'escalier de l'esprit*, or the steps that lead to wit and wisdom. Yet so many people try to climb them and never succeed in reaching the top, given the difficulty of getting there at a single bound. The fact is, you always find that what you did yesterday is no longer in harmony with what you are doing today.

Personally, I am not greatly interested in what is said about art. But if I had to give an opinion, I would put it this way: everything that has a sense of humanity, a sense of modernity, is interesting; everything that lacks these is worthless.

*

[1882]

RECORDED BY GEORGES JEANNIOT   Concision in art is a necessity and a matter of elegance. The concise man makes you think; the verbose man is a bore. Always aim for concision . . . Look for the essential areas of light and shade in a figure; the rest will fall into place, often with no great effort. And because nature can only give you factual information, you must cultivate your memory which will act as a safety net and save you from falling into banality . . . You must always lead the dance and provide entertainment. Don't make it a chore, no, never a chore! . . .

*

[Undated]

RECORDED BY ANTONIN PROUST   If Bacon's definition, that art is man added to nature, *homo additus naturae*, is an absolute truth, you still have to be sure that nature is what you've got. Even the most faithful memory is no substitute.

[On colour and line]   . . . without punctuation there can be neither spelling nor grammar, and it's absurd to try and distinguish between colour and line.

. . . It's true I don't draw the sort of stupid lines one is taught at the École [des Beaux-Arts]. But just ask the illustrious professors who teach there to sketch in a picture with a feeling for light in their fingertips. I defy them to do it. There is such radiance and mobility in the atmosphere that envelops everything in its dazzling splendour! Try telling that to people who pin a figure on a canvas as one pins a butterly in a display case.

[On a portrait by a fashionable artist]   I can see, of course, that he has painted a frock coat. And this frock coat is impeccably cut. But where are the sitter's lungs? He isn't breathing under it. He has no body. It's a portrait for a tailor.

*

[c.1878]

RECORDED BY GASTON LA TOUCHE   Thank you for having thought of me, but I cannot take any pupils. Anyway, what would I teach you? Nothing; or at least a very few things that can be summed up in a couple of words: black does not exist, that's the first precept; don't do anything that is seen through someone else's work, that's the second. So go back home and paint from nature, which is much more important than Messrs X, Y and Z.

*

[1868–78]

RECORDED BY BERTHE MORISOT   You can do *plein air* painting indoors, by painting white in the morning, lilac during the day and orange-toned in the evening.

*

[c.1878–82]

RECORDED BY HENRI GERVEX   [On Robert-Fleury Senior (1797–1890), *bête-noire* of the Impressionist painters]   Isn't he ever going to leave us in peace, that old monster with one foot on the burnt sienna ground and the other in the grave!

*

[1870s]

RECORDED BY GEORGE MOORE   When Degas was painting *Semiramis* [in the early 1860s], I was painting modern Paris.

*

[1870s]

RECORDED BY EDMOND BAZIRE   [To visitors to Manet's studio]   Just look at this Degas, this Renoir, this Monet! Ah, my friends, what talent!

*

[1880–2]

RECORDED BY ANTONIN PROUST   [On Dr Thomas William Evans]   He's been so kind to my mother and me . . . Besides, he's a real artist. It's he who had the idea of creating the avenue du Bois de Boulogne. . . . The Emperor was enthusiastic, he sent for M. Haussmann and M. Alphand, and Thomas W. Evans's avenue was agreed on. How remarkable the democratic régime is in the United States! It produces men who have not only all the qualities of our old French society, but also an instinct for modernity. They understand it. They have a real feeling for it. How on earth did they acquire that? I won't go on about it, but in years to come they're going to amaze the Old World.

*

[1876]

RECORDED BY ANTONIN PROUST Museums have always driven me to despair. I'm deeply depressed when I go in and see how wretched the pictures look. There are visitors and guardians all milling around. The portraits just don't come alive. And yet some of them [clacking his tongue] . . . those by Velasquez, Goya, Hals . . . over here one thinks of the Largillières, the Nattiers, you have to admit, they really knew what they were doing, those fellows. A bit too contrived, but they never lost sight of reality. And the Clouets! To think that Rosso and Primaticcio were given preference over Clouet.

*

[1879–82]

[On the critics' reaction over twenty years]   This war with knives has hurt me very deeply. I've suffered cruelly, but it has been a great stimulus. I wouldn't want any artist to be praised and flattered at the beginning. It would destroy his personality. The fools! They've never stopped telling me I'm inconsistent: they couldn't have said anything more flattering. It has always been my ambition not to remain consistent, not to repeat tomorrow what I did yesterday, but to respond constantly to a fresh vision and seek to make a new voice heard. Ah! the stick-in-the-muds with a formula, who cling to it, and get rich in the process, what has that to do with art, I ask you? On the contrary, the role of a man who knows what he's about is to take a step forward, and a significant step! The people living in the next century will be the lucky ones, my friend; their vision will be better developed than ours. They'll see better. . . . I must be seen whole. And I beg you, if I die, don't let me go piecemeal into the public collections; I would not be judged fairly.

. . . I want to get in complete or not at all. . . . the proper thing in museums would be an appropriate setting, with a wall for each artist and space between the frames. The hanging is inept, the arrangement absurd, the decoration of the rooms ridiculous. It kills the pictures. If I can't have a space to myself, I'd rather have nothing. . . .

[On Proust's proposal that the State acquire some of his pictures]   It would make your colleagues screech like peacocks. Just remember that Courbet is an Old Master compared with me and consider how this Old Master was greeted in the House. The House has recanted, I know. But have the curators at the Louvre mended their ways? They have stuck the Courbets in dark rooms, at absurd heights, and as Gambetta said jokingly, you almost had to hawk your Courbets around in a cart to get the money in, just as Emilie Ambre paraded my *Maximilian (96)* all over America.

In any case I'm not in any hurry. There was a time when I was. Not any more. I've become patient, philosophical, I'll wait or at least my work will wait, because the attacks I've had to bear have sapped my vitality. No one knows what it's like to be constantly insulted. It sickens and destroys you.

. . . please, promise me one thing, never to let me enter a museum piecemeal, at least without making a protest.

Can you imagine me in the Luxembourg with just one canvas, *Olympia (85)* or the *Père Lathuile (208)*? I would be incomplete and I want to remain intact.

[On *Olympia* in the Louvre, after his death]   When I get my wall in the Louvre, with that in the centre, people will be amazed.

[*Art Monthly Review*, 30 September 1876]

RECORDED BY STÉPHANE MALLARMÉ

[Original English translation from the lost French text]

Each time [one] begins a picture . . . [one] plunges headlong into it, and feels like a man who knows that his surest plan to learn to swim safely is, dangerous as it may seem, to throw himself into the water. . . . No one should paint a landscape and a figure by the same process, with the same knowledge, or in the same fashion; nor, what is more, even two landscapes or two figures. Each work should be a new creation of the mind. The hand, it is true, will conserve some of its acquired secrets of manipulation, but the eye should forget all else it has seen, and learn anew from the lessons before it. It should abstract itself from memory, seeing only that which it looks upon, and that as for the first time; and the hand should become an impersonal abstraction guided only by the will, oblivious of all previous cunning.

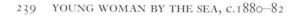

*

239   YOUNG WOMAN BY THE SEA, c.1880–82

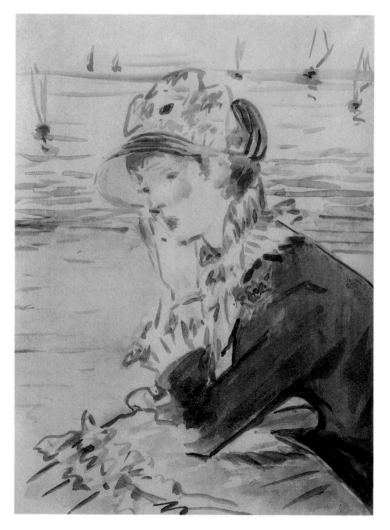

List of Plates

25　LETTER TO THÉODORE DURET, 16 September [1870]
　　Autograph manuscript (text p. 56)
　　Pierpont Morgan Library, New York (MA.3950 Tabarant archive)

26　PORTRAIT OF MME SUZANNE MANET, *c*.1870
　　Oil on canvas, 60 × 50 cm　　RW 116
　　Norton Simon Art Foundation, Pasadena (M.1973.4.P)

27　MME MANET ON A BLUE COUCH, *c*.1873
　　Pastel on paper, 49 × 60 cm　　RW P3, PNY 143
　　Musée d'Orsay, Paris (RF 4507)

28　HEAD OF A RECUMBENT MAN, *c*.1850–56
　　Graphite and white chalk on faded blue paper, 20.6 × 27 cm　　RW D498
　　Musée du Louvre, Arts graphiques, Paris (RF 30.531)

29　HEAD OF A BOY, *c*.1850–56
　　Sold to Faure 1873
　　Pastel on faded blue (?) paper, 37 × 30 cm　　RW P1
　　Detroit Institute of Arts, Gift of Edward E. Rothman (69.2)

30　AFTER TINTORETTO'S SELF-PORTRAIT, *c*.1855
　　Painting in the Louvre. Manet's copy inscribed: *JACOBVS TENTORETVS PICTOR VENTIVS* (spurious inscription on original removed in 1957); *IPSIVS F*; *Manet d'après Tintoret*
　　Oil on canvas, 61 × 50 cm　　RW 5
　　Musée des Beaux-Arts, Dijon (1317)

31　AFTER DELACROIX'S BARQUE OF DANTE, *c*.1858
　　Painting then in the Musée du Luxembourg, now in the Louvre
　　Oil on canvas, 33 × 41 cm　　RW 3
　　Metropolitan Museum of Art, New York (29.100.114)

32　AFTER GHIRLANDAIO'S VISITATION (detail), 1857
　　Fresco in Santa Maria Novella, Florence
　　Graphite, 29 × 21.2 cm　　RW D41
　　Musée du Louvre, Arts graphiques, Paris (RF 30.342)

33　AFTER ANDREA DEL SARTO'S MADONNA DEL SACCO, 1857
　　Fresco lunette in the cloister 'dei Morti', SS. Annunziata, Florence
　　Black and red chalks, 22 × 44.4 cm　　RW D25
　　Jean-Claude Romand Collection, Paris

34　AFTER BERNARDINO POCCETTI'S CONCESSION OF INDULGENCES TO THE SS. ANNUNZIATA (detail), 1857
　　Fresco lunette in the cloister 'dei Morti', SS. Annunziata, Florence
　　Graphite and watercolour, 29 × 21.2 cm　　RW D102
　　Musée du Louvre, Arts graphiques, Paris (RF 30.370)

35　AFTER PARMIGIANINO, VIOL PLAYER AND PUTTO, 1857
　　Drawing in the Uffizi, Florence (10978)
　　Pen and sepia ink with wash, 15.3 × 28.4 cm　　RW D109
　　Musée du Louvre, Arts graphiques, Paris (RF 30.432)

36　AFTER TITIAN'S VENUS OF URBINO, 1857
　　Painting in the Uffizi, Florence
　　Oil on panel, 24 × 37 cm　　RW7
　　Private collection

37　RECLINING NUDE, *c*.1858–60
　　Red chalk, 24.7 × 45.7 cm　　RW D376, PNY 65
　　Musée du Louvre, Arts graphiques, Paris (RF 24.335)

38　STUDY FOR A FINDING OF MOSES, *c*.1858–60
　　Pen and sepia ink with wash over graphite, squared in red chalk, 33.3 × 28.1 cm　　RW D–, 1986 London 3
　　Museum Boymans-van Beuningen, Rotterdam (FII 105)

39　SEATED BATHER, *c*.1858–60
　　Brush and sepia wash, 26.6 × 20.3 cm　　RW D362, PNY 23
　　Private collection, London

40　SKETCH FOR A FINDING OF MOSES (?), *c*.1858–60
　　Oil on panel, 35.5 × 46 cm　　RW 39, PNY 20
　　Nasjonalgalleriet, Oslo (1182)

41　THE SURPRISED NYMPH, d.1861
　　Reworked section of a large composition, see (*40*). Exhibited Imperial Academy, St Petersburg 1861 ('Nymph and Satyr')
　　Oil on canvas, 146 × 114 cm　　RW 40, PNY 19
　　Museo Nacional de Bellas Artes, Buenos Aires (2712)

42　STUDY OF A HEAD IN PROFILE (SUZANNE LEENHOFF), *c*.1858–60
　　Red chalk, 29.7 × 25.4 cm　　RW D356
　　Bibliothèque nationale, Estampes, Paris (Dc300 d, b.I 10)

43　AFTER THE BATH, *c*.1858–60
　　Red chalk, 28 × 20 cm　　RW D363, PNY 24
　　Art Institute of Chicago. Helen Regenstein Collection (1967.30)

44　LA TOILETTE (WOMAN AT HER TOILET), *c*.1861–2
　　Probably after a lost painting by Manet – see the study (*43*) and the preparatory drawing (RW D360) for the print published in 1862 (Cadart) and *c*.1863 (*16*)
　　Etching, 2nd state, 28.7 × 22.5 cm　　G 26, H 20, PNY 25
　　Bibliothèque nationale, Estampes, Paris (Dc300 d)

45　WOMAN POURING WATER (STUDY OF SUZANNE LEENHOFF), *c*.1858–60
　　Reworked, unfinished fragment from a large composition
　　Oil on canvas, 56 × 47.2 cm　　RW 20 (not repr.), 1986 Japan 1
　　Ordrupgaardsamlingen, Charlottenlund-Copenhagen

46　BOY AND DOG, *c*.1862
　　Possibly from a lost painting and based on a drawing (RW D455)
　　Print published in 1862 (Cadart) and *c*.1863 (*16*)
　　Etching and aquatint, 20.5 × 14.5 cm (repr. actual size) G 17, H 11, PNY 9
　　Nationalmuseum, Stockholm (307.1924)

47　BOY WITH CHERRIES (STUDY OF ALEXANDRE), *c*.1858–9
　　Exhibited Martinet 1861
　　Oil on canvas, 65 × 55 cm　　RW 18
　　Calouste Gulbenkian Foundation, Lisbon (395)

48　M. AND MME AUGUSTE MANET, d.1860
　　Salon of 1861 (2099). See page 29
　　Oil on canvas, 111.5 × 91 cm　　RW 30, PNY 3
　　Musée d'Orsay, Paris (RF 1977.12)

49　MME MANET MÈRE (THE ARTIST'S MOTHER), *c*.1863–6
　　Oil on canvas, 98 × 80 cm　　RW 62
　　Isabella Stewart Gardner Museum, Boston (P3s4)

50　THE ABSINTHE DRINKER / PHILOSOPHER, *c*.1858–9/72?
　　Refused Salon of 1859. Extensively reworked between 1859 and its sale to Durand-Ruel in 1872 (p.163). See page 28
　　Oil on canvas, 81 × 106 cm　　RW 19
　　Ny Carlsberg Glyptothek, Copenhagen (1778)

51　THE OLD MUSICIAN, d.1862
　　Exhibited Martinet 1863 (136)
　　Oil on canvas, 186 × 247 cm　　RW 52
　　National Gallery of Art, Washington DC. Chester Dale Collection (1963.10.162) (1826)

52　AFTER VELASQUEZ'S LITTLE CAVALIERS, *c*.1858–9
　　Painting in the Louvre, then attributed to Velasquez
　　Inscribed (lower right) *Manet d'après Velasquez*. Sold to Faure 1878. See page 27
　　Oil on canvas, 47 × 78 cm　　RW 21
　　Chrysler Museum, Norfolk, Virginia (71.679)

53　THE SALAMANCA STUDENTS, d.1860
　　Given or sold to Ambroise Adam (*62*)
　　Oil on canvas, 72.8 × 93 cm　　RW 28, 1986 Japan 2
　　Private collection (Courtesy Sayn-Wittgenstein Fine Art, Inc., New York)

54　BOY WITH A SWORD (STUDY OF LÉON LEENHOFF), *c*.1860–61
　　Exhibited Martinet *c*.1860–61?; Martinet 1863; Brussels 1863; Marseilles 1868. Sold to Durand-Ruel 1872 (p.163). Donated to the Metropolitan Museum in 1889, with (*89*). See page 29
　　Oil on canvas, 131.1 × 93.3 cm　　RW 37, PNY 14
　　Metropolitan Museum of Art, New York (89.21.2)

55 ILLUSTRATED COVER FOR A SET OF PRINTS, d.1862
Unpublished project – see (16); lettered *ETCHINGS By Edouard Manet*
Etching, 32.7 × 24 cm, on blue paper   G 29, H 38, PNY 45
Nationalmuseum, Stockholm (320.1924)

56 THE SPANISH SINGER / THE GUITAR PLAYER, d.1860
Salon of 1861 (2098, honourable mention); Martinet 1861; Marseilles 1868.
Sold to Durand-Ruel 1872 (p.163). See page 29
Oil on canvas, 147.3 × 114.3 cm   RW 32, PNY 10
Metropolitan Museum of Art, New York (49.58.2)

57 MLLE V . . . IN THE COSTUME OF AN ESPADA, d.1862
Salon des Refusés 1863 (365). Sold to Durand-Ruel 1872 (p.163)
Oil on canvas, 165.1 × 127.6 cm   RW 58, PNY 33
Metropolitan Museum of Art, New York (29.100.53)

58 LE DÉJEUNER SUR L'HERBE (LUNCHEON ON THE GRASS), d.1863
Salon des Refusés (363 *Le Bain*). Sold to Faure 1878
Oil on canvas, 208 × 264 cm   RW 67, PNY 62
Musée d'Orsay, Paris (RF 1668)

59 LE DÉJEUNER SUR L'HERBE, c.1863–5
Watercolour with pen and Indian ink over graphite,
40.8 × 47.8 cm   RW D306, PNY 63
Ashmolean Museum, Oxford (1980.83)

60 YOUNG MAN IN THE COSTUME OF A MAJO, d.1862
Salon des Refusés 1863 (364). Sold to Durand-Ruel 1872 (p.163)
Oil on canvas, 188 × 124.8 cm   RW 70, PNY 72
Metropolitan Museum of Art, New York (29.100.54)

61 THE STREET SINGER, c.1862
Exhibited Martinet 1863. Sold to Durand-Ruel 1872 (p.163)
Oil on canvas, 175.2 × 108.5 cm   RW 50, PNY 32
Museum of Fine Arts, Boston (66.304)

62 AMBROISE ADAM IN THE GARDEN AT PRESSAGNY, 1861
Study of Manet's cousin, documented July 1861 and given to Adam
Oil on canvas, 40.7 × 33.4 cm   RW –, Wilson-Bareau 1984
Private collection

63 CHILDREN IN THE TUILERIES, c.1861–2
Oil on canvas, 38 × 46.5 cm   RW –, 1986 Japan 6
Rhode Island School of Design, Museum of Art, Providence, RI (42.190)

64 BAUDELAIRE IN PROFILE, WEARING A HAT, c.1862–5
See the profile portrait of Baudelaire in (65). Print unpublished in Manet's
lifetime. See page 44
Etching, 13 × 7.5 cm   G 30, H 21, PNY 54
Bibliothèque nationale, Estampes, Paris (Dc300 d)

65 MUSIC IN THE TUILERIES, d.1862
Exhibited Martinet 1863 (135). Sold to Faure 1883
Oil on canvas, 76 × 118 cm   RW 51, PNY 38
National Gallery, London (3260)

66 BAUDELAIRE'S MISTRESS RECLINING / STUDY OF JEANNE
DUVAL, c.1862
Oil on canvas, 90 × 113 cm   RW 48, PNY 27
Budapest Museum of Fine Arts (5004.368.B)

67 YOUNG WOMAN RECLINING IN SPANISH COSTUME, c.1862
Exhibited Martinet 1863 (130). Proposed to Martinet 1865 – see (85)?
Dedicated (c.1868?) *to my friend Nadar*. See page 38
Oil on canvas, 94 × 113 cm   RW 59, PNY 29
*Yale University Art Gallery, New Haven. Bequest of Stephen Carlton Clark, BA
1903* (61.18.33)

68 THE SPANISH DANCER, MARIANO CAMPRUBI, 1862–3
Lettered (in Spanish) *don Mariano Camprubi principal dancer at the royal theatre
in Madrid*
Print published c.1863 (16); signed *bon à tirer* proof
Etching, 30.2 × 20 cm   G 24, H 34
Bibliothèque nationale, Estampes, Paris (Dc300 d)

69 LOLA DE VALENCE, COVER FOR A SONGSHEET, 1863
After the painting (RW 53, PNY 50). Words and music by Zacharie Astruc
Print published March 1863. Copy dedicated by Astruc to Fantin-Latour
Lithograph, 24 × 21.5 cm; 35.8 × 27 (sheet)   G 69, H 32, PNY 53
Bibliothèque nationale, Estampes, Paris (Dc300 d)

70 THE SPANISH BALLET, 1862–3
After Manet's painting (RW 55)
Pen and Indian ink with wash, watercolour and gouache, 23 × 41 cm
RW D533, PNY 49
Budapest Museum of Fine Arts (1925.1200)

71 BULLFIGHTERS / THE BULLFIGHT, c.1863–5
Reworked fragment of Manet's Salon painting of 1864 (1282,
'Incident in a Bullfight'), see (72)
Oil on canvas, 48 × 108 cm   RW 73
Frick Collection, New York (14.1.86)

72 THE DEAD TORERO / THE DEAD MAN, c.1863–5
Reworked fragment of Manet's Salon painting of 1864, 'Incident in a
Bullfight', see (71)
Exhibited Martinet 1865? (see letter p.32 (10) '2 the dead Matador');
Le Havre 1868. Sold to Durand-Ruel 1872 (p.163). See page 48
Oil on canvas, 76 × 153.3 cm   RW 72, PNY 73
National Gallery of Art, Washington DC. Widener Collection (636)

73 THE STEAMER, 1864
Double page from a sketchbook, used for (74)
Graphite and watercolour, 14.3 × 18.5 cm (repr. actual size)   RW D222
Private collection (Courtesy Brame et Lorenceau, Paris)

74 THE PORPOISES / SEASCAPE AT BOULOGNE, 1864
Sold to Durand-Ruel 1872 (p.163); 4th London exhibition 1872; exchanged?
and sold to Weiz 1881
Oil on canvas, 81 × 100 cm   RW 79
*Philadelphia Museum of Art. Bequest of Anne Thomson as a memorial to her father,
Frank Thomson, and her mother, Mary Elizabeth Clarke Thomson* (54.66.3)

75 COMBAT OF THE *KEARSARGE* AND THE *ALABAMA*, 1864
Exhibited Cadart 1864; sold to Durand-Ruel (p.163) and exhibited Salon of
1872 (1059). See page 31
Oil on canvas, 134 × 127 cm   RW 76, PNY 83
Philadelphia Museum of Art. John G. Johnson Collection (1027)

76 FISHING BOAT COMING IN BEFORE THE WIND
THE *KEARSARGE* AT BOULOGNE, 1864
Exhibited Martinet 1865? (see letter p.32 (10) '7 the sea, the federal ship
Kearsarge . . .'). Given or sold to Adam (62). See page 31
Oil on canvas, 81 × 99.4 cm   RW 75, PNY 84
Private collection, USA

77 FISH / SALMON, PIKE AND SHRIMP, 1864–5
Exhibited Martinet 1865? (see letter p.32 (10) '5 fish', pendant to (78)
'fruit')
Oil on canvas, 44.5 × 71.8 cm   RW 82
Norton Simon Art Foundation, Pasadena (M 1978.25.P)

78 FRUIT ON A TABLECLOTH, 1864–5
Exhibited Martinet 1865? – see (77). Given to Dr Siredey between 1867
and 1883
Oil on canvas, 45 × 73.5 cm   RW 83, PNY 80
Musée d'Orsay, Paris (RF 1670)

79 PEONIES IN A VASE ON A STAND, 1864
Exhibited Martinet 1865? (see letter p.32 (10) '6 flowers'). Sold to Durand-
Ruel 1872 (p.163)
Oil on canvas, 93.2 × 72 cm   RW 86, PNY 77
Musée d'Orsay, Paris (RF 1669)

80 BRANCH OF WHITE PEONIES WITH SECATEURS, 1864
Given to Champfleury
Oil on canvas, 31 × 46.5 cm   RW 88, PNY 78
Musée d'Orsay, Paris (RF 1995)

81 THE DEAD CHRIST AND THE ANGELS, 1864
Salon of 1864 (1281). Sold to Durand-Ruel 1872 (p.163)
Oil on canvas, 179 × 150 cm   RW 74, PNY 74
Metropolitan Museum of Art, New York (29.100.51)

82 THE DEAD CHRIST AND THE ANGELS, c.1865–7
Exhibited Cercle de l'Union artistique 1870. Given to Zola
Preparatory drawing (composition reversed) for a print (83)
Graphite, watercolour, gouache, pen and Indian ink, 32.4 × 27 cm
RW D130, PNY 75
Musée du Louvre, Arts graphiques, Paris (RF 4520)

83 THE DEAD CHRIST AND THE ANGELS, c.1865–7
Unpublished print (Manet's largest etching)
Etching and aquatint, 1st state, 40.3 × 33.2 cm   G 34, H 51, PNY 76
Bibliothèque nationale, Estampes, Paris (Dc300 d)

84 JESUS MOCKED BY THE SOLDIERS, d.1865
Salon of 1865 (1427). See pages 32, 33
Oil on canvas, 190.8 × 148.3 cm   RW 102, PNY 87
Art Institute of Chicago. Gift of James Deering (1925.703)

85 OLYMPIA, c.1860–65/d.1863
Salon of 1865 (1428); proposed to Martinet February 1865? (see letter p.32
(10) '1 a reclining woman . . .'). Bought by subscription for the Musée du
Luxembourg in 1890. See pages 33, 179
Oil on canvas, 130.5 × 190 cm   RW 69, PNY 64
Musée d'Orsay, Paris (RF 644)

86 THE BULLRING IN MADRID, 1865
Sold to Pertuiset. See page 37
Oil on canvas, 90 × 110 cm   RW 107, PNY 91
Musée d'Orsay, Paris (RF 1976.8)

87 BULLFIGHT, 1865
Sold to Durand-Ruel 1872 (p.163)
Oil on canvas, 48 × 60.3 cm   RW 108
Art Institute of Chicago. Mr and Mrs Martin A. Ryerson Collection (317.1019)

88 THE TRAGIC ACTOR / PHILIBERT ROUVIÈRE IN THE ROLE OF
HAMLET, 1865–6
Refused Salon of 1866. Sold to Durand-Ruel 1872 (p.163). See page 38
Oil on canvas, 187.2 × 108.1 cm   RW 106, PNY 89
National Gallery of Art, Washington DC. Gift of Edith Stuyvesant Gerry (1530)

89 YOUNG LADY IN 1866 / WOMAN WITH A PARROT, 1866
Study of Victorine. Salon of 1868 (1659). Sold to Durand-Ruel 1872
(p.163). Donated to the Metropolitan Museum in 1889, with (54)
Oil on canvas, 185.1 × 128.6 cm   RW 115, PNY 96
Metropolitan Museum of Art, New York, (89.21.3)

90 PORTRAIT OF ZACHARIE ASTRUC, d.1866
Dedicated *to the poet Z. Astruc his friend Manet*
Oil on canvas, 90 × 116 cm   RW 92, PNY 94
Kunsthalle, Bremen (88)

91 PORTRAIT OF ÉMILE ZOLA, 1868
Salon of 1868 (1660). See pages 45, 182
Oil on canvas, 146 × 114 cm   RW 128, PNY 106
Musée d'Orsay, Paris (RF 2205)

92 VIEW OF A RACE IN THE BOIS DE BOULOGNE, d.1864
After a painting exhibited Martinet 1865? – see letter, p.32 (10) '3 view of a
race . . .'; cut and reworked, see (94)
Watercolour, 22.2 × 56.5 cm   RW D548
*Fogg Art Museum, Harvard University, Cambridge, Mass. Bequest of Grenville L.
Winthrop (1943.387)*

93 THE RACES, c.1865–7
Contemporary proof(?), before the posthumous publication 1884
Crayon lithograph, 1st state, 36.6 × 51.3 cm   G 72, H 41, PNY 101
Private collection

94 RACES AT LONGCHAMP IN THE BOIS DE BOULOGNE, d.186(7?)
Reworked fragment of the 1864–5 composition (92). Sold to Delius 1877
Oil on canvas, 43.9 × 84.5 cm   RW 98, PNY 99
Art Institute of Chicago. Potter Palmer Collection (1922.424)

95 THE EXECUTION OF MAXIMILIAN, c.1867–9/d.1867
Extensively reworked sketch for the last of three large compositions: see
(96) and RW 124, 126, and the lithograph (22). Given to Méry Laurent
Oil on canvas, 48 × 58 cm   RW 125
Ny Carlsberg Glyptotek, Copenhagen (924)

96 THE EXECUTION OF MAXIMILIAN, 1868–9/d. 19 June 1867
Third and final 'Salon' composition, suppressed by the authorities.
Exhibited New York and Boston 1879–80. See pages 50, 304
Oil on canvas, 252 × 305 cm   RW 127
Städtische Kunsthalle, Mannheim (281)

97 A MOONLIT SKY, 1868
Double page from a sketchbook
Watercolour, 15 × 20 cm   RW D182
Musée du Louvre, Arts graphiques, Paris (RF 11.169:32)

98 BOULOGNE, MOONLIGHT, 1868
Brussels Salon 1869 (756). Sold to Durand-Ruel 1872 (p.163). See
page 179
Oil on canvas, 82 × 101 cm   RW 143, PNY 118
Musée d'Orsay, Paris (RF 1993)

99 JETTY AT BOULOGNE, 1868
Sold to Durand-Ruel 1873
Oil on canvas, 60 × 73 cm   RW 145, PNY 119
Private collection

100 BEACH AT BOULOGNE, 1868
Sold to Durand-Ruel 1872 (p.163)
Oil on canvas, 32 × 65 cm   RW 148
*Virginia Museum of Art, Richmond, Virginia. Collection of Mr and Mrs Paul
Mellon (85.498)*

101 FANNY CLAUS ON THE BALCONY, 1868
Oil on canvas, 71 × 43 cm   RW 133
Private collection, London

102 THE BALCONY, 1868–9
Salon of 1869 (1616); Brussels Salon 1869 (754). See the sketch (21)
Oil on canvas, 169 × 125 cm   RW 134, PNY 115
Musée d'Orsay, Paris (RF 2772)

103 THE LUNCHEON / LUNCHEON IN THE STUDIO, 1868–9
Salon of 1869 (1617); Brussels Salon 1869 (755). Sold to Faure 1873
Oil on canvas, 118 × 153.9 cm   RW 135, PNY 109
Neue Pinakothek, Bayerische Staatsgemäldesammlungen, Munich (8638)

104 THE SALMON, c.1868–9
Sold to Bassett; bought by Durand-Ruel 1872. See page 52
Oil on canvas, 72 × 92 cm   RW 140
Shelburne Museum, Vermont (27.1.3–24)

105 MELON, PEACHES AND GRAPES, c.1868–9
Sold to Basset; bought by Durand-Ruel 1872. See page 52
Oil on canvas, 69 × 92.2 cm   RW 121, PNY 82
National Gallery of Art, Washington DC. Gift of Eugene and Agnes Meyer (1549)

106 REPOSE / STUDY OF BERTHE MORISOT, 1869–70
Sold to Durand-Ruel 1872 (p.163). Salon of 1873 (998)
Oil on canvas, 147.8 × 111 cm   RW 158, PNY 121
Rhode Island School of Design, Museum of Art, Providence, RI (59.027)

107 PORTRAIT OF EVA GONZALÈS, d.1870
Salon of 1870 (1852). See page 52
Oil on canvas, 191 × 133 cm   RW 154
National Gallery, London (3259)

108 EVA GONZALÈS IN MANET'S STUDIO, 1869–70
Eva Gonzalès painting *L'enfant de troupe* (*The Bugler*), her Salon entry for
1870; on the wall, Manet's *Lola de Valence* (RW 53, PNY 50)
Oil on canvas, 56 × 46 cm   RW 153
Private collection

109 VELASQUEZ IN HIS STUDIO, PAINTING THE LITTLE CAVALIERS,
c.1865–70
For *The Little Cavaliers*, see (52)
Oil on canvas, 46 × 38 cm   RW 25
Private collection

110 THE MUSIC LESSON, 1868–70
Posed by Zacharie Astruc and an unidentified lady. Salon of 1870 (1851)
Oil on canvas, 140 × 173 cm   RW 152
Museum of Fine Arts, Boston (69.1123)

168 MARCELLIN DESBOUTIN, 1875
Watercolour, 22 × 13 cm   RW D474
Fogg Art Museum, Harvard University, Cambridge Mass. Bequest of Grenville L. Winthrop (1943.386)

169 THE ARTIST / STUDY OF MARCELLIN DESBOUTIN, d.1875
Sold to Debrousse 1875. Refused Salon of 1876; exhibited in Manet's studio – see (*131*). See page 183
Oil on canvas, 192 × 128 cm   RW 244, PNY 146
Museu de Arte de Sao Paulo

170 THE PARISIENNE / STUDY OF ELLEN ANDRÉE, 1874–5
Intended for the Salon of 1876; replaced by *Le linge* (*134*)
Oil on canvas, 192 × 125 cm   RW 236
Nationalmuseum, Stockholm (2068)

171 NANA / STUDY OF HENRIETTE HAUSER, d.1877
Refused Salon of 1877; exhibited in Giroux's shop window
Oil on canvas, 154 × 115 cm   RW 259, PNY 157
Hamburger Kunsthalle, Hamburg (2376)

172 BEFORE THE MIRROR, c.1876–9
Exhibited *La Vie moderne* 1880 (8) – see (*193*)
Oil on canvas, 92.1 × 71.4 cm   RW 264, PNY 156
Solomon R. Guggenheim Museum, New York. Justin K. Thannhauser Collection (78.2514 T 27)

173 LA TOILETTE (WOMAN AT HER TOILET), c.1876–9
Exhibited *La Vie moderne* 1880 (16)? – see (*193*)
Pastel on canvas, 54 × 45 cm   RW P24, PNY 179
Musée d'Orsay, Paris (RF 35.739)

174 THE SKATING RINK, 1877
Exhibited *La Vie moderne* 1880 (6) – see (*193*). See page 183
Oil on canvas, 92 × 72 cm   RW 260
Fogg Art Museum, Harvard University, Cambridge Mass. Bequest of Collection of Maurice Wertheim Class of 1906 (1951.50)

175 FAURE IN THE ROLE OF HAMLET AT THE OPERA, 1877
Full-scale study for the painting in the Salon of 1877 (RW 257).
See page 182
Oil on canvas, 196 × 130 cm   RW 256
Hamburger Kunsthalle, Hamburg (1565)

176 ERNEST HOSCHEDÉ AND HIS DAUGHTER MARTHE AT MONTGERON, 1876
See page 180
Oil on canvas, 86 × 130 cm   RW 246
Museo Nacional de Bellas Artes, Buenos Aires (7961)

177 CAROLUS DURAN AT MONTGERON, 1876
Given to Carolus Duran. See page 180
Oil on canvas, 189 × 170 cm   RW 245
Barber Institute of Fine Arts, The University of Birmingham

178 THE RUE MOSNIER WITH PAVERS, 1878
Sold to Portalis 1879
Oil on canvas, 64 × 80 cm   RW 272, PNY 158
Private collection

179 THE RUE MOSNIER, 1878
Project for a lithograph?
Brush and lithographic ink over graphite, 19 × 36 cm   RW D328, PNY 159
Budapest Museum of Fine Arts (1935.2735)

180 LES MENDIANTS (THE BEGGARS), COVER DESIGN FOR A SONGSHEET, 1878
Design with sketched title and 'Music by Cabaner', 'Poems by J. Richepin'
Brush and ink over graphite, 34 × 26.5 cm   RW D478
Huguette Berès Collection, Paris

181 THE RUE MOSNIER DECKED WITH FLAGS (FOR THE FÊTE DE LA PAIX ON 30 JUNE), 1878
Sold 1879 (buyer unidentified)
Oil on canvas, 65 × 81 cm   RW 270
J. Paul Getty Museum, Malibu (89.PA.71)

182 VIEW FROM THE PLACE CLICHY, c.1878
Oil on canvas, 38 × 23 cm   RW 273
Private collection

183 THE TAVERN / AT THE BARRIÈRE DE CLICHY, c.1878
Oil on canvas, 73 × 91 cm   RW 275
Pushkin Museum, Moscow

184 WOMAN WRITING, c.1878
Double page from a notebook
Graphite, 8.2 × 10.4 cm (repr. slightly enlarged)   RW D382
Musée du Louvre, Arts graphiques, Paris (RF 30.467)

185 MAN WRITING IN A CAFÉ / 'CHEZ TORTONI', c.1878?
Oil on canvas, 26 × 34 cm   RW 328
Isabella Stewart Gardner Museum, Boston (P355)

186 AT THE CAFÉ, d.1878
Left half of Manet's 'Reichshoffen' composition – see (*187*). Sold to Barroil 1880, to replace (*187*). See page 247
Oil on canvas, 77 × 83 cm   RW 278
Sammlung Oskar Reinhart 'Am Römerholz', Winterthur

187 CORNER OF A CAFÉ-CONCERT, 1878–80/d.187(8?)
Reworked right half of Manet's 'Reichshoffen' composition – see (*186*). Sold to Barroil 1879; returned and extensively reworked (stage and musicians added). See pages 187, 247
Exhibited *La Vie moderne* 1880 (3) – see (*193*); Lyons 1883
Oil on canvas, 98 × 79 cm   RW 311, PNY 172
National Gallery, London (3858)

188 CAFÉ-CONCERT, 1878–9
Exhibited *La Vie moderne* 1880 (2) – see (*193*). Sold to Boussaton 1881
Oil on canvas, 47.5 × 32 cm   RW 280, PNY 169
Walters Art Gallery, Baltimore (893)

189 THE BEER DRINKERS, c.1878–9
Exhibited *La Vie moderne* 1880 (23) – see (*193*); sold (buyer unidentified)
Pastel on canvas, 61 × 50.8 cm   RW P7
Burrell Collection, Glasgow Art Galleries and Museums (35.305)

190 A CAFÉ ON THE PLACE DU THÉÂTRE FRANÇAIS, c.1876–8
Pastel on canvas, 32.4 × 45.7 cm   RW P64
Burrell Collection, Glasgow Art Galleries and Museums (35.306)

191 LA PRUNE (THE PLUM BRANDY), c.1876–8
Exhibited *La Vie Moderne* 1880 (4) – see (*193*). Sold to Deudon 1881
Oil on canvas, 73.6 × 50.2 cm   RW 282, PNY 165
National Gallery of Art, Washington DC. Collection of Mr and Mrs Paul Mellon (2585)

192 PORTRAIT OF MME ÉMILE ZOLA, 1879
Exhibited *La Vie moderne* 1880 (11) – see (*193*)
Pastel on canvas, 52 × 44 cm   RW P13, PNY 183
Musée d'Orsay, Paris (RF 4519)

193 CATALOGUE OF MANET'S EXHIBITION AT *LA VIE MODERNE*, 1880
With gillotage reproductions of two lost lithographs. See De L 486 and 484 (copy)
Private collection

194 PORTRAIT OF CLAUDE MONET, 1880
Drawing for a gillotage reproduction for Monet's *Vie moderne* exhibition catalogue, 1880
Brush and black ink with gouache, 14 × 12.5 cm (sight)   RW D486
Private collection (Courtesy Galerie Robert Schmit, Paris)

195 WORKING MAN ON A BENCH / COVER OF *LE SALON RÉALISTE*, 1880
With gillotage reproduction of a lost drawing, 12.1 × 8.6 cm (image)   RW D481
Bibliothèque nationale, Imprimés, Paris (8° V3627)

196 LETTER TO ISABELLE LEMONNIER, 11 or 18 July 1880
Autograph manuscript (text p.251) illustrated with brush and grey ink, 4 pages (2r/v), 20 × 12.5 cm (each)   RW D576
Musée du Louvre, Arts graphiques, Paris (RF 11.182)

228   A BAR AT THE FOLIES-BERGÈRE, d.1882
      Salon of 1882 (1753)
      Oil on canvas, 96 × 130 cm   RW 388, PNY 211
      Courtauld Institute Galleries, London. Courtauld Collection

229   SPRING / STUDY OF JEANNE DEMARSY, d.1881
      Salon of 1882 (1754). Sold to A. Proust 1883. See page 265
      Oil on canvas, 73 × 51 cm   RW 372
      Private collection

230   AUTUMN / STUDY OF MÉRY LAURENT, 1882
      Second and last in a projected series of the 'Four Seasons' (the muff
      unfinished and retouched in 1883). See page 259
      Oil on canvas, 73 × 51 cm   RW 393, PNY 215
      Musée des Beaux-Arts, Nancy (1071)

231   JULIE MANET WITH A WATERING CAN AT RUEIL, 1882
      Free, unfinished sketch
      Oil on canvas, 100 × 81 cm   RW 399
      Private collection

232   THE HOUSE AT RUEIL, d.1882
      Sold to Faure 1883
      Oil on canvas, 92 × 73 cm   RW 406
      National Gallery of Victoria, Melbourne

233   THE AMAZON (THE HORSEWOMAN), 1882–3
      Project for the Salon of 1883; allegedly slashed by Manet in front of Pierre
      Prins. Given to Prins by Mme Manet, according to the inscription
      Oil on canvas, 114 × 86 cm   RW 396
      Private collection

234   THE BUGLER, 1882–3
      Project for the Salon of 1883
      Oil on canvas, 73 × 51 cm   RW 392
      Private collection

235   LILAC AND ROSES IN A LITTLE GLASS VASE, c.1882
      Given to Mlle Ginevra Hureau de Villeneuve
      Oil on canvas, 32 × 24 cm   RW 416
      Private collection

236   PINKS AND CLEMATIS IN A GLASS VASE, c.1882
      Oil on canvas, 56 × 35 cm   RW 423, PNY 221
      Musée d'Orsay, Paris (MNR 631)

237   WHITE LILAC IN A GLASS VASE, 1882–3
      One of three flower paintings sold to Marcel Bernstein in 1883
      Oil on canvas, 56 × 46 cm   RW 427
      Staatliche Museen Preussischer Kulturbesitz, Nationalgalerie, Berlin (1333)

238   ROSES IN A GLASS VASE, 1 March 1883
      Manet's last painting, for Ignace Ephrussi
      Oil on canvas, 56 × 35 cm   RW 429
      Private collection, Japan

239   YOUNG WOMAN BY THE SEA, c.1880–82
      Based on a pencil drawing (RW D413) and possibly related to the beach
      scenes of 1880 (*197, 198, 214*) or the illustrations for Mallarmé (*203*)
      Pencil and watercolour, 18 × 13 cm   RW D414
      André Bromberg Collection, France

Biographical Notes

These notes are intended to provide a background to some of the personalities
and families referred to in the text. Other brief notes are included in the index.

ADAM, Ambroise   1800–85
Related by marriage to Henriette Metman, the wife of Edmond Fournier
(Manet's maternal uncle), Adam was a member of the legal profession.
Photographs of him and a letter written in July 1861 have documented an
uncatalogued painting (*62*) as a portrait of Adam sketched in a garden at
Pressagny-l'Orgueilleux, on the Seine between Paris and Rouen (see Map).
J. Wilson-Bareau, 'The Portrait of Ambroise Adam by Edouard Manet', *Burlington
Magazine*, CXXVI, 1984, 750–58

ASTRUC, Zacharie   1835–1907
Artist, writer and composer, hispanophile and japonist, Astruc wrote in support
of Manet's paintings at the Salon des Refusés and collaborated on an illustrated
songsheet (*69*) in 1863, composed a poem for *Olympia* (*85*) and advised Manet on
his visit to Spain in 1865. Fantin showed Manet painting Astruc's portrait, as he
had in fact done (*90*) in 1866, in *A Studio in the Batignolles* of 1870.

BALLEROY, Count Albert de   1828–73
In the 1850s Balleroy, who specialized in hunting scenes, shared with Manet the
studio in which the boy assistant Alexandre (*46, 47*) hung himself. Balleroy
stands next to Manet in *Music in the Tuileries* (*65*). His family property was in
Calvados and as a Deputy to the Assembly in Bordeaux in 1871 he took Manet to
listen to the proceedings.

BANVILLE, Théodore de   1823–91
Poet, dramatist and critic and a friend of Baudelaire, Banville was a central figure
in Manet's artistic and literary circle. In 1873 he composed a cameo portrait of
Eva Gonzalès and the following year Manet devised a delightful image of the
'cloud compelling' poet (*126*).

BAUDELAIRE, Charles   1821–67
In his poetry and critical writings Baudelaire was an advocate of 'modernity', in
an urban, Parisian context. The most important figure in the development of
Manet's attitudes to art, he followed the artist's successes and failures from the
late 1850s, appearing in *Music in the Tuileries* (*65*), and remaining in close touch
after his departure for Belgium (during the Salons of 1864 and 1865) and on his
return to Paris in the year before his death. Two portraits by Manet (see *17*)
appeared in the posthumous biography by Baudelaire's friend Charles Asselineau.
Baudelaire, Correspondance, ed. C. Pichois, Paris 1973. *Lettres à Charles Baudelaire*, ed.
C. Pichois, Neuchâtel 1973. *Baudelaire, Oeuvres complètes*, ed. C. Pichois, 2 vols,
Paris 1975

BRACQUEMOND, Félix   1833–1914
Active in many artistic spheres, Bracquemond led the revival of original
printmaking and the growing enthusiasm for oriental art in the early 1860s. He
helped Manet with his prints and made portraits of him in pastel (*1864*) and
etching (for Zola's 1867 pamphlet).
J.-P. Bouillon, 'Les lettres de Manet à Bracquemond', *Gazette des Beaux-Arts*, April
1983, 145–8

BURTY, Philippe   1830–90
An intimate friend of Bracquemond, Burty shared his wide-ranging interests and
his passion for printmaking, acquiring a unique collection of Manet's prints which
later passed to Degas. He commissioned a print from Manet for a *de luxe* album in
1868 (*19*). Manet regarded the critic's essentially conservative views with some
scepticism in later years but they remained good friends.

CARDART, Alfred   1828–75
Cardart opened a shop and gallery on the rue de Richelieu with facilities for print
making. In 1862 he founded the *Société des aquafortistes* (Society of etchers), and
published prints by Manet. He showed his paintings in 1864 (*75*) and 1865.

CALLIAS, Nina de 1845?–84
Poet and pianist, renowned for her striking looks, extravagant ideas and generosity, Nina's bohemian salon attracted the liveliest talents in the 1870s, including Mallarmé and Manet whose portrait of Nina (*158*) was reproduced to illustrate a poem by her friend Charles Cros.

CHAMPFLEURY (Jules Husson) 1821–89
A writer and critic, friend of Baudelaire and Duranty, Champfleury was closely involved with the realist movement. His interest in caricature and naïve art influenced Manet in the early 1860s (see *55*, *63*), and in 1868 Manet designed an illustration and a striking poster for Champfleury's popular book about cats.

CHARPENTIER, Georges 1846–1905
Charpentier published the naturalist novels of Flaubert, Maupassant, Zola and Goncourt. From the 1870s he and his wife Marguerite (née Lemonnier) held a celebrated Salon and collected the Impressionists, particularly Renoir. Mme Charpentier, whose younger sister Isabelle became one of Manet's favourite models, launched the magazine *La Vie moderne* in 1879.

CHESNEAU, Ernest 1833–90
Writer and critic, Chesneau was secretary to Nieuwerkerke, the Fine Arts administrator. He acquired a small painting by Manet in 1864 and later gave qualified support to the 'new art' of the Impressionists.

COURBET, Gustave 1819–77
Courbet was the most radical artist in the 1850s, whose work was shown at the *Exposition universelle* and in his individual exhibition in 1855. His challenge to the conventions of official, academic art was an inspiration to younger artists and Manet admired him profoundly. Although disillusioned by Courbet's conduct during and after the Commune of 1871, he contributed a lithographic portrait to d'Ideville's memorial biography of 1878 (*8*).

COUTURE, Thomas 1815–79
Manet spent six years in Couture's studio, rejecting his more contrived, 'academic' methods but benefitting from his liberal approach to sketching from nature and the use of relatively free brushwork. Couture painted in a straightforward manner with a dry handling of paint, reflected in Manet's earliest works (*30*).

CROS, Charles 1842–88
Poet and inventor, friend of Nina de Callias, Cros created the *Revue du monde nouveau* to which both Manet and Mallarmé contributed in 1873, asked Manet to illustrate his poem *Le fleuve* (*125*) in 1874, and used *Spring* (*299*) for his first successful experiment in colour photography.

DEGAS, Edgar 1834–1917
Rivals as well as friends and colleagues, Degas and Manet disputed each other's claim to precedence as painters of modern life. Although the Old Masters influenced Degas well into the 1860s, he later devoted himself to urban themes, including some not treated by Manet, the ballet and the brothel.

DESBOUTIN, Marcellin 1823–1902
Writer, artist and brilliant printmaker, Desboutin lived in style near Florence until ruined, then as a penniless but aristocratic bohemian in Paris from 1871. He frequented the café Guerbois and the Nouvelle-Athènes and exhibited with the Impressionists in 1876.

DURAND-RUEL, Paul 1831–1922
A major art dealer with interests in fashionable academic painters as well as the Romantic and Realist schools, Durand-Ruel met Pissarro and Monet in London during the Franco-Prussian War. In January 1872, he made a major purchase from Manet's studio but, in spite of active promotion and exhibitions in London, most of this stock remained unsold until years later.
Impressionists in London, ed. Flint, London 1984, pp. 357–60 (Durand-Ruel and Deschamps exhibitions)

DURANTY, Edmond 1833–80
A prolific novelist and critic, friend of Champfleury and Degas, Duranty supported Courbet and the realist cause and later the Impressionists. In spite of the challenge to a duel in 1870 over an alleged affront, Duranty fully acknowledged Manet's lead in the development of 'the new painting'.

DURET, Théodore 1838–1927
Duret's family cognac business enabled him to pursue his interests in art and politics. An encounter with Manet in Madrid in 1865 led to a life-long association with the Impressionists. Duret helped Manet in many ways, organized the sale of works from his studio after his death, wrote a biography and catalogued his work.

EVANS, Dr Thomas William 1823–97
Celebrated American dentist living in Paris, the protector of Méry Laurent, Evans was a friend of Manet and his mother, and a patron of the artist.

FANTIN-LATOUR, Henri 1836–1904
One of Manet's earliest friends and admirers, Fantin included him in three of his large group portraits (including *A Studio in the Batignolles* of 1870) and painted the portrait (Salon of 1867) that was reproduced in *La Vie moderne* for Manet's 1880 exhibition.

FAURE, Jean-Baptiste 1830–1914
In 1876 Faure's career as a baritone ended with his final role in an operatic version of Shakespeare's *Hamlet*, the subject of Manet's portrait shown at the Salon of 1877 (see *175*). A clever and thrifty patron, Faure acquired many of Manet's paintings, including *Le bon bock* (*151*) which the artist hoped might be purchased by the State in 1879, and later marketed his Manets through Durand-Ruel.

FOURNIER family
Manet's father married Eugénie Désirée Fournier (1811–85) a god-daughter of the elected king of Sweden who, as Marshal Bernadotte, had been a close friend of her father. Her brother Edmond (1800–65), who encouraged Manet's artistic talents as a boy, was a military man and a monarchist who retired to Pontcelles after the Revolution of 1848. Edmond Fournier married a Metman and was thus related to Ambroise Adam (*62*). One of his sons, also called Edmond and born the same year as Manet, is referred to in Manet's letters from Rio. In 1865 the artist stayed with Fournier relatives on his return from Spain.

GAMBETTA, Léon 1838–82
A Republican politician, opponent of the Imperial régime and the war with Prussia, Gambetta proclaimed the Third Republic in 1870. He contributed to the downfall of Mac-Mahon, but did not exercise power until 1881 when his short-lived government nominated Manet for the Legion of Honour.

GONZALÈS, Eva 1849–83
The daughter of Emmanuel Gonzalès (novelist, playwright and journalist), Eva studied with Charles Chaplin, becoming Manet's pupil in 1869 and a long-suffering model for her portrait (*107*). An excellent artist and Berthe Morisot's rival for Manet's approval, she married Henri Guérard in 1879 and died a few days after Manet.

GUÉRARD, Henri 1846–97
An accomplished young artist, Guérard posed with Ellen Andrée for an ambitious café scene (*186*). He was a brilliant printmaker, who helped Manet with the few etchings he produced in later years (*205*) and acquired a remarkable collection of the artist's prints.

HOSCHEDÉ, Ernest 1837–91
A wealthy businessman and speculator, Hoschedé was a major collector of Impressionist paintings. Bankrupted in 1877–8, separated from his wife and family who lived with Monet from 1879, Hoschedé remained active, launching *L'Art de la mode* to rival the Charpentiers' *Vie moderne* in 1880.

LAURENT, Méry 1849–1900
A woman of great charm and beauty, the mistress of Dr Evans, Méry became an intimate friend of Mallarmé and Manet whom she met at his 1876 studio exhibition and who made many portraits of her in oils and pastel.

LEENHOFF family
Manet's wife Suzanne (1830–1906), the daughter of a Dutch organist, was an excellent pianist who taught the young Manet brothers. Her illegitimate son Léon (1852–1927), whose father was named as Köella but was probably someone in the Manet family circle, was always referred to as his mother's younger brother. Suzanne's sculptor brother Ferdinand (1841–1914) posed for *Le déjeuner sur l'herbe*. Her sister Marthe (Martiena) married the artist Jules Vibert and there are references to their children Alexandre and Edouard. Léon Köella-Leenhoff inherited Manet's estate after his mother's death.

LEJOSNE, Hippolyte 1814–84
Commandant Lejosne, a military officer with strong Republican sympathies, and his wife (née Valentine Thérèse(?) Cazalis-Allut) were enthusiastic supporters of the literary, artistic and musical avant garde. Mme Lejosne appears seated in Manet's *Music in the Tuileries* (*65*).

MALLARMÉ, Stéphane   1842–98
The symbolist poet and critic met Manet in the circle of Nina de Callias in 1873 and defended him after the Salon jury rejected his pictures in 1874 and 1876. They collaborated on illustrated editions of *The Raven* by Poe (*127*, *128*) in 1875, Mallarmé's *L'Après-midi d'un faune* (*130*) in 1876 and the poems of Poe (*203*, *204*) in 1881.
Stéphane Mallarmé. Correspondance, ed. H. Mondor and L. J. Austin, Paris 1956–85
Stéphane Mallarmé. Oeuvres complètes, ed. H. Mondor and G. Jean-Aubry, Paris 1945

MANET family
Manet's father Auguste (1797–1862) held important posts in the legal administration, becoming a *chevalier* of the Legion of Honour and a judge. He married Eugénie Désirée Fournier who gave him three sons, Edouard (1832–83), Eugène (1833–92) and Gustave (1835–84). Auguste Manet became partially paralysed in 1858, two years before Manet painted his parents (*48*). Eugène studied medicine, followed no profession and married Berthe Morisot in 1874. Gustave was a lawyer and a Republican politician and friend of Clemenceau, becoming a municipal councillor in 1871. Auguste Manet's elder sister Émilie was the mother of Jules De Jouy (1812–94).

MARTINET, Louis   1814–95
A painter and Fine Arts administrator, Martinet held exhibitions in large premises on the Boulevard des Italiens from 1860 and founded the Société Nationale des Beaux-arts. Changing displays with works for sale, and individual exhibitions (including a Delacroix memorial show) created considerable public interest and an important group of Manet's paintings achieved a *succès de scandale* in 1863. Disillusioned, Manet withdrew his support in 1865.

MEURENT, Victorine Louise   1844–90 +
A perfect artist's model, Victorine was apparently discovered by Manet in 1861–2 and appears in many of his paintings of the 1860s including *Olympia* (see *57*, *58*, *85*, *89*). After a spell in America, she reappeared, posing again for Manet in 1873 (*155*). She took up painting and exhibited at the Salon, but later sank into obscurity.

MEURICE, Paul 1820–1902
Paul Meurice and his wife Eléonore (*née* Granger, 1819–74) were close friends of Baudelaire and fervent admirers of Victor Hugo and Wagner. Their salon was a cultural meeting place in the 1860s and Mme Meurice defended Manet when *Olympia* (*85*) caused a scandal at the Salon of 1865. An excellent pianist, she and Suzanne Manet played Wagner for Baudelaire during his final illness.

MONET, Claude   1840–1926
Early years at Le Havre and contacts with Boudin and Jongkind made Monet a master of the seascape and the influence of Courbet and Manet was also strong. Manet became a firm admirer, painting with Monet at Argenteuil in 1874 and helping him financially. In 1890 Monet organized a public subscription to purchase *Olympia* for the French nation.

MORISOT, Berthe   1841–95
Berthe and her sister Edma (who married Adolphe Pontillon, Manet's naval co-recruit) took painting lessons with Corot and Oudinot, copied in the Louvre alongside Fantin and were introduced to Manet in 1868. Berthe posed for *The Balcony* (*102*) and *Repose* (*106*), and Manet made many portraits of her before her marriage to his brother Eugène in 1874 and the birth of their daughter Julie (Bibi). An accomplished and highly individual artist, she exhibited with the Impressionists. The Morisot family letters are an important source of information.
Correspondance de Berthe Morisot avec sa famille et ses amis, ed. D. Rouart, Paris 1950
The Correspondence of Berthe Morisot, London (1957) ed. K. Adler and T. Garb, London 1986

NADAR (Félix Tournachon)   1820–1910
An enthusiastic Republican and supporter of many interests and causes, Nadar was journalist, novelist, caricaturist, balloonist and the oustanding portrait photographer of his time. He was a close friend of Baudelaire and Manet, and made a studio available for the first Impressionist exhibition in 1874.

NIEUWERKERKE, Count Alfred de   1811–92
A friend of Louis Napoleon Bonaparte, his brilliant administrative career under the Second Empire gave him great power as director general of French museums, with responsibility for the organization of the Paris Salon. He was blamed by Manet for contributing to his failure to gain public recognition.

PROUST, Antonin   1832–1905
Proust, the son of a Deputy, was born in the same year as Manet, attended school and then Couture's studio with him. A life-long friend, his memoirs (first published in 1897) provide the most direct record of Manet's life and opinions. Proust's portrait by Manet (*212*) was shown at the Salon of 1880 and as Minister of Fine Arts during Gambetta's government, he nominated Manet for the Legion of Honour the following year.
A. Proust, 'Edouard Manet Souvenirs', *La revue blanche*, 1897, 125–35, 168–80, 201–7, 306–15, 413–24 (reprint Caen 1988); 'L'Art d'Edouard Manet'. *The Sudio*, 15 January 1901 (reprint Caen 1988); *Edouard Manet Souvenirs*, Paris 1913

POULET-MALASSIS, Auguste   1815–78
Publisher of Banville, Gautier and above all of Baudelaire's *Les Fleurs du mal*, he withdrew to Belgium in 1863, where he brought out works that would have been banned in France, including Baudelaire's *Les Épaves*.

ROCHEFORT, Henri (Count Henri de Rochefort Luçay)   1831–1913
Rochefort was a polemical Republican journalist and scourge of the Empire. He supported Gambetta and the Paris Commune and was tried and deported in 1873. After a spectacular escape, he returned to France only after the 1880 amnesty. Manet painted his portrait and two versions of his escape (*224*, *225*).

STEVENS, Alfred 1823–1906
A Belgian artist living principally in Paris, Stevens painted polished and highly successful pictures. As much at home in *avant-garde* circles in the Batignolles as on the Boulevard, he was a particular friend of Manet and introduced him to Durand-Ruel in 1871.

THIERS, Adolphe   1797–1877
The leader of the liberal opposition to Napoleon III, elected to the National Assembly in Bordeaux in 1871, Thiers' government of national unity provoked the events of the Commune.

TISSOT, James   1836–1902
Tissot was a friend of Whistler, Degas and Stevens and a highly professional and fashionable painter of genre subjects and society portraits. His support for the Commune obliged him to move to London where he remained in touch with Manet, acquiring one of his views of Venice (*164*) and advising him about exhibitions.

WOLFF, Albert   1835–91
Born in Germany, Wolff became a very influential journalist as editor and, from 1868, principal art critic of *Le Figaro*. He promoted mainly academic artists and was deeply hostile to the Impressionists. His reviews of Manet's work were consistently, often grossly uncomprehending although their social relations remained cordial.

ZOLA, Émile   1840–1902
Friendship with Cézanne and a literary career in Paris in the 1860s led to Zola's interest in the new realist school in art. In 1864 he met Gabrielle Alexandrine Meley who posed for Monet and Cézanne and became his companion and, in 1870, his wife. A series of articles on the Salon of 1866 for *L'Événement* marked the start of Zola's courageous defence of Manet in the 1860s. A study in the *Revue du XIXe siècle* was reprinted for Manet's 1867 exhibition, and Zola protested against the censorship of his lithograph and painting of *The execution of Maximilian* (*22*, *96*) in 1869. He wanted Manet to illustrate his *Tales for Ninon* and dedicated the novel *Madeleine Férat* to him in 1868, the year in which Manet painted his portrait and possibly one of Gabrielle.
   Rejected as a volunteer in 1870, Zola took his wife and mother away from Paris during the war, reporting on the provisional Republican government in Bordeaux. In the 1870s he continued his art criticism, championing Manet as leader of the new realist and Impressionist school but with reservations (in 1879 through an article which had appeared in a Russian review, and in 1880 with his articles in *Le Voltaire*). Although Zola was ultimately unable to accept him as the hoped for 'man of genius', Manet remained grateful for his old friend's support and paid tribute to his integrity and courage in 1881 (*202*).
'Letters from Manet to Zola', ed. C. Becker, in F. Cachin *et al* (exh. cat.) Paris/New York 1983, Appendix I, pp. 518–34

Index

Brief notes are provided for some personalities in this selective index and more information is given for others in the Biographical Notes (pages 314–6).

Sources and Bibliography

SOURCES

The documents with their references are followed by the page and plate references to this volume.

FRANCE
ARCHIVES NATIONALES
F21.308 *Turquet* 186
BIBLIOTHÈQUE D'ART ET D'ARCHÉOLOGIE
Carton 59, dossier 1   *Bergerat* (3, 33) 244, *Burty* (20) 31, (8) 40, *Charpentier, Georges* (13) 253, *Charpentier, Mme* (11, 24) 165, (23) 253, *Chesneau* (30) 264, *Duret* (4) 170, *La Rochenoire* (19) 53, *Lemercier* (25) 168, *Manet, Suzanne* (31) 60, (32) 61, *Martinet* (17) 249, *Proust* (35) 254, *Wolff* (2, 29) 181, *Zola* (15) 165; in 8° D677 (see *J. de Biez 1884*)   *L'Art*, editor of 260; see also Dunan Coll. (see *Courthion-Cailler*, 1, 53–74) *Suzanne Manet* 55, 58, 62, 65
BIBLIOTHÈQUE LITTÉRAIRE JACQUES DOUCET
Manuscrits   *Laurent* (*MNR 1630*) 247, (*MNR 1631, 1632*) 266, (*No. 132*) 257
BIBLIOTHÈQUE NATIONALE
Estampes   Cahier Léon Leenhoff I (Yb3.2401a, t.1) *Sale to Durand-Ruel* (130–31) 163, *Sale 1883* (83, 143) 'Demandes de cartes de travail' (*1858: 2361*) 28; Manuscrits   N.a.f. 15816) *Poulet-Malassis* 38 N.a.f. 24022 *Asselineau* 44   N.a.f. 24277 *Nadar* (*f.259*) 40, (*f.257*) 44   N.a.f. 24839 *Burty* (*f.398*) 46, *Goetschy* (*f.395*) 265
MUSÉE DU LOUVRE
Cabinet des Dessins   Boîte BS 8   *Astruc* (*L 55*) 250, *Banville* (*L 48, 49*) 171, *Burty* (*L 47*) 50, *Castagnary* (*L 56*) 178, *Chesneau* (*L 45*) 40, *Duret* (*L 2*) 37, (*L 30*) 46, (*L 3*) 50, (*L 6, 11*) 54, (*L 7, 10*) 160, (*L 14, 9*) 162, (*L 12*) 169, (*L 16*) 170, (*L 19*) 182, (*L 26*) 248, (*L 25*) 249, (*L 28*) 261, *Duret?* (*L 58*) 164, *Ephrussi* (*L 31*) 261, *La Rochenoire* (*L 43*) 53, *Lemercier* (*L 46*) 51, (*L 50*) 168, *Lesclide* (*L 33, 34*) 173, *Martinet* (*L 54*) 29, (*L 53*) 32, *Montrosier* (*L 39*) 167, (*L 40, 35*) 168, (*L 38*) 171, *Wolff* (*L 1*) 177   See plate 10; Lettres et documents   *Duret* (3) 259; Lettres à Isabelle   *Lemonnier* (*RF. 11.176*) 250, (*11.182*) 251, (*11.170, 174, 179, 183*) 252, (*11.177, 181*) 253, (*11.171*) 254 (*11.184*) 256, (*11.175*) 255, (*11.178*) 258   *Mme Guillemet* (*11.186*) 253   See pl. 196, 197, 215
MUSÉE MARMOTTAN
Fonds Rouart I   *Mme Manet* (1) 18, (3) 21, (4, 5) 23 *Eugène Manet* (6) 24 (see *Lettres de jeunesse. Voyage à Rio, 1929*), II   *Berthe Morisot* 259
FONDATION CUSTODIA, INSTITUT NÉERLANDAIS
Pertuiset (*MS 7692a*) 267   *Wolff* (1974, A172) 265
MUSÉE STÉPHANE MALLARMÉ, VULAINES-SUR-SEINE
Mallarmé 167, 173, 174, 176, 177, 180, 186, 247–9, 259, 260, 262, 266   See plates 124, 130, 131
PRIVATE COLLECTIONS
Huguette Berès (see *Bazire 1884* fascimile, *Berès 1978*, 72, 107–9, *Moreau-Nélaton 1926*, I, 127, II, 31, 69, 85)   *Mme Gonzalès* 52, *Eva Gonzalès* 52, 60, 180, 250, 263 *Henri Guérard* 255, 265   See plates 198, 214
Le Blond-Zola   *Zola* (in *Paris/New York 1983*, Appendix I: 1) 38, (2) 39, (3) 40, (4) 41, (5, 6) 42, (7–9, 11, 35) 45, (10) 48, (13) 49, (12) 50, (16) 53, (18) 65, (23, 24) 166, (27) 180, (29, 32) 182, (36) 186, (37) 244, (39) 257, (43) 261   See plate 202
Denise Scheler   *Asselineau* 44
Troyes, Pierre Lévy   *Duret?* 251
Private collections   *Astruc* (*RW D601, Berès 1978*, 100*) 249   *Baudelaire* (See *Lettres à Baudelaire 1973:*

230) 31, (*232*) 32, (*233*) 33, (*236*) 36, (*237*) 37, (*238*) 38 (see also *Vente Sickles* I: 31, II: 292)   *Bergerat* (*Berès 1978*, 102) 245   *Degas* (*Loyrette 1991*, 222) 47 *Fantin* (see *Moreau-Nélaton 1926*, I, 102–4) 42, 47, 49 *Laurent* (*RW D602*) 256   *Manet family and J. De Jouy* (see *Lettres de jeunesse 1929*) 18–25   *Morisot* (Correspondance: 59) 161, (*101–2*) 264   *Portier* (*Berès 1978: 99*) 186
GREAT BRITAIN
Glasgow University Library   *Duret, Whistler* (m 257, see *Gazette des Beaux-Arts, 1986*, 205) 258
HOLLAND
Amsterdam   Stedelijk Museum (lr. F.F.R. Koenigs loan)   *Bracquemond* (*RW D581, Bouillon 10*) 257 see plate 200
SWITZERLAND
Private collections   *Nadar* (*RW D590*) 254 *Unidentified* (*RW D596*) 252
UNITED STATES OF AMERICA
New York   Pierpont Morgan Library   Siege letters *Suzanne Manet* 57–60, 62–64   Tabarant archive *Barret* 164, *Duret* 56, 169 see plate 25   In Heineman 785 (*Zola*, Ed. Manet, *Paris 1867*)   *Noriac* 177; Mrs Alexander Lewyt   *Marthe Hoschedé* 257 see plate 199
UNLOCATED AUTOGRAPH LETTERS
Academy in Florence (see *Berès 1978*, 1) 27 *Bracquemond* (see *Bouillon*, GBA 1983, nos 1, 3, 5) 30, (4) 31, (6) 32, (7, 8) 160–61   Editor of *L'Événement*, 10 *July 1882, p.2* 266   *Gauthier-Lathuile* (photograph, private coll.) 261   *Mme Guillemet* (*RW D583*) 254   *Laurent* (RW D603) 256   *Mlle Marguerite* (*Guiffrey 1929, XX*) 252   *Prefect of the Seine* (*Bazire 142*) 185   *A. Proust* (*Proust 1913*, 102–3) 246   *Saint-Lannes* (in *Le Type* see plate 133) 178 *Unidentified* (in *La Revue artistique*, *Antwerp, 1880–81*, 251) 249
CONTEMPORARY DOCUMENTS
1867   *Manet exhibition catalogue*, 'Motifs d'une exposition particulière' 43
1872   *Memorandum of the sale to Durand-Ruel, January–February 1872* 163
1876   *Manet studio exhibition invitation* (to S. *Mallarmé*) 177   Autograph statement in La Galerie contemporaine, 'Edouard Manet', *April 1876* 178 *Letter and drawing in Le Type, 10 April 1876, p.1* 178 See plates 131–3
1880   *Manet exhibition catalogue*, La Vie moderne, *April 1880* 245   Cover of *Vast-Ricouard and Gros-Kost*, Le Salon réaliste, *May 1880* 248   See plates 193, 195
1882   *Manet's will, 30 September* (in Le Journal des curieux, *10 March 1907, p.12*) 267
1883   *Manet's sales memoranda, January–February* (see *Bibliothèque nationale, Estampes*) 267
CONTEMPORARY RECORDS
Bazire, (Manet, *Paris 1884*, 69) 162, (74) 303   *De Biez* (E. Manet. Conférence..., *Paris 1884*, 8) 171   *Burty* (in Salons de la 'Vie moderne'. Catalogue des Peintures et Pastels de Eva Gonzalès, *Paris 1885*, 9–10) 52   *De Nittis* (Notes et souvenirs, *Paris 1895*, see *Moreau-Nélaton 1926*, II, 49) 264   *Duret* (see *Duret 1906: 100*) 33, (61) 34, (144) 167, (161) 169   *Gervex* (in Bulletin de la Vie artistique, *1920*, 609) 303 *Jeanniot* (in La Grande revue, *10 August 1907*, see *Moreau-Nélaton 1926*, II, 92, 96) 261, 302   *La Touche* (in Journal des artistes, *1884*) 303   *Mallarmé* (in Art Monthly Review, *18*) 305   *Moore* (in Modern Painting, *London 1893*, 37) 303   *Morisot* ('Premier carnet vert', in Morisot exh. cat. *Vevey 1961*, 50) 303   *Toché* (in *A. Vollard*, Souvenirs d'un marchand de tableaux, *Paris* (1937) *1984: 162*) 26, (*160–67*) 172, (*168*) 182   *Zola* (in L'Événement illustré, *10 May 1868*, see *Courthion-Cailler*, II, 75) 45 *Proust* (see *Proust 1897*; Proust's record has been freely rearranged for the purposes of this publication) 25–29, 33, 169, 179, 181, 183–5, 187, 246–7, 302–4; (see *Proust 1901: 72/Caen 89*) 28, (*74–76/Caen 95–101*) 302, 304; (see *Proust 1913: 16*) 29, (*38*) 51 (*102–3*) 246

BIBLIOGRAPHY
LETTERS, DOCUMENTS AND RECORDS
E... M... Lettres de jeunesse, ed. Rouart, Paris 1928
E... M... Voyage en Espagne, ed. Wilson-Bareau, Caen 1988
Lettres illustrées d'E... M..., ed. Guiffrey, Paris 1929
Manet, lettres à Isabelle..., ed. Cachin, Geneva 1985
Manet raconté par lui-même et par ses amis, ed. Courthion and Cailler, 2 vols, Geneva 1953
Manet. A Retrospective, ed. Gronberg, New York 1988
Bibliothèque du Colonel Daniel Sickles, Drouot-Montaigne, Paris, I, 20–21 April, II, 28–29 November 1989
A. Tabarant, *Une correspondance inédite d'E... M... Les lettres du siège de Paris*, (Mercure de France) Paris 1935
See also Notes (pages 314–6): Adam, Baudelaire, Bracquemond, Mallarmé, Morisot, Proust, Zola
BIOGRAPHIES AND CATALOGUES
T. Duret, *Histoire d'E... M... et de son oeuvre*, Paris (1902) 1906
E. Moreau-Nélaton, *M... raconté par lui-même*, 2 vols, Paris 1926
A. Tabarant, *Manet. Histoire catalographique*, Paris 1931
M. Guérin, *L'Oeuvre gravé de Manet*, Paris 1944
A. Tabarant, *Manet et ses oeuvres*, Paris 1947
A. de Leiris, *The Drawings of E... M...*, California 1969
J.C. Harris, *E... M... Graphic works*, New York 1970 (revised ed. San Francisco 1990)
D. Rouart and D. Wildenstein, *E... M..., Catalogue raisonné*, 2 vols, Lausanne/Paris 1975
Complete Paintings..., ed. Pool/Orienti, London 1985
MONOGRAPHS, EXHIBITION CATALOGUES
K. Adler, *Manet*, Oxford 1985
F. Cachin et al. (exh. cat.) *Manet*, Paris/New York 1983
T.J. Clark, *The Painting of Modern Life*, New York 1985
E. Darragon, *Manet*, Paris 1989
A.C. Hanson, *Manet and the Modern Tradition*, New Haven and London 1977
Th. Reff, *Manet and Modern Paris*. (National Gallery of Art), Washington DC and Chicago 1982
J. Richardson, *Edouard Manet Paintings and Drawings*, London (1958), ed. Adler 1982.
C.F. Stuckey and J. Wilson-Bareau, (exh. cat.) *Manet*, Japan 1986
J. Wilson, (exh. cat.) *Manet*, ed. H. Berès, Paris 1978
J. Wilson-Bareau, (exh. cat.) *The Hidden Face of Manet*. (Burlington Magazine, CXXVIII) London 1986
M. Wilson, (exh. cat.) *Manet at Work*, (National Gallery) London 1983
M. Wivel, (exh. cat.) *Manet*, ed. Finsen, Ordrupgaard-Copenhagen 1989

Picture Acknowledgements

The publishers would like to express their gratitude to the museums, galleries and collections credited with the note to each plate for permission to reproduce the works in this book. Photographs were kindly supplied by the collections concerned with the exception of the following: Acquavella Galleries Inc., New York 76; Jörg P. Anders, Berlin 207, 237; Artothek, Peissenberg 103, 161; © 1991 The Art Institute of Chicago. All rights reserved 43, 84, 87, 94; Michael Bodycomb 145; Reproduced by courtesy of the Board of Directors of the Budapest Museum of Fine Arts 66, 70, 142, 179; Jean-Pierre Caron, Levallois-Perret 33, 116, 117, 121, 124, 125, 130, 131, 154, 180, 198, 202, 214, 231; Christie's, New York 109, 217; Photographie Giraudon, Paris 73, 162, 208; David Heald 172; Luiz Hossaka 169; Kent Fine Art, New York 36; Hugo Naertens 230; Reproduced by courtesy of the Trustees, The National Gallery, London 65, 107, 187; Réunion des Musées Nationaux, Paris 4, 5, 6, 7, 10, 14, 27, 28, 32, 34, 35, 37, 48, 58, 78, 79, 80, 82, 85, 86, 91, 97, 98, 99, 102, 111, 112, 118, 119, 126, 129, 136, 146, 149, 158, 159, 173, 184, 192, 196, 197, 215, 236; Courtesy Galerie Schmit, Paris 147; Jim Strong, Inc., New York 120, 209; Courtesy Wolfgang Wittrock, Düsseldorf 93.